CB°°

993

DATE DUE

DEMCO 38-296

Cross-Cultural Performances

Cross-Cultural Performances

Differences in
Women's Re-Visions
of Shakespeare

Edited by
Marianne Novy

UNIVERSITY OF ILLINOIS PRESS
Urbana and Chicago

© 1993 by the Board of Trustees of the University of Illinois
Manufactured in the United States of America
1 2 3 4 5 C P 5 4 3 2 1

This book is printed on acid-free paper.

Library of Congress Cataloging-in-Publication Data

Cross-cultural performances : differences in women's re-visions of
Shakespeare / edited by Marianne Novy.
    p.   cm.
Includes index.
ISBN 0-252-02017-0 (acid-free paper). – ISBN 0-252-06323-6 (pb. :
acid-free paper)
    1. Shakespeare, William, 1564–1616–Adaptations–History and
criticism.   2. Shakespeare, William, 1564–1616–Characters–Women.
3. Literature–Women authors–History and criticism.
4. Shakespeare, William, 1564–1616–Stage history.   5. Authorship–
Sex differences.   6. Feminism and literature.   7. Women in the
theater.   8. Feminism and theater.   9. Women and literature.
I. Novy, Marianne, 1945–
PR2880.A1C76   1993
822.3'3–dc20
                                                                92-44535
                                                                CIP

Contents

Acknowledgments

Early versions of the essays by Diana Brydon, Ania Loomba, Valerie Traub, and Judith Lee were presented at Special Sessions at the Modern Language Association conventions of 1990 and 1987. Margaret Drabble's essay is slightly shortened from the version she delivered as a Celebration Lecture in honor of Gareth Lloyd Evans (1923–84), the Shakespeare scholar and drama critic, at the Shakespeare Centre, Stratford-upon-Avon, in 1988. It was published in an edition of 150 copies by the Celandine Press. I am grateful to Margaret Drabble and Barbara Evans for permission to use it here, and to Gayle Greene for telling me about it. I also thank everyone who helped publicize my call for papers, especially Ann Thompson and Jeanne Roberts. Shirley Nelson Garner, Dennis Kennedy, Peter Erickson, and two very helpful anonymous readers made useful suggestions. Gwendolen Gorzelsky checked quotations. My husband, David Carrier, accompanied me to many Shakespeare plays and held our daughter Elizabeth during her first "grown-up" one, a multiracial, cross-dressed *Midsummer Night's Dream* under the redwoods at Santa Cruz in 1991. He also took many phone messages for this book.

MARIANNE NOVY

Introduction

This anthology combines feminist criticism with black and postcolonial criticism, literature with theater, the study of a male writer with the study of women. It is a companion volume to *Women's Re-Visions of Shakespeare: On the Responses of Dickinson, Woolf, Rich, H.D., George Eliot, and Others.*[1] Let me summarize some history behind these volumes.

In 1979 Elaine Showalter's article "Towards a Feminist Poetics" divided feminist criticism into that concerned with women as readers and that concerned with women as writers.[2] But since the late sixties, feminist Shakespeareans have often read and taught both kinds of criticism, even if we were only writing the first. Many of us were fascinated by the way Showalter and other influential feminist scholars such as Ellen Moers, Sandra Gilbert, and Susan Gubar constructed a literary tradition using comparisons among women, mostly nineteenth-century British novelists and poets, but we began to wonder what more could be said about how women writers related to male literary tradition, particularly to the male writer to whom we ourselves were responding in other moments of our teaching and writing.[3]

These questions converged with arguments among feminists about Shakespeare's portrayal of gender and with challenges from other Shakespeare critics who called all kinds of feminist criticism ahistorical.[4] I decided to explore what could be found out about women's responses to Shakespeare in the past as well as the present. When did women start reading him with a special interest in his female characters? Who praised them? Who criticized them or their treatment? When did women writers begin to evoke his women to tell stories differently? What kinds of attitudes have women held toward the cultural image of Shakespeare himself? How have changes in feminist consciousness changed women's responses?

The project was clearly big enough for a collective effort. Working mainly through the Modern Language Association and the Shakespeare Association of America, I invited others to join me, some of whom were already pursuing similar questions.[5] Our special sessions and seminar developed into *Women's Re-Visions of Shakespeare*. The book crossed genres, genders, and historical periods in connecting Shakespeare and women writers—indeed, many of the women writers of most interest to feminist criticism at the time—but it stayed within the world of white women, particularly Anglo-American women, and it paid very little attention to women of the theater. These limitations are in part symptomatic of institutional barriers between English and theater arts departments, between English and other modern language departments, and between English and African-American literature: they also reflect the related fact that, on the whole, feminist study of Anglo-American novelists and poets is more established and better known beyond specialists than feminist study of theater and of women of color.[6] As the anthology was approaching publication, already too long, it left much room for further exploration in less canonical areas.

This anthology, collected in a time when feminist criticism is more conscious of historical, racial, class, and national differences among women, attempts to be more inclusive. It also benefits from the greater historical and cultural consciousness of women's studies today, from the greater development of feminist theater criticism, and from the way cultural materialists and new historicists as well as feminists have prodded Shakespeareans of all varieties to greater awareness of how particular cultures, indeed particular readers, of past and present construct their own Shakespeares.[7] We are becoming aware that all Shakespeare criticism after the Renaissance is in one sense cross-cultural.[8]

Much more than its predecessor, this anthology includes essays on women whose response to Shakespeare is cross-cultural not just in terms of time but also in terms of race and relation to colonialism. This means writing about the responses to Shakespeare of black women such as Gloria Naylor and Toni Morrison and postcolonial women such as Sarah Murphy and Suniti Namjoshi; it also means considering Aphra Behn's treatment of race, and noticing that among many women's transformations of *The Tempest* discussed here, only Isak Dinesen's pays little attention to colonialism. It means the reader can compare the rewriting of *Hamlet*'s Gertrude in Zora Neale Hurston's purposeful and lusty Lena with the dependent, maternal Gertrude imagined by the noncanonical white Lillie Wyman about the same time.[9]

By selecting a title that describes women's responses to Shakespeare not only as re-visions but also as performances, I have tried to highlight this anthology's attention to theater as well as to cultural crossing. Here we can compare the possibilities for Helen Faucit, Margaret Drabble, Fiona Shaw, and Tilda Swinton in acting Shakespeare, for Joan Littlewood and Deborah Warner in directing, and for Aphra Behn and the Women's Theater Group in playwriting. Furthermore, we can contrast the responses of Drabble and Ania Loomba to productions directed by men in Stratford and in a remote province of India. As Loomba's essay in particular shows, it is especially appropriate that theater be considered in a volume dealing with cross-cultural uses of Shakespeare, since in many different cultures today Shakespeare is known more through performance, in translation, rather than through reading an English text.

But "performance" in a larger sense occurs in writing as well as in the theater. As a term for all the responses discussed, it stresses the fact that they are actions in a specific time, with strategies and with an audience. Thus, like "cross-cultural," it emphasizes the historical location of the works analyzed, helping us to see their use at their time of origin and some of their limitations.

The essays that follow do not take the view that any engagement with Shakespeare inevitably maintains male dominance and a canonical literary hierarchy. But, more than in the first anthology, we see costs as well as benefits in women's appropriations of Shakespeare's characters and cultural images. The perspective of this anthology on women's relation to male literary tradition is close to that used by Ann Rosalind Jones in *The Currency of Eros: Women's Love Lyric in Europe, 1540–1620*. Building on the work of Stuart Hall and Christine Gledhill, Jones uses the concept of "negotiation" to emphasize that "reigning discourses are neither seamless wholes nor swallowed whole": as she shows "the mixed process of acceptance and resistance through which women poets responded to the gender ideologies and poetic norms of early modern Europe," I would stress, similarly, that Shakespeare's texts, and the Shakespeare criticism of each successive period, are not "seamless wholes," nor have women swallowed them whole.[10] As Jones says, "To think in terms of negotiation rather than coerced repetition or romantic rejection of literary models opens up a whole new spectrum of women's responses to the logics of power."[11] Like the women writers Jones discusses, the women discussed in this volume differ in their proportion of adaptation and opposition-ality, in ways strongly influenced by their historical situation and group identifications. The contributors are interested in women's difficulties as well as successes in using Shakespeare. They locate places where women, in Diana Brydon's phrase, "talk back" to him—sometimes about race as well as about gender; they also locate places where Shakespeare may support one woman's power at the cost of another's.

The introduction to *Women's Re-Visions* provided a brief historical overview of responses to Shakespeare by English-speaking women writers, from the 1660s Margaret Cavendish to the 1980s American poet Marilyn

Hacker, British novelist Angela Carter, and Australian playwright Alison Lyssa.[12] This introduction can only hint at the rich and complex history of women as performers of Shakespeare and at the possibilities emerging now that more women are finally in directorial positions: consider the importance today of Tina Packer at Shakespeare & Co., JoAnne Akalaitas in New York, Pina Bausch in Germany, and Ariane Mnouchkine at the Théâtre Du Soleil in France.[13] It can hint even more briefly at the meanings Shakespeare has had in continental Europe, where translating his work often accompanied cultural nationalism, and in the Third World, where nationalist interpretations could mean both appropriation and confrontation.[14] There is still much work to do on the interaction of gender with these theatrical and cultural issues.

In the rest of this introduction, I want to contextualize these essays with regard to problems posed by other uses of Shakespeare by black women, mainly in the U.S., and women of the theater, mainly in England.[15] Women most directly influenced by racial and theatrical institutions have much reason for oppositional approaches to Shakespeare, but they also have a history of claiming Shakespeare on their behalf in opposition to other institutions in their culture. On one hand, Shakespeare's only female character written as black is Cleopatra, and many lines in his plays explicitly assume white standards of beauty and use "Ethiope" as a hostile epithet. Even if postcolonial women want to claim also her attendants Iras and Charmian, the Goth Tamora, Glendower's Welsh daughter, or the Algerian witch Sycorax, appropriation of Shakespeare for black or anticolonial feminism requires much more drastic revision than is needed by white women looking for female characters to claim. Feminists dealing with colonialism and racism also need to come to terms with the cultural history of *The Tempest* and *Othello* in a different way than feminists dealing only with gender: hence the dominance of *The Tempest* in this volume.

On the other hand, black women do not have a consistent history of opposition to Shakespeare, and their readings of him, like those of other readers, have been influenced by the possibilities of their own time. Toni Morrison and Gloria Naylor read Shakespeare under far different conditions than did Anna Julia Cooper, whose 1892 book *A Voice from the South* includes probably the first important published literary criticism by a black woman.[16] Cooper resembles many of the women quoted in *Women's Re-Visions* in her praise of Shakespeare's "all-embracing sympathy, . . . which proved a key to unlock and open every soul that came within his radius."[17] Her aim in this passage, however, is not to evaluate Shakespeare; it is to add his cultural prestige to a plea against racial prejudice. Hearing of an art school denying admission to a black woman whose drawings its critics had pronounced excellent, she asks, "Can anyone conceive a Shakespeare, a Michael Angelo, or a Beethoven putting away any fact of simple merit because the thought, or the suggestion, or the creation emanated from a soul with an unpleasing exterior?" (114).[18] Like George Eliot, from whom she quotes the identification of sympathy with "so much of human insight,"[19] she found the image of the sympathetic Shakespeare particularly important because it coalesced with what she maintained of the nineteenth century's ideal image of women; indeed the praise of Shakespeare is a transition to her argument that women should help humanize America by educating it against prejudice, instead of exemplifying the prejudice that she noted in a National Women's Council paper by Anna Howard Shaw.

Like many white women discussed in *Women's Re-Visions,* Cooper makes Shakespeare into her ally—but against racial prejudice, more than against gender prejudice (which she attacks elsewhere). In another essay, she introduces her analyses of the biases in literary treatment of "descendants of Africans" by saying that "No Shakespeare arose to distil from their unmatched personality and unparalleled situations the exalted poesy and crude grandeur of an immortal Caliban."[20] She is using progressively an image of Shakespeare that today is often used conservatively; she claims Shakespeare on the side of cultural openness and hopes to see "a black man honestly and appreciatively portraying both the Negro as he is, and the white man, occasionally, as seen from the Negro's standpoint."[21] Her use of Shakespeare as an ally against racial exclusion is similar to an attitude that appears in discussions of black women's theatrical performances at that time. In 1884, when Henrietta Vinton Davis performed scenes from *Macbeth* and *Richard III* at Ford's Opera House with two other black actors, a reviewer commented, "Thus leap by leap the colored man and woman encroach upon the ground so long held sacred by their white brother and sister."[22]

The most widely known black female response to Shakespeare of recent years may well be that of Maya Angelou, presented in a palimpsest of rewritings which began with her book *I Know Why the Caged Bird Sings,* published in 1969. In this book she remembers acting out scenes from *The Merchant of Venice* in childhood. She writes, "It was Shakespeare who said, 'When in disgrace with fortune and men's eyes,' " and calls him "my first white love."[23] Young Maya responded to Shakespeare out of her biographical situation as a black girl in a strict household, just as Gloria Naylor's George responds, Valerie Traub shows, out of his situation as an orphan. Neither Maya nor George makes the allusions to Shakespeare's position as an outsider to literary institutions suggested by a number of writers discussed in *Women's Re-Visions*—by their time he was long in the canon—yet both of them are especially interested in his representation of outsiders' voices. Young Maya, like Anna Julia Cooper, is also drawn to writings by blacks; on the same page in *Caged Bird* that she quotes Shakespeare, she remembers her "young and loyal passion for Paul Laurence Dunbar, Langston Hughes, James Weldon Johnston and W. E. B. Dubois' 'Litany of Atlanta.' "[24] In this version of her autobiography she frames her reflections on Shakespeare as her feelings as a child, leaving the audience to infer her mature position.

In 1985 Angelou rewrote her childhood memory for an address to the National Assembly of Local Arts Agencies. In this version, drawn on by Lynne Cheney in her 1988 report *Humanities in America,* she puts her identification with Shakespeare into the present: "I found myself and still find myself, whenever I like, stepping back into Shakespeare. Whenever I like, I *pull* him to me [note the suggestion here of some effort involved]. . . . 'When in disgrace with fortune and men's eyes, / I all alone beweep my outcast state.' . . . Of course, he wrote it for me: that is a condition of the black woman. Of course, he was a black woman. I understand that. Nobody else understands it, but I *know* that William Shakespeare was a black woman. That is the role of art in life."[25] Here Angelou's appropriation of the sonnet is both her claim for the dignity and importance of the black woman's experience before a mainly white audience in Cedar Rapids, Iowa, and her protest against limited access to culture; her invocation of Shakespeare's sympathy as able to transcend racial difference echoes Cooper's.

As Malin LaVon Walther shows, Toni Morrison in 1981 was much more critical of Shakespeare; this shows the difficulty of arguing an absolute trajectory of increased opposition over time among black women. A black woman's response to Shakespeare today, like a white woman's, is influenced not only by race but by many aspects of her biographical, historical, and political location. Even though both identify themselves as black women, such factors as age difference and relative closeness to performing (Angelou) or critical (Morrison) traditions have effects.

Gloria Naylor's work is more involved with Shakespeare than were most of the 1960s and 1970s novels by black women. In both *The Women of Brewster Place* and *Linden Hills,* she occasionally invokes the myth of the black Shakespeare, an analogue to Woolf's myth of Shakespeare's sister.[26] Her *Mama Day,* as Valerie Traub shows, offers a dialogue among many different black ways of responding to Shakespeare; yet she, like our culture generally, offers more space for criticizing him than was available to Cooper. Oppositional possibilities increase over the course of a century, in spite of shorter-term variations. Arguably, Suniti Namjoshi's 1984 rewriting of *The Tempest,* in which Miranda and a female Caliban form a new cultural compact, is the most drastic revision of all considered here, because it deals with sexuality as well as gender, race, and colonialism.[27] Here, as in *Tar Baby,* the Caliban myth and the Miranda myth have replaced the Shakespeare myth; Namjoshi and Morrison reimagine them as an effort in both cultural and social transformation.[28]

Responses of women of the theater to Shakespeare have a similarly complex history, which includes accommodation, confrontation and appropriation, opposition to Shakespeare and oppositional use of him. This anthology studies some examples of how male-dominated theatrical institutions have shaped possibilities and how women directors and performers have negotiated them. Julie Hankey shows that Helen Faucit used Shakespeare both to glorify Victorian womanhood and to promote escapes from its restrictions: Margaret Drabble remembers how the role of Imogen, which seemed liberating to Faucit, seemed constricting in 1960. Lizbeth Goodman discusses contemporary directors and performers who find Shakespearean female parts confining, as well as Fiona Shaw, who acts Rosalind as a critique of gender stereotyping. Dympna Callaghan shows Joan Littlewood using Shakespeare against class prejudice, somewhat as Joyce MacDonald finds Deborah Warner directing *Titus Andronicus* in opposition to violence against women.

Since the articles on theater in this anthology rarely deal with one play's constructions by women in different times, I want to look briefly at changing interpretations of *The Taming of the Shrew,* which provides the most obvious example of how performance history interacts with changing attitudes toward gender.[29] Stage adaptations from 1594 on often suggest some discomfort with the play, but the first performer on record as adding a tone of mockery to Kate's final speech is Margaret Anglin, in 1908 Melbourne and 1914 New York productions.[30] These productions, influenced by the first wave of feminism, may well have been more feminist versions of the play than the 1960 version directed by John Barton, discussed by Margaret Drabble, of which Kenneth Tynan wrote, "Dame Peggy plays the last scene ... with an eager, sensible radiance that almost prompts one to regret the triumph of the suffragette movement."[31] Yet Drabble's own discontent registers the tensions building in 1960, which would soon lead to the reemergence of feminism.

Clamorous Voices, a 1988 collection of dialogues among Royal Shakespeare Company actresses, explicitly allies itself with feminism, yet two of the women are much more positive about the play than is Drabble, and they use language suggesting value placed on freedom and authenticity, rather than on "eager, sensible radiance," in imagining the last scene.[32] Sinead Cusack sees the last speech as not about submission but "about how her spirit has been allowed to soar free. ... He hasn't laid down the rules for her, she has made her own rules."[33] Fiona Shaw's view is similar.

One of the other speakers in *Clamorous Voices,* however, Paola Dionisotti, stresses the male dominance of the play. Like Lavinia in Deborah Warner's production discussed by Joyce MacDonald, her Kate protests the power structures of her society even as she suffers from them. She paraphrases Kate's last speech thus: "To the women she's saying, 'This is what our role is, girls—really explore it; it's like an acting exercise.'... To Petruchio she's saying, 'Is this what you want? Is this what you're asking me to do?... The man I was having gags with in the street, does that man want me to do this?' "[34]

Dionisotti played Kate in Michael Bogdanov's modern-dress production of 1978; Cusack and Shaw in Elizabethan-costumed productions of 1982 and 1987, directed by Barry Kyle and Jonathan Miller, respectively. Bogdanov's interpretation of the play as a critique of male violence responded to the active feminism of 1978; both the time and her own experience of that production no doubt influenced Dionisotti's more critical view of Kate's situation as confirming male dominance. We may wonder, on the other hand, if Shaw's and Cusack's more affirmative view of Kate results from their greater professional commitment to the RSC, which Dionisotti left after 1978, or from whatever in their own histories and self-construction makes that greater professional commitment possible. As we shall see with Tilda Swinton and Margaret Drabble, an emphasis on the male dominance in Shakespeare's plays tends to accompany a career move away from them.

While Cusack and Shaw may also be seen as influenced by a late 1980s dispersal of feminism, their affirmative view of the play approximates that maintained earlier by Juliet Dusinberre, Irene Dash, and John Bean, among others;[35] Dionisotti's approach is closer to that developed by such critics as Linda Woodbridge, Lisa Jardine, and Lynda Boose, though far from identical since she claims that the play ultimately critiques Petruchio's behavior, rather than endorsing it.[36] The juxtaposition of Cusack, Shaw, and Dionisotti suggests approaches to the play that stress its ambiguity, such as Karen Newman's and my own.[37] But while making connections between critics' and actresses' views it is worth noting some differences between their undertakings. An essay can emphasize a critical view of the male power it identifies in a play; in a production, in certain contexts, an emphasis on male power may be received as a celebration of that power.[38] Aiming at the critique of sexism, a production may, in practice, reinforce it; on the other hand, a production that aims at finding female power in Shakespeare runs the risk of implying that Shakespeare anticipated all late twentieth-century concerns and that gender inequality was no problem in his world and is none in our own.

However, one recent production of *Shrew* managed to critique both male dominance and class dominance without claiming that such a critique is inherent in the play. It was a 1985 RSC touring production directed by Di Trevis, which began with a "group of nineteenth century actors, evidently poor and oppressed."[39] After the ending of Shakespeare's text, Sly approached his "lady," who ran away mockingly. Then "the actress who had played Katherina... re-entered, holding a baby and looking again downtrodden and burdened." Sly offers her some of the money the lord has contemptuously thrown at him; the poor man and poor woman gesture towards an alliance. Such historicizing reframing in performance can suggest how a play can have both ideological and utopian elements, in a balance that varies with specific circumstances of production and situation.[40] In discussing appropriations of *The Tempest,* Ania Loomba has suggested "that the struggle over meaning is intensified in the case of a text which is itself polyphonic and that the contradictions within the text and the struggle between its different appropriations are inter-related."[41] We may say this of many of Shakespeare's plays, while keeping in mind that polyphony is not the same as universality.

This last in a long series of epilogues added to *The Taming of the Shrew* indicates how producing Shakespeare with a feminist historical consciousness can readily merge with rewriting him, and parallels the Miranda-Caliban compact imagined by Namjoshi and Sarah Murphy. Like this volume in general, it places Shakespeare within what Peter Erickson calls "the larger project of cultural change we are undergoing with respect to race, gender, and class."[42] If Kate can join with Sly, and Miranda can talk back to Prospero and ally herself with Calibans male and female, who knows what may happen next?

NOTES

1. Marianne Novy, ed. *Women's Re-Visions of Shakespeare: On the Responses of Dickinson, Woolf, H.D., George Eliot, and Others* (Urbana: University of Illinois Press, 1990.

2. Elaine Showalter, "Towards a Feminist Poetics," *Women's Writing and Writing about Women,* ed. Mary Jacobus (London: Croom Helm, 1979), 22–41.

3. Elaine Showalter, *A Literature of Their Own* (Princeton: Princeton University Press, 1977); Ellen Moers, *Literary Women* (Garden City, N.Y.: Doubleday, 1976); Sandra Gilbert and Susan Gubar, *The Madwoman in the Attic* (New Haven: Yale University Press, 1979). I cite specific disagreements with Gilbert and Gubar in the introduction to *Women's Re-Visions;* they are the feminist critics whose writing on women's relation to male literary tradition has had most influence, but see also Myra Jehlen, "Archimedes and the Paradox of Feminist Criticism," *Signs* 6, no. 4 (Summer 1981): 575–601.

4. For presentation of those arguments, see, for example, Carol Thomas Neely, "Feminist Criticism in Motion," in *For Alma Mater,* ed. Paula Treichler, Cheris Kramarae, and Beth Stafford (Urbana: University of Illinois Press, 1985), 65–90; and Kathleen McLuskie, "The Patriarchal Bard: Feminist Criticism and Shakespeare," in *Political Shakespeare,* ed. Jonathan Dollimore and Alan Sinfield (Ithaca: Cornell University Press, 1985), 88–108. McLuskie's emphasis on the relations of gender ideology to production choices points to questions raised more in the current anthology than in *Women's Re-Visions.*

5. The critic whose work has most consistently studied these issues, with a focus on changes since 1970, is Peter Erickson: see his *Rewriting Shakespeare, Rewriting Ourselves* (Berkeley: University of California Press, 1991).

6. My attempts to get essays on black women's responses to Shakespeare produced a gracious refusal from Gloria Naylor, acknowledging use of his language and images. I also unsuccessfully attempted to publish a version of Hortense Spillers's conference paper "Sycorax's Sister," which I presume became part of the discussion of Sycorax in the Introduction to her anthology *Comparative American Identities* (New York: Routledge, 1991).

7. For feminist theater criticism, see, for example, Sue-Ellen Case, *Feminism and Theatre* (New York: Routledge, 1988), and her anthology *Performing Feminisms: Feminist Critical Theory and Theatre* (Baltimore: Johns Hopkins University Press, 1990). Case's introduction to the anthology discusses "tardiness" in feminist theater studies (2). For feminist historical consciousness, see, for example, Judith Newton, "Making—and Remaking—History: Another Look at 'Patriarchy,'" in *Feminist Issues in Literary Scholarship,* ed. Shari Benstock (Bloomington: Indiana University Press, 1987), 124–40; for consciousness of other differences, see, for example, Gayatri Spivak, "Three Women's Texts and a Critique of Imperialism," *Critical Inquiry* 12 (1985): 243–61; and *Feminist Criticism and Social Change,* ed. Judith Newton and Deborah Rosenfelt (New York: Methuen, 1985). For cultural materialism, see especially *Political Shakespeare,* ed. Dollimore and Sinfield; *Alternative Shakespeares,* ed. John Drakakis (New York: Methuen, 1985); and Terence Hawkes, *That Shakespeherian Rag* (New York: Methuen, 1986). For new historicism, see especially Stephen Greenblatt, *Renaissance Self-Fashioning* (Chicago: University of Chicago Press, 1980). See the discussion of cultural materialism and new historicism in Peter Erickson's afterword to this volume. Other recent works that historicize Shakespeare studies are *Shakespeare Reproduced,* ed. Jean Howard and Marion O'Connor (New York: Methuen, 1987); Jonathan Bate, *Shakespearean Constitutions: Politics, Theatre, Criticism 1730–1830* (Oxford: Clarendon Press, 1989); Gary Taylor, *Reinventing Shakespeare* (New York: Weidenfeld and Nicolson, 1989); Annabel Patterson, *Shakespeare and the Popular Voice* (New York: Basil Blackwell, 1989); and *The Appropriation of Shakespeare,* ed. Jean Marsden (New York: St. Martin's Press, 1992).

8. Compare Dennis Kennedy's observation, in the introduction to his anthology *Foreign Shakespeare* (Cambridge: Cambridge University Press, 1993), "Shakespeare is foreign to all of us."

9. White women can, however, imagine purposeful and lusty versions of

Gertrude: see, most recently, Margaret Atwood, "Gertrude Talks Back," in *Good Bones* (Toronto: Coach House Press, 1992), 15–18. Her Gertrude reveals she killed Old Hamlet herself.

10. Ann Rosalind Jones, *The Currency of Eros: Women's Love Lyric in Europe, 1540–1620* (Bloomington: University of Indiana Press, 1990). The initial discussion of negotiation occurs on p. 2, referring to Christine Gledhill's "Pleasurable Negotiations," in *Female Spectators: Looking at Film and Television,* ed. E. Deirdre Pribram (London: Verso, 1988), 67.

11. Jones, *The Currency of Eros,* 4. She is drawing on Stuart Hall's "Encoding/Decoding," in *Culture, Media, Language,* ed. Stuart Hall et al. (London: Hutchinson, 1980), 136.

12. Carter quotes from *As You Like It* in *Nights at the Circus* (New York: Penguin, 1984), 280–81. Both Hacker and Lyssa appropriate Shakespeare explicitly in works dealing with love between women, Hacker in her sonnet sequence *Love, Death, and the Changing of the Seasons* (New York: Arbor House, 1986), and Lyssa in her play *Pinball,* in *Plays by Women,* vol. 4, ed. Michelene Wandor (New York: Methuen, 1985).

13. Some studies of this history, influential in the development of this project, are Nina Auerbach, *Women and the Demon* (Cambridge: Harvard University Press, 1982), 207–17, and her *Ellen Terry: Player in Her Time* (New York: W. W. Norton, 1987); and Elaine Showalter, "Representing Ophelia: Women, Madness, and the Responsibilities of Feminist Criticism," in *Shakespeare and the Question of Theory,* ed. Patricia Parker and Geoffrey Hartman (New York: Methuen, 1985), 80–94. On Mnouchkine see Dennis Kennedy, *Looking at Shakespeare* (Cambridge: Cambridge University Press, 1992). Women are also directing Shakespeare on film and television today; see, for example, the discussion of Liz White's *Othello* in Peter Donaldson, *Shakespearean Films/Shakespearean Directors* (Boston: Unwin Hyman, 1990). On feminist projects at Shakespeare & Co.—Packer's "Women of Will" and Kristin Linklater's work with Carol Gilligan in The Company of Women—see Patti Hartigan, "Women Rediscover Their Voices," *The Boston Sunday Globe,* 2 Aug. 1992: B25–26. Thanks to Carol Thomas Neely for this reference.

14. To European romantics of France and Germany, Shakespeare was a model of artistic freedom in contrast to the strict rules of neoclassicism: this tradition may be relevant to Dinesen's view of Shakespeare as well as to recent appropriations by Hélène Cixous, for example in "Sorties," in *The Newly Born Woman,* by Hélène Cixous and Catherine Clément (Minneapolis: University of Minnesota Press, 1986), 98, 122–30. On Shakespeare and cultural nationalism in Europe, see Kennedy, *Foreign Shakespeare.* See also Ania Loomba, *Gender, Race, Renaissance Drama* (New York: Manchester University Press, 1989), on Shakespeare and nationalism in India.

15. The lack of discussion of American theater in this collection reflects, in part, the fact that Shakespeare does not dominate the American stage as he does the British; women's experimental theater in the United States does not need to be seen as "alternatives to Shakespeare," and American actresses are under less

pressure to define their attitude to Shakespeare. With the help of Stratford, Ontario, Shakespeare probably does dominate Canadian theater more: see Ann-Marie MacDonald's play *Goodnight Desdemona (Good Morning Juliet)* (Toronto: Coach House Press, 1990), which won the Canadian Governor General's Award.

16. Anna Julia Cooper, *A Voice from the South* (1892; rpt. New York: Oxford University Press, 1989). Cooper seems to have been best known and most influential in her own day as principal of Dunbar High School, which was at the time the only black high school in Washington, D.C.: she oriented it towards preparing students for college, in opposition to a view—held by Booker T. Washington and many blacks as well as whites—that vocational and industrial training was more appropriate for blacks: see Mary Helen Washington's introduction to *A Voice from the South,* and Hazel Carby's discussion in *Reconstructing Womanhood* (New York: Oxford University Press, 1987), 97–107, for a sense of how she could combine attacks on racism, sexism, and imperialism with remnants of "the cult of true womanhood."

17. Cooper, *A Voice from the South,* 115.

18. Ibid., 114. This does not mean that she thinks of a black "exterior" as unattractive, but that she knows the art school authorities do.

19. On 115 Cooper quotes Eliot, without specifics, paraphrasing chapter 50 of *Adam Bede:* "sympathy—the one poor word which includes all our best insight and all our best love." The passage can be found in *Adam Bede* (Boston: Houghton Mifflin, 1968), 407. On Eliot's own uses of the sympathetic Shakespeare, see Novy, *"Daniel Deronda* and George Eliot's Female Re-Vision of Shakespeare," in *Women's Re-Visions,* 89–107.

20. Cooper, *A Voice from the South,* 178.

21. Ibid., 225.

22. Quoted from the May 17 *New York Globe* by Errol Hill in *Shakespeare in Sable* (Amherst: University of Massachusetts Press, 1984), 68.

23. Maya Angelou, *I Know Why the Caged Bird Sings* (1969; New York: Bantam, 1970), 11.

24. Ibid., 11.

25. Maya Angelou, "Journey to the Heartland," transcription of address delivered at the 1985 National Assembly of Local Arts Agencies Convention, 5. Much of this passage—but not "I pull him to me," which stresses the effort of appropriation—is quoted by Lynne Cheney, *Humanities in America* (Washington, D.C.: National Endowment for the Humanities, 1988), 14. Peter Erickson (*Rewriting Shakespeare,* 111–23) shows how Cheney's use of it against considering literature with regard to "accidents of class, race, and gender" (*Humanities,* 14) misrepresents Angelou. See also Marjorie Garber, "Shakespeare as Fetish," *Shakespeare Quarterly* 41 (1990): 242–50. The irony of Angelou's memorization of "The Rape of Lucrece" has been earlier discussed by Christine Froula, "The Daughter's Seduction: Sexual Violence and Literary History," *Signs* 11 (1986): 621–44.

26. Naylor's uses of Shakespeare are further discussed in my forthcoming book on women novelists' uses of Shakespeare, as well as in Erickson, *Rewriting Shakespeare,* 124–45.

27. Women whose sexuality is not "straight," whether they should be called lesbians, bisexuals, romantic friends—as in Lillian Faderman, *Surpassing the Love of Men* (New York: Morrow, 1981)—or something else, are prominent in *Women's Re-Visions:* see the essays on Woolf, H.D., Dickinson, and Rich, as well as the introduction's discussion of Hacker and Lyssa. Paula Bennett argues, in "Gender as Performance: Ambiguity and the Lesbian Reader," in *Sexual Practice, Textual Theory: Lesbian Cultural Criticism,* ed. Julia Penelope and Susan J. Wolfe (Boston: Basil Blackwell, 1993), that she herself as a lesbian was particularly drawn to Shakespeare because of his critique of gender roles. See also Marjorie Garber, *Vested Interests* (New York: Routledge, 1992), on transvestites' interest in Shakespeare. Rich, by contrast, as Peter Erickson's essay in *Women's Re-Visions* shows, moves away from Shakespeare because she does not see enough critique of sexism and racism in him. The degree and kind of oppositionality in a woman's response to Shakespeare thus depends in part on the balance among different aspects of her own identity at her historical moment; "minority" sexuality may at times contribute to a woman's identification with Shakespeare.

28. See Ann Thompson's suggestion, in " 'The Warrant of Womanhood': Shakespeare and Feminist Criticism," for studies of " 'the Cordelia myth,' 'the Cleopatra myth' and so on," in *The Shakespeare Myth,* ed. Graham Holderness (New York: Manchester University Press, 1988), 82.

29. See Ann Thompson's introduction to *The Taming of the Shrew,* ed. Ann Thompson (Cambridge: Cambridge University Press, 1984), 18–24; and Graham Holderness, *The Taming of the Shrew: Shakespeare in Performance* (New York: Manchester University Press, 1989). According to Errol Hill, *Shakespeare in Sable,* 156, Kate is one of the few female Shakespearean roles conventionally available to black actresses; the cultural meaning of this would repay study, as would the fact that, as I learned in Dennis Kennedy's 1990 SAA seminar on Foreign Shakespeare, *Shrew* is by far the most frequently performed of Shakespeare's comedies in Eastern Europe.

30. W. Winter, *Shakespeare on the Stage,* Second Series, (New York, 1915), quoted in the introduction to *The Taming of the Shrew,* ed. H. J. Oliver (New York: Oxford University Press, 1984), 72. In the 1929 film version Mary Pickford winked: see Thompson, ed., *The Taming of the Shrew,* 22. On pp. 18–24 Thompson discusses the changes in stage adaptations from 1594 to 1978. On pp. 21–22 she quotes a 1933 reviewer as attributing annual performances of *Shrew* at Stratford (England) for eight years from 1909 onwards to intended criticism of suffrage activists ("vote-hungry viragoes . . . militant Furies"). The change from mockery to winking might, perhaps, reflect something of the privatist belief that women's major battles have been won, characteristic of many of the late 1920s essays edited by Elaine Showalter in *These Modern Women* (1979; New York: Feminist Press, 1989). The term "post-feminist" dates from this period.

31. Kenneth Tynan, *Observer,* 26 June 1960, quoted in Holderness, *The Taming of the Shrew,* 41. The reference is to Dame Peggy Ashcroft.

32. Carol Rutter, et al., *Clamorous Voices* (London: Women's Press, 1988).

33. Ibid., 22.

34. Ibid., 23.

35. Juliet Dusinberre, *Shakespeare and the Nature of Women* (New York: Barnes and Noble, 1975); Irene Dash, *Wooing, Wedding and Power* (New York: Columbia University Press, 1981); John Bean, "Comic Structure and the Humanizing of Kate in *The Taming of the Shrew,*" in *The Woman's Part,* ed. Carolyn Ruth Swift Lenz, Gayle Greene, and Carol Thomas Neely (Urbana: University of Illinois Press, 1980), 65–78.

36. Woodbridge, *Women and the English Renaissance: Literature and the Nature of Womankind* (Urbana: University of Illinois Press, 1984); Boose, "Scolding Brides and Bridling Scolds," *Shakespeare Quarterly* 42 (1991): 179–213; Jardine, *Still Harping on Daughters* (1983; New York: Columbia University Press, 1989), 59–60.

37. Newman, *Fashioning Femininity and English Renaissance Drama* (Chicago: University of Chicago Press, 1991), 33–50; Novy, *Love's Argument* (Chapel Hill: University of North Carolina Press, 1984), 45–62.

38. Michael Bogdanov, for example, intended the emphasis on Petruchio's menace and violence in his 1978 production as a critique, but Graham Holderness's study of reviews, *The Taming of the Shrew,* 85–86, shows that some spectators, instead, identified with Petruchio's brutality.

39. Holderness, *The Taming of the Shrew,* 46. The discussion continues through p. 48.

40. See Patrocinio Schweikart, "Reading Ourselves: Toward a Feminist Theory of Reading," in *Gender and Reading,* ed. Elizabeth A. Flynn and Patrocinio P. Schweickart (Baltimore: Johns Hopkins University Press, 1986), 42, using terms from Fredric Jameson, *The Political Unconscious* (Ithaca, N.Y.: Cornell University Press, 1981), 286.

41. Loomba, *Gender, Race, Renaissance Drama,* 146.

42. Erickson, *Rewriting Shakespeare,* 176.

MARGARET FERGUSON

Transmuting Othello: Aphra Behn's *Oroonoko*

BOY	Our Curl'd embraces shall delight
	To checker Limbs with black and white.
NYMPH	Thy ink, my Paper, make me guess
	Our nuptial-bed will prove a press;
	And in our Sports, if any come,
	They'll read a wanton epigram.

(John Cleveland, "A Fair Nymph Scorning a
Black Boy Courting Her," 1687)

In her introduction to *Women's Re-Visions of Shakespeare,* Marianne Novy calls attention to an early example of a woman writer, Aphra Behn, using a cultural image of Shakespeare "to her own advantage."[1] I shall argue in this essay that Behn draws specifically on Shakespeare's *Othello* to dramatize, for the late seventeenth-century readers of her novella *Oroonoko,* novel or news-worthy relations between white and nonwhite persons. One of my chief aims is to explore some of the problems that attend the notion of a woman's "advantage" when we think of her as playing a social game involving different rules (and handicaps) for members not only of different genders but also of different races, nationalities, and classes. "Advantage," as both an economic and a recreational concept, will be a central focus here because it implies an arena of competition in which modern feminist anglophone literary critics, the majority of whom are white and economically privileged, are no less implicated than was Aphra Behn herself. Her ways of using Shakespeare "to her own advantage" in *Oroonoko* highlight the need to distinguish *among* women even as we attempt to analyze how some women in the past sought to redress disadvantages they suffered because they weren't born men.

"Plays," wrote Behn in an early "Epistle to the Reader," "have no great room for that which is men's great advantage over women, that is Learning; We all well know that the immortal Shakespeare's Plays (who was not guilty of much more of this than often falls to women's share) have better

pleas'd the World than Johnson's works, though by the way 'tis said that
Benjamin was no such Rabbi neither, for I am inform'd that his Learning
was but Grammar high; (sufficient indeed to rob poor Salust of his best
orations)."[2] With these characteristically witty and breezy clauses, Behn
becomes the first, to my knowledge, in a line of English women writers
who have defended or justified their own writing practices (which, like
Shakespeare's and Jonson's, often included substantial imitations or "thefts"
from predecessors) by allying themselves with the paradoxical authority
of a supposedly unlearned Shakespeare, a figure whose greatness is held
to derive more from "nature" than from "art," and who is therefore an
appealing imaginary model for the writer who is, because of her gender,
excluded from, or only partially welcomed into, institutions of higher
learning.[3]

When I suggest that the authority invested in this image of the
"unlearned" or nonacademic Shakespeare is paradoxical, I do so in part
because I want to avoid sentimentalizing the idea of the "outsider" as it
applies either to Shakespeare or to an Englishwoman such as Aphra Behn,
who possessed the ability to read and write despite her lack of access to
academic citadels like Cambridge and Oxford. Without denying the material and ideological disadvantages that stem from being barred from the
treasures of Trinity College Library—as Virginia Woolf so vividly describes
herself being barred by a Miltonic bad-angel-Beadle in *A Room of One's
Own*[4]—I want also to emphasize the fact that academic privileges and
prowess have not been unequivocally valued during most periods of
British (or North American) history, and hence exclusion from higher
educational institutions may be, on occasion, an advantage for a writer.
Aphra Behn, addressing both the privileged habitués of the Restoration
London theater and also the reader who could buy the printed playbook,
as she observes, for a shilling (*Works,* 1:223), is clearly tapping a well of
popular sentiment, including jibes at pedantic pretensions, that has many
counterparts in late twentieth-century America. She is indeed capitalizing
on an early version of an ideological topos that has arguably bolstered
Shakespeare's prestige through the last several centuries of his increasingly
global dissemination: the topos of the great "popular" dramatist who
speaks not arcane truths but universal ones that transcend political and
linguistic divisions.

That ideological reproduction of Shakespeare, a phenomenon illustrated early on in Ben Jonson's famous line, "He was not of an age, but for
all time" (and in the fact that this line is almost always quoted out of its
original nationalist context), has been interrogated in recent years by a
relatively small band of cultural critics including many feminists; but
partly because the attacks have circulated mainly along elite academic

routes, the force or import of the critique remains an open question.[5] In what follows, I shall adopt a stance of hermeneutical suspicion not only toward this image of the unlearned Shakespeare but also toward that line in feminist writing which constructs a sympathetic alliance between Shakespeare and women on the grounds of a shared "outsiderness" to educational privilege. Outsider status is, after all, relative, and that point becomes especially useful to keep in mind when analyzing English texts that represent "exotic" characters.

Oroonoko, or the Royal Slave was written and published in the year before Aphra Behn's death; born sometime in the 1640s, she died in April, 1689. Like her posthumously staged drama *The Widow Ranter, or the History of Bacon in Virginia, Oroonoko* dramatizes, and profits from, exotic "news" from the new world.[6] In the novella, the news is explicitly drawn from an experience Behn herself claimed to have had in the British colony of Surinam when she was a young woman. To grasp the import of this claim to eyewitness representation of the tragic story of an African prince named Oroonoko who was enslaved but then oddly exempted from slave labor by English planters who eventually kill him, we need to consider briefly some of the historical narratives with which Behn's story intersects.

Key Contexts

Let us look first at the biographical contextual narrative, which is extremely vexed, for the facts about Aphra Behn's life continue to be the subject of speculation and dispute, partly because she herself contributed to the biographical narrative(s) in ways that show her to have been an adroit self-fashioner.[7] If we know more about Behn's life than we do about Shakespeare's, we nonetheless face problems similar to those which plague students of Defoe; like Defoe, Behn "counterfeited" herself in many ostensibly autobiographical moments, and she did so by means of a pen which, as she observed to the readers of her play *Sir Patient Fancy,* she was "forced" to use to earn her bread, "and [was] not ashamed to owne it" (*Works,* 4:7). It was clearly to her advantage to represent herself as belonging to the gentry, though she may well have been humbly born or even illegitimate. Unable to follow Shakespeare's upwardly mobile tactic of gentrifying himself by buying his father a knighthood, she adopted many narrative tactics of self-promotion, among which is her portrait of herself, in *Oroonoko,* as the daughter of a "gentleman" with connections to the powerful Lord Willoughby. The gentleman, surnamed Johnson, was very probably her adoptive rather than natural father, and in any case he left her without a dowry when he died in 1663, during a voyage with his family to Surinam.[8]

Whatever the "facts" of Behn's birth or of the trip to Surinam—compelling historical evidence exists for her having at least really made the trip rather than having made it up with the help of plagiarism, as one early critic complained—there is no doubt that her education was more determinative of her social status than her bloodlines were.[9] Although she had no Latin or Greek—and in later life lamented that women in her society had less access to education than men—her ability to read and write English, as well as several other European languages including French and Dutch, nonetheless allowed her to earn a living (albeit never a stable one).[10] After working for several years as a spy in the Netherlands for Charles II—during which period she perhaps met and married a Dutch merchant whose surname she took—she was arrested and briefly imprisoned, back in England, for debt, the King having ignored her letters pleading for her promised remuneration for spying. Released from prison through friends (no evidence of Mr. Behn's presence exists, so critics have assumed widowhood for Mrs. Behn), she began to earn her living by writing highly successful plays for the London stage; in her later years, hindered in her access to the theater after she imprudently included an attack on Charles II's disloyal (illegitimate) son Monmouth in one of her plays—for which attack she was arrested and perhaps briefly imprisoned—she also published poems, translations, and short fictions including *Oroonoko*.[11]

Interwoven with the biographical story is one we can call the cultural narrative of female "nature." Feminist scholars have done much to excavate this complex narrative in recent years, and two areas of research are particularly relevant to an understanding of Behn's—and her society's—construction of her persona of female author. The discourse of "normative" womanhood, which proclaimed that women should be "chaste, silent, and obedient," is a dark ground upon which Behn's figure shines brightly (for modern readers seeking models of rebellion from constricting norms of female nature) or luridly (for contemporaries assessing Behn's status as a "licentious" widow who earned her own living).[12] And this discourse of "normative" womanhood had an old misogynist obverse which was being newly inflected, during the seventeenth century, in a set of texts about colonial life that depicted Englishwomen seeking their erotic and marital fortunes "licentiously" in the New World.[13]

At the same time, however, there was an emergent cultural narrative of protofeminist protest against the subordinate role prescribed for women, which is equally important for understanding Behn's colonialist writings. According to this narrative, British women, especially wives, are unjustly treated like (black male) slaves: both groups are demeaned by being the "property" of white men, and members of both groups are objects of

sentimental concern to the producers of this cultural discourse.[14] Linked
to, possibly even enabling, this emergent cultural narrative protesting
women's legal and ideological status as property of men is a version of a
skeptical Renaissance narrative we can call "perspectivism." This emergent narrative had led European writers from Peter Martyr through
Montaigne to Thomas Browne and George Herbert to interrogate ideologies of ethnocentrism and early modes of color prejudice that would
develop, over the course of the next few centuries, into what we call
racism.[15] Behind the apparently liberal views of a character like Desdemona
or the first-person female narrator of Behn's *Oroonoko,* both of whom
find great beauty in a black man, lies a strong, if by no means culturally
dominant, line of philosophical speculation and its accompanying pleasures,
among them the erotic pleasure of experimenting with the unfamiliar.
Such erotic pleasure could be legitimized, like so much else in early
modern culture, by reference to biblical authority: "Thus we that are of
contrary complexions," Thomas Browne wrote, "accuse the blackness
of the Moors as ugly. But the Spouse in the *Canticles* excuseth this
conceit, in that description of hers, I am black, but comely."[16] The witty
poem by Cleveland cited in my epigraph and several remarkable poems by
George Herbert and his brother Edward elaborate on this significant,
albeit relatively unfamiliar, view of black-skinned people as beautiful.

The third contextual narrative (really a set of narratives) that I want to
adduce for this discussion of Behn pertains to two significant, and complexly
linked, institutions of seventeenth-century England, the theater and book
publishing. Behn's efforts to construct marketable authorial personae were
shaped by, and addressed to, the specific kinds of audience—and patrons—
available to her. Catherine Gallagher, who has brilliantly analyzed Behn's
material circumstances as a writer, usefully cautions us against misunderstanding Behn's claim to have earned her "bread" by her pen.[17] Mediating
in crucial ways between pen and profits were the institution of the theater
and also the need to appeal to actual or potential patrons of printed
books; for as Gallagher shows, Behn could not have supported herself just
on her income from her published books, numerous though these were
(*British Women Writers,* 12). Unable to acquire patrons at all during her
early career, as Deborah Payne has argued, Behn was trapped—as were
Dryden and other nonaristocratic members of her generation of writers—
"between a regressive system of patronage and an emergent marketplace
of print" (Payne, 111). And, as Gallagher has persuasively demonstrated,

Behn like most of the age's 'professional writers,' . . . was a playwright partly because the structure and financing of drama allowed
for the support of writers. The theater as an institution changed

abruptly when, after a twenty-year hiatus, it was restored along with the monarchy. The changes made playwrighting a much more discreet, potentially independently lucrative and chancy activity than it had been. Earlier playwrights had either been members of the theater companies that produced their scripts and therefore simply shared in the company's profits, ... or ... were heavily reliant on aristocratic or royal patronage. In contrast, Restoration playwrights were paid the receipts (above the House Charges) for the third day's performance of their plays. . . . Consequently, if a play was not popular enough to hold the stage for three days, the playwright got nothing; if it lasted until the "author's benefit" performance, the playwright's fee would be roughly proportionate to the play's reputation based on its first and second nights' reception. The London theater-going population was small enough for word-of-mouth reporting to spread rapidly through the potential audience. (13–14)

Gallagher goes on to suggest that Behn's construction of an authorial persona, especially in her Epistles to her readers and in the spoken prologues and epilogues of her plays, needs to be understood in the context of this "quite specialized financial arrangement"; like other Restoration playwrights, she tries "to engender a relationship of mutual obligation that will bring in an audience on the third night" (19). As part of this seduction effort, she must work "to keep herself interesting, to dispel the boredom of familiarity." And it is here that Gallagher locates one of Behn's most striking gender-marked innovations, namely her construction, from common misogynist stereotypes of female sexuality, of an unprecedented persona: "the professional woman playwright as a new-fangled whore" (20). Part of the "new-fangledness" displayed in *Oroonoko* depends, I would argue, on an implicit erotic rule, developed by and for the female author, that draws a line between titillation or seduction, on the one hand, and, on the other, any sexual behavior, or pleasure, connected with procreation.

Behn not only adapts the image of the prostitute for her own purposes; she also seeks to revise and partly to revalue the common cultural association of the color black with female unchastity. She herself had been satirized for her literary ambitions in a poem that bawdily alludes to the female genitals as a "black ace." Written (anonymously) in 1676, the satire depicts "the Poetess Aphra" as an aging whore (she was then 36) whose designs on the Laureate's crown come too late. Though she swears "by her poetry and her black ace / The laurel by a double right was her own / For the plays she had writ and the conquests she's won," Apollo denies her plea, suggesting that she's a dozen years too old for sexual conquest.[18]

Barely a year later, Behn obliquely counters this type of attack by creating a prostitute heroine in *The Rover* whose name not only wittily inverts the stereotype of "moral color" but also points teasingly to Aphra Behn herself as a maker of signs or masks. This character, named Angellica Bianca, recalls Cassio's mistress in *Othello* as well as numerous other less than physically or morally pure women named Bianca in English Renaissance drama. This witty character, moreover, bears Aphra Behn's initials, as Janet Todd observes, and also displays an inviting and provocative sign of herself to attract male patrons.[19] Behn underscores her identification with Angellica when she lays paradoxical claim to that sign in a fascinating passage affixed to the first edition of the play, a passage defending it against the charge that it was a piece of rampant plagiarism (from Thomas Killigrew's *Thomaso, or The Wanderer* of 1663–64). Though she has, she confesses, "stol'n some hints," unlike other poets who *conceal* their thefts, she has taken the (by implication superior) tack of calling attention both to her source and to her own witty ways of "appropriating" it: "I, vainly proud of my Judgment, hung out the Sign of Angelica [sic] (the only Stol'n Object) to give notice where a great part of the Wit dwelt" (*Works*, 1:107). Angellica "the White's" sign, as Behn erects it to advertise the products of her own wit, is clearly analogous to the black masks worn by prostitutes in the theater; as Gallagher remarks in her discussion of Behn's prologue to her first play, *The Forc'd Marriage* of 1670, "the poetess like the prostitute is she who 'stands out' . . . by virtue of her mask," the "black velvet case" which, as the Prologue says, "disguises"— but also paradoxically identifies—"every face" of a prostitute in all parts of the theater (Gallagher, *British Women Writers*, 30–31).

What I have called the "institutional" contextual narrative clearly coincides, at key points, with a fourth set of stories, refracting changing and contested practices, which we can very roughly label "the economic." When we consider Behn's economic interests first from the perspective of her situation as an English and specifically a London writer, we can see her relation to Shakespeare in a new light. She allies herself with Shakespeare not only on the grounds of their shared lack of learning but also, and perhaps more surprisingly for the modern reader, on the grounds that certain aspects of her plays that had been excoriated for obscenity should be justified because similar representations occur in Shakespeare's plays. Replying indignantly to the charge that her plays contain indecent episodes, Behn insists that a sexual double standard underpins the unjust criticisms. She adduces Shakespeare's "*The Moor of Venice* in many places," along with other instances of licentious sexual drama (for example, "Valentinian all loose and ruffld a Moment after the Rape"), to support her claim that "had the Plays I have writ come forth under any Mans Name, and never

known to have been mine; I appeal to all unbyast Judges of Sense, if they
had not said that Person had made as many good Comedies, as any one
Man that has writ in our Age" (*Works,* 3:186). The modern reader or
viewer of *Othello* probably doesn't think of that play as the epitome of
"Indecency," but for Restoration audiences, a scene such as 4.3, in which
Desdemona undresses and sings the "willow song"—and also, to many
critics' perplexity, tells Emilia to "unpin me here. / This Ludovico is a
proper man" (ll. 35–36)—was evidently charged with an extraordinary,
and highly marketable, eroticism.[20] Behn uses a version of that charge for
her own purposes in *Oroonoko,* and the ways she does so indicate that
the charge comes not only from Shakespeare's text but from complex
mediations of Restoration stage practices refracting ideologies of race and
gender that had changed significantly with alterations in England's economy that affected not only the institutions of the theater and publishing
but also England's relation to her European rivals for the lucrative markets
of the New World.

    Though I can only gesture toward the epochal changes in the realm
of political economy that occurred between 1607, when *Othello* was
first staged, and 1688, when Behn published *Oroonoko,* it is important
to note that in the years between the reigns of James I and James II,
England had gone from being a small island nation seeking to whittle
away the monopolies which Spain and Portugal held on New World
treasure to enjoying, in Eric Williams's phrase, an "astounding commercial efflorescence" based largely on the profits of the "triangular
trade."[21] That phenomenon consisted of "the combination of the Negro
[African] slave trade, Negro slavery and Caribbean sugar production"
(Williams, 140). By 1697, to the great joy of mercantilist theorists
intent on promoting the ideal of a favorable balance of trade, the "triangular" trade had given an enormous stimulus to England's own
industry (especially in wool) and agriculture, and represented, in the
view of an able seventeenth-century economist named Charles Davenant,
"a minimum of 36 per cent of Britain's commercial profits" (cited in
Williams, 143). By the time Behn wrote her colonialist novella, England
was well on the way to becoming, in Folarin Shyllon's phrase, "the leading
slave mistress, slave trader, and slave carrier of the world."[22] Inevitably,
this development affected how a member of an English audience perceived Othello's "theft" of Desdemona from her father, although in-
ferences about precisely *how* perceptions changed, and how they were
shaped by differences of class and gender, are extremely difficult to make.
I want nonetheless to contribute to that intellectual task, and conclude
this sketchy survey of contextual narratives important for *Oroonoko,*
by using Thomas Rymer's notorious and very funny attack on *Othello*

to dramatize changing perspectives on Othello's love as an offense against (white English) property.

In his *Short View of Tragedy* (1693), Rymer expresses mock astonishment at *Othello*'s enormous popularity on the Restoration stage. What, he wonders, "raises Othello above all other Tragedies on our theatres?"[23] How can it be that English audiences can so admire a play Rymer sees as a "Bloody Farce" (255)? One of his particular objections is to the play's apparent naturalization of the strange novelty of an upper-class white woman marrying a black man: "Instead of starting at the prodigy," he complains, each of Shakespeare's Venetian lords is as "familiar with Desdemona as if he were her own natural Father, rejoice in her good fortune, and wish their own several Daughters as hopefully married" (229). Brabantio, of course, doesn't take the news so well; indeed he equates the loss of his treasured daughter to the state's potential loss of one of its treasured colonies, Cyprus—the island Othello is sent to defend against the Turks. Brabantio, though, shares precisely the upper-class paternal viewpoint Rymer advocates when he writes, "Should the Poet have provided such a Husband for an only Daughter of any noble Peer in England, the Black-amoor must have chang'd his Skin, to look our House of Lords in the Face" (229). Shakespeare's Brabantio is impotent to save Desdemona from what *he* regards as the real tragedy of an exogamous and miscegenous match. And it is precisely such paternal impotence that Rymer laments and imputes, intriguingly, to the playwright himself: "A noble Venetian Lady is to be murdered by our Poet—in sober sadness, purely for being a Fool. No Pagan Poet but wou'd have found some Machine for her deliverance. . . . Has our Christian Poetry no generosity, nor bowels? Ha, Sir Lancelot! ha, St. George! will no ghost leave the shades for us in extremity to save a distressed Damosel?" (249–50).

One of my arguments in what follows is that the deficiency in English chivalry and hardihood which Rymer comically laments—and locates in the author of *Othello*—was perceived as a golden professional opportunity by Aphra Behn, whose poem "The Disappointment" laments, from the point of view of an amorous nymph, the failure of a male lover to rise successfully to an erotic occasion.[24] I propose, in other words, that Behn, England's first professional female writer, deliberately sought to capitalize on *Othello*'s popularity during the Restoration era—which popularity was clearly related to the titillating and novel fact that Desdemona was played now by women rather than boys[25]—by recasting the play's plot for her own professional purposes. Those purposes, which were conditioned by all the historical contexts I have adduced, arguably involved an attempt to legitimate an exercise of female agency within an ideological and socio-economic system that defined "public" women as prostitutes.[26] Because

Behn had to work with as well as against cultural perceptions of the
female playwright as indecent, and because that role had traditional
associations with blackness, she was in a peculiarly apt position to articulate a paradoxical perspective on England's colonizing venture, a perspective I would describe as *partially critical.* Behn's professional and economic
interests deviated just enough from those we may ascribe to England's
dominant male property owners and investors in the colonies to provide a
fascinating example of a female author oscillating among multiple subject
positions and between complicity with and critique of the emergent
institution of New World slavery.

A Partial Reading of the Text

Let me turn now to look more closely at the uses Behn makes of *Othello*
in her late novella. Seeking, I have suggested, to make Shakespeare's old
but still popular play new—or, more precisely, newsworthy—by adding a
spicy ingredient, the phenomenon of female authorship itself, to *Othello's*
explicit dramatization of miscegenous romance and its implicit meditation on England's early colonial encounters with non-white "others,"
Behn also appeals to her audience's hunger for pamphlets and plays
detailing the changes that were occurring in England's imperial mission.
That mission, which had first been articulated for a variety of literate
English people by Hakluyt in the 1580s and first seriously implemented
by Cromwell, was rapidly expanding, at the time Behn wrote, under the
restored Stuart monarchy.[27] An ardent if by no means uncritical supporter
of the Stuarts by the late 1680s,[28] Behn weaves a complex brand of
domestic royalist ideology into her portrait of her princely black hero
whose tragedy unfolds "abroad."

In *Oroonoko,* the hero follows Othello's example by killing his (virtuous) wife before colluding in his own death. Though Oroonoko differs
from Othello in knowing his wife to be chaste even as he kills her, he
shares Othello's desperate fear of being cuckolded; more precisely, he fears
that his beloved wife will become a "slave" to other men's lust after his
death, and he therefore seeks to ensure that she remains his by the extreme
expedient of killing her. Behn's heroine resembles Desdemona in a number of ways; but there is a significant difference: Imoinda is black-skinned.
Oroonoko's characterization, mediated by Shakespeare's portrait of Othello
and also, as I shall suggest, by more villainous black characters like Aaron
of *Titus Andronicus* and his various Restoration reincarnations, derives
according to Behn herself from the unvarnished truth of (her) history.[29]
He is, she insists in her first paragraph, no "feigned hero," and she was
herself an "Eye-witness" to most of the events recounted in the story.[30]

What she could not witness, she "received from the Mouth of the chief Actor in this History, the Hero himself" (1). Such a claim to verisimilitude is of course not uncommon in fictions of this period; but the particular way in which the claim is eroded solicits attention, for late in the story the narrator herself stresses that she was lamentably *absent* from—and impotent to prevent—two scenes in which her hero was tortured. In the second of these he was castrated and killed; he was therefore quite unable to narrate the events to the young Aphra Behn.

The difficulty of establishing the mixture of fact and fiction in Oroonoko's character is nicely epitomized by his name itself: while it could derive from the Yoruba language of the West African coast, the name also recalls the South American river (Orinoco) mentioned by Sir Walter Ralegh in his *Discoverie of the large, rich, and beautifull Empire of Guiana* (1596).[31] Described by Behn as an "ebony" prince with a "rising and Roman" nose, Oroonoko is immediately presented as superior to other Africans, who have flat noses and "brown Rusty-Black" skin (8). A royalist ideology of "natural" nobility infuses Behn's descriptions of Oroonoko's military prowess in his native Coramantien, a part of the West African "Gold Coast" (now Ghana) renowned and feared among colonists for its fierce fighters. Oroonoko's prowess allows him to acquire slaves through war and sell them for profit with no apparent censure from Behn. She does deplore the "ignoble" slave-gaining methods of the white Europeans, however, and satirizes the hypocrisy of the "Christians" while empathizing with her hero's outrage when he is entrapped by a lying English captain and transported to Surinam just when Behn says she arrived there with her mother and sister; her (putative) father, had he lived, would have assumed the post of Lieutenant-Governor of the colony, thus making her, in effect or in fantasy, a "princess" in relation to the princely Oroonoko.

The narrator's perceptions of Africa and the New World are clearly mediated through European conventions of heroic romance and through a set of ideological inconsistencies quite typical of colonial discourse, namely those which arise from the tendency both to conflate and abruptly to distinguish American Indians and Africans as representatives of "otherness" and also as persons who are, or are not, currently enslaved. In Behn's novella, the condition of slavery itself, as well as the differences of skin color which (partly) determine one's vulnerability to a literal or economic form of slavery, are products of overlapping, and sometimes competing, signifying codes, chief among them the erotic, the moral, the economic, and the political.

Oroonoko behaves and is characterized in ways that make him politically labile, indeed overdetermined with reference to any topical allegory. Although modern critics have almost all read Oroonoko as a royalist hero and even, more specifically, as a figure for the martyred Charles I and the soon-to-be-deposed James II (the Stuarts' color was black), this reading neglects the fact that Oroonoko rebels against a villainous tyrant figure, William Byam. Byam was a rabid Royalist and was opposed, according to the historical record and in Behn's novella as well, to Behn's family and to one of the characters she treats admiringly, Colonel George Martin, "brother to the Oliverian" (that is, brother to the regicide Henry Martin).[32]

Behn's Oroonoko, ironically renamed Caesar by his English owners, intriguingly invokes a black hero from Roman history, Hannibal, as his model at a late moment in the story; in the context of urging his fellow slaves to revolt against the English, Oroonoko describes Hannibal as "a great Captain" who "cut his way through Mountains of solid Rocks" (62).[33] He doesn't, however, tell his less well-educated followers about Hannibal's ultimate fate in his battles against Rome. Oroonoko has obviously had a European education (he was tutored by an atheist Frenchman during his boyhood); and the description of his "Roman" nose which I remarked above seems strikingly to anticipate M. R. Ridley's efforts to assure (white) readers, in his 1957 introduction to the Arden *Othello,* that the black hero isn't one of those "subhuman"-looking Negroes with "wooly hair" and "thick lips."[34] Reshaped both mentally and physically to comply with European tastes, Oroonoko nonetheless shares with Othello an inability to transcend his "otherness" sufficiently to be seen as an equal—much less a potential son-in-law—by English men.

In women's eyes, however, Oroonoko and Othello find more favor. "He was pretty tall, but of a Shape the most exact that can be fancy'd," the narrator says admiringly upon first seeing him and finding him "so beyond all Report" (8). Like Othello, then, Oroonoko occupies an ambiguous outside/inside position with respect to the ruling culture; he's officially a slave but is not made to work and has been promised his freedom by one of the "middle-level managers," Trefry, and also by the narrator herself, who tells us she occupies a high social position, and the best house in the colony, and who is, at the time she meets Oroonoko, an "outsider" to the chief patriarchal institutions governing women in Restoration England, the family and marriage. When she arrives in South America, she is a fatherless, unmarried young woman, far from home and without a dowry.[35]

In contrast to the female narrator, Oroonoko is apparently allowed to fulfill his sexual desires according to a hoary romance formula: a pair of young lovers is separated by a *senex* figure, Oroonoko's erotically greedy but, as it turns out, physically impotent grandfather, who takes the prince's beloved Imoinda into his own harem in the novella's opening section; in the second part of the story, set in the American colonies, the lovers are miraculously reunited, in a scene which the narrator calls a pleasing "Novel" (44). The lovers' bliss, however, is shadowed by their condition of chattel slavery and filtered, for the reader, through the observing consciousness of the narrator, who jarringly mixes social and Petrarchan or courtly-love notions of "service" when she tells us that Oroonoko regarded her as his "Great Mistress" (46).

Soon after Oroonoko learns that Imoinda is pregnant, the complex heroic romance turns tragic: Oroonoko follows the example of Othello by killing his beloved. Sexual jealousy reinforced by a principle of patriarchal property rights in women and children looms almost as largely among Oroonoko's motives as it does among Othello's, though the former imagines others occupying his erotic place *in the future* rather than in the past or present. Specifically, he fears that Imoinda may be "ravished by every Brute," thus becoming a "Slave to the enraged Multitude" (71) after his own death comes—and he's sure it soon will—as the result of his scheme for avenging himself on the cruel Deputy Governor of the colony, Colonel Byam. With Imoinda's prompt approval of his plan of revenge, Oroonoko gives her the "fatal Stroke, first cutting her Throat, and then severing her yet smiling Face from that delicate Body, pregnant as it was with the Fruits of tenderest Love" (72). Imoinda is clearly much more compliant in her fate than Desdemona is, and also, perhaps not coincidentally, more innocent in her husband's eyes; paradoxically, therefore, Imoinda can appropriately be seen as a creature worthy of "sacrifice," the "fairest, dearest, softest Creature that ever Nature made" (73), whereas Desdemona, in Othello's eyes, becomes a "black weed" (4.3.69) or a book whose white pages, as Karen Newman acutely observes, "are blackened by writing when Othello imagines 'whore' inscribed acress them."[36] In this condition, which Desdemona herself seems to internalize when she "identifies herself with her mother's maid Barbary, whose name indicates blackness" (Newman, 151), she becomes an object Othello can consider suitable only for murder, not, as he initially thought, for "sacrifice." Othello like Oroonoko comes to value his lady more in death than he ever did in life: once her body is invulnerable to sexual use or abuse, Othello can see it again as "white," a "pearl" and Oroonoko can stare fixedly at the "Sight of this dear Object," the beheaded woman, "now more beloved, and more ador'd than ever" (73).

The complex reasons for Imoinda's death include two centered on property. Oroonoko is unable to bear the thought that his child will be born a slave, the property of others; and he is equally outraged by the idea that Imoinda will perhaps also be alienated from his patriarchal ownership— she may become, after his death (or indeed at anytime), the sexual slave of a white man. Interestingly, when Oroonoko first hears, from Trefry, of

Imoinda's presence in Surinam, but before he learns her name and recognizes her as his own long-lost wife, he expresses considerable surprise that her owner should be pining fruitlessly for her favors: he asks Trefry "why, being your Slave, you do not oblige her to yield?" (42). Here is a moment in the text where a gender ideology of masculine dominance clearly overshadows differences *among* men arising from skin color or social class. Nonetheless, in the end Oroonoko's black skin color and his slave status outweigh the solidarity effects, as we might call them, associated with male gender and shared "noble" class origins. Though Oroonoko like Othello has evidently internalized many of the less savory parts of the intertwined European codes of male honor and male sexual prerogatives—codes which are built, as Stephen Greenblatt and Edward Snow have argued, on profound fears of women and of sexuality itself—both heroes are ultimately destroyed because of the threat their "outsider" status poses to the dominant social group and, specifically, to the male property owners of that group.[37]

That threat, complex and differently articulated as it is in the two texts, nonetheless elicits an eerily similar response: in both texts a sexually powerful black man is depicted as taking out terrible impulses of anger and revenge not on the bodies of white male property holders—though Oroonoko attempts to do just that in his abortive slave rebellion—but rather on a defenseless woman and on himself: Othello, after famously characterizing himself as an alien, a "malignant and a turban'd Turk," stabs himself in the throat. He thus at once silences himself and, by implication, also wreaks a symbolic self-castration: "I took by th' throat the circumcised dog / and smote him—thus" (5.2.351–52).[38] Oroonoko suffers a longer process of death in which others' hands as well as his own carry out a gruesome dismemberment of his body—a punishment he has knowingly incurred by pursuing his schemes of revolt and, subsequently, vengeance. After leading the slave rebellion he is brutally whipped and has "Indian Pepper" rubbed into his wounds by the "civilized" white Governor and his party. The violation of Oroonoko's own body continues after he has violated Imoinda's by severing her head. Discovered by the white property owners after two days when he has lain impotently by his slain wife's side, Oroonoko holds up his knife, declares histrionically that he is unafraid of dying, "and, at that word, cut a piece of Flesh from his Throat" (75). Thus he is represented as actively participating in the process by which he is ultimately silenced so the narrator can fulfill her chosen role of telling his "glorious" story for him. Several long paragraphs later, he undergoes a literal rather than a symbolic castration: "the Executioner came, and first cut off his Members, and threw them into the Fire" (77).

To appreciate the ideological significance of such a death scene, in which a black hero is hideously made to occupy a "feminized" position after he has killed his wife and unborn child, we need to consider briefly not only the *Othello* subtext but also other Shakespearean texts and their Restoration reincarnations. Both Caliban from *The Tempest* (which Dryden had rewritten in 1667) and Aaron from *Titus Andronicus* exert pressure on Behn's creation of a lurid aura of potential danger around her ostensibly admirable and docile black hero. I would suggest, indeed, that the villainous Aaron, along with his several highly popular Restoration reincarnations, necessarily competes for ideological space with any version of Shakespeare's "noble" Moor Othello. As a stereotypically lustful Moor who fathers a black child on a white queen and who also aspires to "mount aloft" in Roman society with his "imperial mistress" Tamora (2.1.13), Shakespeare's Aaron is the model for Thomas Dekker's Eleazer in *Lusts Dominion* (1600) and hence for the villain-hero of Behn's adaptation of that play, *Abdelazar, or the Moor's Revenge*. First performed in 1677, Behn's play stresses not only the Moor's lust but also his political ambitions. Shakespeare's Aaron also resurfaces in the black villain in Ravencroft's 1686 play *Titus Andronicus, or the Rape of Lavinia* (1686).[39] Both as a sexual danger and as a potential usurper of political power reserved for white Europeans (such as Prospero), Aaron like Caliban helps shape the plot of *Oroonoko*. The black hero's nobility may be instantly undermined by the powerful *fantasies* of the story's colonial women, fantasies that transform Othello into Aaron at the first "news" that a black man is seeking freedom and political power.

Behn makes use of *Othello* and its cultural resonances, then, by sensationalizing and rendering more visible precisely that aspect of Othello's relation to a metropolitan state which we might call the "Aaron potential"—the possibility, rendered fearsome by widespread prejudices against black-skinned men, that a black male slave will seize any chance to usurp the white leader's political and erotic places. If we see a *potential* Aaron lurking as an ideological construct in most versions of "noble savage" stories by white authors of the early modern period, then we can better appreciate why such stories are invariably cast as tragedies. What makes Behn's dramatization of this tendency so interesting, however, is that she repeatedly makes small rents in the ideological fabric which justifies the tragic plot as "necessary," "inevitable." In *Oroonoko,* she performs this rending activity chiefly through recording the white female narrator's intermittent sense of anxiety and guilt about the hero's fate. The narrator's responses are of course safely retroactive—the hero is long dead—but as she sometimes uneasily calls attention to the temporal layering and complexity of her story, we are reminded, as an English reader might well have been in 1688, that Britain's saga as an imperial slave trader competing with Dutch rivals had by no means ended on the eve of what seemed to Behn's Tory (and probably Catholic) eyes an invasion of the English throne by a Protestant Dutchman.

Signalling her continuing implication in the imperial project that caused Oroonoko's death, Behn remarks, for instance, that she deeply regrets Surinam's loss to the Dutch soon after she had left "that Country," a country which, she suggests, was an undervalued paradise: "had his late Majesty [Charles II] but seen and known what a vast and charming World he had been Master of in that Continent, he would never have parted so easily with it to the Dutch" (48). The lost colony, the hero who deserved a "better Fate" than to provide "frightful Spectacles of a mangled King," (77–78), and a proleptic lament for the demise of the Stuart line all seem intertwined in Behn's narrative in a way that suggests the narrator's confusion about her own degree of responsibility for past and imminent tragedies. She was "obliged," she says, to leave Surinam after only a brief stay (because of the untimely death of her father); and the absence of a sympathetic male authority figure also seems somehow a (partial) cause of her inability to prevent Oroonoko's torture and death. She relates that she had "assured" Caesar of his liberty "as soon as the Governor arrived" (45), but she is unable to fulfill this promise against the forces of the wicked substitute governor Byam and also—intriguingly—against the forces of her own female "nature," which turns out, whether accidentally or necessarily we can't discern, to be subject to mysterious illnesses and fantasies at crucial moments. As a female novelist and playwright re- calling herself as a young woman in an exotic colony, the narrator presents herself as peculiarly implicated in a market for *ornament* and fantasy that has erotic, rhetorical, theatrical, and economic dimensions.

"We trade for feathers," Behn writes, and the "we," a complex shifter throughout the novella, clearly refers here to English persons of both sexes who are trading with the Indians, a group designated as "other," "them," in this passage. The Indians, Behn goes on to explain, order the feathers "into all Shapes, make themselves little short Habits of 'em, and glorious Wreaths for their Heads, Necks, Arms and Legs, whose Tinc- tures are unconceivable. I had a Set of these presented to me, and I gave 'em to the King's Theatre; it was the Dress of the Indian Queen, infinitely admir'd by Persons of Quality" (2). Though she gives rather than sells the "inimitable" feathers to the "King's Theatre" (actually, the Theatre Royal where the King's Company played), it seems clear that the gift is made in the hope of future authorial benefit; Behn's own plays were produced by the King's Company, and though she was unable to get a play per- formed in 1688, she evidently hoped to do so again in the future. She may even have meant this passage to advertise her own as yet unstaged *Widow Ranter*, which was written nearly contemporaneously with *Oroonoko*, and which had as its tragic heroine an "Indian Queen" who was clearly modeled on the heroine of Dryden's *Indian Queen* (1665) to whom Behn alludes in the quotation above. An actress playing Behn's Indian Queen (Anne Bracegirdle, who also played Desdemona in several Restoration productions of *Othello*) wears a gorgeous feather headress in a mezzotint by W. Vincent.[40]

Unlike some English visitors to the colonies who brought Native American persons home with them as "curiosities," Aphra Behn brought instead theatrical feathers, "some rare flies, of amazing forms and colors" (2), and of course material for the verbal representations of exotic bodies contained in the book she wrote many years later. Imoinda's body is described in a way that highlights its status—and value—as an exotic ornamented artifact: as Catherine Gallagher has shrewdly observed, it is a body described as if its "natural" state were artificial (*British Women Writers*, 104). Behn tells us that all nobly born Coramantiens "are so delicately cut and raised all over the Fore-part of the Trunk of their Bodies, that it looks as if it were japan'd, the Works being raised like high Point around the edges of the Flowers" (45). Some, she goes on to explain, are only carved "with a little Flower or bird"; this is the case with Caesar-Oroonoko. Others, however—the example suggests yet another significant asymmetry of gender—are carved all over. Imoinda, the narrator remarks as if it were an afterthought ("I had forgot to tell you"), has "fine Flowers and Birds all over her Body" (45).[41]

Behn goes on to suggest that carvings such as those on Imoinda's body are "more delicate" than those on "our antient Picts that are figur'd in the Chronicles"; this observation alludes, almost certainly, to a famous set of engravings by Theodor deBry based on paintings by John White. Published in 1590 with Thomas Hariot's *Briefe and True Report of the New Found Lande* (1588), White's paintings of Indians were accompanied by "drawings of ancient Picts and Britons who looked very much like his Indians, particularly in dress and body decorations."[42] Behn's passage, then, with its allusion to a famous work of travel literature, dramatizes her effort to establish a scale of comparative value for an emergent market in which books and bodies and bodily adornments all jostled as commodities. I want to argue, indeed, that *Oroonoko* uses echoes of Othello in particularly intriguing ways to construct an ambiguous reflection on the role of intellectual producers and consumers, especially female ones, in this international market. Oroonoko's physical beauty is particularly admired by an audience of women, Behn suggests: "He came into the Room," she says of her first meeting with her hero, "and addressed himself to me, and

some other Women, with the best Grace in the World" (8). He leads
a group of English women on "Adventures" to explore the wonders
of the new world, and so long as "we had Caesar in our Company on
these Designs, we fear'd no Harm" (49). The narrator explicitly describes
him, moreover, as preferring "the Company of us Women much above
the Men," partly, she explains, because "he could not drink" (46),
but also partly, we surmise, because he enjoys the position of (relative)
power he acquires through being an object of fascination for a female
audience.

In this "true" account of things that happened in the "new Colonies,"
Oroonoko and Imoinda are presented not only as the object of the
author's interest and sympathy; they are also "curiosities" she offers her
readers back in England. As she is well aware, she must offer "Novelty" to
pique her metropolitan reader's interest (for "where there is no Novelty,
there can be no Curiosity" [3]). The author herself, as we have also seen, is
both a producer and a consumer of novelty or "news" whether oral or
written. Indeed, in a fascinating passage about her own role in one of the
novella's climactic episodes, the slave rebellion, Behn represents her female
identity as well as her problematic agency as an ambiguous function of
the *circulation* of information.

In the passage in question, Behn evokes, as Shakespeare does in *Othello,*
what I have called the "Aaron potential"; here a group of sexually
vulnerable (and valuable) English women are pitted against a black man
they momentarily *imagine* as a villainous rapist. After describing how
Oroonoko leads other male slaves to revolt, is deserted by all but one of
his fellows, and is then recaptured and brutally punished by white male
property owners, the narrator interrupts the plot's temporal progression
to return to a point in the just-recounted story when the outcome of
Oroonoko's rebellion was still uncertain. That uncertainty is oddly pre-
served for Behn's readers by her shift from the simple past tense to a
subjunctive formulation that mixes past, present, and the possibility of
a different future:

You must know, that when the News was brought . . . that Caesar
had betaken himself to the Woods, and carry'd with him all the
Negroes, we were possess'd with extreme Fear, which no Persua-
sions could dissipate, that he would secure himself till night, and
then, that he would come down and cut all our Throats. This
Apprehension made all the Females of us fly down the River to be
secured; and while we were away, they acted this Cruelty; for I
suppose I had Authority and Interest enough there, had I suspected
any such thing, to have prevented it: but we had not gone many

Leagues, but the News overtook us, that Caesar was taken and whipped like a common Slave. (67–68)

In this passage, the authorial "I" seems at once extraordinarily lucid and disturbingly blind about her own complicity in her hero's capture and humiliating punishment. Had she been present, she "supposes" she could have prevented the cruelty which "they"—white men—wrought upon the black male slave.[43] Her claim to possess some singular social authority, however, is belied by her representation of herself as part of a group of weak females, a passive group prone to illness: as Martine Brownley has noted, Behn later rather guiltily claims sickness as an excuse for her absence from Oroonoko's final torture.[44] In the earlier scene of female flight, the women are possessed not by men, black or white, but rather by an agent named Fear and quickly renamed Apprehension. That oddly abstract agent turns out, if we look closely, to be a product of something the passage twice calls "News"—a mode of verbal production that is often defined in this text as unreliable and which belongs, as we have seen, to a semantic complex that names crucial features of Behn's own discourse in *Oroonoko*.

Here as in many other parts of the book, the narrative oscillates between criticizing and profiting from a "system" of circulation which includes both bodies and words, among them the lies Oroonoko discovers to be characteristic of Englishmen and even, the text obliquely suggests, of the narrator herself.[45] Aspects of this disturbing oscillation have been shrewdly analyzed by Laura Brown and Michael McKeon but have prompted other critics less comfortable with ideological contradictions to (mis)represent Behn's text either as an "anti-slavery" document or as a royalist allegory which is not at all opposed to the institution of slavery but only to the enslavement of kings.[46] Building especially on Brown's work, I would argue that in Behn's shifting and sometimes contradictory perspectives on her hero and on the slave trade, we can see the lineaments of a complex model of European colonization that limns the relation between Old World and New not only in terms of a binary opposition between self and other but also in terms of a highly unstable triangular model. This model, in its simplest version, draws relations of sameness and difference among a black African slave, a white English woman, and a group of native Americans who are described, in the book's opening pages, as innocents "so unadorned" and beautiful that they resemble "our first parents before the fall" (3). Neither the white English woman nor the black African man share the Indians' imputed quality of primeval innocence—a quality that seems indeed highly paradoxical since the narrator describes the Indians as "unadorned" immediately after describing how the English traded beads and trinkets, subsequently used as ornaments by the Indians, for the feathered clothes and wreathes made by the natives.

If the Indians are seen both as "pre-fallen" and as "falling" (via their trade in ornament), the narrator and Oroonoko-Caesar are, by contrast, definitely post-fall beings. Both have received the adornments of a European education, albeit less good, we may suppose, than those accorded to privileged white men; and both are at once victims and beneficiaries of socioeconomic systems that discriminate kings from commoners and support the privileges of the nobility with the profits of the slave trade. Oroonoko is described as having captured and sold black slaves in African wars before he was himself enslaved; and the narrator not only belongs to a slave-owning class but, as we have seen, voices intermittent support for the nationalistic colonizing enterprise which fueled and depended on the African slave trade. She laments the loss of Surinam to the Dutch a few years after the events of the novella take place (interestingly, the English traded that colony for New Amsterdam, in "our" America, in 1667) and even uses a lush description of a gold-prospecting river trip to suggest the desirability—in 1688, on the eve of William of Orange's accession to the British throne—of retaking the lost colony and its lost profits: "And 'tis to be bemoaned what his majesty lost by losing part of America," she remarks (59).[47] At the same time, the narrator deplores the lies told by white slavers and represents Oroonoko's rousing encomium of freedom to his fellow slaves with an enthusiasm that Thomas Southerne prudently censors in his 1696 stage version of Behn's novella.[48]

By thus presenting a narrator and a hero who are victims, ambivalent critics, and also of course beneficiaries of the international system of the slave trade, and by contrasting and comparing both characters, at different moments, to the exotic and quasi-innocent Indians, Behn provides a perspective on the conquest of America that complicates, among other binary oppositions, the ethical one, infinitely labile in the literature of the imperial venture, between "we" as good and "them" as evil—or vice versa. The "triangulation effects" of Behn's text have, as one of their several hermeneutic horizons, I would argue, the "triangular trade" analyzed by Eric Williams and mentioned early in this essay.

What even this account of the complexity of Behn's novella leaves out, however, is the specific ideological modality of the "other" black slave in the story, the character who is, indeed, a major if relatively silent player in the book's shadowy plot about an erotic triangle. Imoinda is doubly enslaved—to the whites, male and female, who have bought her and also, as the narrative insists, to her black husband. In striking contrast to the unmarried narrator, who as we have seen plays the role of the Petrarchan mistress and lady-lord toward Oroonoko as vassal, Imoinda is an uncanny

amalgam of European ideals of wifely subservience and European fantasies about wives of Oriental despots. She is thus the perfect embodiment,
with the exception of her dark hue, of an image of the ideal English wife
as the property, body and soul, of her husband. Wives like Imoinda—that
is, *African* wives, as refracted in the mirror a white English woman holds
up to this example of the "other"—"have a respect for their Husbands
equal to what other People pay a Deity; and when a Man finds any
occasion to quit his Wife, if he love her, she dies by his hand; if not he sells
her, or suffers some other to kill her" (72).

In this passage, which rationalizes and immediately precedes the gruesome scene in which Oroonoko severs Imoinda's head from her pregnant
body, the narrator's relation to her black heroine is revealed to be anything
but straightforwardly sympathetic. On the contrary, I want to argue, Behn
as author uses Imoinda's death scene to inscribe the authority and agency
of the white woman writer, figured in the narrator, as a function of a set of
finely calibrated differences from the female "other" embodied in Imoinda.
That "other," against which Behn constructs her authorial agency, is a
creature of extremes. On the one hand, Imoinda appears utterly passive
and obedient; on the other, however, she is violent and powerful, a
creature which threatens the white civilization in ways that are arguably
analogous, as we shall see, to those dramatized when Oroonoko kills not
one but two mother tigers. Imoinda is, significantly, the only nonwhite
character in the story who is allowed actually to wound, with an arrow,
the supreme figure of white patriarchal authority, Colonel Byam.[49] Her
deed of Amazonian aggression is, however, described by the narrator as
being quite literally undone—and by another woman of color. Byam's life
is saved, though the narrator clearly regrets this, by his Indian mistress,
who sucks the poison from his wound (65, 68). The narrator's own
ambivalent relation to male English authority is figured here—but also
symbolically divested of its power to harm—by the device of splitting
"other" women into the extreme roles of dangerous rebel and erotically
complicitous slave.

Behn implicitly associates both these extremes with Imoinda, through
the symbol of a mother tiger and also through the anagrammatic link
between the unnamed Indian woman who nurses Byam and the black
woman whose name, intriguingly, means "honey mixed with wealth" in
the Yoruba language; when seen through a European linguistic lens, the
name also suggests "I'm Indian" or even more punningly, "I-me [moi] am
Indian."[50] Effectively presenting her own agency as safe—or safe enough—by
contrast to Imoinda's figure, Behn thus implicitly both stages and preor-
dains the outcome of a competition between the white female author and
the nonwhite female slave and potential rebel. The competition is focused

on possession of Oroonoko's body and its symbolic power to engender
something that will outlive it. That power remains latent, in the sense of
impotent, without a female counterpart, and for this Behn offers two
distinct images: Imoinda's pregnant body, holding a potential slave-laborer
("for," as the text reminds us, "all the Breed is theirs to whom the Parents
belong" [45]); and, alternatively, the author's own "Female Pen" (40),
which she deploys to describe, with an unnerving blend of relish and
horror, the novella's concluding scenes of Oroonoko's dismemberment.
She uses that pen also, as she tells the reader in the final paragraph, in
hopes of making Oroonoko's "glorious Name to survive all Ages" (78).

The narrator seems to win the competition hands down, though the
production of the text, years after the events it describes, testifies to a
certain intractible residue or psychic fallout from the narrator's comport-
ment toward her slaves. If, however, she signals guilt and some chagrin at
her impotence to save Oroonoko (she deserts him in the middle of his
torture, for instance, because his smell is too much for her suddenly
acquired and typically "feminine" delicacy, [76]), she also demonstrates
the powers of her pen and implies some degree of choice in how she
deploys her verbal skills, oral and written. Through her "Female Pen" flow
at least some of the prerogatives of the English empire and its language, a
language she shows herself using, in one remarkable scene, as a potent
instrument of sexual and political domination. In this scene, which explicitly
pits an image of politically "dangerous" biological reproduction against
an image of "safe" verbal production, the author presents herself most
paradoxically as both a servant and a beneficiary of the eroticized socio-
economic *system* of domination she describes. When some unnamed
English authority figures perceive that Oroonoko is growing sullen because
of the "Thought" that his child will belong not to him but to his owners,
the narrator is "obliged," she tells us, to use her fiction-making powers to
"divert" Oroonoko (and Imoinda too) from thoughts of mutiny. Mutiny is
specifically tied to a problem in population management, a problem about
which Behn's text—like much colonialist discourse, including chilling
debates on whether it is better to "buy or breed" one's slaves—is fundamentally ambivalent.[51] Mutiny, the narrator observes, "is very fatal sometimes in those Colonies that abound so with Slaves, that they exceed the
Whites in vast numbers" (46). It is to abort the potential mutiny that
the narrator is "obliged" to "discourse with Caesar, and to give him all the
Satisfaction I possibly could"—which she does, entertaining him with
stories about "the Loves of the Romans and great Men, which charmed
him to my Company" (46). In an interestingly gendered division of
narrative goods, she tells Imoinda stories about nuns.[52]

Playing a version of Othello to both her slaves, and thus dramatizing a complex mode of authorial "ownership" of characters cast in the role of enthralled—and feminized—audience, Behn represents herself creating a paradoxical *facsimile* of freedom, for herself, her immediate audience, and by implication, her readers back home. In this facsimile, servitude, which Oroonoko during his revolt describes scornfully as a condition of being "Sport for Women" (61), is rendered (perhaps only temporarily) tolerable by being eroticized, fantasized, "diverted" from activities, either sexual or military, that might work to dislodge the English from their precarious lordship in this new world. Just how precarious their possession was the narrative acknowledges by repeatedly lamenting their loss of the land to the Dutch; but the deeper problems of the logic of colonialism are also signalled, albeit confusedly, by the contrast between the description of slave mutiny quoted above and the explanation offered early in the story for why the British do *not* enslave the native Indians, a group which, like the Africans, is essential to the colonists' welfare; "they being on all occasions very useful to us," the narrator says, "we find it absolutely necessary to caress 'em as Friends, and not to treat 'em as Slaves, nor dare we do other, their numbers so far surpassing ours in that Continent" (5)[53] This passage sheds an ironic light on the later moment when the narrator uses stories to divert Oroonoko from thoughts of mutiny, for we see that one logical solution to the mutiny problem, a solution that her stories to Oroonoko suppress but which her larger narrative only partially represses, is the possibility of *not* enslaving a group of "others" who outnumber you. Such a solution, with respect both to Africans and to Indians, had been recommended by a few early critics of the colonial enterprise; but Behn is far from joining the tiny group who voiced criticisms of the whole system of international trade based on forced labor by persons of many skin colors, including freckled Irish white.[54]

   In its characteristically disturbing way, Behn's novella shows us just enough about the author's competition with Imoinda, and the enmeshment of that competition within a larger socio-sexual-economic system, to make us uneasy when we hold the book *Oroonoko* in our hands and realize that the text itself invites us to see the book as a safe-sex substitute for the potentially mutinous but also economically valuable black slave child Oroonoko might have had with Imoinda—or indeed with Aphra Behn, had she given physical rather than verbal "satisfaction," playing Tamora, as it were, to Oroonoko's Aaron and thereby activating longstanding English anxieties about the "genetic" strength of blackness (babies born of mixed unions were thought inevitably to follow the darker and "lower" parental hue).[55]

   In an apparently conservative and reassuring twist of the old trope of book as child, however, Behn offers her contemporary English readers a representation of a white woman who is apparently attracted to a strong black hero but who in the end refrains—as Desdemona did not—from taking her sexual "treasure" from its rightful owner and disposer, her father, to give to an alien. That contemporary readers would have remarked the text's coy dramatization of an erotic "road not taken" on the narrator's part—the road excoriated by Thomas Rymer among others—is suggested by Southerne's revisionary dramatization of Behn's tale; in Southerne's play, Oroonoko loves a *white* Imoinda.[56] The frontispiece from a 1735 production of Southerne's highly popular play (fig. 1) is reproduced, intriguingly, on the cover of the Norton edition of Behn's story, and this representation—like Southerne's play—arguably capitalizes on the cultural prestige of *Othello*'s drama of tragic miscegenous romance. Southerne's play and its frontispiece also arguably exploit the posthumous notoriety of Behn herself, a notoriety which Behn herself may well have helped fashion. In 1696, the same year that Southerne's play was first produced, a biography of Behn appeared as a preface and advertisement to a posthumous collection of her fictions. The anonymous biography, elaborately and titillatingly *denies* a rumor that the author of *Oroonoko* had a romance with her hero: "I knew her intimately well," the author affirms, "and I believe she wou'd not have conceal'd any Love-affair from me ... which makes me assure the World, there was no Affair between that Prince and Astrea."[57]

Whatever the status of this rumor (which is reproduced, again only to be denied "credit," in the introduction to Norton edition of the text, [x]), it arguably forms part of the larger discursive field in which Behn's text was and continues to be read. At least a part of this field is evidently governed by an ideological economy in which the white woman's book is born, quite starkly, from a self-willed (albeit partial) censoring of her own sexuality and from the death and silencing of black persons, one of them pregnant. Behind the scene of Oroonoko's final torture is the murder-sacrifice of the black woman and her unborn child. And the threat represented by the black woman, I would suggest, is obscurely acknowledged to be even greater than the threat represented by the black man, so that the text finally has to enlist him, through enticements of various codes of masculine honor, to suppress the one character who uses physical force rather than words to attack the highest legal representative of the colonial system, namely the male Lieutenant Governor. According to the old Renaissance commonplace, deeds are masculine, words are feminine; but Imoinda, like the Amazon maidens Sir Walter Ralegh sought in Guiana, performs the kind of deed that Desdemona, Othello's "fair warrior," is never allowed.[70]

Imoinda's rebellious power—and the need to destroy or at least dis-

Figure 1. Frontispiece, Thomas Southerne, *Oroonoko,* London, 1735. From the Rare Books and Manuscripts Division, New York Public Library; Astor, Lenox and Tilden Foundations.

guise it—are figured most strikingly, I think, in the two juxtaposed episodes in which Oroonoko first kills a mother tiger and lays the whelp at the author's feet (51) and then kills a property-destroying tiger—again female—and extracts her bullet-ridden heart to give to the English audience. At this moment Oroonoko is most transparently shown as a figure for the author of *Oroonoko,* a repository of novel curiosities which Behn offers to her readers as he offers the tiger's cub, and then heart, to his owner-admirers: "This heart the conqueror brought up to us, and 'twas a very great curiosity, which all the country came to see, and which gave Caesar occasion of making many fine Discourses, of Accidents in War, and strange Escapes" (53). Here Oroonoko woos his "Great Mistress" and other English ladies as Othello wooed Desdemona with his eloquent story of his "most disastrous chances...moving accidents...hair breadth-scapes i' th' imminent deadly breach" (1.3.134–36). With respect to the power relation between a narrator and an audience, this scene offers a mirror reversal of that in which the narrator entertains her sullen, potentially mutinous hero with *her* culture's stories of "great [Roman] men." The "ground" of both scenes, the "material," as it were, from which the production and reception of exotic stories derives, is the silent figure of the black woman—silent but by no means safe, as is suggested by the image of the female tiger and the narrative device of duplicating it.

In *Oroonoko,* then, we see Aphra Behn using her "Female Pen" to ward off the overdetermined set of dangers she associates with or projects onto the nonwhite heroine; among these dangers, I have suggested, lurks pregnancy, the consequence and all too visible sign, for women, of one form of sexual pleasure.[59] Behn not only kills the African woman off in the end but performs an ideologically significant gesture of cultural appropriation and justification by making the heroine voice, as if it were her own, a desire for death at the hands of a lover, a desire founded, moreover, on precisely the European ideal of female "honor" as chastity which Behn mocks and interrogates in so many of her works. In thus making her nonwhite heroine participate verbally in the mystification of the complex causes of her death, Behn makes Imoinda into an interesting variation of the Desdemona who lies for love at the moment of her death: in response to Emilia's question "O, who hath done this deed?" she famously insists, "Nobody—I myself" (5.2.122–23). Behn thus exposes some of the dire contradictions of her society's ideologies of gender and at the same time takes advantage, we might fairly say, of the particular historical condition of silence which affected the vast majority of nonwhite women who lived in England's early imperial territories. That point may seem obvious, but is therefore all the more likely to be grist for the mills of forgetfulness upon which ideologies feed. Among those ideologies are versions of academic feminism that forget that literate metropolitan women sometimes promoted and rationalized, as well as interrogated, the colonizing process which was figured so often and so profoundly as a rape of a female, or feminized, "other."

Trying not to forget the implications of that fact for my own work as a teacher of English, I shall end with a provisional and necessarily mixed assessment of what Behn accomplishes in her reworking of *Othello.* She clearly perpetuates a tradition of misrepresenting nonwhite characters on English stages and in the pages of English books. But she also invites us to see and ponder the fact that we are *not* seeing the "whole truth" about either her white or her nonwhite characters. Representing herself as (effectively if not deliberately) lying to Oroonoko by breaking her promise that he would be freed by the English, Behn's narrator implicitly belongs to the group of white English Christians whose collective Word Oroonoko painfully learns to scorn. Like the paradoxical Cretan Liar ("All Cretans are liars; I am a Cretan"), however, Behn produces some quantity of skepticism about the believability or "credit" of her colonial narrative. And in so doing, she is arguably a better interpreter and maker of news from the New World than many who have followed her.

NOTES

For help with this essay I am indebted to many students and colleagues; I am especially grateful to Ann R. Jones, David Kastan, Karen Newman, Marianne Novy, David Simpson, and Betty Travitsky. Professors Jones and Travitsky organized an MLA Forum on Renaissance women in 1989 for which I worked out some of the ideas developed in the present essay; the Forum papers, including my "Juggling the Categories of Race, Class and Gender: Aphra Behn's *Oroonoko*," were published in *Women's Studies: An Interdisciplinary Journal* 19 (Spring 1991).

1. Marianne Novy, ed., *Women's Re-Visions of Shakespeare* (Urbana: University of Illinois Press, 1990), 3.

2. Aphra Behn, Preface to *The Dutch Lover,* in *The Works of Aphra Behn,* ed. Montague Summers (1915; rpt. New York: Phaeton, 1967), 1:224; cited in Novy, 12*n5*. Subsequent references will be noted in the text.

3. On Aphra Behn's education—unusually good for a seventeenth-century woman of any class but described by Behn herself as grossly inadequate in comparison to the (classical) education afforded to middle- and upper-class English men—see Angeline Goreau, *Reconstructing Aphra: A Social Biography of Aphra Behn* (New York: Dial Press, 1980), chap. 4.

4. Virginia Woolf, *A Room of One's Own* (1929; rpt. New York: Harcourt, Brace, Jovanovich, 1957), 5–6.

5. For a discussion of Ben Jonson's oft-quoted lines, see my afterword to *Shakespeare Reproduced: The Text in History and Ideology,* ed. Jean E. Howard and Marion F. O'Connor (London: Methuen, 1987), 281.

6. I discuss the parallels between Behn's *Widow Ranter* and *Oroonoko* in an essay in *The Production of English Renaissance Culture,* ed. David Lee Miller, Sharon O'Brian, and Harold Weber, forthcoming from Cornell University Press.

7. The first biography of Behn, which states that she was a "Gentlewoman, by Birth" (sig. A7v), was published anonymously as a preface and advertisement for the earliest edition (1696) of her collected *Histories and Novels,* "Printed for S. Briscoe" in London (Wing B 1711). This biography, entitled in its earliest and shortest version "Memoirs on the Life of Mrs. Behn. Written by a Gentlewoman of her Acquaintance," is an odd mixture of fact and fiction and was almost certainly compiled from semi-autobiographical materials written by Behn herself. For a discussion of the (probable) authorship and multiple versions of this biography, see R. A. Day, "Aphra Behn's First Biographer," *Studies in Bibliography* 22 (1969): 227–40. For modern discussions of Behn's family, see Goreau, *Reconstructing Aphra,* 8–10; Maureen Duffy, *The Passionate Shepherdess: Aphra Behn, 1640–89* (London: Jonathan Cape, 1977), chap. 1; Sara Mendelson, *The Mental World of Stuart Women: Three Studies* (Brighton: Harvester, 1967), 116–20; and Mary Ann O'Donnell, *Aphra Behn: An Annotated Bibliography of Primary and Secondary Sources* (New York: Garland, 1986), 2–3.

8. On Behn's situation after her father died, impoverished but also freer of paternal constraint than was thought proper, see Goreau, *Reconstructing Aphra,* 42.

9. See Goreau, *Reconstructing Aphra*, 12–13, for a discussion of how Behn's education constitutes a strong objection to the theory that a lower-class girl might have been simply "adopted" by a gentry family; "a possible exception to this rule of class might have been an illegitimate child passed off as a relative of some sort." For the theory that Behn never really went to Surinam but rather plagiarized her descriptions of the colony from George Warren's *Impartial Description of Surinam upon the Continent of Guinea in America* (1667), see Ernest Bernbaum, "Mrs. Behn's Biography a Fiction," *PMLA* 28 (1913): 432–53. For bibliography on the evidence for Behn's trip to Surinam, see O'Donnell, *Aphra Behn: An Annotated Bibliography*, 3; and see also Elaine Campbell, "Aphra Behn's Surinam Interlude," *Kunapipi* 7, nos. 2–3 (1985): 25–35.

10. See Behn's "To Mr. Creech (under the name of Daphnis) on his Excellent Translation of Lucretius," in which she describes herself as "unlearn'd in Schools," a victim of her birth, her education, and "the scanted Customes of the Nation" that don't permit "the Female Sex to tread, / The mighty Paths of Learned Heroes dead" (*Works*, 6:166). The best account of how she earned her living is by Catherine Gallagher in the chapters on Behn in her forthcoming book *British Women Writers and the Literary Marketplace from 1670–1820* (New York: Oxford University Press, 1993). Gallagher has kindly allowed me to read and quote from a draft of her manuscript. One chapter, entitled "Who Was That Masked Woman? The Prostitute and the Playwright in the Comedies of Aphra Behn," has been published in *Last Laughs: Perspectives on Women in Comedy*, ed. Regina Barreca (New York: Gordon & Breach, 1988), 23–42.

11. For this very condensed biographical account I have drawn on materials in Goreau, *Reconstructing Aphra*; Duffy, *The Passionate Shepherdess*; and Mendelson, *The Mental World of Stuart Women*. For more details on the financially conse-quential attack on Monmouth—in the epilogue she wrote for an anonymous play called *Romulus and Hersilia* (August 1682)—see Goreau, 251–52. As Goreau observes, it was not only Behn's arrest, however, but a general depression in the London theater that prompted her turn to the (less lucrative) role of poetry and fiction writer. The theatrical depression was the result, in large part, of the amalgamation of the two great companies in 1682, which meant "new plays were for a time hardly required" (Janet Todd, *The Sign of Angellica: Women, Writing and Fiction, 1660–1800* [New York: Columbia University Press, 1989], 74). See also O'Donnell, *Aphra Behn: An Annotated Bibliography*, 5–6; she remarks that between 1682, "when her slur of Monmouth in the epilogue to the anonymous *Romulus and Hersilia* resulted in the warrant for her arrest," and her death, Behn produced and published only two more plays (though she wrote two others); but "all her prose fiction was written (although not all was published) . . . along with her three poetry miscellanies."

12. For an excellent account and bibliography of the Renaissance ideology of normative femininity, see Ann Rosalind Jones, *The Currency of Eros: Women's Love Lyric in Europe, 1540–1620* (Bloomington: University of Indiana Press, 1990), chap. 1. For a discussion of the attacks on Behn mounted by some of her contemporaries, see Goreau, *Reconstructing Aphra*, chap. 11.

13. For examples of this gendered colonial cultural discourse, see David Brion Davis, *The Problem of Slavery in Western Culture* (Ithaca: Cornell University Press, 1966), 277, where he notes that the State of Maryland reversed the old convention of *partus sequitur ventrum* (the child follows the mother) in the late seventeenth century in order to "inhibit the 'lustful desires' of white women." Davis also cites an eighteenth-century colonialist document by Edward Long that displays a fear of female sexuality that is yoked with, or channeled through, an ideology of class: "The lower class of women in England," wrote Long in 1772, "are remarkably fond of the blacks, for reasons too brutal to mention; they would connect themselves with horses and asses, if the law permitted them" (qtd. in Davis, 277).

14. See, for instance, Lady Mary Chudleigh's argument, in "To The Ladies" (1703), that "Wife and servant are the same, / But only differ in the name," in *First Feminists: British Women Writers 1578–1799,* ed. Moira Ferguson (Bloomington and Old Westbury: Indiana University Press and The Feminist Press, 1985), 237. Cf. the statement in a famous pamphlet entitled *The Levellers,* also from 1703, that "Matrimony is indeed become a meer Trade[.] They carry their daughters to *Smithfield* as they do Horses, and sell to the highest bidder," quoted in Maximillian E. Novak and David Stuart Rodes's edition of Thomas Southerne's *Oroonoko* (Lincoln: University of Nebraska Press, 1976), xxiv. And see Jacqueline Pearson, *The Prostituted Muse: Images of Women and Women Dramatists, 1642–1737* (New York: St. Martin's Press, 1988), 114, on the way in which Southerne followed Behn in making a "symbolic equivalence between women and slaves."

15. For a concise account of the (relatively small) group of early Renaissance texts which remarked the fact that "ethnocentrism works in two directions," see Elliot H. Tokson, *The Popular Image of the Black Man in English Drama, 1550–1688* (Boston: G. K. Hall, 1982), 6–7; and see also his discussion in chap. 2 of a set of English lyric poems (by George Herbert and his brother Edward, Henry King, Henry Rainolds, and John Cleveland) which offer more complex depictions of black persons as objects and subjects of erotic passion than most English Renaissance texts do.

16. *The Works of Sir Thomas Browne,* ed. Charles Sayle (Edinburgh: John Grant, 1912) 2:386; cited in Tokson, *The Popular Image,* 6.

17. See Catherine Gallagher, *British Women Writers;* and also Deborah C. Payne, "'And Poets Shall by Patron-Princes Live': Aphra Behn and Patronage," *Curtain Calls: British and American Women and the Theater, 1660–1820,* ed. Mary Anne Schofield and Cecilia Macheski (Athens: Ohio University Press, 1991), 105–19.

18. "A Session of the Poets," in *Poems on Affairs of State,* ed. George de F. Lord (New Haven: Yale University Press, 1963), 1:355; cited in Goreau, *Reconstructing Aphra,* 232–33.

19. Janet Todd, *The Sign of Angellica,* 1.

20. See for instance the Prologue which Thomas Jordan wrote for the first production of *Othello* after the Restoration (by the King's Company in November or December 1660); this text focuses, in a strikingly prurient way, on the histori-

cally specific novelty of a female body in Desdemona's clothes: "I come, unknown to any of the rest, / To tell you news, I saw the Lady drest. / The Woman plays to day: mistake me not, / No man in gown, or Page in petty coat; / A Woman to my knowledge, yet I cann't / (If I should dye) make affidavidt on't" ("A Prologue, to Introduce the First Woman that Came to Act on the Stage, in the Tragedy Called The Moor of Venice," in *A Royal Arbour of Loyal Poesie* [London, 1664], 22). For directing my attention to Jordan's text I am indebted to Katherine Eisaman Maus, "Playhouse Flesh and Blood: Sexual Ideology and the Restoration Actress," *ELH* 46 (1979): 595–617; she discusses the Prologue and quotes another passage from it on pp. 596–97. On the circumstances of *Othello*'s Restoration revival, see Bryan Forbes, *That Despicable Race: A History of the British Acting Tradition* (London: Elm Tree Books, 1980), 28; and also Rosamund Gilder, *Enter the Actress: The First Women in the Theatre* (New York: Theatre Arts Books, 1931), 141.

21. Eric Williams, *From Columbus To Castro: The History of the Caribbean* (1970; rpt. New York: Vintage, 1984), 140.

22. Folarin Shyllon, *Black People in Britain, 1553–1883* (London: Oxford University Press for the Institute of Race Relations, 1977), 8.

23. Thomas Rymer, *A Short View of Tragedy,* in *Critical Essays of the Seventeenth Century,* ed. Joel Spingarn (Oxford: Oxford University Press, 1908), 2:238.

24. For the text of "The Disappointment," see *Works,* 6:178–82. This poem, a fine gloss on the comic representation of male impotence in the first part of *Oroonoko,* is a brilliantly revisionary instance of the Restoration subgenre of "imperfect enjoyment" poems; on Behn's deviation from male-authored poetic representations of impotence, see Judith Kegan Gardiner, "Aphra Behn: Sexuality and Self-respect," *Women's Studies* 7 (1980): 67–78, esp. 74–77; and also Margaret W. Ferguson, "A Room Not Their Own: Renaissance Women as Readers and Writers," in *The Comparative Perspective on Literature,* ed. Clayton Koelb and Susan Noakes (Ithaca: Cornell University Press, 1988), 112–14.

25. Cf. Gallagher's observation, made with reference to Dryden's revision of Shakespeare's *The Tempest,* that the Restoration playwright "revised the Renaissance to make the revelation of the woman the wonder. The brave new world of the Restoration stage was indeed the female body" (*British Women Writers,* 47).

26. On the cultural perception of both actresses and (published) female authors as whores, see Goreau, *Reconstructing Aphra,* chap. 9. "From the moment a woman set pen to paper her sexuality came into question," remarks Goreau, citing a passage from Robert Gould's *A Satyrical Epistle to the Female Author of a Poem Called 'Sylvia's Revenge,'* (1691) "whore's the like reproachful name, as poetess—the luckless twins of shame" (Goreau, 158). The idea that not only female authors but actresses were by definition unchaste was, of course, a common theme of Restoration drama as well as a phenomenon grounded in historical fact and caused, in part, by the asymmetries between male and female actors' economic situations.

27. For useful summaries of the early history of English imperialism, see Williams, *From Columbus to Castro,* chap. 1; and Laura Brown, "The Romance of

Empire: *Oroonoko* and the Trade in Slaves," in *The New Eighteenth Century,* ed. L. Brown and Felicity Nussbaum (New York: Methuen, 1987), 40–61.

28. Though critics regularly insist on Behn's Tory politics—and note that a number of her plays from the period of the Exclusion crisis are highly propagandistic—her political views in the 1660s, when she went to Surinam, cannot simply be assumed to have been identical with those she held twenty years later; moreover, even in the 1680s, her obvious sympathies with the Stuart absolutists did not preclude her from criticizing James's incompetence in the period just before he lost his throne; see Mendelson, *The Mental World of Stuart Women,* 174, for the discussion of Behn's satire on James's 1686 Hounslow Heath encampment in a poem entitled "Caesar's Ghost."

29. Scholars differ substantially on the dating (and duration) of Behn's Surinam visit: see Goreau, *Reconstructing Aphra,* 49–69; and Mendelson, *The Mental World of Stuart Women,* 118.

30. All quotations from *Oroonoko* are cited by page number of the text edited by Lore Metzger (New York: W. W. Norton, 1973). The passage cited here is from p. 1.

31. I am grateful to my colleague Adélékè Adéèkó for explaining that Oroonoko's name could perfectly well come directly from the Yoruba language spoken in modern Nigeria. We know too little about how much an English writer like Behn might have known about African languages and cultures through information circulated by early explorers and slave traders. It does seem likely that Ralegh's *Discoverie*—with its famous description of Guiana as a country "that hath yet her maidenhead"—exerted some influence on Behn's choice of her hero's name. Ralegh's text, first published in 1596 and reissued in three editions that year, was even more widely read when it appeared in the second edition of Richard Hakluyt's *Principal Navigations* (1600); the text is available in the modern edition of the *Navigations* by Walter Ralegh, 12 vols. (Glasgow: J. MacLehose, 1903–5), 10:338–431. I am indebted for bibliographical information and for my general understanding of Ralegh's *Discoverie* both as text and as event (the published work includes in its full title the phrase *Performed in the yeere 1595*) to Louis Montrose, "The Work of Gender in the Discourse of Discovery," *Representations* 33 (Winter 1991): 1–41. See also Joyce Lorimer, "Ralegh's First Reconnaissance of Guiana? An English Survey of the Orinoco in 1587," *Terrae Incognitae* 9 (1977): 7–21.

32. I am indebted for this point to Mendelson, *The Mental World of Stuart Women,* 120; alone among the scholars I have read, she comments on the "unexpected" Republican perspective that pervades (I wouldn't follow her in assuming that it governs) the novella—unexpected because Behn had become a "fanatical royalist" only two years after the events of *Oroonoko* took place. It seems to me, however, that Mendelson too oversimplifies the question of the novella's political allegory (or rather, its overlapping allegories) when she explains the Republicanism of the story—written after all in 1688, long after Behn had "matured" into Tory views—as a function simply of her youth and the fact that her lover, a man named William Scot who does not appear (as such) in the narrative, was an exiled Republican and son of a regicide. For Martin, see *Oroonoko,* 50.

33. See Laura Brown's acute discussion of this typical ideological gesture of remaking the African "other" into a version of the European (aristocratic) "self," "The Romance of Empire: *Oroonoko* and the Trade in Slaves," in *The New Eighteenth Century,* ed. Brown and Nussbaum, 47.

34. For an analysis of Ridley's racist remaking of Othello (which follows in the critical tradition of the "tawny" Moor), see Karen Newman, "And Wash th' Ethiop White: Femininity and the Monstrous in *Othello,*" in *Shakespeare Reproduced,* ed. Jean Howard and Marion O'Connor (London: Methuen, 1987), 143–62, esp. 154, where Newman explicitly compares Ridley's description of Othello to Behn's of Oroonoko.

35. The text is, however, significantly ambiguous about whether Behn could or did own slaves in her own right, as an unfathered, unmarried woman. In her prefatory letter to Maitland, she refers to Oroonoko as "my Slave," but as we have seen, in the novella she is unable to free him in the absence of a male authority figure. Her assertion that she occupies the "best house" in the colony is on p. 45 of the Norton edition; in her prefatory epistle to Lord Maitland—not printed in the Norton edition—she states that "I had none above me in that Country, yet I wanted power to preserve this Great Man [Oroonoko]" (qtd. from *Oroonoko,* ed. Adelaide P. Amore [Washington: University Press of America, 1987], 3).

36. Newman, "And Wash th' Ethiop White," 151; my quotations from *Othello* are from the Signet edition by Alvin Kernan (New York: New American Library, 1963).

37. See Snow's "Sexual Ideology and the Male Order of Things in *Othello,*" *English Literary Renaissance* 10 (1980): 384–412; and Greenblatt's *Renaissance Self-Fashioning From More To Shakespeare* (Chicago: University of Chicago Press, 1980), chap. 6.

38. See Peter Erickson's fine discussion of this moment when Othello "is both the heroic Othello and the evil cultural outsider" in *Patriarchal Structures in Shakespeare's Drama* (Berkeley: University of California Press, 1985), 100.

39. This paragraph is indebted to Anthony Barthelemy, *Black Face, Maligned Race: The Representation of Blacks in English Drama from Shakespeare to Southerne* (Baton Rouge: Louisiana State University Press, 1987), 90–92. See also, for useful discussions of Shakespeare's Aaron and his theatrical double, Eleazer, Eldred Jones, *Othello's Countrymen: The African in English Renaissance Drama* (London: Oxford University Press, 1965), 52–68; and Tokson, *The Popular Image.*

40. The mezzotint is reproduced in Gilder, *Enter the Actress,* 166.

41. Gallagher remarks, with reference to Behn's parenthetical gesture of "I had forgot to tell you," the "clumsy yet strong scoring" of Imoinda's body (*British Women Writers,* 103–4).

42. Karen Kupperman, *Settling With the Indians: The Meeting of English and Indian Cultures in America, 1580–1640* (Totowa, N.J.: Rowman and Littlefield, 1980), 113.

43. Note that the most logical syntactic antecedent of "they" would be a group of *black* men composed of Oroonoko and his band, perpetrating the rape which one might easily construe as the referent for "this cruelty." The grammati-

cal ambiguity points, it seems, to the struggle between the narrator's original perception of danger and her "corrected" but guiltily impotent retroactive perception that the white men, not the black ones, were her true enemies.

44. See Martine W. Brownley, "The Narrator in *Oroonoko,*" *Essays in Literature* 4, no. 2 (1977): 174–81.

45. See, for instance, the passage discussed below where the narrator explicitly invites her reader to reflect on her manipulative narrative powers when she tells Oroonoko stories to "divert" him from thoughts of mutiny. I credit her with considerably more authorial self-consciousness, especially with regard to her complicity in Oroonoko's fate and in his "education" about the little "credit" that should be accorded to white men's (and women's) words (66), than Michael McKeon does in his generally illuminating remarks on the epistemological "instability" of the novella (*The Origins of the English Novel, 1600–1740* [Baltimore: Johns Hopkins University Press, 1987], 113).

46. See Brown, "The Romance of Empire"; and McKeon, *Origins of the English Novel,* esp. 111–13 and 249–50. For examples of opposed critical accounts that don't allow for symptomatic contradictions and ambivalences in Behn's novella, see George Guffey, *Two English Novelists: Aphra Behn and Anthony Trollope,* co-authored by Andrew White (Los Angeles: William Andrews Clark Memorial Library, 1975), 15–16; and Goreau, *Reconstructing Aphra,* 289.

47. On the British loss of Surinam (later Guiana) in exchange for New York, see Williams, *From Columbus to Castro,* 81.

48. And even Southerne's tame version of Oroonoko's advocacy of a slave revolt was felt to be too dangerous for representation in one eighteenth-century English port; according to Mrs. Inchbald, "The tragedy of 'Oroonoko' is never acted in Liverpool, for the very reason why it ought to be acted there oftener than at any other place—The Merchants of that great city acquire their riches by the slave trade" (quoted from Thomas Southerne, *Oroonoko,* ed. Maximillian E. Novak and David Stuart Rodes [Lincoln: University of Nebraska Press, 1976], xxix*n*48).

49. See *Oroonoko,* 64–65, where Imoinda's exploit is first described as incontrovertible "fact"; and 68, where it is oddly described again, this time through the epistemological filter of "news": "the first News we heard was that the Governour was dead of a wound Imoinda had given him; but it was not so well."

50. For the Yoruba meaning of "Imoinda" I am again grateful to my colleague Adélékè Adéèkó.

51. On the "buy or breed" debates, see Daniel P. Mannix in collaboration with Malcolm Cowley, *Black Cargoes: A History of the Atlantic Slave Trade 1518–1865* (New York: Viking, 1962), 52.

52. See Amore's introduction to *Oroonoko* for the hypothesis of Behn's Catholicism, a hypothesis which I think is well founded but which does not adequately gloss the "sexual division of narrative labor" whereby Imoinda is given stories of nuns. For Behn's own nuns' stories (and the late tale *Oroonoko* seems to be full of authorial self-citations), see *The History of the Nun; or, The Fair Vow Breaker* and *The Nun; or, the Perjured Beauty,* both in *Works,* vol. 5.

53. Since the blacks also greatly outnumbered the whites in the colony, Behn's explanation for the distinction in the English treatment of the two nonwhite groups is clearly problematic. The matter continues to be a site of debate in modern histories of slavery in the New World; see Winthrop Jordan, *White Over Black: American Attitudes toward the Negro, 1550–1812* (Chapel Hill: University of North Carolina Press, 1968); Davis, *The Problem of Slavery,* 178; and William D. Phillips, Jr., *Slavery from Roman Times to the Early Transatlantic Trade* (Minneapolis: University of Minnesota Press, 1985), 184.

54. For discussions of early critics of slavery such as Las Casas (who came only late in life to decry the enslavement of blacks as well as Indians) and Albornoz, see Davis, *The Problem of Slavery,* 189; Eric Williams, *From Columbus to Castro,* 43–44; and Goreau, *Reconstructing Aphra,* 289 (on the Quaker Fox's opposition to slavery). On the legal and ideological distinctions very unevenly and gradually introduced between white and black slaves, see Phillips, *Slavery from Roman Times,* 183.

55. See, for instance, George Best's *Discourse* (1578): "I my selfe have seene an Ethiopian as blacke as a cole brought into England, who taking a faire English women to wife, begat a sonne in all respects as blacke as the father was, although England were his native countrey, and an English woman his mother" (rpt. in Hakluyt, *Principal Navigations,* ed. Ralegh, 7:262). I am indebted to Karen Newman's discussion of this passage in "Femininity and the Monstrous," 146. Folarin Shyllon also discusses this passage by Best; its formulation of a theory of racial domination is clearly significant for understanding the first racially discriminatory law in England, namely the one passed in 1596, under Elizabeth I: "Her Majesty, understanding that there are late divers blackamoores brought into this realme, of which kind there are already too manie, considering how God hath blessed this land with great increase of people of our owne nation . . . those kinds of people should be sent forth the lande" (*Acts of the Privy Council of England (New Series), 1596–97,* ed. John R. Dasent, 26: 16–17; cited in Shyllon, *Black People in England,* 93).

56. For a discussion of this "recoloring" of Behn's hero and other significant changes Southerne makes, see Novak and Rodes's introduction to their edition of Southerne's *Oroonoko,* esp. xxxviii.

57. "Memoirs on the Life of Mrs. Behn," sig. B1r.

58. On Ralegh's quest for Amazons as described in his *Discoverie* ("I was very desirous to understand the truth of those warlike woman, because of some it is beleeved, of others not"), see Louis Montrose, "The Work of Gender," 25–29.

59. The narrator's lavish descriptions of Imoinda's "carved" body suggest, of course, the possibility of female homoerotic pleasure as yet another alternative to procreative sexuality. I am grateful to Michèle Barale for this suggestion, which is supported by Behn's publication, in the same year as *Oroonoko,* of a poem "To the Fair Clarinda, who made love to me, imagined more than woman." This poem praises Clarinda for combining virtues of males and females in one body—the same vein of praise that one of Behn's admirers accorded her in a poem printed in the same volume—and thanks the nymph for bringing to "our sex" a way "That

we might love, and yet be innocent" (qtd. from "Poems Appended to *Lycidus,*" *Works,* 6:363; cited and discussed in Goreau, *Reconstructing Aphra,* 205). For the poem by Daniel Kendrick praising Behn as the sole exemplar of a super "Third Sex," see *Works,* 6:296–98.

JULIE HANKEY

Helen Faucit and Shakespeare:
Womanly Theater

When John Ruskin baldly declared in his lecture "Of Queen's Gardens" (1865) that "Shakespeare has no heroes;—only heroines" he condensed into an abrupt conclusion a process that had in fact been evolving over the previous half century and more.[1] If his audience were theatergoers or readers of Shakespearean criticism they would have been only momentarily surprised, for they would not only have been accustomed to the adulation of Shakespeare's women, but also undismayed by the way they could be used (as in Ruskin) to sanction a modern writer's own idealizing conceptions of womanhood. In 1832, after more than a generation of scattered comments and short pieces extolling Shakespeare's women, Anna Jameson devoted a whole book to the subject, which she significantly called *Characteristics of Women,* the object being quite unembarrassedly to exploit Shakespeare's women for feminine purposes—"feminine," that is, in its traditional sense.[2] The elevation of Shakespeare in the eighteenth century to the post of national poet was followed in the nineteenth century by his virtual canonization. This was itself closely paralleled by the promotion of women, or rather Woman, within the Victorian system of values. But a small cloud had traditionally hung over the question of Shakespeare's treatment of womanhood, so that a defense of the nation's greatest poet against the charge of slighting women fitted nicely with a defense of Woman against the charge of being slight. By the time Ruskin gave his lecture, the two mutually influencing processes were complete and women—for good or ill—were provided with a powerful patron saint. "Such in broad light," Ruskin concludes, "is Shakespeare's testimony to the position and character of women in human life. He represents them as infallibly faithful and wise counsellors—incorruptibly just and pure examples—strong always to sanctify, even when they cannot save."[3]

The reputation, as it developed among critics and on the stage, of Shakespeare's female roles has been outlined by Carol J. Carlisle in "The

Critics Discover Shakespeare's Women."[4] It is a story of general neglect, of a prejudice (established by Dryden[5]) in favor of Fletcher as the poet of the "softer" sex, up until the last quarter of the eighteenth century and then of a slowly gathering interest. This latter she accounts for mainly by the growing ideal of "the womanly woman"—that angel in the house who listened to the promptings of the heart, all too often silent in men, buffeted as they were by the exigencies of the commercial world. It was an ideal which seemed to be served by Shakespeare's heroines and which found critical and theatrical exponents to "confirm" it—most notably the Victorian Shakespearean actress Helen Faucit. The present essay takes Carlisle's work as a starting point from which to try to understand the convergence of these multiple canonizations—of Shakespeare, of Shakespeare's women, of Woman, and lastly of Helen Faucit, for she shared in, while helping to create, the reputation of the women she represented.

"I do not suppose it is possible," wrote one admirer to the actress's husband, "to estimate the influence she has had for good. . . . One woman (herself an actress) wrote to me: 'One grows tender over her acting, and any attempt at criticism hurts and angers one. It is the only acting that is perfectly sympathetic.' And a young girl . . . said to me yesterday, 'One felt so grateful to her—I cannot bear to hear anyone speak of it. . . . She has put to silence the ignorance of foolish people, and as to myself I have no words to utter her praise.' "[6] And yet, in contrast to Sarah Siddons at the end of the eighteenth century or to Ellen Terry at the end of the nineteenth, Helen Faucit (debut: 1837) is little remembered now. The reason lies possibly in the very thing that made her so beloved of audiences then— her femininity. But her enshrinement was not an effortless achievement. Being "of a period," which she was, suggests a simple yielding to the flow of contemporary opinion. But in fact she represented an extraordinary paradox: an eminently public woman, practicing not only a profession but a questionable one, celebrated as a symbol of that utterly private and virtuous person, the "womanly woman." The paradox feels a little limp now when the two worlds seem not to threaten each other so fiercely, but the whole subject bristled for the Victorians. In *A Woman's Thoughts about Women* (1858), Dinah Mulock Craik rehearses the arguments against women taking up that profession—arguments that occur repeatedly in periodicals and novels throughout the century. In an often-quoted passage, she describes the female writer who, though known over half the world, can "sit as quiet by the chimney corner, live a life as simple and peaceful as any happy 'common woman' of them all." But, she goes on, with the actress it is different: "She needs to be constantly before the public, not only mentally, but physically: the general eye becomes familiar,

not merely with her genius, but her corporeality; . . . This of itself is a
position contrary to the instinctive something—call it reticence, modesty,
shyness, what you will—which is inherent in every one of Eve's daughters."[7]
Beyond that, she fears the egotism that the profession breeds. Men are
naturally egotistical, but in a woman "it is the most lamentable of all
results, not absolutely vicious, which the world and the necessity of
working in it, effects on women." In short, the actress puts her "tempera-
ment, character, and mode of thought" at risk. Mulock Craik allows that
genius is refining, and that even necessity, where there are old parents or a
"fiddler husband" to support, can be purifying, so she concludes with a
piece of advice to the aspirant: follow your art if you must, but remember
you are "the woman first, the artiste afterwards."[8]

These are measured tones, but some of the same opinions were no
doubt more furiously expressed by others, as is suggested by the following diatribe of a male character in a novel of the late 1840s. Aimed, for
good measure, at both women writers and actresses, it sheds an interesting light on contemporary attitudes and is worth quoting at length:

> A woman who makes her mind public, or exhibits herself in any way
> . . . seems to me no better than a woman of a nameless class. . . .
> there is something revolting in the notion of a woman who professes
> to love and belong to you alone going and printing the secrets of her
> inmost heart, the most sacred workings of her soul for the benefit of
> all who can pay for them. . . . The stage is still worse, for that is
> publishing both mind and body too. Everybody may go to the
> theatre to see an actress, and may pass whatever gross comments on
> her they will; and she has no protection, is open to every species of
> proposal. . . . I could not love a professional woman. . . . no wife or
> daughter of mine should ever . . . form an acquaintance with actress,
> artist, singer or musician.[9]

The passage comes from *The Half-Sisters* (1848), written by one of
Helen Faucit's greatest friends and admirers, Geraldine Jewsbury, to whom
the actress dedicated one of the series of "letters" she published about
Shakespeare's heroines.[10] The external circumstances of Jewsbury's actress-
heroine, Bianca, bear no resemblance to Faucit's, but their difficulties as
women and artists, their alienation, as we would now call it, from a
profession which seemed to threaten something essentially "womanly,"
these were suffered by both, and the resulting anguish was regarded by
them both as a trial of their artistic and personal integrity. Bianca, with
Jewsbury's evident sympathy, protests bitterly against the kind of social
disapproval expressed in the passage quoted above: "The stage is to me a
passion as well as a profession. . . . You don't know what it is to be

devoted to an art. . . . it is a sacred necessity laid upon me, which I cannot help obeying." But in order to defend her "art," she concedes everything to do with "the profession" to her accusers, as Jewsbury comments: "No one could have a keener perception than herself of the tinsel tawdry reality of all stage effects, and no one could loathe the details of the profession more than she did. It required all her imagination and enthusiasm for her art, to carry her through the coarse, gaudy, glaring accessories."[11] Faucit had written to a friend in 1846 in similar terms: "Oh, dear friend, you do not know, you cannot tell what my profession is when you are forced to deal with only the mechanical, matter-of-fact side of it! . . . If you could sit by and listen to the insipid things that I am obliged to hear, generally summed up by praise or dispraise of a dress, or a bunch of feathers, or what not, you would not be surprised that my heart sinks into a very deep pit now and then. It may be all an illusion; and my art may not be the instrument for good and the help of all high and noble things I believe it. . . . As it is, I feel like a person suffering a slow death by pincers."[12]

The consequence for both the real and the fictional actress was to force them, not as professionals, but as women, into the closest possible embrace with their characters. When Bianca, for example, plays Juliet especially finely, it was good because "it was not acting, it was her own heart and life she was embodying."[13] One is reminded of the virtuous and intensely private Mirah in George Eliot's *Daniel Deronda,* who knew that her "acting was not good, except when it was not really acting, but the part was one that I could be myself in."[14] Similarly Faucit, although a professional for at least thirty years, liked to insist that her effects came spontaneously, and that if they were repeated it was because the same unforeseen impulse struck her again and again: "I have often been asked . . . how I did this, how I did that. . . . Questions of this kind irritated me, because they seemed to imply that the actor's art was wholly mechanical, to which the impulse of the moment was a stranger, and that no part of what I did at its best was to be regarded as the unconscious emanation of one's very own self."[15] If this was so for the details of execution, how much more for her interpretations as a whole. As I hope to show, both she and her biographer-husband, Theodore Martin, stress again and again the same private and personal sources for these as well.

In this context, where actresses were suspected of betraying, if not their actual chastity, then Mulock Craik's "instinctive something," Shakespeare represented a haven. The morally fastidious American actress Mary Anderson, one of Helen Faucit's immediate successors, expressed a "sense of comfort and joy," after a period of not playing Shakespeare "at being again under the protecting wing of the great Bard."[16] Shakespeare was

more than just morally safe, of course (local indecencies had been ironed
out of playhouse copies). He was, according to Carlyle, "a blessed heaven-
sent Bringer of Light."[17] His heroines—the ones most often performed,
that is, Desdemona rather than Cressida, Juliet rather than Cleopatra, and
of course, Portia, Viola, Imogen, Rosalind, and the others from the
romantic comedies—were "pure" women, so much so that they could be
regarded as a test of purity in those who played them.[18] According to
Theodore Martin, the morally "impure" French actress Mlle Rachel was
all very well as Phèdre or Andromaque, but she would have fallen at the
first hurdle in Shakespeare.[19]

But for an actress in the thick of professional life, at risk from the taint
of theatricality, there was a cluster of purifying ideas associated with
Shakespeare that could set her apart more radically than could the mere
guarantee of moral rectitude. Crucially, in the light of what has been said,
he had been "privatised," as Jonathan Bate puts it.[20] His plays still formed
a prominent part of the theater repertoire, but a whole inner world, of the
mind and the imagination, had been staked out for him by the Romantics.
They felt not only that the theater was often too crude a medium for him,
but that there were some aspects of Shakespeare that defied any theatrical
treatment at all, however subtle. Charles Lamb's celebrated doubts about
the stage had been echoed by Hazlitt and Coleridge who, though they
made partial exceptions for Kean and Siddons, agreed that at his greatest,
Shakespeare properly belonged in the reader's mind: "the principal and
only genuine excitement ought to come from within," wrote Coleridge in
his discussion of The Tempest, "from the moved and sympathetic
imagination."[21] The stage, wrote Hazlitt, dealt in "the pantomime of
tragedy," the physical display. Everything that "appeals to our profounder
feelings, to reflection and imagination, all that affects us most deeply in
our closets, and in fact constitutes the glory of Shakespeare, is little else
than an interruption and a drag on the business of the stage."[22]

One of these glories was discovered to be Shakespeare's women,
though as it happens, they did not figure centrally in Romantic criticism.
The Romantics' adoration of them, together with their belief, as we shall
see, that women were regulated not by the mind but by feeling, slackened
their critical grip. Hazlitt commented illuminatingly on that problem in a
different context. Comparing the two actors Elizabeth O'Neill and Edmund
Kean, he noticed a difference in kind. The male actor (necessarily, he
implies) had roles which, through the "restraint put upon the feelings by
the understanding and the will," "[afford] a never-failing source of observation and discussion." By contrast, the actress's "simple, obvious and
natural" expression of passion not only gave her "less scope for the
exercise of intellect, and for the distinct and complicated reaction of

the character upon circumstances," but left the critic with little to say but "praise or blame."[23]

If only in passing then, the Romantics nevertheless etherealized the heroines for their Victorian successors, as though in illustration of their concept of the poet's inwardness. Perhaps Coleridge himself recognized the connection when he said, "I have often thought of Shakespeare as the mighty wizard himself [meaning Prospero], introducing as the first and fairest pledge of his so potent art, the female character in all its charms, as if conscious that he first had represented womanhood as a dramatist." The phrase "in all its charms" has a curiously neoclassical ring, suggesting that "the female character" here stands as a symbol rather than an instance of Shakespeare's "potent art." Coleridge believed that "in Shakespeare all the elements of womanhood were holy," and that the "want of prominence" with which they had formerly been taxed was really "their blessed beauty." What had to earlier critics seemed a fault—that they were untheatrical—now seemed a virtue. Shakespeare understood, he goes on, that it arose from "the more exquisite harmony of all the parts of the moral being, constituting one living total of head and heart. He has drawn it, indeed, in all its distinctive energies of faith, patience, constancy, fortitude—shown in all of them as following the heart, which gives its results by a nice tact and happy intuition, without the intervention of the discursive faculty—sees all things by the light of the affections. . . . In all the Shakespearean women there is essentially the same foundation and principle; the distinct individuality and variety are merely the result of the modification of circumstances."[24]

This is more than holiness; it is a theory of womanhood. The two flow into one another, and together they constitute an essentially nontheatrical version of Shakespeare's (and therefore of "real") women. Hazlitt similarly had defined them against the heroines of the eighteenth-century repertoire as being "certainly very unlike stage-heroines; the reverse of tragedy-queens";[25] as for Shakespeare's comic heroines, he would "rather have seen Mrs Abington's Millamant than any Rosalind that ever appeared on the stage," Millamant being essentially "more artificial, more theatrical, more meretricious."[26] Shakespeare's women, he said, "are pure abstractions of the affections. We think as little of their persons as they do themselves, because we are let into the secrets of their hearts, which are more important."[27]

No actress could welcome this reduction to shadowy abstraction—this decorporealization—however sanctified. And yet Helen Faucit absorbed their version of Shakespeare—one that "psychologizes and internalizes, which Romanticizes and novelizes."[28] Her conclusions as to the individuality of the heroines, their weight and prominence, were often entirely at odds with those of the Romantics, but the point is that, like them, she jealously appropriated Shakespeare to herself. She could not insist that he properly belonged only in the mind and imagination of the reader, but if not there, then he or his heroines could belong in an anterior place, as it were, closer in kind to the one they had originally sprung from, that is, her very nature. In the "Envoie" to her letters she writes, "I have had the great advantage of throwing my own nature into theirs, of becoming moved by their emotions: I have, as it were thought their thoughts and spoken their words straight from my own living heart and mind" (viii). This comes close to claiming creative kinship with Shakespeare, the more so because it was in just such terms that the Romantics had described his creative imagination. Shakespeare, above all others, was the poet who "darts himself forth," in Coleridge's phrase, "and passes into all the forms of human character and passion."[29] He had, said Hazlitt, "the faculty of transforming himself at will into whatever he chose: his originality was the power of seeing every object from the exact point of view in which others would see it. He was the Proteus of the human intellect."[30] But put like that, creative genius provides an exact analogy for the actor's function.

In some ways there was nothing new in this. Great actors had always been said to "be," to possess themselves of, their characters. As Earl R. Wasserman has shown, treatises on acting from about the middle of the eighteenth century onwards argue as urgently as treatises on poetry for the importance of the creative or 'sympathetic' imagination. Actors themselves were especially extravagant on the subject of their own imaginations. In 1825 the French tragedian Talma extolled "that imagination which, creative, active, powerful, . . . associates the actor with the inspirations of the poet."[31] But for all these writers the actor was still an associate, sometimes even a very junior associate, not a usurper of the poet. Faucit presses closer. It was not just that she threw her nature into the characters when she acted them, but that that nature had itself been partly defined by them: "Juliet seems inwoven with my life" (85); "she seemed to become 'my very life of life,' " she says of Imogen (160); "Juliet, Desdemona, Cordelia, Imogen, I had brooded over until they had become, as it were part of my life" (231). Without perhaps intending it, she virtually offers herself as an alternative origin, the source of a second birth for Shakespeare's heroines.

Moreover, during the course of her career Shakespeare himself seemed to take a step towards the actor, coming to be exclusively identified with the specific powers of characterization—"Portrait-painting," said Carlyle, was where "all the greatness of the man comes out."[32] The distinction between actor and poet almost melts away, and it becomes possible to write of actors in terms formerly reserved for Shakespeare: "great actors are stewards of the mysteries of nature, gifted to probe her most recondite recesses, to apprehend the spirit of all forms and passions."[33] These are the words of Theodore Martin, Helen Faucit's husband-to-be, and he might have come fresh from reading Schlegel, who had written long before of Shakespeare that he was "the plenipotentiary of the whole human race," possessed of "the gift of looking into the inmost recesses of [his characters'] minds."[34] When Martin turns to the actress herself, he goes further and suggests not just equivalence with, but priority over Shakespeare: "she is the greatest poetess of our time, in the power, the variety, the beauty of the images . . . [and] sentiments she awakens. . . . Words, however powerful, produce no such impression, do not so permeate and steal into the very depths of our being as the unwritten poetry of this lady's acting. . . . Her performances not merely send us away filled with brighter and higher conceptions of the creatures of the poet's world, . . . but better men, inspired with something of the Ideal, the study of which has made her . . . the great instructress of her time."[35]

It is a bold claim. But there is a certain logic in the fact that the Victorians' veneration of Shakespeare should have rubbed off like this, and especially onto an actress. For if the essence of creativity was sympathy, so was it pre-eminently of womanhood.[36] Of course in one case it is imaginative and in the other moral, but there was a leakage between the two, as Hazlitt had demonstrated: "It has been said that tragedy purifies the affections by terror and pity. That is, it substitutes imaginary sympathy for mere selfishness. It gives us a high and permanent interest, beyond ourselves, in humanity as such. . . . It makes man a partaker with his kind. It subdues and softens the stubbornness of his will. . . . It opens the chambers of the human heart. . . . It is the refiner of the species; a discipline of humanity."[37] The "chambers of the human heart" are precisely where women were meant to preside. The "discursive faculty" was a closed door, but feeling, intuition, love—love, which according to Coleridge was itself creative, giving "to every object in nature a power of the heart without which it would indeed be spiritless"[38]—these were the prerogatives of women and therefore of the actress. The Romantics themselves did not pursue the connection. Their "colonization of the feminine,"[39] as it has been called, their assimilation of qualities previously regarded as belonging to women, was no invitation to their sisters to join the great line of the Poets. In their view genius was male, so much so that, as John Barrell has ingeniously argued, the feminizing terms of Coleridge's definition of Shakespeare's genius (where "knowledge . . . wedded . . . to his habitual feelings . . . gave birth to that stupendous power") had to be tortuously obfuscated by the surrounding language.[40] Later critics of the feminine school such as George Fletcher, a devotee of Helen Faucit, were less exercised. Reflecting on the variousness of her powers, he confesses to the belief that "truly there is something in female genius and female energy—something worthy of Shakespeare, worthy to be cherished with the holiest of all sacred feelings, that of affectionate veneration."[41]

Helen Faucit herself would not have analyzed and calculated the "advantages" for the Shakespearean actress of this whole convergence of ideas. On the contrary, as we have seen, it sometimes seemed at the time as if there were no lofty ideas at all about acting, least of all about actresses. But with hindsight and with the no doubt unconscious shaping and smoothing of her book on Shakespeare's heroines, written at the end of her life, and of her husband's biography, the connections can be made and the influences noted. As we have seen, the boundary between art and life, between the heroines of Shakespeare and reality, was not regarded at the time. The only sense in which it existed for Helen Faucit was that it freed his women from an independent bodily existence. She could speak of them not only as friends, which was common at the time, but as part of herself. By personally and passionately appropriating Shakespeare's women, she made the actual business of the stage almost incidental. Physically playing them was the unlooked-for outpouring of an inner reality that had been formed long before. She steals a march, as it were, on the theater, and makes of Shakespeare's heroines an oblique form of autobiography.

Her childhood was ideal for the purpose. Her parents, though theater people themselves, did not intend their daughter for the stage, and actually forbad visits to the theater. She and her sister were sent to a boarding school in Greenwich and left very much alone. After her parents separated she never saw her father, and her mother visited only rarely. Her health was delicate. She was sent to the seaside and put in the charge of people who also left her largely alone. She spent hours on the beach reading the *Arabian Nights, Pilgrim's Progress, Paradise Lost,* declaiming to the waves Satan's address to the council. She had too a translation of Dante, and of course, Shakespeare.[42] Thus was formed the pattern followed by many little girls of the period of solitary reading and daydreaming,[43] of living "again and again," as she says of herself, "through the whole childhood and lives of many of Shakespeare's heroines" (6). At that time these were the "suffering" heroines: "Pathos, heroism, trial, suffering—in these my imagination revelled," she says (231). "Ophelia was one of the pet dreams of my girlhood—partly perhaps from the mystery of her madness" (4); Desdemona was a "heroine into whose life I had entered with a passionate sympathy which I cannot even now recall without emotion.... Owing I suppose to delicate health and the weak action of my heart, the fear of being smothered haunted me continually. The very thought of being in a crowd, of any pressure near me, would fill me with terror" (47–48); in her imagination, Juliet's tomb lay in Lee churchyard on one of her school walks in Greenwich, and she used to terrify herself with imagining the toads and frogs she saw there hopping over Juliet's face (89).

There is a certain mystique about this Shakespeareanized childhood. Her husband describes her as a "dreaming girl," "grave and thoughtful," "shy and sensitive . . . unconsciously preparing herself to be the interpreter of what Shakespeare . . . had dreamed of ideal womanhood" (Martin, 2–4). Childhood and childlikeness, heavily dwelt on by them both, are obvious routes to the privatization of Shakespeare. At the cost of some mawkishness, they tell us that her sister's pet name for her was little "birdie" (Faucit, 86; Martin, 2); that her schoolmates called her "fairy"; (Martin, 3); that when she had started her career, Percy Farren, her mentor, still referred to her always as his "child" (Faucit, 92); and that Charles Kemble, her first manager, called her "Baby": "I cannot tell why, unless it were because of the contrast he found between his own wide knowledge of the world and of art, and my innocent ignorance and youth. . . . I knew perhaps far less of the world and its ways than even most girls of my age" (296n). It is significant in that it connects Shakespeare with the most innocent level of her life, with all that was peculiar to her and most romantically interesting: her loneliness, her ill-health, her phobias. Looking back, or even at the time, she seems to have become her own heroine. Even when a character was not especially associated with her pretheatrical childhood, she emphasizes, when she can, the next best thing—that she was extremely young when she first played it.

Reinforcing this theme was Faucit's habit of novelizing her heroines, inventing her own continuations of their lives both before the opening of the plays and after their endings. Imogen she imagines dying of the lasting wound to her love and faithfulness: "Tremblingly, gradually and oh how reluctantly! the hearts to whom that life is so precious will see the sweet smile which greets them grow fainter, will hear the loved voice grow feebler!" The doctor will do his best, but she will gently fade away, and those left behind will be inspired to live worthily for her sake (225). For Portia she composes an elaborate epilogue, the holy and difficult task, as she calls it, of converting Shylock. Portia (unrecognized as the young lawyer) visits him, tends him in body and mind, softens his heart, and lifts him slowly out of moral darkness. Jessica, under her influence, repents of her cruelty in leaving her father and throws herself at his feet, "sobbing out her grief and her contrition." Shylock dies at last understanding the quality of mercy (39–43). In this way, Faucit possessed her roles in secret.

In the performance of some of these heroines, her childhood was extended into adulthood by a certain artless naiveté. On the stage she was in the frontline, at risk from theatrical tradition, and even sometimes from

Shakespeare himself (in spite of the censored playhouse copies). As Beatrice, she says, "I was amazed at some of the odd things I had to say,—not at all from knowing their meaning, but simply because I did not surmise it" (295). Ignorance of other actresses was also a great help: "It was well for me that I never saw Desdemona, or indeed any of Shakespeare's heroines, on the stage before I had to impersonate them myself. I was thus hampered by no traditions and my ideals were not interfered with. . . . I struggled as best I could . . . ignoring all commentators and critics" (49). This was especially important for comedy. Rosalind struck fear into the youthful Helen for that reason alone. Though she had never seen the part acted, "I had heard enough of what Mrs Jordan and others had done with the character to add fresh alarm to my misgivings" (231). But in performance, her artlessness served her well. Shakespeare brings Rosalind, for example, up to "the verge of impropriety," according to Sir Archibald Alison, but Helen Faucit "never lets her pass the limit, and her joyous spirit bounds away with so much naivete and sprightliness, that the incipient impression is dissipated."[44]

Beatrice was more difficult. She is scarcely ingenuous. Her wit stabs; she "has a quick eye to see what is weak, or ludicrous in man or woman" (Faucit, 292). By stage tradition she was a cross between a shrew and a termagant. But again Faucit steered her way through, making her into "a creature overflowing with joyousness—raillery itself being in her nothing more than an excess of animal spirits, tempered by passing through a soul of goodness."[45] Goodness, especially in women, was essentially serious. Anna Jameson had written that "a humorous woman, whether in high or low life, has always a tinge of vulgarity" (25), and by vulgarity she meant not only indecency but anything that smacked of satire or ridicule. She found it contrary to female nature: "women . . . are by nature too much subjected to suffering in many forms—have too much of fancy and sensibility, and too much of that faculty which some philosophers call veneration, to be naturally satirical" (Jameson, 11). She believed, like Dinah Mulock Craik, that whatever else women were, they were women first, "affectionate, thinking beings, and moral agents; and *then* witty as if by accident" (Jameson, 25) It was this modified, tactful kind of wit that Faucit was particularly adept at. As the *Manchester Guardian* observed, "Miss Faucit has . . . a charm of manner which the strongest salt of the witticisms of Beatrice is unable to impair. Such is the intellectual tact of this actress, that she could be trusted . . . with the delivery of badinage which Queen Elizabeth herself would have thought effective. . . . This is the perfection of the art of high comedy, in which everything is made subordinate to character" (qtd. in Martin, 323).

But the qualities that were above all characteristic of her Shakespearean acting were, as the admirer's letter quoted earlier indicates, tenderness and sympathy. Artlessness was childlike, but tenderness was the badge of womanliness, and although Helen Faucit sometimes sounds like a child-woman, it wasn't ultimately what she was known for. Tenderness more than anything else, she felt, was the mark of Shakespeare's comedy: "It was surely a strange perversion which . . . assigned Rosalind . . . to actresses whose strength lay only in comedy. Even the joyous, buoyant side of her nature could hardly have justice done to it in their hands; for that is so inextricably mingled with deep womanly tenderness" (238).

Faucit's analyses of the comic heroines and the accounts of her performances show how easy it was to stray, how careful (almost artful) she needed to be not to hit the "wrong" note. So when in her description of Rosalind "wit and fancy" modulates swiftly into "pretty womanly waywardness playing like summer lightening over her throbbing tenderness of heart" (239), one can see not just sentimentality but a sort of code too, deflecting the implications of "wit." In performance, she says, she never approached the scene in which Rosalind suggests that Orlando should woo Ganymede as though wooing Rosalind "without a sort of pleasing dread, so strongly did I feel the importance of striking the true note in it" (265). All through her essay on the part she stresses the tenderness, "the strong emotion which is palpitating at the speaker's heart," as she puts it at one point (273). At the mock marriage, she says she "could never speak these words without a trembling of the voice, and the involuntary rushing of happy tears into the eyes, which made it necessary for me to turn my eyes away from Orlando" (274). Similarly with Beatrice, though she cannot "write with the full heart, or the same glow of sympathy" about her, for "sorrow and wrong have not softened her nature, nor taken off the keen edge of her wit . . . the sacred fountain of tears has never been stirred within her" (292). Nevertheless it was said of her that in performance the keenness had gone: "the heart of a true woman appeared through all the effervescence of humour" and "the undercurrent of a sympathetic earnest heart beneath the rich laughter of this transparent soul, deepened the poetry."[46] Archibald Alison, though a devoted admirer, interestingly observed of her Rosalind that "above two thirds of the charming image . . . is entirely her own. It is quite Shakespearean, but it is not to be found in Shakespeare."[47]

If the artlessness and tenderness of Rosalind and Beatrice had to be nursed a little, Imogen was a gift. Unlike them, she belonged to Faucit's childhood, for she and her friends had put on *Cymbeline* to surprise her governess on her birthday. Imogen was "one of the great favourites of my girlhood" (161), she writes, and in this Faucit was part of what amounted almost to a cult for Imogen. It had been started by Hazlitt, who in the opening essay of his *Characters of Shakespeare's Plays* crowned this heroine, unregarded at the time, "the most tender and the most artless" of them all.[48] Imogen might have been made for a Victorian afterlife. Not only is she a faithful, long-suffering wife, falsely accused, but Shakespeare has given her feminine domestic detail to match. Her needle simile; her likening of herself to an old rich garment that must be ripped; her cooking:[49] "How womanly are Imogen's similes. . . . Shakespeare thought woman's thoughts, with no woman to embody them!" wrote Faucit (194n). And in a rapturous celebration of hearth and home she describes how she imagined Imogen keeping house for the brothers: "For the first time their cave is felt to be home. On their return from their day's sport . . . a fresh smell of newly strewn rushes . . . pervades it . . . dainty wild flowers . . . Fresh water from the brook. . . . The vegetables are washed, and cut into 'quaint characters.' . . . a savoury odour of herbs comes from the 'sauced' broth, and a smile, sweet in their eyes beyond all other sweetness, salutes them as they hurry in" (203). In performance she fulfilled all expectations, "modestly clinging to her husband" in the first scene, "shrinking from the rough life outside their love, and stretching out to him, as he departs, the hands that return to her empty." Some thought it her greatest role, just as it was the "purest and most womanly of Shakespeare's women; in the whole range of poetry the most delicate embodiment of all the qualities that blend to form womanly perfection."[50]

But in her repertoire there was one Shakespearean challenge to the whole concept of womanliness—namely Lady Macbeth—and Helen Faucit's success and failure in the part are both equally significant. If she "succeeded" (with her audiences) she was a great actress; if she failed it was because she was too womanly. But in this part theatrical tradition was not easily ignored. Sarah Siddons had identified herself so closely with Lady Macbeth that critics took their cue from her. Faucit may not have seen her, but she could not have been unaware of how she acted the part. Siddons died in 1831, and the next year Anna Jameson dared to suggest that the Siddons myth was due for a reappraisal: "the generation that beheld Mrs Siddons in her glory is passing away, and we are again left to our own unassisted feelings" (Jameson, 409). Those feelings were decidedly more sympathetic than the ones Siddons had appealed to (though Siddons did have a theory about Lady Macbeth, untried by her, that was closer to these later interpretations). The traditional view of the matter was that, between Lady Macbeth and Macbeth, the evil was all on her side; Macbeth was a fundamentally virtuous and reluctant murderer, corrupted and driven on by his wife. Thus Dr. Johnson had been able to say that she was "merely detested."[51] Siddons, however, had made her more than "merely." Her Lady Macbeth was sublime. She realized Hazlitt's description of her as "a great, bad woman": she was, he said, "above nature. It seemed almost as if a being of a superior order had dropped from a higher sphere. . . . Power was seated on her brow, passion emanated from her breast as from a shrine; she was tragedy personified."[52] Rather than humanizing her, Siddons supernaturalized her: "she is a splendid picture of evil," wrote Campbell, her biographer, "a sort of sister of Milton's Lucifer."[53]

But the Victorians were not really interested in other spheres. If fiends or angels were wanted at all, they were wanted in the house. Anna Jameson used loaded vocabulary in insisting that Lady Macbeth was "a woman to the last—still linked with her sex and humanity" (Jameson, 410); George Fletcher wrote an analysis of the play, showing it to be Macbeth who is essentially depraved and cowardly, while Lady Macbeth is so devoted a wife that she is prepared to sacrifice her own lively and remorseful conscience for his sake. Painstakingly, he goes through all the places in the play where either the critics or the accounts of Sarah Siddons had shown Lady Macbeth to be "imperious," "commanding," or "triumphant," substituting his own view of her as being in "earnest entreaty," or "tremulous anxiety," and stressing the "continual struggle between her compunction . . . and her devotion." Knowing what kind of an actress Helen Faucit was, he put in a plea for her to bring her provincial production, which he had not seen, to London.[54] Whether she read Anna Jameson or George Fletcher (for his book, though published in 1847, consists of periodical articles published two and three years earlier) is not clear, but her portrayal of the character in 1846 should have satisfied them. "Instead of a domineering, hard and selfish woman," remembered one admirer, "the Lady Macbeth of Helen Faucit was a wife, whose strongest passion is for her husband."[55] William Carleton wrote to a friend that she made it appear to him that "this woman . . . is simply urging her husband forward through her love for him, which prompts her to wish for the gratification of his ambition. . . . In such a case it is not necessary that she should label herself a murderess, and wantonly parade that inhuman ferocity by which she has hitherto been distinguished. . . . This . . . keeps [the character] within the category of humanity, and gives a beautiful moral to the closing scenes of the queen's life" (qtd. in Martin, 177).

In fact, as Carol J. Carlisle has shown in her study of Faucit's Lady Macbeth,[56] she did also try to represent "ferocity," but perhaps not "wantonly." Some reviewers praise her "perception of the lofty, the revolting characteristics of human nature,"[57] which suggests an attempt at the Siddons tradition alongside her own. Clearly she herself felt repulsed, in spite of her innovations, for although urged to, she never made Lady Macbeth the subject of one of her "letters." She made it plain that it was a part she dreaded: "I had no misgivings after reaching the third act, but the first two always filled me with a shrinking horror." Neither her childhood nor her artlessness served her here. She did what she could to be tender, and to imagine Lady Macbeth's upbringing at a violent court—"amid such scenes, . . . one murder more seemed little to her" (234). But her invention, so fertile over Portia, fails her. As the *Blackwood's* correspondent wrote, "I doubted her ability to perform this character knowing how opposed to it all her own feelings must be, and that instead of being able to throw herself into the part, and identify it with her own nature, success must entirely depend upon the power of imagination unaided by sympathy of feeling" (Stokes, 759). The writer was, in fact, impressed, and it is difficult to find a dissenting note in the adulation accorded to the actress, even in this part. But her Lady Macbeth was not universally admired: "Miss Faucit is too essentially feminine, too exclusively gifted with the art of expressing all that is most graceful and beautiful in womanhood, to succeed in inspiring anything like awe and terror. The lines beginning 'Come all you spirits / That tend on mortal thoughts, unsex me here', are simply spouted. The famous passage . . . 'I have given suck' etc, . . . is poured out by Miss Faucit in a way that, by tones and gestures, vividly recalls . . . a scold at the door of a gin shop."[58] It is an ironic form of failure for someone who struck people as representing what her husband, in a surprising phrase, called "the exquisite ladyhood of nature."[59] The part marked the limits for her of autobiographical Shakespeare.

But just as her most successful Shakespearean interpretations were those that derived in some sense from her own nature, so her own nature seemed to acquire a collective glory brighter than any one of them. We have seen Sir Archibald Alison observing that two thirds of her Rosalind was her own—Shakespearean, but not in Shakespeare. And we have seen Theodore Martin say that her acting surpassed in effect the words she had to utter. As her reputation rose and she added to her roles, her commentators fall into a habit of alluding to the heroines as though they were all aspects of the same thing. In a review of her letters and of her career as a whole, the correspondent for *Blackwood's Magazine* wrote, "For thousands she opened up a world of poetry . . . filled their eyes with visions of beauty, grace and dignity . . . and by her delineations of all that is best in womanhood, woke up feelings which, but for the magic touch of her genius, might have slumbered all unknown" (Stokes, 741). It hardly seems to matter what the individual delineations were; the sum was greater than the parts. Together they blur into a dream of womanliness, with Helen Faucit as the one common denominator. She herself spoke of her career as having a purpose beyond the interpretation of each part: "Whatever gifts I had as an actress were ever regarded by me as a sacred trust to be used for widening and refining the sympathies of my audiences" (Martin, 405). In that sense each of Shakespeare's heroines was subsumed within a larger, unifying whole.

Thus the circle of canonizations is virtually complete, from Shakespeare, through his heroines, to herself. But a secular saint is nothing without worshippers, as Helen Faucit knew well. "It is hard to say whether in those days we women or the men were most in love with Helen Faucit. The women were all gratitude to her for the noble pictures of her sex which they owed to her. The men were no doubt animated by a more mixed feeling."[60] There is an element of coquetry in Faucit's delight. Writing to her future husband from Paris where she went in 1845 with William Charles Macready, her leading man at the time, she remarked: "I am told I have admirers among all the first literary ladywriters here. . . . I do love to attract women, do I not?" (Martin, 143). Theophile Gautier, with a touch of cynicism, likened her then to the pictures in the "keepsakes" or "Books of Beauty": "you are familiar with it . . . the pensive smile, the liquid eyes, the dishevelled hair . . . a certain display and . . . confusion in her mode of dress—a haphazard effect . . . of gauze and feathers and ribbons."[61] But cynicism was rare. George Eliot "fell in love" with her, and called her "the most poetic woman I have seen for a long time" (Martin, 237). Between the keepsakes and poetry, Faucit's appeal was wide. Macready could growl at her reputation, gloat over her failures, and insist that "she is not Mrs Siddons, not Miss O'Neill, not Mlle Rachel."[62] He may have been right, but the irony was that her public probably liked her the more for it.

This essay has been about the successful construction of an icon. And yet the icon's very perfection makes it suspect. One looks for something stray, something loose, a fragment of a self that wasn't entirely contained by it. The evidence of Helen Faucit's diaries appears to have been destroyed. We only know what her husband has chosen from them. The splenetic and self-absorbed diaries of Charles Macready should perhaps be read warily, but they do give us refreshing glimpses of her being, on occasion, as petulant, indiscreet, and ambitious as anyone else. We know that her acting in tragic parts was often stormy and violent and, as we have seen with her Lady Macbeth, sometimes uncontrolled and shrill. There are frustratingly few clues, and it is beyond the scope of this present study to track them down. But there is in her "letter" on Imogen one extraordinarily suggestive passage. Imogen was the heroine that Faucit felt closest to, it being "next to impossible to put her so far away from me that I can look at her as a being to be scanned and measured and written about." When she comes to Imogen's decision to escape to Milford Haven, Faucit exclaims, "Oh, how I enjoyed acting this scene! All had been so sad before. What a burst of happiness, what play of loving fancy had scope here! It was like a bit of Rosalind in the forest. The sense of liberty, of breathing in the free air, and for a while escaping from the trammels of the Court . . . gave light to the eyes and buoyancy to the step. . . . Imogen is already in imagination at that height of happiness . . . which brings her into the presence of her banished lord. . . . We can imagine with what delighted haste Imogen dons the riding suit of the franklin's housewife!" (191).

Theodore Martin records her embarrassment over the disguise itself (56–57),[63] but the feeling here transcends such scruples. It almost transcends the banished lord. Of course he is there in her imagination, but her buoyancy seems somehow autonomous too; it has to do with liberty, with "breathing in the free air," with escaping the "courtly prison-house," as she later calls her home. Briefly like Rosalind, she is roofless, neither fathered nor husbanded. In that condition her burst of happiness reverberates further perhaps than she thought, beyond the particular circumstances of each heroine. It becomes an intimation that Shakespeare, while apparently hymning Victorian womanhood, could open a door and simultaneously offer, if not an escape, then a holiday from it.

NOTES

1. John Ruskin, "Of Queen's Gardens," in *Sesame and Lilies* (London: George Allen, 1904), 92.

2. See Elaine Showalter's division of the phases of women's writing into "Feminine, Feminist, and Female" in *A Literature of Their Own* (London: Virago, 1984), 13.

3. Ruskin, "Of Queen's Gardens," 96.

4. Carol J. Carlisle, "The Critics Discover Shakespeare's Women," in *Renaissance Papers* 1979, ed. A. Leigh DeNeef and M. Thomas Hester (Southern Renaissance Conference, 1980), 59–73.

5. In his preface to *Troilus and Cressida*, "Containing the Grounds of Criticism in Tragedy," Dryden asserts that Shakespeare's excellence lay "in the more manly passions; Fletcher's in the softer; Shakespeare writ better betwixt man and man; Fletcher betwixt man and woman" (*Essays of John Dryden*, 2 vols., ed. W. P. Ker [Oxford: Clarendon Press, 1900], 1:227–28). This view became a casual critical assumption (Carlisle points to Nicholas Rowe's prologue to *The Ambitious Mother* [1700], William Collins's "Epistle: Addressed to Sir Thomas Hanmer on His Edition of Shakespeare's Works" [1744], and John Upton's *Critical Observations on Shakespeare*, 2d ed. [1748])—so much so that later apologists for Shakespeare's treatment of women, such as William Richardson in his *On Shakespeare's Imitation of Female Characters, Addressed to a Friend* (1788), make a point of countering the commonly held view to the contrary. Even in 1832 Anna Jameson is still on the defensive: "You know the prevalent idea is, that Shakespeare's

women are inferior to his men. This assertion is constantly repeated, and has been but tamely refuted" (*Characteristics of Women: Moral, Poetical and Historical,* 17). This and subsequent quotations come from an undated, but clearly late nineteenth-century edition, published by George Routledge, London.

6. Quoted by Theodore Martin in *Helena Faucit, Lady Martin* (London: William Blackwood and Sons, 1900), 285.

7. Dinah Mulock Craik, *A Woman's Thoughts about Women* (London: Hurst and Blackett, 1858), 58–59.

8. Ibid., 60–61.

9. Geraldine Jewsbury, *The Half-Sisters,* 2 vols. (London: Chapman and Hall, 1848), 2:18–19.

10. Helena Faucit, Lady Martin, *On Some of Shakespeare's Female Characters* (London: William Blackwood and Sons, 1887). Further citations will be given by page number in the text.

11. Jewsbury, *The Half-Sisters,* 1:205, 222.

12. Quoted in Martin, *Helena Faucit,* 166.

13. Jewsbury, *The Half-Sisters,* 1:217.

14. George Eliot, *Daniel Deronda* (Harmondsworth: Penguin, 1970), 258.

15. Quoted in Martin, *Helena Faucit,* 404, from a preface prepared by Helen Faucit for the 1893 edition of her book, but abandoned "out of a rooted dislike she had to speaking of herself," he says (403).

16. Mary Anderson (Mme de Navarro), *A Few Memories* (London: Osgood, McIlvaine and Co., 1896), 233.

17. Thomas Carlyle, "The Hero as Poet. Dante; Shakespeare," in *On Heroes and Hero Worship* (London: Chapman and Hall, 1891), 103. The lecture was originally given in 1840.

18. For the efforts made to tweak some of these heroines into the "right" Victorian shape, see Russell Jackson, " 'Perfect Types of Womanhood': Rosalind, Beatrice and Viola in Victorian Criticism and Performance," *Shakespeare Survey* 32 (1979): 15–26.

19. See Theodore Martin, "Rachel," *Blackwood's Magazine,* Sept. 1882: 271–95.

20. Jonathan Bate, *Shakespearean Constitutions: Politics, Theatre, Criticism 1730–1830* (Oxford: Oxford University Press, 1989), 131. The whole interesting discussion, to which I am indebted, continues on this and the following three pages.

21. "*The Tempest,*" in *Coleridge on Shakespeare,* ed. Terence Hawkes (Harmondsworth: Penguin, 1969), 224.

22. William Hazlitt, "Mr. Kean's Richard II," *The Examiner,* 19 Mar. 1815, in *The Complete Works of William Hazlitt,* 21 vols., ed. P. P. Howe (London: J. M. Dent and Sons, 1930–34), 5:222.

23. Hazlitt, "Mr. Kean and Miss O'Neill," in *Works,* 18:266.

24. *Coleridge on Shakespeare,* 224–26.

25. William Hazlitt, "Cymbeline," in *Characters of Shakespeare's Plays and Lectures on the English Poets* (London: Macmillan, 1903), 3.

26. Hazlitt, "On Wycherley, Congreve, Van Brugh, and Farquhar," in *Works,* 6:74.

27. Hazlitt, "Cymbeline," 2.

28. Bate, *Shakespearean Constitutions*, 132.

29. Samuel Taylor Coleridge, *Biographia Literaria*, quoted by Jonathan Bate in *Shakespeare and the English Romantic Imagination* (Oxford: Oxford University Press, 1989), 16. I am indebted to Bate's discussion of the Romantics and their understanding of Shakespeare's creativity.

30. Hazlitt, "The Same Subject Continued [On Genius and Common Sense]," in *Works*, 8:42.

31. Earl R. Wasserman, "The Sympathetic Imagination in Eighteenth-Century Theories of Acting," *Journal of English and Germanic Philology* 46 (1947): 264–72. The quotation from Talma is on p. 270.

32. Carlyle, "The Hero as Poet," 96–97.

33. Theodore Martin, "The Drama in Connexion with the Fine Arts," *Dublin University Magazine*, July 1846: 102.

34. Augustus William Schlegel, *A Course of Lectures on Dramatic Art and Literature*, 2 vols., trans. John Black (London: Baldwin, Cradock and Joy, 1815), 2:128–29.

35. Martin, "The Drama," 103–4.

36. Marianne Novy makes the same point in the introduction to *Women's Re-Visions of Shakespeare: On the Responses of Dickinson, Woolf, Rich, H.D., George Eliot, and Others* (Urbana: University of Illinois Press, 1990), 4.

37. Hazlitt, "Othello," in *Works*, 4:200.

38. In his lecture on *Romeo and Juliet*, in *Coleridge on Shakespeare*, 154.

39. See Alan Richardson, "Romanticism and the Colonization of the Feminine," in *Romanticism and Feminism*, ed. Anne K. Mellor (Bloomington: Indiana University Press, 1988), 13–25. He argues that the Romantic poet, heir to the Man of Feeling, incorporated qualities that had previously been regarded as exclusively feminine, and that, in the process, women themselves stood "to risk obliteration." He gives the example, among others, of Byron's Manfred who destroys Astarte "because his end is not union with [her], but the assimilation of her" (19).

40. John Barrell, *Poetry, Language and Politics* (Manchester: Manchester University Press, 1988), 64–74. The quotation from Coleridge comes from his *Biographia Literaria*, 2 vols., eds. James Engell and W. Jackson Bate (London: Routledge and Kegan Paul, 1983), 2:26–28.

41. Quoted in Martin, *Helena Faucit*, 93.

42. See Faucit, *Shakespeare's Female Characters*, 4–5; and Martin, *Helena Faucit*, 2–4.

43. See Valerie Sanders, *The Private Lives of Victorian Women: Autobiography in Nineteenth-Century England* (New York: Harvester, 1989). Sanders's discussion of the solitary and "alienated" childhoods as they appear in the autobiographies of Victorian women, and their later consequences, has been useful and interesting.

44. Sir Archibald Alison, "The British Theater," *Dublin University Magazine*, Nov. and Dec. 1846, in *Essays, Political, Historical, and Miscellaneous*, 3 vols., (London: William Blackwood and Sons, 1850), 3:587.

45. "A chance critic" quoted by Faucit, *Shakespeare's Female Characters,* 300.

46. Margaret Stokes, "Helen Faucit," *Blackwood's Magazine,* Dec. 1885: 748.

47. Alison, "The British Theater," 587.

48. Hazlitt, "Cymbeline," 3.

49. At 1.3.17–19, 3.4.51–53, and 4.2.49–50, in *The Riverside Shakespeare,* ed. G. Blakemore Evans (Boston: Houghton Mifflin, 1974).

50. Henry Morley, *Journal of a London Playgoer from 1851–1866,* ed. M. R. Booth (Leicester: Leicester University Press, 1974), 292–93.

51. *Dr. Johnson on Shakespeare,* ed. W. K. Wimsatt (Harmondsworth: Penguin, 1969), 134.

52. Hazlitt, "Macbeth," in *Characters of Shakespeare's Plays,* 12, 14.

53. Quoted by George Fletcher in *Studies of Shakespeare* (London: Longman's, 1847), 187.

54. George Fletcher, "False Acting of the Two Principal Characters," in *Studies of Shakespeare,* 191–92, 197–98.

55. Stokes, "Helen Faucit," 757.

56. Carol J. Carlisle, "Helen Faucit's Lady Macbeth," *Shakespeare Studies* 16 (1983): 205–33.

57. *Liverpool Albion,* 27 Apr. 1846, quoted by Carlisle, "Helen Faucit's Lady Macbeth," 209.

58. Morley, *Journal,* 289–90.

59. *Dublin University Magazine,* July 1846: 104.

60. Stokes, "Helen Faucit," 742.

61. Quoted in Frederic Whyte, *Actors of the Century: A Playlover's Gleanings from Theatrical Annals* (London: G. Bell and Sons, 1898), 106.

62. *The Diaries of William Charles Macready,* 2 vols., ed. William Toynbee (London: Chapman and Hall, 1912), 2:308.

63. Martin quotes Faucit on the subject: "I can never forget Mr Macready's finding fault with my page's dress, which I had ordered to be made with a tunic that descended to the ankles." Macready apparently apologized but said that the story would not be clear without an alteration to her costume. "With many tears, I had to yield. . . . I managed however to devise a compromise by swathing myself in the 'franklin' housewife's 'riding cloak' " (Martin, 57).

MARTHA TUCK ROZETT

Gertrude's Ghost Tells Her Story:
Lillie Wyman's *Gertrude of Denmark*

"Was it in a dream or reverie," asks the narrator of *Gertrude of Denmark,* "that Gertrude of Denmark came and begged me to tell her story to the world?" Prince Hamlet, the Gertrude-ghost remarks, had Horatio "to report him and his 'cause aright.' I had no chance, before I died, to ask anybody to protect me from the writers, the critics,—and the actresses."[1] Thus begins Lillie Buffum Chace Wyman's "interpretive romance," a *Hamlet* transformation that appeared in 1924 when its author was seventy-seven years old.

This re-vision of *Hamlet* constitutes a critique, not so much of Shakespeare's text, but of the play's performance history and the lore surrounding it, a Hamlet-centered tradition that Lillie Wyman observed from her own distinctively feminine (if not entirely feminist) perspective. Wyman was able to create a fictional work of "criticism" in a way that links her to the nineteenth rather than the twentieth century, a time when criticism was not yet the purview of a class of academic specialists but was instead written for the "cultivated public and disseminated in editions of the works, public lectures, books, and—above all—in magazines and newspapers." So observes Hugh Grady, who adds that the plays "were assumed to be the intellectual property of men (and increasingly of women) of any cultural pretensions."[2] Wyman's text not only implies the incompleteness of Shakespeare's; it resists every reading of *Hamlet* that dismisses Gertrude as a relatively unimportant character while Hamlet occupies center stage and an undisputed claim on the reader or spectator's sympathies.

Gertrude of Denmark re-imagines the Hamlet story as an exploration of the nineteenth-century cult of the devoted, self-sacrificing mother, a cult that, as Ann Douglas has remarked, enabled American women "to exonerate almost any action performed in the sacred name of motherhood."[3] Gertrude is defined by her role as a mother: "She was not quite sixteen when Hamlet was born. She became a Madonna at once. There were two or three children afterwards, but not one of them lived many hours. She had not quite come out of her gulf of maternal pain, before each of those children had turned itself into the memory of a thwarted hope. It was Hamlet therefore always with her—Hamlet first and last and all the time." One afternoon, Wyman continues, the two brothers see Gertrude sitting on a high-backed chair holding her child on her knee.

"She looks like the Holy Mother," said the King. "I think that I will give her to the church here to take the place of their wooden image of the Mother."

"She is the most sacred creature on earth," answered Claudius, as he whirled on his heels and walked away. (10–11)

The two men view Gertrude as the quintessential idealized mother, here represented by the conventional icon of the self-effacing madonna with the child at her breast.

Uncle Tom's Cabin, a book Lillie Wyman allegedly read at age six (though she doubts the truth of this family legend), told the story of salvation through motherly love to a culture that sanctified motherhood and the family and celebrated the redemptive power of "motherly loving kindness."[4] Lillie's childhood reading included the works of Louisa May Alcott and could conceivably have also included the books on the mothers of famous men—George Washington's mother Mary, for instance—which became immensely popular in mid-nineteenth-century America.[5] Jane Tompkins has suggested that *Uncle Tom's Cabin,* while seemingly a conservative novel harking back to "an older way of life," is actually radical in its "removal of the male from the center to the periphery of the human sphere."[6] Wyman's *Gertrude of Denmark* and the biographies of famous men's mothers do likewise. Wyman's text is a temporally "cross-cultural" re-vision inasmuch as it employs nineteenth-century assumptions about women and motherhood to revise a legend that, from Saxo-Grammaticus onward, had been told and retold from the perspective of its male "hero."

But Wyman's re-vision, while drawing on the cult of motherhood, also interrogates its inherent assumptions. Just as a certain ambiguity attaches to the role and obligations of the hero-revenger as the Hamlet story changes through time, so Gertrude's role as the self-sacrificing mother is treated with a certain ambivalence. For a woman to define herself wholly as a mother, Wyman seems to imply, is to risk losing her sense of self when the child, now an adult, no longer needs and depends upon her. Building upon the sixty-eight times Gertrude speaks in Shakespeare's play, Wyman probes the inner life of Hamlet's mother in the form of a romance, a text for women readers to experience privately in their homes

rather than publicly in the theaters. And in doing so, she speaks to women
readers not only about the way a male-dominated theatrical establishment
has long represented this particular mother and wife, but also about their
own experiences as mothers and wives.

As Wyman depicts her, Gertrude is fiercely devoted to her only son,
but extends her mother's arms to Ophelia, Laertes, and even Osric as the
story unfolds. For Gertrude, motherhood has been a supremely rewarding—
and sensuous—state of being; in her imagination, Hamlet will always
remain the little boy on her lap. As he announces his intent to return to
Wittenberg, "she remembered just how soft his little body had felt, and
how he had been wont to gaze at her and then lay his head on her
shoulder" (15). Her refusal to relinquish the past suggests the emptiness
of the stereotypical mother's life once her child no longer needs her. The
narrator tells us, with characteristic understatement, that "when her husband died, Gertrude had been a queen for thirty years. She did not know
how to be anything but a queen with a prince for a son—both of them
upheld in their station by a king" (14). Wyman recasts Gertrude as a
familiar figure, the wife whose comfortable and sheltered existence renders her unprepared for sudden widowhood. A less idealized character
type than the self-sacrificing mother, the widow whose early marriage
prevented her from developing an identity or existence apart from her
husband was a sufficiently familiar figure in late nineteenth- and early
twentieth-century America that women readers would be able to see their
experience or that of an acquaintance or relative reflected in Wyman's
Gertrude. She is at once the devoted but rejected mother of an adult son
and the widow who wants to continue living the married life she has
always known.

Wyman rewrites *Hamlet* by beginning with the characters and events
of the play, assuming the reader's acquaintance with Shakespeare's text,
but fleshes them out according to the conventions of the nineteenth-
century novelist. She adds a few scenes, but only when Gertrude is
involved; most of the additions take the form of the narrator's commentary.
Just as Tom Stoppard places Rosencrantz and Guildenstern in the foreground of *Rosencrantz and Guildenstern Are Dead,* expands the roles of
the players, and relegates the "major characters," including Hamlet, to
minor roles, so Wyman enlarges the roles of Gertrude, Claudius, and
Ophelia, and removes Hamlet to the periphery of the novel. Claudius's
and Ophelia's unspoken thoughts and feelings are occasionally recounted;
Hamlet's, almost never. In each case the redistribution of attention constitutes a statement about the relative importance of men and women,
princes and attendants, "heroes" and minor characters.

The appendix that follows the romance makes explicit Wyman's challenge to a predominantly male community of actors, directors, and critics. Wyman calls into question the Ghost's remark about his "seeming virtuous queen" by transforming him into a variation on the irrationally jealous husband. The King Hamlet who "declared that he was jealous of her love for 'that baby' " (11) and who was frequently away on hunting expeditions and official business later develops "a posthumous but unfounded suspicion and jealousy" (250), posthumous and unfounded, presumably, because he had no reason to suspect his wife during his lifetime and doesn't know her well enough to understand her reasons for remarrying. Wyman's depiction of the Prince also seeks to refute the views of audiences and readers whom she dismisses, in the appendix, as "enamoured of Hamlet." (241) Wyman would firmly disagree, for example, with C. L. Barber and Richard Wheeler, who maintain that *Hamlet* "calls for an identification with the hero's alienation that excludes critical perspective," so that we can see Hamlet only from his own vantage point.[7] What about Gertrude's and Ophelia's alienation, Wyman seems to be asking—the alienation experienced by misrepresented and largely ignored women in a world both dominated and imaginatively recreated by men? Why is the emphasis on how Gertrude's remarriage is perceived, not on why and under what circumstances it occurred?

Lillie Buffum Chace Wyman was born in 1847, the eighth of ten children in a family of New England Quakers. Her mother, Elizabeth Buffum Chace, was a well-known activist in the abolitionist and women's rights movements, an indefatigable woman who lived to the age of ninety-three. In 1914, Lillie and her son Arthur Crawford Wyman published a two-volume biography entitled *Elizabeth Buffum Chace: Her Life and its Environment.* This was not Lillie's first literary endeavor; she had published a collection of stories (*Poverty Grass,* 1886), a collection of poetry (*Interludes,* 1913) and *American Chivalry* (1913), a series of memoir-like portraits of her mother, her husband John Crawford Wyman, her mother's sister Rebecca Buffum Spring, and her mother's friends Wendell Phillips and Sojourner Truth. The books were published by well-known publishing houses (*Poverty Grass* by Houghton-Mifflin, the subsequent books by W. B. Clarke), but no reviews are extant. It seems curious that twenty-seven years passed between Lillie's first publication at the age of thirty-nine and the prolific years of 1913–14, when three works appeared, just as it seems unlikely that Lillie wrote *Gertrude of Denmark* as late as the early 1920s.

　　Lillie says remarkably little about herself in *Elizabeth Buffum Chace* and *American Chivalry;* the impression one gets is of a self-effacing daughter overshadowed by her powerful mother, a daughter who had chosen the private occupation of poetry-writing rather than public service as her life's work. It may be that Lillie Wyman's portrait of Gertrude is a veiled attempt to explain her own role as "attendant lord, one that will do / To swell a progress, start a scene or two" (to appropriate Prufrock's description of himself). Why, she might be asking, do we always pay so much attention to life's Hamlets and so little to the other characters in the drama?

Although the biography focuses on Elizabeth Chace's public life, Wyman's study of her mother *as a mother* is especially revealing. Mrs. Chace (as the Wymans refer to her in their narrative) was born in 1806, married Samuel Chace in 1828, and had five sons in the early years of her marriage, all of whom died in the late 1830s. After an interim of several years, during which time she was very active in the New England Anti-Slavery Society (founded by her father, Arnold Buffum, with William Lloyd Garrison and others in 1832), Mrs. Chace had five more children, from 1843 to 1852. Of her mother, Lillie says that "she grew to be a dominant, though intensely feminine monarch. . . . she was a brooding and solicitous rather than a caressing mother. Perhaps she was different as to that in her younger life, but I remember her as personally demonstrative only to her very youngest son, the ninth of her ten children; and yet I am certain that an older one was really her best beloved child while his brief, beautiful life lasted."[8] Lillie recalls having had whooping cough when her brother Edward was born; because he was a sickly baby, her mother "never left him" for six months, thus effectively abandoning her fifteen-month-old daughter.[9]

Lillie's son Arthur was born in 1879 or 1880, the only child of her marriage to John Crawford Wyman, a widower twenty-five years her senior. The biography offers glimpses of both Mrs. Chace and Lillie as devoted, self-sacrificing mothers of sons. Like Wyman's Gertrude, the Lillie that emerges revered her much older husband but was probably closer to her son, although, unlike her mother and the Gertrude of her interpretive romance, she does not seem to have lost any children to early death.

We can speculate that Lillie Wyman was drawn to the Hamlet story at least in part by her own complex identification with the characters: she is at once the widowed Gertrude to Arthur's Hamlet and the motherless Ophelia to Mrs. Chace's Polonius. As much as she admired her accomplished and charismatic mother, she never ceased to resent her indifference to a daughter's childhood needs.[10] Speaking of the close friendship between her mother and her husband, Lillie acknowledged that her mother "was better fitted by nature to get on with men than with women" (II, 103).[11] Such a mother could understandably have been the earliest source of Lillie's ambivalent feelings about women as wives and mothers.

Both Anna Jameson's *Characteristics of Women, Moral, Poetical and Historical* (1832) and Mary Cowden Clarke's *Girlhood of Shakespeare's Heroines* (1850–52) attempt to explore and account for the personalities and motivation of the female characters in Shakespeare's plays, in ways that somewhat anticipate Wyman's. However, Gertrude does not figure in either Jameson's twenty-three portraits or Cowden Clarke's fifteen novella-like tales; she is referred to only in passing by Jameson in her section on Ophelia. Wyman had read Jameson,[12] and would certainly have taken issue with her characterization of Gertrude as a "wicked queen" who is nevertheless "not so wholly abandoned but that there remains within her some sense of the virtue she has forfeited."[13] Rather, Wyman's portrayal of Gertrude resembles Jameson's description of Constance in *King John:* "Whenever we think of Constance, it is in her maternal character. . . . the maternal affections are a powerful instinct. . . . We think of her as a mother, because, as a mother distracted for the loss of her son, she is immediately presented before us, and calls forth our sympathy and our tears; but we infer the rest of her character from what we see, as certainly and completely as if we had known her whole course of life." Constance, says Jameson, experienced "a mother's heart-rending, soul-absorbing grief" at the death of Arthur, a grief as "natural" as her ambitions for her son, proud as she was "of his high birth and royal rights, and violent in defending them."[14]

This Constance's grief anticipates the self-sacrificing devotion Wyman's Gertrude would feel toward her son, a devotion felt inwardly rather than expressed passionately. Christy Desmet notes that Jameson represents Constance as "not merely a mother or victim," but also "a powerful and defiant ruler"; she quotes Jameson on Constance's "power—power of imagination, of will, of passion, of affection, of pride."[15] It may be that Gertrude's powerlessness made her uninteresting to Jameson. Wyman, by contrast, makes no claims for her subject's heroism or moral power, but finds her interesting precisely because she exemplifies the kind of woman who lacks the imagination and assertiveness Jameson finds in Constance and Lady Macbeth. Gertrude, Wyman's narrator remarks, was "not a profound thinker nor a very wise judge of the motives which actuated people around her. Yet not commonplace was the personality of this woman, whom a great king had loved and trusted all his life" (4).

It is difficult to believe that Lillie Wyman was unacquainted with Mary Cowden Clarke's reconstruction of the early lives of Shakespeare's "heroines," for the two works, although published at a remove of seventy years, approach literary characters from a common vantage point.[16] As Clarke states in her preface, her intent is "to imagine the possible circumstances and influences of scene, event, and associate . . . which might have conduced to originate and foster those germs of character recognized in their maturity."[17] Nina Auerbach observes that Cowden Clarke's *Girlhood of Shakespeare's Heroines* allows its subjects to "move freely in the conditional tense"; Desdemona, for instance, is "freed from her author's single-minded cause."[18] Wyman employs a similar strategy, although her Gertrude, perhaps more realistically, lacks the autonomy and self-reliance of Cowden Clarke's heroines.

The mother-child bond is clearly as important to Cowden Clarke as it was to Wyman and Jameson; equally important is the conviction that childhood experiences are crucial in shaping the disposition of the adult. Cowden Clarke's story of Lady Macbeth, for example, depicts a motherless girl (like Wyman's Gertrude), whose childhood was spent longing to "pour some of her own spirit into that placid nature" of her "unmanly" father.[19] Young Gruoch eventually grows up to be the proud and ambitious wife of the admired hero Macbeth, yet her marriage does not satisfy her aspirations: she always wishes she had been born a man. Like Elizabeth, Lillie, and Gertrude, Gruoch nurses a young son through an illness, but "fate decreed that he shall not live." She suffers a "fierce pang for the loss of her offspring," but bears it "with stern composure, that she may stimulate her more irrepressible husband."[20] The tale ends where Lady Macbeth's role begins in the play, with the letter announcing the witches' prophecy. Cowden Clarke's portrait of Lady Macbeth, like Jameson's, emphasizes her subject's desire for independence and passionate nature, qualities that Wyman's Gertrude does not possess.

Although Cowden Clarke's Lady Macbeth and Wyman's Gertrude are clearly different characters, both texts employ a fictional strategy of characterization that presents a series of influential events in the protagonists' past lives as daughters, wives, and mothers that make their behavior in the "present" of the plays' main action seem understandable and inevitable. It should be noted that Wyman employs this same approach to character as the consequence of formative past events (remembered through fictional flashbacks) in her handling of characters other than Gertrude. For example, as Hamlet looks upon the kneeling Claudius in the prayer scene, "odd memories" come back to him and he recalls that as a child "he had often heard his father mock at Claudius a little for his athletic failures. . . . the boy Hamlet, with the uncomprehending, almost innocent cruelty of childhood, had delighted in his father's taunting raillery" (118).

Wyman also uses novelistic strategies to fill what she perceives as the gaps in *Hamlet* by dwelling on the inner life and feelings of her subject.

Working from a single line in the play, she offers a lengthy gloss on Gertrude's line "I will not speak with her" (4.5.1). Gertrude dreads an encounter with Ophelia because "to face another encounter with a lunatic was horrible to this woman who, except for that frightful hour with Hamlet, had throughout all her adult life been cloistered in splendor and sheathed in courtesy." Uncertain of herself, she "feared, as she had from the beginning, that, if she saw the daughter, she would in some way reveal the awful secret of that stab through the arras. This fear, and the knowledge from which it grew, wrought an uneasiness like that of guilt within her" (161). Yet Gertrude's maternal instincts overcome her fear and guilt, and she steps forward, saying "How now, Ophelia?" in a spirit of pity and love (162).

This moment of moral courage anticipates an even more impressive one later in the scene. As before, Gertrude derives strength from her maternal role at a crucial, and potentially dangerous, moment for her husband. Laertes has just entered the room, hurling angry threats at Claudius:

> Gertrude let go of the King's hand, went close to the young man and took hold of his. She had often held him on her knee when he was a child. Custom paralyzed him. He stood still.
> "Calmly, good Laertes," she said with a smile, that was only a little more dauntless than it was gracious. (167)

In constructing a life for Gertrude before the events of the play *Hamlet* begin, Lillie Wyman confronts head-on a crucial unanswered question: how did Gertrude come to marry Claudius after her husband's death? Wyman depicts Gertrude as a soft and sheltered woman "bruised" at the thought of being "any kind of personage" other than a queen (13–14). When a court lady informs her "that speculation was busy in the palace as to whom the new king would marry, for marry now and speedily he must," Gertrude retreats to her closet for ten days of intense and agonizing reflection (15). "No son of Claudius shall ever sit in my Hamlet's place," she resolves, then recoils in horror from an image of herself "with fell intent stealthily approaching an unguarded infant" (19). As "her brain was still whirling," a messenger comes from the king to "beg" an interview. This fortuitous event presents her with an opportunity she might not have sought on her own:

> They were entirely alone. "Gertrude," he said, "*marry* me! The people who loved my brother best will see, in such a marriage, a plain augury of my future policy. You and I will front the world,

clothed in double dignity. The nobles elected me king. Through your clasp of my hand, my brother will bestow his blessing. . . . Your Hamlet will become my son; no other son will ever be born to me. His princely future lies in your hands, Gertrude. Together, we will persuade him not to go back to Wittenberg and lead a bookish life. At our side, he will become a seasoned prince, fit to share my power as I grow old,—certain to win the election after my death." (20)

As Gertrude walks into his outstretched arms, the narrator observes that "perhaps he was sincere for the moment, perhaps he had even forgotten his guilt for that instant. He had refrained from unholy expression of love for this woman so long." Gertrude sees nothing, feels nothing, but tenderness and solace. "Mother of God, I thank thee," she murmurs, "Hamlet's father has sent you to save my boy and me" (21).

This Gertrude is not an idealized, heroic woman; rather, she is a more familiar and human character, the suddenly widowed woman confronted with choices for the first time, with no one to turn to for help and advice. That she agrees to marry a man she has known for her entire adult life, a man whose devotion she has probably recognized and taken for granted, is hardly surprising.[21]

For her portrait of Gertrude to be convincing, Wyman must first of all clear her of the charges of adultery. Speaking of Hamlet's encounter with the Ghost in act 1, scene 5, the narrator firmly asserts that "there is no word in this scene or elsewhere, in the whole of Shakespeare's dramatic rendition of the story, which even intimates that the King, during his existence upon the earth, had ever doubted his wife's fidelity" (52). This interpretation lodges a direct challenge to the formidable Shakespeare scholar A. C. Bradley, whose *Shakespearian Tragedy* (1904) had become widely influential by the time Wyman published her romance. Bradley proclaims that it is "practically certain" that Gertrude was "false to her husband while he lived," though he adds that "she was *not* privy to the murder of her husband, either before the deed or after it."[22] To this Wyman's Gertrude would respond, as her ghost cries indignantly to the narrator, "Whatever Claudius may have done, there was one indecorous thing he never would have done. He would never have made his mistress the queen of Denmark" (53).

Wyman doesn't try to explain why Claudius killed his brother, perhaps because she knows that such an explanation is beyond her skill. She speaks briefly of his ambition, of the "kind of self-love which makes a man at once brave and cowardly," of the parts played by both hatred and love in "his onward progress toward criminality." Passing quickly over both "the deed which entailed upon him the 'primal eldest curse' and his election to the throne (11–12), she dwells instead on his role in bringing about Gertrude's "fatal mistake." This "mistake" is made as convincing as possible. Gertrude's hesitantly whispered objections to the immediacy of the marriage are swept aside by Claudius's shrewd awareness that his advisers might try to pressure him to marry a woman of childbearing age. When Gertrude asks about "the notion that such a marriage was incestuous" Claudius assures her "that he has seen the priests, and everything has been made right as to that," an ambiguous response Gertrude accepts because "she held a solemn conviction that angels . . . had inspired Claudius to offer the ring which would insure her own and her son's future safety and dignity" (23).

This response is characteristic of Wyman's Gertrude; like many self-deluding tragic characters, she believes that which most comfortably supports her own self-image and aspirations, and willingly accepts what she is told without further inquiry. Yet like other tragic characters, she remains plagued by doubts. When Hamlet violently accuses her in the closet scene, she experiences "this feeling coming upon her and gripping her throat. . . . had she, after all, been moved to that marriage by the slightest unworthy desire? Oh God, had she? Had she in the least, wanted throne and royalty, for herself, and not merely for Hamlet? This thought hissed its awful question in her ears" (135).

The question is an "awful" one because it is very hard for Gertrude to accept the truth that "she wanted something for herself. She had preferred life to stagnation" (135). Wyman is fully aware that other possibilities existed: "There were, indeed, women, even in her period, who, as spinsters or widows, could, and did carve out and carry on interesting careers for themselves in politics or other action" (135). The "interesting career" of which Gertrude is incapable, a medieval version of Elizabeth Chace's career, perhaps, is utterly beyond Gertrude, as the narrator realizes. Gertrude is "not that kind, and nothing, in her experience as King Hamlet's wife, had fitted her to become such." Neither, perhaps, was Lillie. And so the narrator concludes, defending her heroine in an understated way: "She had made the normal choice" (136). "Normal" is a loaded word here; Gertrude, it appears, acts as the woman reader for whom Wyman was writing might have acted—as Lillie herself might as done or wanted to do—if as a young widow she was offered "something for herself." One can only assume that many readers in 1924, like readers of the 1990s, would sympathize with this choice.

In her appendix, Wyman observes that "the critics have generally denounced Gertrude's second marriage as sinful in its very nature. It is rather absurd to echo Hamlet so completely as to this." She goes on to remind the reader that the Catholic Church upheld the marriage of

Katherine of Aragon to Henry VIII after the death of his brother Arthur, and that Shakespeare "did not represent Katherine as a loathsome creature in his drama on that subject" (238). The novel presents Gertrude as a sheltered, rather childlike woman, trained to defer to male authority, with little knowledge of the world outside her palace garden. Gertrude is placed "amid tragical circumstances" (250), as Wyman says at the end of the appendix, not the least of which are the circumstances created by an uprearing from which she emerges as a passive, dependent woman, able to act assertively and confidently only when she assumes her maternal role on behalf of another. Equally tragic, perhaps, is the way her beloved son misunderstands and misrepresents her; this son is a "monstrous egotist, who could question all things in the Universe, himself included, but who could not see the answers to his questions, because his egoism imposed itself like a tangible substance between the eyes of his mind and everything in the Universe" (222).

Wyman's evident distaste for Hamlet does not prevent her from providing her heroine with the illusion of a satisfying final moment as she watches the fifth-act duel. Her posture during the duel is that of a pleased mother, enjoying the prospect of "her darling . . . restored to health, lovely in his powerful manhood" (217). The narrator speaks of "a mystical kind of vision" that comes over her, and it is in this mood of exultant self-affirmation that she drinks to Hamlet, and then, a few lines later, realizes that she is poisoned. "Then," says the narrator, "a mother died" (220).

Wyman's Gertrude lives and dies in a world where the only socially acceptable or legitimate reason for the marriage would be the selfless one—to protect Hamlet's claim to the throne. To expiate the sin of having possibly acted selfishly, Gertrude feels she must immerse herself in selfless, wifely ministrations to a king whose love, the narrator observes judgmentally, is "selfish, unmoral love . . . [an] overdevelopment of aestheticism, which rots downward into the heart of man, and turns the love of anything which is beautiful . . . into self-love and the desire for self-gratification" (177). Although she could not achieve the perfect selflessness and womanly devotion to the interests of husband and child to which she felt she should aspire, the romance convinces us that her desire to remain in the court world where she has lived all her adult life is understandable and forgivable, particularly when her husband and son are so undeserving of her attentiveness and self-sacrifice. The sympathy for Gertrude that Wyman allows her narrator to voice might appear as a critique of a society that placed unfair expectations upon women. Wyman's upbringing among feminists and abolitionists could easily have prepared her for the role of social critic, but it would be a mistake to view *Gertrude of Denmark* as an overtly ideological work. The dominant tone of the romance is one of gentle, decorous sympathy and respect for a character left unfinished by her original creator.

Rather than a victim of society, Wyman's Gertrude can be seen as a casualty of the limitations of a play centered on its male protagonist. The romance interrogates the "maleness" of *Hamlet* as a sacrosanct canonical text far more than Jameson, for example, does: Jameson's portrait of Ophelia speaks of its subject's "relative beauty and delicacy when considered in relation to that of Hamlet, which is the delineation of a man of genius in contest with the powers of this world." Hamlet, Jameson continues, has "an immense intellectual power [which] renders him unspeakably interesting. . . . undoubtedly Shakespeare loved him beyond all his other creations."[23]

In 1924, the year *Gertrude of Denmark* appeared (although we do not know when it was actually written), Agnes Mure MacKenzie published *The Women in Shakespeare's Plays: A Critical Study from the Dramatic and the Psychological Points of View.* There are certain similarities between her portrait of Gertrude and Wyman's: "the whole tragedy has its root in Gertrude's weakness—weakness, not wickedness, for she is not at all an evil woman. She is passive and obtuse, and she loves comfort—one always pictures her as being a little fat, with podgy white fingers heavily beringed—but she is nothing worse, at bottom. Only that 'nothing worse' is the direct cause of nine violent deaths, besides a hell of agony for her own son."[24] MacKenzie condescends to Gertrude, something Wyman never does: "She has the qualities of a pleasant animal—docility, kindliness, affection for her offspring, a courage in the defence of her mate."[25] The urgency of Wyman's felt need to tell Gertrude's story may owe something to the unfairness of MacKenzie's view of her, particularly her final, extraordinary paragraph. Gertrude, she concludes, "kills both husbands, she kills Ophelia, she kills her son . . . [and] Rosencrantz and Guildenstern . . . and Polonius. . . . And she has not a particle of ill-will or ill-intentions in her. Simply she is stupid, coarse, and shallow."[26]

The review of *Gertrude of Denmark* in *Theatre Arts Monthly* (August 1924) laments that Wyman's "frankly intuitional and sentimental" presentation "weakens the value of what critically and historically handled might be an interesting contribution to the study of *Hamlet.*" Other reviewers were more positive: *Bookman* calls it a "friendly, 'civilized,' humorous, beautiful, and assertive entry into the lists of Shakespeariana," and the *Springfield Republican* observes that "whether we are convinced or not, this romance of Hamlet and his mother . . . is likely to stay in our memory."[27]

Gertrude of Denmark does not seem to have had any influence on

Shakespeare criticism, however. When Carolyn Heilbrun published her defense of Gertrude in *Shakespeare Quarterly* in 1957 (recently reissued as the leading essay in a volume called *Hamlet's Mother and Other Women*), there was no mention either of Wyman's book or the ideas contained within it. After surveying the critics' assessments of Gertrude, Heilbrun concludes that without exception they agree to define Gertrude by her "frailty." The best they can say of her is that she is "well-meaning but shallow and feminine in the pejorative sense of the word: incapable of any sustained rational process, superficial and flighty." Heilbrun sets out to refute this view, by looking at everything Gertrude says and every scene in which she appears. She asserts that Gertrude's speeches are "human," "direct," "courageous," and that except for her "single flaw," she is a "strong-minded, intelligent, succinct . . . [and] sensible" woman. The flaw that stands against and undermines all these fine qualities is "lust, the desire for sexual relations," which causes Gertrude to cry "O Hamlet, speak no more! / Thou turn'st my [eyes into my very] soul," when he accuses her of shameless and "compulsive ardure" (3.4.86–90). Heilbrun sees this as a moment of recognition for Gertrude (she knows "that this is her sin") and as a key element in the plot ("Gertrude's flaw of lust made Claudius's ambition possible").[28] It would be interesting to know what the Heilbrun of the 1990s would say about Wyman's theory of the "normal choice," a natural preference for the married state that resists the imposed constraints of widowhood. Curiously, Heilbrun says nothing about Gertrude's maternal feelings; perhaps she was making a deliberate break with the ideology of the 1950s and anticipating the feminism of the next decade.

By 1980 it had become possible once again to depict Gertrude as a devoted mother. Rebecca Smith's essay on Gertrude in *The Woman's Part* emphasizes Gertrude's "persistent extreme love for her son," a love that conflicts with her love for Claudius (hence the "heart cleft in twain" of the essay's title). Gertrude is "merely a quiet, biddable, careful mother and wife," a "compliant, loving, unimaginative woman whose only concern is pleasing others," one "easily led and [who] makes no decisions for herself except, ironically, the one that precipitates her death." Smith ends by saying that if Gertrude "were presented on stage and film as only her own words create her, she might become another stereotypical character: the nurturing, loving, careful mother and wife—malleable, submissive, totally dependent, and solicitous of others at the expense of herself."[29]

One wonders how either Heilbrun or Smith would have reacted to Wyman's description of Gertrude's thoughts as Hamlet delivers his long and excoriating speech. Gertrude's conviction that she had made the "normal choice" falters in the presence of Hamlet's fury, so that

it seemed that every motive which had influenced her must have been stained through by some terrible stream of selfishness. . . . And now returned her earlier moral question. Was the marriage really one that was forbidden by God's law. And, if it were, had she herself become an odious creature?
        Then it was that she sobbed,
        "O Hamlet, speak no more. . . . "
Out of her very innocence, as many another stormily distracted one has done, she confessed to a comparatively small fault, in language which sounded like the admission of a great sin. (136)

The "terrible stream of selfishness" that torments Gertrude is in many ways a more interesting "sin" than Heilbrun's lust, precisely because it is a more ambiguous one. It is also more akin to a tragic "mistake," or hamartia, originating as it does in a misguided effort to preserve her own identity as a queen and protect her son's future.
        And yet Wyman does not attempt to present Gertrude as a tragic figure. *Gertrude of Denmark* sets out to dislodge Prince Hamlet as the hero of the play, but without offering his mother in his place. Gertrude never becomes a heroine who invites the reader's profound sympathy and admiration, partly because she remains constrained by Wyman's decision not to add extensively to or alter the words Shakespeare gives her, and partly because Wyman never really decides how she feels about Gertrude's reasons for remarrying. Wyman imposed a very restrictive set of rules upon her enterprise, for she viewed herself as an interpreter who "had no right to alter [the play] in order to harmonize it with my fancies" (233), a self-characterization paradoxically at odds with the powerful novelistic invention she brings to her transformation of *Hamlet*. Wyman's Gertrude is thus a curious hybrid, at once a critical challenge to the literary establishment's adulation of Hamlet, a romance exhibiting many of the traits of nineteenth-century novels written for and about women, an indirect analysis of the limitations inherent in Shakespeare's view of women, and a record of Wyman's own ambivalence about the problems women face when they define themselves as wives and mothers.

NOTES

        1. Lillie Buffum Chace Wyman, *Gertrude of Denmark: An Interpretive Romance* (Boston: Marshall Jones Company, 1924), 1–2. Further citations will be given by page number in the text.
        2. Hugh Grady, *The Modernist Shakespeare: Critical Texts in a Material World* (Oxford: The Clarendon Press, 1991), 35. Grady cites L. M. Griffiths's 1889

handbook of instructions on setting up Shakespeare societies as evidence of an egalitarian system of study, independent of academic institutions, designed to lead to "self-cultivation." Hundreds of these Shakespeare societies existed in late nineteenth-century America (41).

3. Ann Douglas, *The Feminization of American Culture* (1977; rpt. New York: Avon, 1978), 89. Douglas devotes considerable attention to Henry Ward Beecher, "who, like all his siblings, made his dead mother the rationale and center for a feminized theology, [and] told his hearers that a mother's love is 'a revelation of the love of God' " (130–31).

4. Jane Tompkins, *Sensational Designs: The Cultural Work of American Fiction 1790–1860* (New York: Oxford University Press, 1985), 124–25.

5. Douglas, *Feminization,* 87.

6. Tompkins, *Sensational Designs,* 144–45.

7. C. L. Barber and Richard Wheeler, *The Whole Journey: Shakespeare's Power of Development* (Berkeley: University of California Press, 1986), 272.

8. Lillie Buffum Chace Wyman and Arthur Crawford Wyman, *Elizabeth Buffum Chace: Her Life and its Environment,* 2 vols. (Boston: W. B. Clarke Co, 1914), 1:33.

9. Ibid., 1:115.

10. In *Elizabeth Buffum Chace,* Lillie remarks that her mother "did not invite the little girls I met at Mrs. Greene's school to visit me. She did not try to get me chances to visit their homes. She did not seem to know their parents" (1:126).

11. Ibid., 2:103.

12. In her appendix to *Gertrude of Denmark* Wyman refers approvingly to Jameson's explanation of Ophelia's songs (244).

13. Anna Jameson, *Characteristics of Women, Moral, Poetical, and Historical* (New York: Wiley and Putnam, 1847), 111. The book was variously published under the titles *Shakespeare's Heroines* and *Characteristics of Women.* . . .

14. Ibid., 269–71.

15. Christy Desmet, "Intercepting the Dewdrop: Female Readers and Readings in Anna Jameson's Shakespearean Criticism," in *Women's Re-Visions of Shakespeare,* ed. Marianne Novy (Urbana: University of Illinois Press, 1990), 44.

16. Mary Cowden Clarke, *The Girlhood of Shakespeare's Heroines,* 3 vols. (1850–52; rpt. London: J. M. Dent, n.d.). Mary Cowden Clarke was married to the distinguished Shakespeare scholar Arthur Cowden Clarke, with whom she labored for sixteen years on a *Concordance of Shakespeare* (1844–45).

17. Ibid., xi.

18. Nina Auerbach, *The Woman and the Demon: The Life of a Victorian Myth* (Cambridge: Harvard University Press, 1982), 212.

19. Clarke, *Girlhood,* 104.

20. Ibid., 147–48.

21. It is also a literary formula familiar to readers of nineteenth-century novels: the heroine's first love or husband is a conventionally, perhaps superficially attractive man, whom she chooses over the less charming but far more intelligent and truly devoted rival. The rival finally wins her hand through persistence and

unflagging devotion, once she is sufficiently mature to recognize his worth. *War and Peace* is an example Wyman would have been familiar with.

22. A. C. Bradley, *Shakespearean Tragedy* (1904; rpt. New York: Fawcett, 1965), 140.

23. Jameson, *Characteristics,* 115, 117–18.

24. Agnes Mure MacKenzie, *The Women in Shakespeare's Plays: A Critical Study from the Dramatic and the Psychological Point of View* (Garden City: Doubleday, 1924), 200.

25. Ibid., 224.

26. Ibid., 225.

27. *Book Review Digest* (1924): 648. *Gertrude of Denmark* was also reviewed by the *Boston Transcript* and the *New York Times,* an indication that it received a fair amount of attention. None of the reviews mentions her previous works, and the entry in *Who's Who in America* for 1924–25 lists her publications but gives no indication of any honors or recognition associated with them.

28. Carolyn Heilbrun, "The Character of Hamlet's Mother," *Shakespeare Quarterly* 8, no. 2 (1957): 201–7. Baldwin Maxwell's 1964 essay entitled "Hamlet's Mother" seems to take issue with Heilbrun's theory, offering instead John Draper's argument that Gertrude is "no slave to lust." Like Wyman, he wonders about the accuracy of the Ghost's characterization of Gertrude. For Maxwell, Gertrude's first gesture of independence comes when she defies Claudius's order not to drink the poisoned cup. Her moment of recognition comes immediately afterwards: only in this last speech does she recognize or admit to herself the villainy of her second husband (*Shakespeare Quarterly* 15, no. 2 [1964]: 235–55). The quote from Draper is from *The Hamlet of Shakespeare's Audience* (Durham: Duke University Press, 1938).

29. Rebecca Smith, "A Heart Cleft in Twain: The Dilemma of Shakespeare's Gertrude," in *The Woman's Part: Feminist Criticism of Shakespeare,* ed. Carolyn Ruth Smith Lenz, Gayle Greene, and Carol Thomas Neely (Urbana: University of Illinois Press, 1980), 201, 207. Smith's notes indicate that she read the appendix of *Gertrude of Denmark,* which she quotes in connection with Henry's marriage to Katherine of Aragon.

JUDITH LEE

Rough Magic:
Isak Dinesen's Re-Visions of
The Tempest

I live ... halfway between that island in *The Tempest* and wherever
I am.
— Isak Dinesen, interview with Eugene Walter (1957)

Ariel was in fact rather heartless ... but so pure, compared with
earthly beings on the island, clear, honest, without reservations,
transparent—in short, like air.
— Isak Dinesen, letter to Ellen Dahl (1930)

Isak Dinesen's last volume of tales, *Anecdotes of Destiny,* constitutes a
dialogue with Shakespeare's *The Tempest.* In her transformations of its
characters and in her treatment of its representations of power and
dislocation, we discover a dialectic between gender and authority that
informs all her writing.[1] Here Dinesen plays out her relationship not only
with Shakespeare but with the canonical figures and texts that appear
frequently in her earlier tales and letters and represent a literary authority
she both reveres and resists. She claims a different but equivalent, female
and metahistorical, authority when she describes herself as woman who is
"three thousand years old and [who] dined with Socrates,"[2] and as a
storyteller who "belongs to an ancient, idle, wild and useless tribe."[3]
When she wrote these tales, moreover, she had achieved an international
status that in some ways depended upon her being an outsider to the
British tradition her tales repeatedly evoked, an ex-colonialist who dis-
avowed expansionist politics, and a woman writer who rejected the social
realism espoused by her Danish male contemporaries.[4] Her allusions to
Shakespeare's play in her final volume of tales trace her own ambivalence
toward the cultural politics this position entailed: although they authorize
her own "rough magic," they also register changes that counter the
cultural authority she invokes.

Shakespeare is a continuing presence in Dinesen's writings, not as the "bogey" that Milton was for other women writers, but as a paternal figure and friendly adversary.[5] She once said that when at the age of fifteen she read Shakespeare for the first time it was "one of the really great events of my life."[6] She called Viola her "favourite female character in all of literature,"[7] and she often referred to the fact that her home, Rungstedlund, was not far from Elsinore. Her letters express her familiarity with Shakespeare's plays. She does not discuss them to the extent that she discusses some contemporary fiction, but her informal references to Shakespeare suggest that his plays were a staple of her reading. She attributes the pleasure of her friendship with a government official, for example, to their shared enthusiasm for Shakespeare: "He is such a great devotee of Shakespeare, so we always talk very enthusiastically about him."[8] Elsewhere, she remarks that Shakespeare's enduring popularity rests in the fact that "he has represented humanity and freedom."[9] Yet she was also at times irreverent toward the authority he represented. Her reflections on Portia in a 1953 essay, "Oration at a Bonfire, Fourteen Years Late," could refer to her own negotiations with this authority, and they suggest why she did not feel disempowered by the authority she acknowledged: "And her magic lies precisely in her duplicity, the pretended deep respect for the paragraphs of the law which overlies her kind heart and her quite fearless heresy."[10]

We shall return to this essay, but at this point it is important to look more closely at Dinesen's apparent affinity with nineteenth-century writers who idealized Shakespeare's universality.[11] She herself attributed her enthusiasm for Shakespeare (indeed for all literature) to the Danish critic Georg Brandes, whose three-volume study of Shakespeare influenced her early reading of the plays.[12] Calling Shakespeare "co-equal with Michael Angelo in pathos and with Cervantes in humour," Brandes proposes that the plays and sonnets express Shakespeare's own inner experience, and he attempts to trace "the human spirit concealed and revealed in a great artist's work" by identifying Shakespeare's personal voice in each of his dramatic heroes.[13] Thus, Shakespeare "transforms himself in imagination" in portraying Richard III because, although he had not suffered physical deformity, he had endured poverty and humiliation as an actor: "Poverty is itself a deformity; and the condition of an actor was a blemish like a hump on his back."[14] And King Lear embodies his own bitterness at the ingratitude of friends and colleagues: "But he hated and despised ingratitude above all vices, because it at once impoverished and belittled his soul."[15]

Dinesen did not practice the same reductive identification between playwright and character, but she did follow Brandes by depoliticizing Shakespeare's characters, subordinating specific social issues to the contingencies of personal relationships and spiritual struggles. Take, for example,

her criticism that a performance of *King Lear* in Berlin during the war
offered too narrow an interpretation of Lear's character: "Balser played
Lear as a kind of grand, humane philosopher in the midst of a brutal and
deranged world; but one did not understand that he had for long pre-
served his faith in its value or that he was finally struck to the ground by
its unworthiness."[16] As a consequence, she remarks, in this production
"the play became, not a tragedy of human life, but a tragedy of old age."[17]
From Dinesen's own point of view, in contrast, Lear is a Job-like figure
who represents a universal (metacultural and gender-free) desire to believe
in the world's value and meaning. At the same time, her comments on
Edgar's role echo Brandes's portrait of the transcendent artist and betray
her assumption that Shakespeare worked effortlessly, for she implicitly
attributes to him a power and vision that no ordinary writer could
achieve: "all things did his [Edgar's] bidding as they came, and for him
everything was in a way undifferentiated, just as it must have been for
Shakespeare himself."[18]

Dinesen's adaptations of *The Tempest,* which omit the play's colonialist issues, call attention to the more problematic aspects of her
insistence upon subordinating the political to the poetical and, for the
most part, ignoring the cultural determinants in all behavior, her own
included. Indeed, this view has made her relationship to colonialist
discourse particularly controversial, for it leads to political equivoca-
tion at best and to moral myopia at worst.[19] Although our present
purpose does not allow for a full discussion of Dinesen's problematic
insistence upon depoliticizing her own colonialist privileges, a brief consideration of her allusions to *King Lear* in *Out of Africa* will illustrate
how she places herself outside the hierarchical relations upon which
colonialism is based. When she compares losing her farm to Lear's
loss of his kingdom, she places the Africans (not herself) in Lear's position. She recalls the government officials objecting to the Africans' request
that they be allowed to continue living together when they are relocated:
" 'O reason not the need,' I thought, 'our basest beggars are in the
poorest things superfluous',—and so on. All my life I have held that
you can class people according to how they may be imagined behaving
to King Lear. You could not reason with King Lear, any more than
with an old Kikuyu, and from the first he demanded too much of everybody; but he was a king."[20] By identifying the Kikuyu with the displaced
king, Dinesen not only inverts the power relation presumed by the
European settlers and the government authorities, but perhaps more
importantly she places herself—with Shakespeare—outside that relation.
Neither king nor daughter nor subject, she uses Shakespeare's language to
depoliticize the process by which her farm and its social network were

being dismantled. She assigns Shakespeare a metacultural authority that she then appropriates.

Not only is it telling that Dinesen finds Lear, rather than Prospero, her reference point in recreating her place in Africa, but this brief example of the way she mythologizes her own colonialist position suggests why, unlike many other post-Romantic adaptations, her versions of *The Tempest* eliminate the play's colonialist aspects.[21] This is perhaps the more surprising in that Brandes provided the basis for a re-vision based specifically on her African experience: "The entire drama is permeated by the atmosphere of that age of discovery and struggling colonists... [including] theories on the civilisation and government of new countries."[22] If she did not see herself as part of the colonialist enterprise, one can understand why she would not portray Prospero in political terms. Nevertheless, she does not portray the idealist Prospero, a figure who undergoes a spiritual education to orchestrate a personal and political reconciliation and, ultimately, achieves a marvelous harmony between Art and Nature. Brandes gives the paradigmatic reading that Dinesen revises: "He [Prospero] is a creature of princely mould, who has subdued outward Nature, has brought his own turbulent inner self under perfect control, and has overpowered the bitterness caused by the wrongs he has suffered in the harmony emanating from his own richly spiritual life.... Prospero is the master-mind, the man of the future, as shown by his control over the forces of nature."[23] As we shall see, Dinesen's figures of Prospero are antithetical to this "master-mind," and indeed she rejects the very concepts of power and control on which Brandes's reading is based.

It is Ariel, not Prospero, who occupies center stage in Dinesen's adaptations of *The Tempest*. Unlike other post-Romantic revisionist writers (who usually subordinate or ignore Ariel), Dinesen assigns Caliban only a minor role.[24] Although she spoke and wrote of the Africans as Other, she did not believe they were the inferior primitive figures that lie behind the allegorical and racist representations that engendered other re-visions in which Caliban is a central figure. Again, Brandes, who suggests that Ariel is the embodiment of "the highest culture,"[25] articulates the idealist view that Dinesen modifies: "He [Ariel] is a non-christian angel, a sprite, an elf, the messenger of Prospero's thought, the fulfiller of his will.... His longing for freedom after prolonged servitude has a peculiar and touching significance as a symbol of the yearning of the poet's own genius for rest."[26] Brandes emphasizes Ariel's lack of physicality: "In every essence of his nature... he is a spirit of the air, a mirage, a hallucination of light and sound."[27] As we shall see, Dinesen not only rejects this characterization, but her figures of Ariel discover and ultimately affirm not only that their (gendered and culturally inscribed) bodies are inescapable, but that this very bodily existence requires dislocation.

The five tales in *Anecdotes of Destiny* incorporate the relationships between art, exile, and power represented in *The Tempest*. In all of them, exile is a condition to be embraced, for it makes possible an art that is redemptive precisely because it is transgressive. Because gender and race are the basis for Dinesen's re-vision in "The Immortal Story" and "Tempests," these two tales exemplify most clearly how she departs from the interpretive traditions in which her work originates. In these two tales, she combines Shakespeare's figure with the prophet Ariel to displace Prospero: both prophet and trickster, her artists are marginal figures who remain *between* Shakespeare's patriarchal island and the promised land of (female) desire.

Dinesen wrote "Tempests," which Judith Thurman has called her "compressed retelling of her own life," in 1957, after seeing Sir John Gielgud play the role of Prospero at Stratford in a production directed by Peter Brook, the first performance of *The Tempest* that she had ever attended.[28] It is worth noting that Gielgud's Prospero was apparently more psychologically ambiguous than the powerful "master-mind" described by Brandes. Reviewing the performance in *Shakespeare Survey*, Roy Walker observes, "Until the end, this was no rich-robed and short-tempered magician but an ascetic hermit in brief tunic, burning with resentment of past wrongs which threatened to overthrow his reason altogether."[29] Miranda wore a sarong, and both "an ashen" Ariel and Caliban were portrayed as projections of Prospero's "disordered imagination."[30] Interpreting the play as a "charming pastoral [that] naturally encompasses rape, murder, conspiracy, and violence . . . [and] deals with the whole condition of man,"[31] Peter Brook designed a set dominated by caves and overgrown vegetation.

"Tempests" may thus be read as a re-vision not only of Brandes's idealized "man of the future" but also of a staging that is an unremittingly Prospero-centered psychomachia. Although the tale's title points toward the inner turmoil that is central to the tale and the production, it designates the female protagonist rather than the Prospero figure. Dinesen decenters the male artist-ruler and focuses on the female artist-outsider. She consequently changes the father-daughter/master-servant relationships at the heart of *The Tempest*. In the tale's first five episodes, Dinesen recreates Prospero and Ariel in the interaction between Malli, an actress learning the role of Ariel in a travelling theater troupe, and Herr Soerenson, the director of the troupe who himself prepares to perform as Prospero. Because Herr Soerensen is also surrogate father to Malli, Dinesen introduces a correspondence between Ariel and Miranda that becomes central to the tale's revisionist myth of redemption. After the troupe is shipwrecked on an island and Malli prepares to marry the shipowner's son, whom she ultimately leaves, Dinesen rewrites the story of Miranda and Ferdinand. In the end, by identifying Malli with the Ariel of Isaiah as well as with Shakespeare's character, Dinesen eliminates both the possibility and desirability for reconciliation and integration, calling attention to the ambivalence in the play also noted by other modern writers.[32]

Dinesen's most significant change in this adaptation of The Tempest is "Miranda's" relationship with her father, in which she inscribes her own relation to Shakespeare. In Shakespeare's play, Miranda's absent mother is suppressed (Prospero displaces both Miranda's mother and Caliban's).[33] But in Dinesen's tale Malli's decision to be an actress, which involves rejecting the placid comfort of both her mother's village and the town where she might marry, shows that she remains aware of her father's continuing presence. Malli herself never knew her father, a Scotch sea captain who stayed with her mother only briefly. He assumes a mythic identity among the townspeople; rumor has it that he, like a demon or a god, was married to another woman, even that he was The Flying Dutchman. After Malli has read Shakespeare for the first time, she imagines that her father is "a Shakespearean hero" (82). She inherits his mysterious lawlessness, his "wild, carefree madness," and in her mother's eyes she has the same "foreign, rich and enrapturing power" (85) and her manner is "as insinuating and enticing" as his (86).[34] When she leaves her mother's home to join Herr Soerensen's theatrical company, Malli affirms a kinship with her father that she had hitherto repressed: "All the vigor and longing in her, which for years had been forcibly mastered, were released into perfect clarity and bliss" (84).[35]

Because Malli's father is an outsider associated with lawlessness, Dinesen problematizes "Miranda's" relation to patriarchal discourse as Shakespeare does not. Not only does Malli's father reject the social and legal structures that Miranda's father embodies, but Malli expresses her self-assertion through loyalty to her father, Miranda through rebellion against hers. Although the maternal is displaced in the tale and the play, Malli's affirmation of her father's primacy is itself a sign that she will never be integrated into the social order. By having Malli discover Shakespeare through the tutelage of a witch-like, self-exiled old woman (a "dried-up, beaky-nosed Englishwoman" [82]), moreover, Dinesen complicates her own relation to her literary "father": Malli is liberated by her reading and finds in Shakespeare's alien language the means by which she can liberate and reinvent herself—a discourse in which she can, paradoxically, legitimize her bastardy.[36]

Herr Soerensen, the travelling troupe's director, becomes Malli's surrogate father, and he seems to free her from the constraints of her

female destiny. Despite her own doubt that she is too large and too slow
for the part, Herr Soerensen casts her to play Ariel: "So moved was he
that he overlooked his pupil's sex" (75). However, a narrative aside
implies a skepticism that emphasizes the differences between the tale and
Shakespeare's play: "Still, no theatre man but one with the eyes of genius
would ever have imagined her in the part of Ariel" (76). With these words,
Dinesen on the one hand admits the authority of a play and a theatrical
practice (of casting a male to play Ariel) that resists transformation; on the
other hand, however, she reiterates the double gender change she herself
has brought about: not only has she substituted a female for the traditional
boy actor, but she has replaced patriarchal stereotypes of female beauty,
and she has invented an Ariel who is not constrained by the material and
bodily limits embodied in the female.[37]

At the same time, Dinesen's aside displaces and subordinates the
playwright himself, for Herr Soerensen is a figure for both Prospero and
Shakespeare.[38] He claims credit for having "created" Malli, and in him
Dinesen treats ironically the kind of power that Brandes attributes to
Prospero—and indirectly to Shakespeare: "he was a man of a mighty,
independent character, which demanded the creation and control of his
own world around him. . . . Herr Soerensen in his nature had a kind of
duplicity which might well confuse and disturb his surroundings and
might even be called demoniacal, but with which he himself managed to
exist on harmonious terms. He was on the one hand a wide-awake
shrewd and untiring businessman. . . . And he was at one and the same
time his art's obedient servant, a humble old priest in the temple, with the
words 'Domine, non sum dignus' graven in his heart" (71, 72).

Dinesen's Prospero is a pragmatist who, despite at one time "neglecting
worldly ends" (1.2.89), can take advantage of an "accident most strange"
(1.2.178) and manipulate others to achieve his own ends.[39] A worldly and
sublime artist whose authority can be both irresistible and inescapable, his
relationship with Malli mirrors that between the storyteller and the dramatist.

In the episode that takes place on the island after the shipwreck,
Dinesen transforms Shakespeare's island into a bourgeois paradise where
Malli cannot survive and where the promised marriage of "Miranda and
Ferdinand" must be endlessly deferred. When the troupe is shipwrecked
in a storm and takes refuge on an island, Malli saves the ship by guiding it
to within reach of the harbor, and as a result the island people treat her
like a fairy-tale heroine. When Arndt Hosewinckel (who as the son of the
shipowner is the bourgeois equivalent to a fairy-tale prince) picks her up
and carries her to shore, Dinesen describes Malli's response in language
that echoes Miranda's first response to Ferdinand: "Malli stared into his
face, and thought that she had never seen so beautiful a human face" (95).

Thus, Dinesen begins where the traditional fairy tale ends: "It was once again the happy ending, both surprising and foreseen, to the old tale in which Cinderella marries the Prince. . . . Inasmuch as she symbolized the sea, the breadwinner and the fate of all, she united, even as the sea itself, the town's humble folk with its richest citizen" (111).

Malli herself at first believes that her new identity is as real as that which she has imagined for herself, and she mistakenly believes that she can fly: "She had once been given wings; they had grown miraculously and had been able to carry her, ever upward, to this unspeakable glory. She stood on a dizzying height, but she could fearlessly cast herself out from it anywhere, because anywhere Arndt's arm would catch her and bear her" (114). To live out the fairy-tale romance, to be idealized, is to achieve a kind of immortality. For Dinesen, however, Miranda-Cinderella is merely a figure of desire that denies female subjectivity. She ironically shows that Malli's fearlessness is a bourgeois maid's flight of fancy that involves no risk. Malli believes she can have it both ways: while she continues to experience the freedom of (gender-free) "Ariel," she enjoys "Miranda's" privileged invulnerability.

Seeing no difference between being Ariel and being Miranda, Malli assumes she has a redeemer's power while she is on the island. At a ball held in her honor, she sings Ariel's song to Ferdinand ("Come unto these yellow sands, / And then take hands . . . " [1.2.377–83; quoted on 105]), addressing it to Arndt. Her initial attraction to Arndt is based not only upon recognizing his status among the townspeople (especially in the eyes of the other young women), but more decisively upon her belief that she can help him: "She thought: 'God! what deep need!' And again: 'I can help there. I can help him in his need and save him!' " (106). She agrees to marry him by quoting the words of Christ: " 'Yes. "I am the resurrection and the life," ' said Malli. " 'He that believeth in me, though he were dead, yet shall he live. And whosoever liveth and believeth in me, shall never die, but have everlasting life" ' " (117).

Malli confronts the difference between this illusory power and immortality, which she identifies with Ariel, and the inescapable mortality that constrains gendered persons when she visits the home of the character Dinesen actually names Ferdinand, a sailor who dies of injuries he received during the storm. Ferdinand's death is devastating for Malli because it forces her to recognize the absolute difference between the role and gender-free immortality that her art allows her as Ariel and the gendered social expectations and mortality she must endure as a woman. The erotically charged detail of Malli's meditation on Ferdinand's body shows Malli ironically coming to life in the very process of confronting her own mortality: "she stretched out her hand and touched his face. Death's icy chill penetrated through her fingers; she felt it go right into her heart and withdrew her hand. But a little after she laid it back again, let it rest on the boy's cheek until she thought that her hand had become as cold as that cheek itself, and so began slowly to stroke the still face. She felt the cheekbones and the eyesockets against the tips of her fingers. Her own face the while took on the dead sailor boy's face; the two grew to resemble each other like brother and sister" (120–21).

Focusing on the paradoxical difference and identity that resemblance involves, Dinesen here shows Malli discovering that she is both mortal and female: she is gendered body, not mere spirit. When Ferdinand's mother tells Malli stories about Ferdinand's childhood and relations with his family, her lamenting makes her a choric figure from a maternal land of the dead: "Malli listened, and deep in her heart recognized this sub-dued woman's wailing. It was her own mother's anxiety about bread for herself and her child. She looked about her, and now also recognized the needy, narrow room. This was the room of her own home; here she had grown up. The old familiar, bare world came back to her, so strangely gentle, and so inescapable" (121).

By identifying the maternal with death and contingency, Dinesen trans-forms Shakespeare's romance into a kind of *danse macabre*. In this scene, particularly, she places Malli in an impossible liminal position between being a "demi-devil" who inherits her father's immortality and eternal exile and a woman who inherits her mother's mortality and inescapable confinement.

When she leaves Arndt and the island, Malli abjures a magic as power-ful as Prospero's. Before Ferdinand's death, she was fearless because she believed she had nothing to fear: "And I understand now, and see well, that in a human being it is beautiful to fear, and also I see clearly that the one who does not fear is all alone, and is rejected, an outcast from among people. But I, I was not in the least afraid" (149). She felt no fear during the storm, she confesses, because she believed that she *was* Ariel, and that she could thus escape any impending danger.

But if the storm is not imaginary, then of course this island is not the "lovely island full of tones, sounds and music sweet" where the imaginary Ariel could roam freely (150). Upon recognizing this, Malli realizes that she has deceived Arndt because by imagining she could be "Ariel" when others believed her to be "Miranda" she has not been herself: "I belong elsewhere and must now go there," she explains (150). She abjures the immortality implied by the mythical identity created for her by the townspeople—and by her own desire.

When Malli comes to Herr Soerensen to acknowledge that neither of them could live in the safe comfort of the island's bourgeois society, she nevertheless disavows the union the two had achieved before the shipwreck.

Herr Soerensen is himself healed and his capacity to invent himself restored. For the first time since the storm that brought them to the island, he can speak, and when he admits that he secretly left his wife many years before, Dinesen reinforces his similarity to Malli's father. The two figures sitting in silence, Malli "beseeching or caressing" the old man (140–41), recall Lear's reunion with Cordelia as well as the scene in which Prospero tells Miranda their history. Herr Soerensen himself is at first unsure which "plot" their lives will follow: "He at first felt that their group was taking form like that of the old unhappy king and his loving daughter [Lear and Cordelia]. But presently the center of gravity was shifted and he became fully conscious of his authority and responsibility. . . . He once more became the man powerful above others: Prospero. And with Prospero's mantle round his shoulders, without lessening his pity of the despairing girl by his side, he was aware of a growing, happy consciousness of fulfillment and reunion. He was not to abandon his precious possession, but she was still his and would remain with him, and he was to see his life's great project realized" (141).

In a reversal of *The Tempest,* Dinesen has him then announce his plans to leave the island with Malli by quoting the lines with which Prospero promises Miranda that they will soon be restored to their true positions ("Now I arise / Sit still, and hear the last of our sea-sorrow" [1.2.169–70 quoted on 141]); in Dinesen's tale, however, such restoration involves permanent displacement. More importantly, Malli rejects the role of Miranda to speak as an Ariel who, unlike Shakespeare's character, claims her own freedom. In response to the pronouncement that they will leave in two days, Malli speaks the words with which Ariel claims his right to freedom from Prospero in *The Tempest.* Dinesen changes the meaning of Shakespeare's dialogue, however. First, she reverses the original order of Ariel's speeches: Malli first recites Ariel's reminder that Prospero has promised him freedom (1.2.246–49), and then his report that he has successfully followed Prospero's orders during the storm (1.2.189–93). As a result, Malli-Ariel's freedom is not a reward but a condition with which both must live. Second, and more importantly, she changes the words of Ariel's song to Ferdinand (1.2.397–403):

> Full fathom five my body [thy father] lies
> Of my [his] bones are coral made,
> Those are the pearls that were my [his] eyes,
> Nothing of me [him] that doth fade,
> But doth suffer a sea-change
> Into something rich and strange.
> Sea-nymphs hourly ring my [his] knell.
> (144 [words from *The Tempest* in brackets])

When Malli identifies both with her own father and with the dead
Ferdinand in these lines, Dinesen reiterates her liminal status as the
illegitimate daughter of a mythic figure (implicitly like Caliban, a "demi-
devil" [5.1.272]) and a mortal woman.[40] At the same time, speaking
as Ariel, Malli refuses the position assigned her by Herr Soerensen
(and Shakespeare), insisting upon a "sea-change / Into something rich and
strange"—a new identity she herself invents whereby she becomes both
spirit and woman, neither wholly imaginary nor wholly real. Just as Malli
thereby proclaims her difference from her absent father even while she
reaffirms her kinship with him, so also, by changing the Shakespearean
text, Dinesen both admits and distances herself from the origins of her
own "rough magic."

Dinesen does not portray Malli as a figure who invents her own
identity, however, or whose choice of self-exile is arbitrary. She displaces
both Shakespeare's sprite and the fairy-tale heroine with the figure of the
prophet Ariel. From the Bible Malli learns another meaning of the name
she has imagined for herself, and she discovers that she is no redeemer but
a harbinger of doom; the book opens to Isaiah 29:1–8, a passage that
builds upon the ironic double meaning of Ariel's name: "Ariel" signifies
both hero and shade, both City of God and underworld:[41] "Woe to Ariel,
to Ariel! . . . And thou shalt be brought down, and thou shalt speak out of
the ground . . . and thy voice shall be as of one that hath a familiar spirit,
out of the ground, and thy speech shall whisper out of the dust! . . . It shall
be as when an hungry man dreameth, and behold, he eateth; but he
awaketh, and his soul is empty; or as when a thirsty man dreameth, and
behold he drinketh; but he awaketh, and behold, he is faint, and his soul
hath appetite" (147–48).

In discovering a story older than Shakespeare's, a story of doom rather
than of regeneration, Malli at once awakens from her dream that she will
be redeemed and rediscovers her ability to speak. The words of Isaiah
interrupt her silence and move her to reject the illusion of redemption
promised in the tale of Miranda-Cinderella. Unlike Shakespeare's Ariel,
moreover, Dinesen's Ariel cannot be liberated (redeemed) by a more
powerful master; she can only redeem herself by remaining "in between"
the island where she would be an object of desire and an imaginary world
where she can "fly" as she desires.[42]

In "The Immortal Story" Dinesen treats with darker irony the power of
the male artist that Brandes identifies in Prospero, and instead of recreating
either an idealist artist-ruler who controls Nature or a revisionary tyranni-
cal racist, she presents a man dehumanized by capitalist greed. In this
master-servant relationship the artist is again not "Prospero" but a displaced

and marginalized "Ariel," an exiled Jew.[43] In contrast to Shakespeare's (and Brandes's) focus on the artist's desire for control—which the artist-as-Prospero abjures—Dinesen centers on the transforming power of art itself—to which the artist-as-Ariel submits.

The story takes place in China and centers on the relationship between an old and unscrupulous businessman, a parody of Prospero aptly named Mr. Clay, and his assistant Elishama, a Polish Jew whose family had been killed in the Pogrom of 1848. Obsessed with the power brought by money, Mr. Clay maneuvers to ruin his partner, whose home and assets he subsequently usurps. He insists that he can bring about the events recounted in a story retold by sailors. This "immortal story" is as follows: When a young sailor goes ashore he is approached by an old gentleman who asks him if he wants to earn five guineas. When the sailor says yes, the old man takes him to his home, serves a wonderful meal, and tells him that he has a young wife but no children to whom he can leave his wealth. After dinner, he leads the sailor to his wife's bedroom, gives him the gold pieces, and leaves him with his wife. In the morning, the sailor returns to his ship, having spent the night with the young woman. Elishama insists that the story exists only because it can never come true: "If they [the sailors] had believed that it could ever happen they would not have told it," Elishama tells him (172). Mr. Clay nevertheless insists upon hiring an actress to play his wife, inviting a young sailor to his home and paying him five guineas, leaving them to spend the night together.

Written in 1953, when Dinesen was frustrated in her attempts to orchestrate the lives of the young writers who gathered at Rungstedlund, this tale's "Prospero" could, as Thurman has suggested, be seen as her own parodic self-portrait.[44] However, her other references to Shakespeare suggest that she inscribes her own position in the displaced and reawakened Elishama. In telling how Elishama arranges to dramatize the sailor's story, Dinesen creates an Ariel who is subversive in his subservience. In some ways, Elishama is more spirit than man. He has neither desire nor ambition: "Desire, in any form, had been washed, bleached, and burnt out of him before he had learned to read" (160–61). He is also, we are told, "without any illusions whatever of the world or of humanity" (160); his single passion is "a fanatical craving for security and for being left alone" (161). He succeeds in recruiting the female lead because he has a "deep innate sympathy or compassion toward all women of this world" (178). In organizing the production, Elishama (like Ariel obeying Prospero and, differently, Dinesen adapting Shakespeare) discovers that he is paradoxically empowered by his subordinate relation to his master: "he realized that from this moment he was indispensable to his master, and could get out of him whatever he wanted. He did not intend to derive any advantage from the circumstance, but the idea pleased him" (176). Just as Elishama does not confuse Mr. Clay's drama with the original story, Dinesen repeatedly distinguishes her story from the drama in which it originates, and, as we shall see, she differentiates that play from the "immortal story" of redemption that is its source.

In the performance itself, a parody of Prospero's masque, Dinesen rewrites the Miranda-Ferdinand story to show that it cannot be incorporated in her own narrative. She draws her names from *Paul et Virginie,* a romance by J. H. B. Saint-Pierre. Saint-Pierre tells the story of a man and woman who enjoy an idyllic romance on an island until Virginie decides she must leave; she drowns when her ship is caught in a storm and she is unwilling to undress in order to swim to safety. When Paul discovers her body, his picture in her hands, he himself dies of heartbreak.[45]

Dinesen's Virginie-Miranda is, in contrast to both Shakespeare's and Saint-Pierre's characters, a worldly woman who has lost faith in the transforming and regenerative power of love. A demimondaine aware that her youthful beauty is ephemeral, she is seeking a way to France and a career in the theater. Like Malli, she feels greater affinity with her absent father, who was Mr. Clay's former business partner, than with her mother; when she was a little girl he used to tell her tales of fantasy and adventure. When she agrees to perform in exchange for three hundred pounds, the exact amount of the debt her father owed Mr. Clay, she wants to avenge his suicide and to reclaim his belief that the world and the imagination hold infinite possibilities. As in "Tempests," Dinesen opposes this paternal absence and fantastic freedom to maternal presence and confinement when, after her performance, Virginie recovers her bond with her mother who (like Malli's mother) figures domestic solitude: "In the middle of the night she suddenly remembered things which her mother had told her about her own people, the seafaring men of Brittany. Old French songs of the sailor's dangers, and of his homecoming, came back to her as on their own. In the end, from far away, came the sailor-wife's cradlesong" (219). Virginie affirms her kinship with her father and displaces her mother when she refuses to abjure the "rough magic" with which she appropriates and perpetuates romance, conjuring an "airy charm" that is the source, literally, of her life and livelihood.

Dinesen makes Paul, the sailor who agrees to Mr. Clay's invitation, a comic version of the fairy-tale hero by drawing upon Shakespeare's portrayal of Caliban. Paul's boorish clumsiness parallels Caliban's. Before arriving in China, Paul had spent a year alone on an island where, he says, there were "many sounds on my island, but no one ever spoke" (205). Dinesen's allusion to Caliban's speech ("Be not afeard: the isle is full of

noises, / Sounds and sweet airs that give delight and hurt not" [3.2.132–33])
underscores the parallel between Ferdinand and Caliban suggested in the
play while ignoring the implications of Caliban's speech for the play's
colonialist subtext. Dinesen translates the play's reference to rape and
Caliban's violent sexuality into a comic description of Paul's naiveté that
ironically re-views romantic idealizations of love. When Virginie first sees
Paul, she reacts as Miranda does to Caliban: "For the figure by the end of
the bed was not a casual sailor out of the streets of Canton. It was a huge
wild animal brought in to crush her beneath him" (216). At the same time,
in Paul's eyes she is "the most beautiful girl in the world" (216), a girl his
own age. Despite being bound by his contract with Mr. Clay, however,
Paul knows he has created a new story: "But that story is not in the least
like what happened to me," he tells Elishama. It is a story he will never
tell: "To whom would I tell it?" he asks. "Who in the world would believe
it if I told it?" (229).

As in "Tempests," the prophecy of Isaiah subordinates Shakespeare's
play and Dinesen's tale to an older myth of redemption. Mr. Clay becomes
especially resolved to make the sailors' story come true after Elishama
reads to him Isaiah's prophecy of a redeemer (Isaiah 35:1–7), the other
"immortal story" of the tale. This passage expresses the desire for healing
and regeneration, but it also announces the inevitability of divine retribution:
"Then shall the lame man leap as a hart, and the tongue of the dumb
sing. . . . And the desert shall rejoice, and blossom as the rose. It shall
blossom abundantly. . . . And the parched ground shall become a pool,
and the thirsty land springs of water" (quoted 165–66). Unable to tolerate
the idea that the desire expressed in the story and the prophecy alike
cannot be satisfied, Mr. Clay's resolve intensifies: "He felt that he was
getting the better of Elishama and the Prophet Isaiah. He was still going to
prove to them his omnipotence" (173). Similarly, when his "masque" is
about to begin, "Dimly he felt that he was about to triumph over the
person who had attempted to upset his own idea of the world—the
Prophet Isaiah" (213).

However, Dinesen emphasizes the difference between Mr. Clay's desire
for control and the artist-as-Ariel's visionary power when, upon arriving
at Mr. Clay's home at dawn the next day, Elishama discovers his employer
sitting "propped up on cushions in his deep armchair," like a discarded
marionette: "The whole proud rigid figure, envied and feared by thousands,
this morning looked like a jumping-jack when the hand which has pulled
the strings has suddenly let them go" (226). In addition, by having
Elishama repeat lines from Isaiah when he realizes Mr. Clay is dead ("And
sorrow and sighing shall flee away" [226]) Dinesen makes her tale a
revisionist continuation of Isaiah's prophecy. Similarly, when Elishama

overhears Virginie's and Paul's tearful farewell, he interprets it as an ironic fulfillment of the prophecy of Isaiah: "In the wilderness shall waters break out, and streams in the desert. And the parched ground shall become a pool" (227). By making Elishama a figure of the Wandering Jew (the unredeemed), who witnesses this "revelation," Dinesen implies that she is writing a new myth of redemption, one in which *anyone* can—indeed must—redeem oneself.

For our last sight of Elishama is of a man free and desiring—redeemed. As Paul leaves, he gives Elishama a shell that he wants Virginie to have. In this shell echoes of the sea bring "an attentive, peaceful look" to both Paul and Elishama as each holds it to his ear. The last lines of the tale describe Elishama listening to the shell, a sound both new and familiar: "He had a strange, gentle, profound shock, from the sound of a new voice in the house, and in the story. 'I have heard it before,' he thought, 'long ago. Long, long ago. But where?' He let his hand sink" (231). No jumping-jack, he exercises his own movement. He awakens to the beginnings of desire in the incipient reawakening of his memory. His final movement closes a dramatic scene, but it marks the beginning of a new story that is at the same time a retelling of one even older than the prophecy of Isaiah, a story as yet unspeakable, unimaginable.

In these tales Dinesen transforms Shakespeare's "spirit" into human characters who cannot escape the contingencies of patriarchal discourse. Like Ariel, Malli (because she is a woman) and Elishama (because he is a Jew) are both outsiders; however, unlike Ariel, they can never be entirely free: there is no "island" they can claim as their own. Neither is included in any promise of reconciliation and social reintegration that earlier critics had discovered in the play. Nevertheless, they are both ultimately empowered by the very "spirit" that makes them (unredeemed) outsiders, even though their endings differ significantly—Malli's with a sense of doom, Elishama's with hope.

Like the artist-figures in "Babette's Feast" and "The Diver"—also in *Anecdotes of Destiny*—Elishama and Malli exercise a "rough magic" that involves participation in the ordinary, natural world, an art that brings healing because it involves transgression.[46] For these artists, as for Malli and Elishama, art does not involve *making* or acting upon the world, but rather discovering and revealing what remains immanent. Exile makes this possible, indeed is a necessary prerequisite.

By displacing Prospero with Ariel, Dinesen both acknowledges the importance of the power relations represented in the play and downplays their political dimension. Her transformations of Ariel in these tales echo her reflections upon gender in her controversial essay, "Oration at a

Bonfire, Fourteen Years Late," where, as I have noted, her description of Portia could be a self-portrait. She argues in this essay that the difference between men and women lies fundamentally in the fact that a man *does,* while a woman *is:* "A man's center of gravity, the substance of his being, consists in what he has executed and performed in life; the woman's, in what she is."[47] A man "creates something by himself but outside of himself," while a woman's creation extends her own being: "Though it can spread out like the crown of a tall tree, it still has its root in her ego."[48] In elaborating this point, Dinesen advocates an apolitical stance, arguing that women should find in sexual difference their own independence: "That which itself has no independent being—or is without any loyalty to such a being—is unable to create. Now I have not meant that women are trees and men are motors, but I wish to insinuate into the minds of the women of our time as well as those of the men, that they should meditate not only upon what they may accomplish but most profoundly upon what they are."[49] Dinesen presents a paradoxical position here: that by turning their attention from *doing* to *being,* women will bring a new ethical consciousness to the world, the awareness that what we create is rooted in our being. The origin for women's art, in particular, is in a metacultural identity that a woman can discover and express by affirming gender difference.

This paradox bespeaks the desire for authority and autonomy that Dinesen realized in Ariel, whose double identity as imaginary sprite and prophet reminds us that this desire is both inevitable and insatiable. It is a desire that Dinesen herself expressed in saying she was an ageless story-teller who finds her home in no one place. She claimed a position both de-centered and self-centered and, like Ariel's, her art both demonstrates and modifies her "master's" authority.

NOTES

All references to Dinesen's tales in the text are to *Anecdotes of Destiny* (1958; rpt. New York: Random House, 1974) and are indicated by page number. References to *The Tempest* are to the Arden Shakespeare edition by Frank Kermode (1954; rpt. New York: Routledge, 1988) and are indicated by act, scene, and line number.

1. Robert Langbaum discusses the importance of *The Tempest* to *Anecdotes of Destiny,* finding in Ariel a figure for desire, but he emphasizes the similarities, rather than the differences, between Dinesen's vision and Shakespeare's: see *Isak Dinesen's Art: The Gayety of Vision* (1964; rpt. Chicago: University of Chicago Press, 1975). Nadia Setti emphasizes the themes of loss and redemption developed in allusions to *The Tempest* and *King Lear* in Dinesen's "Tempests," in "Visions of Life's Tempest: From Shakespeare to Karen Blixen," trans. Susan Sellers, in

Writing Differences: Readings from the Seminar of Helene Cixous, ed. Susan Sellers (New York: St. Martin's Press, 1988), 71–80. Hans Holmberg discusses the significance of Dinesen's uses of *The Tempest* in "The Wing-Clipped Ariel: Later Attitudes to the Relation Between Life and Art," in *Proceedings of the International Symposium on Karen Blixen / Isak Dinesen: Tradition, Modernity, and Other Ambiguities,* ed. Poul Houe and Donna Dacus (Minneapolis: University of Minnesota, 1985), 74–77. Drawing upon poststructuralist feminist theory, Susan Hardy Aiken offers the most comprehensive discussion of Dinesen's negotiations with issues of gender and authority, in *Isak Dinesen and the Engendering of Narrative* (Chicago: University of Chicago Press, 1990).

2. In 1957, in an interview with Eugene Walter, *Writers At Work: The Paris Review Interviews,* 4th series, ed. George Plimpton (New York: Penguin, 1977), 16.

3. Quoted by Donald Hannah, *"Isak Dinesen" and Karen Blixen: The Mask and the Reality* (New York: Random House, 1971), 60.

4. During the last fifteen years of her life Dinesen had very complicated relationships with the young male writers of Denmark, who revered and opposed her with equal passion. Judith Thurman gives a full portrait of this period of her life in *Isak Dinesen: The Life of a Storyteller* (New York: St. Martin's Press, 1982); but the most moving and revealing accounts of Dinesen's charismatic power are by Thorkild Bjornvig (*The Pact: My Friendship with Isak Dinesen,* trans. Ingvar Schousboe and William Jay Smith [Baton Rouge: Louisiana State University Press, 1983]) and Aage Henriksen ("The Messenger" and "At Rungstedlund," in *Karen Blixen / Isak Dinesen,* trans. William Mishler [New York: St. Martin's Press, 1988], 40–45 and 123–76). Aage Westenholz describes what he, and Dinesen herself, called "the Power" in *The Power of Aries: Myth and Reality in Karen Blixen's Life,* trans. Lise Kure-Jensen (Baton Rouge: Louisiana State University Press, 1982), esp. 1–9. Dinesen explains her own aesthetic principles most fully in her 1949 essay "H. C. Branner: *The Riding Master,*" in *Daguerrotypes and Other Essays* (Chicago: University of Chicago Press, 1979), 157–94.

5. Allusions to Shakespeare's plays recur frequently in her tales. References to *Hamlet* appear with particular frequency, most significantly in "The Supper at Elsinore" and "Converse at Night in Copenhagen," and *The Winter's Tale* is an explicit reference point for her second volume of tales, *Winter's Tales.* Bernhard Glienke cites all Dinesen's references to Shakespeare in *Fatale Präzedenz: Karen Blixen's Mythologie* (Neumunster: Karl Wachholtz, 1986).

6. Quoted by Parmenia Migel, *Titania* (New York: Random House, 1967), 16.

7. Quoted by Thurman, *Isak Dinesen,* 51.

8. Isak Dinesen, *Letters From Africa: 1914–1931,* ed. Frans Lasson, trans. Anne Born (Chicago: University of Chicago Press, 1981), 410.

9. Ibid., 235.

10. Dinesen, "Oration at a Bonfire, Fourteen Years Late," in *Daguerrotypes,* 83. The title of this essay alludes to the fact that Dinesen had been invited to speak at the International Women's Congress being held in Copenhagen in 1939, but she had been unable to attend.

11. Meredith Skura's perceptive analysis of "idealist" and "revisionist" readings of *The Tempest* provides a useful framework for understanding Dinesen's adaptations: see "Discourse and the Individual: The Case of Colonialism in *The Tempest*," *Shakespeare Quarterly* 40, no. 1 (Spring 1989): 42–69. For a discussion of how Shakespeare's reputation evolved during the nineteenth century see Gary Taylor, *Reinventing Shakespeare* (New York: Oxford University Press, 1989), 162–230. See also Jonathan Bate, *Shakespeare and the English Romantic Imagination* (New York: Oxford, 1986).

12. Thurman, *Isak Dinesen*, 50–51.

13. Georg Brandes, *William Shakespeare*, 2 vols., trans. William Archer, Mary Morison, and Diana White (London: William Heinemann, 1909), 1:1. On Edward Dowden's influence on Brandes see Bertil Nolin, *Georg Brandes* (Boston: G. K. Hall, 1976); for a pertinent analysis of Dowden's work see Taylor, *Reinventing Shakespeare*, 173–82.

14. Brandes, *William Shakespeare*, 1:129.

15. Ibid., 1:451.

16. Dinesen, "Letters from a Land at War," in *Daguerrotypes*, 127.

17. Ibid., 128.

18. Ibid., 129.

19. The most comprehensive discussions of the relationship between Dinesen's writings on Africa and other colonialist texts are by Thurman (*Isak Dinesen: The Life of a Storyteller*), Aiken (*Isak Dinesen and the Engendering of Narrative*), and Abdul JanMohamed, *Manichean Aesthetics: The Politics of Literature in Colonial Africa* (Amherst: University of Massachusetts Press, 1983). Ngugi wa Thiong'o has offered the most vehement and perhaps most articulate criticism of Dinesen's complicity in the colonialist enterprise: see *Prison Notes*, African Writers Series (London: Heinemann, 1981), and *Homecoming* (1972; rpt. Westport, Conn.: Lawrence Hill, 1983), where he argues that Dinesen exemplifies how European colonialists enacted Prospero's dominance over Caliban (9–10).

20. Dinesen, *Out of Africa* (1937; rpt. New York: Random House, 1989), 361. She quotes from *King Lear*, 2.4.262–63.

21. Skura ("Discourse and the Individual," 43) points out that the New World has provided the context for interpreting the play since the early nineteenth century. For an early critical history of the play see Frank Kermode, ed., *The Tempest*, The Arden Shakespeare (1954; rpt. New York: Routledge, 1988), lxxxi–lxxxix. Ruby Cohn discusses several nineteenth-century adaptations of *The Tempest* in *Modern Shakespeare Offshoots* (Princeton: Princeton University Press, 1976), 267–309. Thomas Cartelli examines the tensions between colonialist and anticolonialist discourse engendered by the play in "Prospero in Africa: *The Tempest* as Colonialist Text and Pretext," in *Shakespeare Reproduced*, ed. Jean Howard and Marion O'Connor (New York: Methuen, 1987), 99–115.

22. Brandes, *William Shakespeare*, 2:368. Although there is no evidence that Dinesen would have had Brandes's commentary beside her, so to speak, she was clearly familiar with his interpretation and demonstrated a remarkably detailed memory for what she had read, both of his work and of other texts.

23. Ibid., 2:379, 380.

24. Ruby Cohn points out that Caliban was of particular interest to the post-Darwinian imagination (*Modern Shakespeare Offshoots*). Ania Loomba offers a brief history of how Caliban has been portrayed in *Gender, Race, and Renaissance Drama* (New York: St. Martin's Press, 1989).

25. Brandes, *William Shakespeare,* 2:384.

26. Ibid., 2:381.

27. Ibid., 2:382.

28. Thurman, *Isak Dinesen,* 410. According to Thurman, Dinesen intended to send a copy of "Tempests" to Sir John Gielgud.

29. Roy Walker, "Unto Caesar: A Review of Recent Productions," *Shakespeare Survey 11,* ed. Allardyce Nicoll (New York: Cambridge University Press, 1958), 128. William Babula paraphrases Walker's review and a review from the *London Times* (which describes the more sexualized Prospero that appears in the photograph accompanying Walker's review: "clean-shaven with the grizzled hair of virile middle age and half-bared to the waist, rather like the symbolic figure of a workman about to strike an anvil") in *Shakespeare in Production, 1935–1978* (New York: Garland, 1981), 310. See also J. C. Trewin, *Shakespeare on the English Stage, 1900–1964* (London: Barrie and Rockliff, 1964). Placing this production in the context of the play's theatrical history, David Bevington notes that Brook omitted the spectacular theatrical effects and romance of nineteenth- and earlier twentieth-century productions: "*The Tempest* in Performance," in *The Tempest,* ed. David Bevington (New York: Bantam, 1988), xxxiii–xxxv.

30. Walker, "Unto Caesar," 135.

31. Peter Brook, *The Empty Stage* (New York: Macmillan, 1975), 102.

32. See, for example, W. H. Auden, *The Sea and the Mirror* (New York: Random House, 1944). More recently, critics have explored the ambivalence with which *The Tempest* ends; see, for example, Stephen Orgel, "Prospero's Wife," in *Rewriting the Renaissance,* ed. Margaret Ferguson et al. (Chicago: University of Chicago Press, 1986), 50–64; and "Shakespeare and the Cannibals," in *Cannibals, Witches, and Divorce: Estranging the Renaissance,* ed. Marjorie Garber (Baltimore: Johns Hopkins University Press, 1987), 40–66.

33. Ania Loomba (*Gender, Race, and Renaissance Drama,* 143–55) offers a very different perspective on the suppression of the maternal by exploring the implications of Prospero's rivalry with Sycorax and of the play's juxtaposition of Miranda, Caliban, and Sycorax. Louise A. DeSalvo demonstrates how the incestuous subtext in the play is illuminated by Djuna Barnes's re-vision of the relationship between Miranda and Prospero in *The Antiphon:* see " 'To Make Her Mutton at Sixteen': Rape, Incest, and Child Abuse in *The Antiphon,* " in *Silence and Power: A Reevaluation of Djuna Barnes,* ed. Mary Lynn Broe (Carbondale: Southern Illinois University Press, 1991), 300–315.

34. Malli is named after a girl in a folk song that her father used to sing, who was "all in all complete" (80). It is also possible that in naming Malli, Dinesen recalled Marie Jorgensen, the children's nurse when she was a child and whom they called "Malla." Thus evoking the time before her own father's death by

suicide when she was ten, Dinesen inscribes her own loss in the very sign of Malli's bond with her father.

35. It is not unusual to find in Dinesen's tales the identification of the mother with bourgeois values and a constraining domesticity, and the identification of the father (often absent) with adventure, freedom, the ability to leave behind him a bourgeois community in which he is inevitably an outsider. This is a dichotomy that Dinesen identified in her own family. Her father had been an adventurer and traveller, and Dinesen herself always felt frustrated with her mother's side of the family; see Thurman, *Isak Dinesen;* and Dinesen, *Letters from Africa.*

36. The implied correspondence between Malli's relation to her father on the one hand and Dinesen's to "father" Shakespeare on the other is further complicated if we recognize that Malli's old teacher is like the old, witch-like women in Dinesen's tales who parody cultural stereotypes of feminine beauty and domesticity and who act as surrogate mothers; they are also Dinesen's parodic self-portraits. Thus, we find figures of Dinesen herself in both the unmarried and exiled old woman and the young girl, in teacher and in student.

37. Although, according to Bevington ("*The Tempest* in Performance," xxxiii), Leslie French was the first male to play the role of Ariel since 1734—in a 1930 production at the Old Vic—it is not clear how familiar Dinesen was with earlier theatrical traditions, and Malli contrasts in every possible way to the performance she herself attended. She creates a double irony here by having the asexual Ariel best represented by a woman whose size and lack of grace contradicts our expectations (as readers of "Tempests" and *The Tempest*) of what either Ariel or Miranda might look like. It is not clear how deliberately she was reversing Shakespeare's practice of using boy actors here, but this tale and the tale that closes the volume, "The Ring," are centrally concerned with the kind of struggle engendered by cultural stereotypes of female behavior that some critics argue is signified by the Elizabethan stage conventions of cross-dressing. See Jean E. Howard's analysis of how this convention allows the Elizabethan audience both to recuperate and to contain the gender stereotypes in "Crossdressing, the Theatre, and Gender Struggle in Early Modern England," *Shakespeare Quarterly* 39, no. 4 (Winter 1988): 418–40; Howard offers a cogent summary of the critical debate surrounding this issue. Certainly, Dinesen repeatedly returns to the question of how unstable cultural stereotypes are, and she consistently identifies the idealization of women with the male desire to dominate and possess, showing how women subvert this desire by means of the very erotic behavior that evokes it; she was, additionally, acutely aware of the ways in which dress and appearance determined a woman's identity. She does not, however, allow for the possibility that gender categories themselves might be destabilized. For an opposing argument see in particular Aiken (*Isak Dinesen and the Engendering of Narrative*) and Eve Pederson, "An Essay Analysis of Karen Blixen's *Bonfire Speech,*" in *Proceedings,* ed. Houe and Dacus, 136–41.

38. I am indebted to Marianne Novy for this insight. The ambiguity of Herr Soerensen's character is reinforced by the fact that, as Judith Thurman (*Isak

Dinesen, 415) has pointed out, "Soerensen" draws upon the Danish "soeren," a nickname for the devil.

39. Note the similarity between Herr Soerensen and Brandes's portrait of Shakespeare: "He [Shakespeare] was a competent, energetic business man, who spared and saved in order to gain an independence and restore the fallen fortunes of his family. But none the less he was evidently a good comrade in practical, a benefactor in intellectual life" (*William Shakespeare,* 1:451).

40. Nadia Setti ("Visions of Life's Tempest," 78) points out that in transforming Shakespeare's text Malli first substitutes her own body for Ferdinand's and transforms both into "something rich and strange" as a way of working through her grief. She argues that at this point Malli ceases to be Ariel and is instead "a mortal angel fallen to earth." I argue, however, that Dinesen seems not to forsake Ariel, but carefully and significantly to transform Shakespeare's figure.

41. John H. Hayes and Stuart A. Irvine, *Isaiah* (Nashville: Abingdon Press, 1987), 332–33.

42. Lorie Jerrell Leininger offers a very different but intriguing interpretation of *The Tempest* that considers Miranda ten years later: see "The Miranda Trap: Sexism and Racism in Shakespeare's *Tempest,*" in *The Woman's Part: Feminist Criticism of Shakespeare,* ed. Carolyn Ruth Swift Lenz, Gayle Greene, and Carol Thomas Neely (Urbana: University of Illinois Press, 1980), 285–94.

43. Although race is not an explicit subject in "The Immortal Story," Dinesen draws upon the archetype of the Wandering Jew (a recurring figure in her tales) to show that Elishama, the exiled Jew, is as "unredeemable" as Caliban is sometimes portrayed to be, albeit for different reasons.

44. Thurman, *Isak Dinesen,* 158–59. Langbaum (*Isak Dinesen's Art,* 263) also notes the parallels between Elishama and Ariel. Although both Thurman and Bjornvig (*The Past*) point out that the description of Elishama is based upon Jorgen Brandt, a young poet who was a follower of Dinesen's and a frequent guest at Rungstedlund during this period, the conceptual similarities between Dinesen's storyteller, Ariel, and Elishama indicate that Dinesen's transformation of her experience (and gender) was more significant than these critics have allowed.

45. I am indebted to Langbaum's summary of *Paul et Virginie* (*Isak Dinesen's Art,* 270). While Langbaum sees the masque as the fulfillment of romance, I argue that, particularly by placing emphasis on Virginie's response rather than on Paul's, Dinesen ironically dramatizes that romance is mere illusion.

46. Dinesen depoliticizes representations of power and art in the other three tales in the volume, especially in "Babette's Feast." Unlike the tales that center on a male Prospero-figure, this tale about a female artist does not shift attention to her helper. A political exile like Prospero, Babette lives in the isolated village of Berlevaag for twelve years before the events described in the tale. When she learns that she has won enough money in the French lottery to pay for her return to Paris, she decides instead to use it to prepare a feast in celebration of the one hundredth birthday of the father of the two women for whom she works, the founder of a religious sect that denies the reality of physical existence. Working not with "spirits" but with the very substance of mortal existence,

Babette's art reflects not merely her "vanity" but additionally the true transformative power of art. Sarah Webster Goodwin argues that Babette's artistry implies a feminist utopia made possible through art: see "Knowing Betters: Feminism and Utopian Discourse in *Pride and Prejudice, Villette,* and "Babette's Feast,"" in *Feminism, Utopia, and Narrative,* ed. Libby Falk Jones and Sarah Webster Goodwin (Knoxville: University of Tennessee Press, 1990), 1–20. Using a different framework, Marleen Barr argues that "Babette's Feast" exemplifies what she calls "feminist fabulation," in "Food for Postmodern Thought: Isak Dinesen's Female Artists as Precursors to Contemporary Feminist Fabulators," in *Feminism, Utopia, and Narrative,* ed. Jones and Webster, 21–33.

47. Dinesen, "Oration at a Bonfire," 73.
48. Ibid., 73.
49. Ibid., 86.

Shakespeare at the Fun Palace:
Joan Littlewood

In a recent assessment of the arts in Britain after the devastation of the Thatcher years, Howard Brenton describes culture as potentially robust yet inherently vulnerable to the ruthless logic of capitalism: "a meeting place which can be raucous at times, both political assembly and place of entertainment, dance floor and theatre, with all kinds of rooms in it." This, he writes, "was the thinking behind Joan Littlewood's great, but now forgotten, idea for a 'fun palace.'"[1] Amid the detritus of post-Thatcher culture, the claim that "politics, in its fullest sense, means the affairs of the people and in this sense . . . plays . . . are political"—the manifesto of one of the early theater groups founded by Joan Littlewood[2]—has been patently and painfully established. More specifically, the connection between the demise of the concept of culture crystallized in Littlewood's fun palace and the advent of an ominous trend in Shakespeare production is now inescapable: "Right-wing theatre has found its voice not in new work but in a particular style of reviving Shakespeare's plays, draining their social content and sentimentalising their psychology" (Brenton 26). In the fun palace, Littlewood's unorthodox Marxist ideas about pleasure, culture, and politics converge to exemplify the principles which most characterize her productions of Shakespeare and are most useful in helping us recognize the degree of oppositionality those productions posed to bourgeois, marketplace culture.

Despite her origins in a working-class family in London, Joan Littlewood developed an early interest in Shakespeare. At the age of eleven she directed impromptu productions of *Hamlet,* playing all the parts herself.[3] Later she attended the Royal Academy for Dramatic Arts, which she left in 1933 to devote her life in British theater to a systematic rebellion against everything she had learned there. On 1 September of that year, while working for BBC radio, she gave her first broadcast, a reading of the role of Cleopatra in "Scenes from Shakespeare" for Empire Services to Canada. Dismissed—"because I was Red" (qtd. in Goodman 7)—she joined

Manchester Repertory, where she worked until she and Ewan MacColl founded Theatre Union, the basis of the subsequent Theatre Workshop, with which her name has become synonymous.

Theatre Workshop began as an itinerant company after the Second World War and was based from 1953 at what became aptly known as the "Other Stratford" in Stratford-Atte-Bowe in London's East End. Like earlier political theater, which had utilized "agit-prop" (agitation and propaganda) techniques, Theatre Workshop rejected bourgeois natural-ism as the theater of the ruling class.[4] At Stratford, running the company for the most part on a shoestring budget with general manager Gerry Raffles, Littlewood became the unmistakable and inassimilable "other" of British theater, engaging in a rigorously oppositional theater practice, which traditional critical assessment typically designates as a fringe enterprise, a satellite of the putative "revolution" in British theater initi-ated by John Osborne's *Look Back in Anger*.[5] Yet Theatre Workshop pioneered modern dramatic techniques and established an international reputation[6] despite battles with the establishment in its various guises— Arts Council funding policies, the censorship of the Lord Chamberlain's office, and the critics. Theatre Workshop performed a mixture of classics and new plays; Shakespeare's *Richard II* and *Henry IV* were two of their most notable productions. After 1963, Littlewood continued to work in London, but without a regular company. She also devoted time to other theater projects, including productions in Nigeria and Tunisia, and her fun palace proposal, which, alas, never came to fruition.[7]

Littlewood's work is an important part of the history of women's responses to Shakespeare even though it is not explicitly feminist. The following analysis strives to situate the role of Shakespeare production in Littlewood's agenda for a theater of social transformation, particularly in terms of her theory and critique of culture as it was embodied in the fun palace proposal.

The concept of the fun palace was based on eighteenth-century plea-sure gardens, the most famous of which was at Vauxhall. These were elaborate parks, consisting of arbors, statuaries, and fish ponds, where commingled classes could enjoy the assembly of entertainments and delights. For Littlewood, the pleasure gardens offered the basis of a more comprehensive concept of theater, which pursued the aims of a political theater to its logical conclusion, to a disavowal of the local practices of theater as such: "I'm not really interested in films or the theatre, I'm interested in all *this*—in what's going on around us, in being alert to life. I don't really want a theatre; I'd rather have a marvelous fun palace like Vauxhall gardens" (qtd. in Goodman 113). Thus for Littlewood, theater was not confined to the stage because the concept of politically transformative theater is founded upon an acute awareness of its ideological function in culture—as the way society "makes sense of itself," reproduces, and potentially transforms itself.

Littlewood's vision of transformation entailed a drastic reconfiguration of traditional theatrical space and an attendant shift from theater *for* the people, as in didactic Marxist models, to theater *of* the people. In specific productions this resulted in radical staging techniques, as for example at the 1952 Edinburgh Festival. Ewan MacColl recalls,

> instead of having two stages, this time we drove a wedge through the audience, from the top to the bottom of the audience. The audience was on either side. . . . Suddenly, all your previous notions of acting had changed . . . because the normal feeling you get on stage is the enemy's outside there, all around you, you're surrounded by enemies who are willing you to fail, and your intelligence is telling you that this is nonsense, and of course it is nonsense, people want you to succeed because they want to be part of it. . . . Suddenly, you felt that everybody was with you, every actor in the show experienced this, as great access of strength from everybody in the audience. (qtd. in Goodman 44)

Littlewood also believed theater should be an integral part of a locality, although it was never simply a matter of a building; for instance, because she recognized the inherent theatricality of children's play, she devoted time to constructing a playground for the children of Stratford East. Theater belonged to its community, its audience, its actors: "people were made to feel that the theater was as much theirs as anybody else's."[8] Littlewood explained her expansive understanding of theater as follows: "Theatre is not just the putting on of plays. It is everywhere; the transformation scene, in the markets, processions, meetings, partings, in the clothes we wear, our manners and mores and the front we put on. At its best it is the great educator, keeping our language alive, giving us the music and poetry which seem to identify us and add some value to our brief journey. Theatre knows no boundaries and only withers where it is confined" (qtd. in Goorney 133).

Nor was Littlewood speaking from misplaced idealism, but from years of taking plays to provincial outposts during the depression, even taking Shakespeare on the back of an unreliable lorry to Welsh mining villages where, since culture was equated with effeminacy, it was widely held that only women attended plays (Goodman 41).

Littlewood's reconceptualization of theatrical space, which reconfigured the relation between drama and society as much as the acting arena itself, reached its apex in her futuristic plan for the fun palace as a "university of the streets," which she described as "A place of toys for adults, a place to waste time without guilt or discomfort, to develop unused talents, to discover the fund of joy and fun and sadness within us" (qtd. in Goorney 133). Yet the fun palace was not intended to monumentalize Littlewood's aesthetic transformation of social relations, but rather to embody the use of unstructured space developed by Theatre Workshop, an arena in which the distinction between performer and audience is dissolved. Littlewood wrote,

> the essence of the place will be its informality: nothing is obligatory, anything goes. There will be no permanent structures. Nothing is to last for more than ten years, some things not even ten days: no concrete stadia, stained and cracking; no legacy of noble contemporary architecture, quickly dating; no municipal geranium beds or fixed teak benches.
>
> With informality goes flexibility. The "areas" that have been listed are not segregated enclosures. The whole plan is open, but on many levels. So the greatest pleasure of traditional parks is preserved—the pleasure of strolling casually, looking in at one or another of these areas or (if this is preferred settling down for several hours of work-play). (qtd. in Goodman 114)

Both the fun palace and Theatre Workshop productions entailed the obliteration of a stifling bourgeois tradition based on the exclusion of the mass of humanity from theater and culture.[9] Littlewood inveighed tirelessly against it: "In England the infantile, snobbish theatre which we have had for so long is showing obvious signs of decay and now the doors are opening to new talent. The talent was always there, but in the England of ascendant imperialism, it was kept strictly in the workhouse" ("Plays for the People," 289). Littlewood discerned early on the ideological function of Shakespeare production, which currently worked for bourgeois class interests. She made the revolutionary recognition that bourgeois Shakespeare was devoid of vitality precisely because it reproduced the values of the dominant class, and that using Shakespeare as a catalyst of social transformation would revitalize the community in which his works were performed as well as the plays themselves. A practical strategy involved in her appropriation of Shakespeare for the people was the removal of the proscenium arch (Coren 60)—that essential device for transmitting the imperatives of the dominant ideology as natural and immutable rather than as socially constructed and changeable.

It has been said that Theatre Workshop "was the first theatre to stop pretending that the audience didn't exist" (Coren 61). While Littlewood claimed the theater as part of a tradition of popular entertainment dating back from ancient Greek drama, she could also use the rhetoric of irreverence to debunk tradition. Shakespeare, as Littlewood notoriously put it, "wasn't a bad old hack" (qtd. in Goodman 125): "We [Theatre Workshop] have no respect for Shakespeare. In Scotland, England, the whole world they are bogged down with respect for the past. We are not. You can attack the poor Queen Mum but don't attack art. Ever since Queen Victoria, you lot have been so artistic. . . . Let's have something of meaning to people" (qtd. in Goorney 131). Yet Littlewood believed in Shakespeare's inherently revolutionary potential: "The bourgeoisie have tried to turn Shakespeare's revolutionary humanism into cheap philanthropy—translate his philosophy into submissiveness—his disregard for religion and meta-physics into philosophical and religious tolerance. It is for us the revolu-tionary therein to translate Shakespeare and Marlowe and the rest into the living criticism of the bourgeois which they represent" (qtd. in Runkel 38–39).[10]

When Theatre Workshop took up residence at the unpromising East End location of working-class Stratford-Atte-Bowe, the goal was to have the theater be a part of the community and to attract local audiences despite social precedent. As Kenneth Tynan put it, Littlewood formed Theatre Workshop "in pursuit of a dream of theatre as a place of commu-nal celebration, a Left-wing shrine of Dionysus dedicated to wiping the puritan frown off the popular image of Socialist art."[11] This was com-bined with a vigorous endeavor to foreground the popular in the plays themselves. Shakespeare, conceived as a popular playwright, wrested from the bourgeois grasp of the West End and Stratford-upon-Avon, was an integral part of this strategy. A contemporary critic observed, "Joan Littlewood's company have built up a huge eager public from the local working-class residents establishing what is a genuine social center for the exchanging of ideas. The theatre has become a stimulating part of the life of the community."[12] A review of a 1953 production of *Twelfth Night* in the *Stratford Express* clearly demonstrates local appreciation of Theatre Workshop (though not, it must be said, on grounds of its political oppositionality) long before it attracted national attention: "John Blanshard, a roaring boisterous Toby, Maureen Daly, delightful and brimming with vitality as Maria, George Cooper's Malvolio, Gerry Raffles' Orsino—could hardly be bettered by the Old Vic, and Anna Korwin's Olivia is a model of dignity and grace" (qtd. in Goodman 48). Reporter John Ennis writing for *Reynolds News* on 16 October 1960 in a retrospective piece entitled "The Theatre Workshop Story" observed, "Only the big time critics failed to make the Tube ride. They hung back until sensational events forced the East End theatre into their ken. Then grumbling, they braved the terrors and discomforts of the six-mile journey and stayed, most of them, to cheer and fight for the credit of discovering something that had been there for the discovering for . . . years" (qtd. in Goodman 61).

Popularizing Shakespeare meant open rebellion against the prevailing static, Edwardian acting style Littlewood deplored. The actor, she said, even if Gielgud or Olivier, "with aid of his profile, his charming figure, his gift of mimicry, his elegant gestures . . . offers a dead mask instead of live acting to the audience" (qtd. in Runkel 41–42). In contrast, Littlewood used new methods that de-aestheticized theater and rebelled against "beauty" and "dignity," those aphorisms for a drama devoid of social reality (Goorney 25).

Yet hers was at the same time a profoundly intellectual enterprise, which involved bringing modern European dramatic theory and practice to bear on all her productions, including those of Shakespeare. In so doing, she challenged peculiarly British mores and icons of the stage (Coren 30). Brecht was an enormous influence: she directed and performed in the first English *Mother Courage*. She also utilized much other continental theory, especially Stanislavsky's *An Actor Prepares*, Meyerhold's theory of biomechanics, Rudolph Laban's theories of movement, Adolph Appia's theory that light was the visual counterpart of music, capable of controlling theatrical production, Vakhtangov's "fantastic realism" (a combination of Stanislavsky's realism and Meyerhold's theories of movement), and Leon Moussinac's *New Movement in the Theatre* (1932) (Runkel 9–28). For Littlewood this was compatible with the concept of a popular theater because "The working people have an instinctive appreciation of good technique acquired in their education at the loom, coal face, or engineering bench" (qtd. in Runkel 40).

Littlewood's theater practice entailed training actors in a broad spectrum of theater arts. Artists, technicians, and actors experimented with stagecraft, which included new uses of lighting, makeup, sound, dance, and acting style to create "a flexible theater art, as swift moving and plastic as the cinema" (Goorney 41–42). In British theater it was Littlewood who pioneered the subordination of the voice to physical expression and who altered genre conventions by integrating singing and music into theater forms other than musicals per se (Goorney 183). Furthermore, for her actors, discussions and readings were an integral part of preparing for performance. Actress Shirley Dynevor recalls, "everyone would be asked to go to the library to do their own research. We were all part of a whole. . . . Joan was a most marvelous teacher. I never learned from anyone what I learned from her" (qtd. in Goorney 171). Similarly, Brian Murphy comments, "you never just talked about the play, you had to know the history, the social, economic and political background. I doubt whether a university could provide what Joan did in Theatre Workshop in those days of 1955" (qtd. in Goorney 171). This, combined with social and political awareness, quasi communal living (especially in the early years of Theatre Workshop), and equal, meager salaries for everyone fed into actors' new understanding of the relation between theater and society, an understanding that profoundly affected their performances (Goorney 191).

Goorney recalls that in preparation for *Richard II* "Joan would get a scene, say, 'All right, this is a market in the time, in the period of Richard II.' And she'd outline a scene about someone, perhaps, who tries to steal something, and they're caught, they're stabbed in the back, and a fight breaks out . . . and build up atmosphere of the period, rather than the characters" (qtd. in Runkel 200). Actors exchanged roles so that they understood the text from different points of view, rather than having a proprietal relation to the character they were to portray on opening night. Brian Murphy recalled, "By not feeling responsible about one particular character, you could be free and uninhibited in your own contributions to the play and its characters" (qtd. in Runkel 200). Swapping parts and other acting exercises also forged connections between performers that would not be severed once the rehearsal turned into performance.[13]

Unusual treatment of verse speaking was a vital element of Littlewood's directoral approach. Howard Goorney remembers her saying "Always come back to the truth of the situation. . . . The meaning is there. Shakespeare was a good playwright. Find the situation, and the words will do the rest. Don't bother with the words. Don't think about the words. Don't play with the words" (qtd. in Goodman 70). One Theatre Workshop actor offers an insightful example of Littlewood's work on the language in *Macbeth:*

> With a classical play in verse, once the improvisations have enabled the actors to grasp the tenor of the play and their characters, she will spend hours on the verse and its rhythms. She will not allow decoration—as soon as you spout "poetry," you are stopped. The hard, driving rhythms which elucidate the meaning—and sometimes *are* the meaning—are all-important. Sometimes an actor is made to physically punch his way through a speech, beating out the meter with his fists like a shadow-boxer. This is making him physically move the verse—"Is this a dagger, which I see before me"—actually pacing it out. When you have the physical movement which underlies the verse its meaning is brought right out. The movement might eventually be used in a modified way in the production itself. "Is this a dagger" was helped by a four-pace forward movement; while not actually retained, it gave the grasping surge of movement behind the line ("Come, let me clutch thee").[14]

Littlewood often typed out lines without attention to verse, avoiding "beautiful language" and set speeches in order to make actors create the most suitable rhythms (Runkel 200). In contrast, when rehearsing Marlowe's *Edward II,* she began with verse speaking, probably because Marlowe's language had not become calcified with bourgeois reverence. Thus, Littlewood's objection to "poetry" was not a refusal to acknowledge the power of its aesthetic, but rather an attempt to reconsider the beauty of Shakespearean language from a nonhegemonic perspective. Murray Melvin comments, "I went to see *Richard II,* and I'd never heard the English language spoken like that. They [commercial theater] still, even today, are speaking Edwardian Shakespeare. Nobody really speaks that wonderful, wonderful language like it was there. It was an eye-opener, a rare treat" (qtd. in Runkel 263).

Such techniques were again a deliberate reaction against prevailing codes of dramatic practice, particularly those of Shakespearean dramaturgy. Littlewood remarked, "I couldn't stand it [Royal Academy of Dramatic Arts acting] because it was so posed, static, so unexciting—this dishonest acting, of showing how very clever, exquisite or ugly I am and how well I do this—all that dishonest exhibitionist stuff. A kid goes to R.A.D.A. and she's told to stop talking like a northerner, a southerner, or a Welsh girl—she's told to talk like a puppet, you see? So language is despised, all the virility of language, and inside were girls being taught to play this tennis-club, French window stuff" (qtd. in Goodman 6). There is here a male-identified condemnation of the elite as effete and effeminate, and a corresponding valorization of the proletarian as potent and masculine, which was characteristic of 1930s radicalism.[15] Certainly, Littlewood's equation of political vitality with virility is apparent in her notorious pronouncement that "A bloke like Ben Jonson only sat down to write 'classics' when he was old and couldn't fuck his audiences any more" (qtd. in Ansorge 20). Littlewood invoked Shakespeare as part of an appropriation of working-class masculinity at a time when his works were firmly established in the public mind as models of the rhetoric of privilege, gentility, and propriety, which produced, among other undesirable social effects, the exclusion of young actresses from the power of dramatic enunciation—the "virility" of language. The importance of Littlewood's appropriation of the vulgar, in both its senses, cannot be overestimated in Britain, where social stigma is still attached to provincial, working-class accents, and where there was nothing woman-identified in the pseudofeminized, refined, sex-repressed accents of the aristocracy and bourgeoisie:

I find the accents of Leeds and Manchester as acceptable as those of St. John's Wood, Eaton, Oxford or hangovers from Edwardian dressing rooms. It is easier to attack the Royal Family than attempt to scrape off the patina of age and the dreary respect which stifles Elizabethan verse. Shakespeare's company was made up of leery misfits, anarchists, out of work soldiers and wits who worked at their ideas in pubs and performed them as throwaways to an uninhibited pre-Puritan audience.

My company works without the assistance of smart direction, fancy dress, beards and greasepaint and was prepared for the wave of opposition which we knew would come. (qtd. in Goorney 130)

In the Theatre Workshop's sensational production of *Richard II*, language and action were made to work together instead of the traditional approach to Shakespeare that subsumed "drama" to "poetry" and reduced the collaborative process of theater to a showcase for the actor in the title role. Rather, the production was a deliberate showcase for Theatre Workshop technique, a vivid exemplification of Littlewood's radical theater consciously staged against a more stolid version of the same play directed by Michael Benthall at the Old Vic. Benthall had a cast of forty-five, while Theatre Workshop had only fourteen, with a great deal of doubling and trebling. Howard Goorney describes the disparity between the two productions: "At the Old Vic all was pomp and ceremony. On a stage full of light, coloured pennants flew, fanfares played, and the attendant Lords and spear carriers manoeuvred into position, while everyone waited for the scenes to begin. The actors were elegantly dressed and beautifully spoken. John Neville's Richard, as befitted an actor who had been compared to the young Gielgud, was a truly regal figure always aware of bearing the poetry of his lines, even when chained to the floor of his cell." At Stratford, in contrast, "[with] John Bury's stark setting, conceived to emphasize fear and oppression, we aimed to bring out the hatred and cruelty of the period. Light was used to break up the stage, scenes were able to merge swiftly one into another, and there was no pause for spectacle. Our concern always was for the inner action behind the lines— what they meant, rather than the poetry of the words" (Goorney 101).

The vast differences in style were the result of two antithetical political and aesthetic perspectives. On 19 January 1955, the *Evening Standard* reported that the two theaters had "come up with such widely differing Richards that by comparison Jekyll and Hyde would appear to be a nicely adjusted, thoroughly uncomplicated fellow" (qtd. in Goodman 70). Ewan MacColl summarizes the disparity between the Old Vic's tradition and Littlewood's innovation as follows:

Joan's direction was basically characterized by the swiftness of the action. No pause. The scenes flowed one into the other. At the Old

Vic, you heard deafening flourishes, trumpets, there were banners unfurling, processions. . . . There was no sustained action but great pauses during which the court assembled according to protocol. We were all sitting there, watching and thinking how Joan had the right idea. At Theatre Workshop there wasn't a single point on the stage where the action wasn't progressing visibly. The Old Vic, with its pomp, didn't hit on anything necessary. They were making a spectacle. Obviously, they cared a lot about the poetry. They took pains so it would sound beautiful. We hadn't bothered about that. When Mowbray and Bolingbroke met they spat, literally. They spat in each other's faces. There was nothing gentlemanly about it.

At the Old Vic, when John of Gaunt made his speech, he didn't look in the least like a dying man. But, in fact, he was dying, on the stage at that very moment. They were going to carry him off. He wouldn't be seen again. That's how Joan understood it. She made me play it as a dying man. Literally. There was none of that at the Old Vic. Their John of Gaunt came on; now for the big speech: "This royal throne of kings, this scepter'd isle, this earth of Majesty, etc," and he went off. He could have been going to dinner, the effect would have been the same. (qtd. in Goodman 70–71)

The Theatre Workshop set was also built to shape the actors' performances, in a way that has subsequently become commonplace in theater production. The stage designer, John Bury (whose work was later widely used by the Royal Shakespeare Company) was directed to build a low arch of unplaned wood so that actors would enter crouched with their cloaks behind them (Runkel 253). There was a raked stage with various levels of ramps; tunnels combined with heavy coats and helmets "to determine and restrict the actors' movements: emphasizing the script's tension and suspense" (Runkel 263).

Predictably, the *Sunday Times* found the Theatre Workshop production less successful than Old Vic's but conceded that "of the two, it is the more interesting, controversial, and subtle" (qtd. in Runkel 259). On the other hand, the *Evening Standard* maintained that Stratford Richard was out of his mind:

Miss Littlewood seizes the Queen's rhetorical hints at Richard's madness: "Has Bolingbroke deposed thine intellect?"—and builds her production—excessively grim in scenery and lighting—upon it. From the start Mr. Corbett's Richard is more than half-mad. His high, treacherous, sing-song voice, his glazed eyes, his up-tilted chin, his fancifully managed hands, his swift, light, stooping little runs and leaps are all marks of a man who has only a distorted grasp

of reality and is living in an interior world of his own that touches
objective existence only with disastrous obliqueness. You may not
like this sort of performance, you may say that it would have
surprised Shakespeare considerably: what you cannot maintain is
that Mr. Corbett does not do it magnificently and disturbingly. (qtd.
in Goodman 73–75)

The overall effect of Littlewood's theater practice was so devoid of the
traditional accoutrements that critics seemed to have difficulty recognizing it as Shakespeare at all. A *Times* critic reported, "In all this there are
moments of real power, but it is not, all in all, an interpretation of *Richard
II* in which we can recognize the play that Shakespeare wrote" (Runkel
259). Milton Shulman of the *Evening Standard* described Theatre Workshop's Richard as "an arrogant, volatile, and angry homosexual . . . an
ugly, loathsome creature at the play's end for whom we can certainly feel
no pity. And without pity, what is there to *Richard II?*" (Runkel 259–61).
Littlewood defended her approach in the *Observer:* "When we play
Richard II, the critics can't stand it because we're playing in what they call
a vulgar fashion—we're playing it for action and dynamic rather than for
decoration" (Goodman 70).

Her work often met with critical displeasure. A condensed version of
both parts of *Henry IV* performed at the 1964 Edinburgh Festival was
savaged by the critics despite the fact that it played to consistently full
houses. The primary objects of attack were the "radical staging," the
lack of poetry (Prince Hal had a Cockney accent), the acting, and the
mixture of modern and period costumes. Sparse scenery was unusually
combined with music and dance; the actors, who wore pullovers, or
collars and string ties, purposely visible under cloaks and ermine, alter-
nated between presentational and representational acting styles in a way
one critic thought symptomatic of the production's "general anarchy"
(Runkel 304–5). The *Times* called the production "an act of theatrical
pillage which in its combination of muddled and bungled execution rivals
the expedition to the Bay of Pigs," and wrote further, "Miss Littlewood
has gone on record as considering Shakespeare to be 'not a bad old hack,'
and she treated him with no more respect than a blushing Stratford
newcomer might expect" (qtd. in Goodman 125). Critics also deplored
what they called "textual tampering" with *Henry IV:* "an invertebrate
succession of political and comic scenes calculated to bewilder even
audiences who know the plays let alone Edinburgh's foreign visitors
coming to them for the first time" (qtd. in Runkel 304).

Theatre Workshop did not treat Shakespeare's texts as the sanctified
iconic objects of traditional theater, but rather as opportunities for collabo-

ration and improvisation—though contrary to popular belief, Littlewood never permitted altering the author's actual words (Coren 37). Tom Milne remembers, "In her rehearsals for *Macbeth,* for example, the actors began by playing at cowboys and Indians, moving gradually to an improvised battle, and finally to the opening scene of the play, using Shakespeare's text. This may sound crude, but it undoubtedly ensures a completely unstereotyped attitude to the play" (Runkel 202). Sometimes Littlewood would have her actors improvise an unscripted scene. In *Macbeth,* the cast were directed to work up a scene between Macbeth and the murderers in a pub (Runkel 202). Tom Milne recalls that "Theatre Workshop produced Shakespeare or Marlowe as though the play had only just been written, and the playwright were commenting on life as we know it today" (qtd. in Runkel 258). Indeed, "Theatre," Littlewood wrote, "must be in the present tense" ("Plays for the People" 286).

But such an approach was invariably thought to be inappropriate for Shakespeare. For example, the 1957 production of *Macbeth* was greeted by the critics "with dismay and muttering about political overtones because it was Shakespeare, and, moreover, the modern dress lent a touch of satire to the army and (most horrible) to royalty" (Milne and Goodwin 81). Predictably, the critic for the *Times* observed that Littlewood "seemed anxious to strip the titanic central figures of their dignity" (qtd. in Runkel 258). One senses that this perspective on the production is unbalanced given the fact that Littlewood did include touches of sentiment (such as the highland lament sung over the bodies of Lady Macduff and her son by an anonymous woman), but did so in parts of the play not usually emphasized by traditional productions focusing on the grandeur of the tragic hero (Rudisill 190).[16]

Littlewood, then, treated the text as the basis rather than the essence of dramatic performance. Her theater thrived on spontaneity, which she sought from the first rehearsal, when actors would improvise around the play's themes, up to moments before the performance when the production was not finished but merely entering a different phase. Her aesthetic demanded "an ensemble working together" to perfect, technically, and artistically, a style which would reflect the tempo of the time (Littlewood, "Plays for the People" 283–84). She wrote, "I do not believe in the supremacy of the director, designer, actor, or even the writer. It is through collaboration that this knockabout art of theatre survives and kicks."[17] In "A Personal Manifesto," she declared theater as a model of social praxis: "The noteworthy epochs of the theatre have been the result of one of the highest forms of human collaboration, the combining of the talents of many people in order to create a living work of art" (283).

Notably, Theatre Workshop was collaborative rather than a collective enterprise because Littlewood always retained a strong directoral authority. Nonetheless, her belief in the powers of collaboration seems to have empowered those who worked with her. As one critic wrote, "whether these advantages come directly from Joan Littlewood herself or indirectly from working with the company she has created almost single-handed— there is no denying that many actors and writers have seemed much better when working at Stratford than they ever have again" (qtd. in Taylor 9).

For Littlewood, the theater was a liminal space where challenges to the dominant order could be posed, where pleasure could be offered to all social classes, and where social transformation could begin. Fredric Jameson's essay "Pleasure: A Political Issue" makes a similar claim for the political necessity that cultural interventions orient themselves toward the transformative politics they seek to effect, rather than merely toward the immediate local, specific, and isolated act of intervention:

> The point, however, . . . is to draw the lesson of what might be a radically different political use of pleasure as such. I will suggest, then, that the proper political use of pleasure must always be *allegorical*. . . . the thematizing of a particular pleasure as a political issue (to fight, for example . . . for access to certain kinds of cultural activities; or for an aesthetic transformation of social relations or a politics of the body) must always involve a dual focus, in which the local issue is meaningful and desirable in and of itself, but is also *at one and the same time* taken as the *figure* for Utopia in general, and for the systematic revolutionary transformation of society as a whole. Without these simultaneous dimensions, the political demand becomes reduced to yet another local "issue" in the micropolitics of this or that limited group or its particular hobby or specialization, and a slogan that once satisfied, leads no further politically.

This dual or "allegorical" focus is what constitutes the Marxist problematic, Jameson explains, because the revolutionary formation of the dialectic demands that the exigencies of the present prefigure global, Utopian goals.[18]

In theater, Littlewood was able to negotiate those marginal territories between specific text and actual production, current intervention and revolutionary aim, and use them to dramatic and political advantage. Littlewood herself theorized this: "No one mind or imagination can foresee what a play will become until all the physical or intellectual stimuli which are crystallized in the poetry of the author, have been understood by a company, and then tried out in terms of mime, discussion and the precise music of grammar; word and movement allied and integrated."[19] Imagination, the utopian vision necessary for any cultural program for

social transformation as much as actor's technique, was a palpable component of the Littlewood aesthetic, as John Wells points out: "She shook
people into the realisation that theatre has to be about thinking, what she
calls the use of the imagination muscle, the progress by which the actor's
imaginings on the stage are transferred to the audience. That is something
which I think you will find any person working in the theatre now would
agree with. When Joan began working before the war, the idea was to
produce beautiful productions in which everything was well-oiled and
perfect. I think her great contribution was to change the centre of gravity
of theatre from what seems to be there to the reality of thinking and the
real interpretation of plays" (qtd. in Goorney 183). In terms of her
productions of Shakespearean plays, the effect of such a shift in gravity—
the company's group playing and the stark simplicity of the sets—has
been described as "one of remarkable textual clarity. . . . it was like watching
Shakespeare in one continuous shaft of lightning" (Milne and Goodwin
118).

Littlewood was marginal and anomalous not simply because of her
politics but also because of her gender: "You must realise the awful shock
this was," said David Scase of his first opportunity to work with Joan
Littlewood's Theatre Workshop, "to work with a woman—it was unknown
in the profession, unbelievable, it was going against the laws of nature"
(qtd. in Goorney 189). Kenneth Tynan commented in a similar vein: "she
would have been burnt as a witch a few years ago."[20] Nonetheless,
Littlewood's relation as a woman to Shakespeare is finally difficult to
summarize since she was far more class-identified than gender-identified.
Nor does the relative sparsity of production details offer much assistance
in making a judgment in this matter, although critic's concerns about the
portrayal of male homosexuality in her productions (*Richard II, Edward
II,* and *A Taste of Honey*) seem to indicate a more enlightened attitude
towards sexuality than that of most of her contemporaries. On the other
hand, like many successful women, judging by the difficulties experienced
by many of the actresses who worked with her, Joan Littlewood seems to
have been thoroughly male-identified. Avis Bunage recollects, "Of the
women, I think I survived longer than any of them because I wouldn't
always give in to Joan. There was always a girl in tears somewhere because
Joan was very hard on women. The men she got on with fabulously" (qtd.
in Goorney 171).

Especially in her productions of Shakespeare, Littlewood inaugurated
many of the practices now commonplace in contemporary theater such as
"the working-class actor," sophisticated lighting techniques, and the interplay of verse and action. She also pioneered techniques and concepts
which have become vital aspects of selfconsciously feminist theater, espe-

cially collaboration, and the recognition that theater practices must be transformed as much as the content of plays. Littlewood approached Shakespeare as a political ally, someone who like herself found that his politics made him an outsider to established institutions.[21] Stratford East became literally and symbolically a site for counterhegemonic Shakespeare. When she left for what was to be a triumphant debut at the Paris Festival, an envious West End manager sent a telegram to the organizers: "You have made a terrible mistake. The Workshop are nobodies. They are from Stratford East, not from Stratford-on-Avon" (Rudisill 187). The symbolic association of the Avon players with true professionals versus the East End imposters offers a sense of why Littlewood's assault on bourgeois Shakespeare was so important.

Yet the "success" of even self-consciously political, marginal theater is usually judged by the degree to which it has been assimilated by the center, rather than the extent to which it holds on to marginal territory as an ever-present challenge to dominant theatrical practices. This exacerbates the difficulty of determining the effectiveness of Littlewood's Shakespeare productions, regardless of whether they emphasized class issues more than those of gender. Her work on Shakespeare never suffered the fate of her productions of modern plays, especially *Oh, What A Lovely War* and *The Hostage,* which were assimilated in their entirety by the West End in the early 1970s, and in the process, politically neutralized: "Each community should have a theatre; the West End has plundered our talent and diluted our ideas."[22] But mainstream theater, particularly the Royal Shakespeare Company, appropriated the aesthetics of Littlewood's theater practice and utterly divorced them from her politics, as in the use of depoliticized "radical" techniques in any number of contemporary productions.[23]

Littlewood cannot be said to have foregrounded "women's issues" or to have had even the glimmerings of a feminist consciousness, and we cannot classify her as a feminist Shakespearean. Rather, her contribution to a feminist politics of theater is a concern for class, culture, and transformation of institutions and techniques. Viewed in this light, Littlewood's conception of theater, although formulated prior to the full emergence of feminism either as a social category or a political movement, approaches something akin to a protofeminist aesthetic. Further, it is indisputable that she held Shakespeare as the model of politically committed theater, and that Shakespeare was central to her own theater politics and to her vision of the transformation of culture.

Nowadays, when the term "fun palace" is more likely to summon up images of some Disneyesque simulacrum where pleasure is totally colonized by consumption, the prospect of Shakespeare at the fun palace, that is, of an oppositional popular aesthetic in which Shakespeare might be central, seems increasingly unfeasible.[23] In such times, Littlewood's achievement should be recorded not as an unrecoverable moment for the post-Thatcher era, but as a concrete goal for future feminist Shakespeare production and analysis.

NOTES

1. Howard Brenton, "The Art of Survival," *The Guardian Weekly*, 9 Dec. 1990: 25.

2. Qtd. in Judith Lea Goodman, "Joan Littlewood and Her Theatre Workshop" (Ph.D. diss., New York University, 1975), 13.

3. Amanda Sue Rudisill, "The Contributions of Eva Le Gallienne, Margaret Webster, Margo Jones, and Joan Littlewood to the Establishment of Repertory Theatre in the United States and Great Britain" (Ph.D. diss., Northwestern University, 1972), 176.

4. See Howard Goorney, *The Theatre Workshop Story* (London: Eyre Methuen, 1981), 1.

5. See also John Russell Taylor, *Anger and After* (Harmondsworth: Penguin, 1963); Michelene Wandor, "The Personal Is Political: Feminism and Theatre," in *Dreams and Deconstructions: Alternative Theatre In Britain,* ed. Sandy Craig (Ambergate, U.K.: Amber Lane Press, 1980); Alan Sinfield, "The Theatre and Its Audiences," in *Society and Literature 1945–1970,* ed. Alan Sinfield (New York: Holmes and Meier, 1983), 173–97.

6. Theatre Workshop toured in Czechoslovakia, Sweden, and Moscow, and had enormous success at the Paris Festival.

7. With Littlewood, as with the work of women in general and the work of women theater directors in particular, the amount of information available rarely matches the cultural contribution. For another instance of this problem in relation to a woman director, see Dympna Callaghan, "Buzz Goodbody: Directing For Change," in *The Appropriation of Shakespeare: Post-Renaissance Reconstructions of the Works and the Myth,* ed. Jean Marsden (Hemel Hempstead: Harvester, 1991), 163–81. There are three dissertations which treat Littlewood's work: Goodman, "Joan Littlewood"; Rudisill, "Contributions"; and Richard Runkel, "Theatre Workshop: Its Philosophy, Plays, Process and Productions" (Ph.D. diss., University of Texas at Austin, 1987). The other major document is Goorney's *Theatre Workshop Story,* and while this is a marvelously informative resource, it is more of a lively history than a systematic analysis of the group. There are no detailed descriptions of the productions extant, even among the Littlewood papers at the Library of the University of Texas at Austin.

Important pieces authored by Littlewood herself are "A Personal Manifesto," *Encore* 7 (1956): 283; and "Plays for the People," *World Theatre* 8/4 (1959): 286.

8. Michael Coren, *Theatre Royal: One Hundred Years of Stratford East* (New York: Quartet Books, 1984), 55.

9. Littlewood was equally contemptuous of the "arty" Left who despised the "uneducated masses" (Littlewood, "Plays for the People," 286).

10. Runkel points out that these unpublished speeches were not intended for the reader's gaze and therefore contain the irregularities of a rough draft. Although Runkel transcribes these verbatim, I have emended grammar and spelling where it seemed appropriate.

11. Qtd. in John McGrath, *A Good Night Out: Popular Theatre, Audience, Class and Form* (1981; rpt. New York: Methuen, 1984), 44.

12. "They Want a New Audience," *Plays and Players*, Jan. 1955: 25. Critics have sometimes claimed, quite inaccurately, that Littlewood failed to attract the working-class audience she intended. J. L. Styan in his three-volume study, *Modern Drama in Theory and Practice* (New York: Cambridge University Press, 1981), gives only passing reference to Littlewood and then only to make this highly contentious allegation: "she wanted to create a popular theatre for a working-class audience in opposition to a middle-class theatre of false values, but... she failed" (3:185). Similarly Ronald Hayman's *British Theatre Since 1955: A Reassessment* (Oxford: Oxford University Press, 1979) does nothing to reassess, but much to distort Littlewood's contribution since she is once again dubbed as a failure, in an account which totally ignores the importance of the economic conditions in which theater is produced: "But Arts Council subsidy was of little help to Joan Littlewood, who made a most strenuous and serious attempt to create a theatre for the people.... but though her inclinations were anti-literary and her productions drew robustly on the techniques of popular theatre, she was unable to attract the East End audience she wanted.... She was working-class by birth and anti-intellectual by disposition; paradoxically, it was writers and directors of middle-class origin and university education who were to take more successful initiatives in persuading a working-class audience into theatre-going habits—Jim Haynes; Michael Kustow and Terry Hands... David Hare and Tony Bicat" (131). Hayman's endeavor to defend capitalist "free market theater" leads him to omit the fact that Littlewood secured few, meager, and grudging monies from the Arts Council and to condemn her aesthetic in theater.

John McGrath resoundingly debunks this view as a gross distortion and gives accounts of how his own company is frequently met by working-class audiences who reminisce about Littlewood's well-attended entertainments which years ago came to their community (*A Good Night Out*, 42–52).

13. Peter Ansorge, "Lots of Lovely Human Contact," *Plays and Players* 19, no. 10 (July 1972): 21.

14. Tom Milne and Clive Goodwin, "Working with Joan," in *Theatre at Work: Playwrights and Productions in Modern British Theatre*, ed. Charles Marowitz and Simon Trussler (New York: Hill and Wang, 1967), 119.

15. A recent American anthology addresses the promulgation of working-class masculinity as the acme of political radicalism. Thus, no allowance is made for women's different social position from men, and women are then excluded from radical movements, or included only as token men: see *Writing Red: An Anthology of American Women Writers, 1930–1940*, ed. Charlotte Nekola and

Paula Rabinowitz (New York: The Feminist Press, 1987), 1–13. However, in the United States, class differences aren't nearly so deeply engraved in people's speech and demeanor as they are in England, where the assertion of coarse language and behavior (albeit traditionally coded as "masculine") can be an effective strategy in the attack on bourgeois mores, and where it does not necessarily imply the disavowal of women's specific relation to the social order. Similarly, of course, upper-class refinement (traditionally coded as feminine) does not imply the assertion of gender equality, so that the male and female lower orders by virtue of their capacity for manual labor are always in some sense constructed as "masculine" by the dominant classes.

16. On the problematic centrality of the tragic hero, see Dympna Callaghan, *Woman and Gender in Renaissance Tragedy: A Study of King Lear, Othello, The Duchess of Malfi, and The White Devil* (Atlantic Highlands, N.J.: Humanities Press, 1989).

17. Joan Littlewood, "Goodbye Note From Joan," in *New Theatre Voices of the Fifties and Sixties: Selections from Encore Magazine 1956–1963,* ed. Charles Marowitz, Tom Milne, and Owen Hale (London: Eyre Methuen, 1965), 133. See also Tom Milne, "Art in Angel Lane," in the same volume, pp. 80–91.

18. Fredric Jameson, "Pleasure: A Political Issue," in *The Ideologies of Theory: Essays 1971–86, Vol. 2: The History of Syntax* (Minneapolis: University of Minnesota Press, 1988), 73–74.

19. Qtd. in Charles Marowitz, "Littlewood Pays A Dividend," *Encore* 10, no. 3 (May–June 1963): 64.

20. Philip Barnes, *A Companion to Post-War British Theatre* (Totowa, N.J.: Barnes and Noble, 1986), 141.

21. The identification with Shakespeare as outsider is a conception Marianne Novy has shown to be a common theme in women's interpretations of Shakespeare. What is distinctive in Littlewood's case is that she regards Shakespeare as sharing her own highly politicized oppositional consciousness. See *Women's Re-Visions of Shakespeare: On the Responses of Dickinson, Woolf, Rich, H. D., George Eliot, and Others,* ed. Marianne Novy (Urbana: University of Illinois Press, 1990), 2.

22. West End transfers of *The Hostage* and *Oh What a Lovely War* became sentimental frolics instead of hard-hitting political dramas. *The Hostage* became something of an Irish joke instead of a play with chilling relevance given the escalation of violence in Northern Ireland, while the ending of *Oh What A Lovely War,* with its explicit parallel with atomic warfare, was cut from the West End production. See Alan Sinfield, *Literature, Politics, and Culture in Postwar Britain* (Berkeley: University of California Press, 1989), 179.

23. Littlewood registered her pessimism about the assimilation of new materials for reactionary ends: "Young actors and actresses, don't be puppets any longer! The directors and the critics won't help you; in television, film or theatre they ask for the dregs of the old acting, mere 'expression,' exploitation of your 'type.' In Shaftsbury Avenue or in the Brecht theatre, it's all the same" ("Goodbye Note" 16). On contemporary conservative appropriations of radical technique, see Dympna

Callaghan, "Resistance and Recuperation: Kenneth Branagh's *Henry V,*" *Shakespeare On Film Newsletter* 15, no. 2 (April 1991): 5–6.

24. Fredric Jameson poses the problem as follows: "How do we distinguish . . . between real pleasure and mere diversion—the degradation of free time into that very different commodity called 'leisure,' the form of commodity consumption stamped on the most intimate former pleasures from sexuality to reading?" (63).

MARGARET DRABBLE

Stratford Revisited: A Legacy of the Sixties

In many ways, I hated Stratford. I suppose you could say I have a love-hate relationship with Stratford. These feelings are muddled up with many personal matters which I shall not bore or embarrass you by describing here, for this is the town where I came when I was first married, this is the town where I first tried to keep house, where I boiled my first pound of sprouts, where I gave my first dinner party. I can remember the guest list and the menu now. This is the town where I pushed my first baby in his push-chair, and learned to play Scrabble, and failed my driving test, and met some of my closest friends, and helped to found a Theatre Nursery Group, and understudied Judi Dench and Vanessa Redgrave. It is a town with many reverberations and echoes, echoes which sound in an intertextual or intersonic sort of way through my writings. I spent the first night of my honeymoon here, alone, in the audience, watching, ominously, John Barton's production of *The Taming of the Shrew,* in 1960, with Peggy Ashcroft and Peter O'Toole. I lived here for two seasons, in various digs, some of which I cannot now locate, and some of which I can find blindfold. I rarely come back to Stratford. Too many memories are stirred, too many painful and ridiculous episodes revive. And yet, if I had not come to Stratford, I doubt if I would have become a writer at all. I owe a great deal to this town.

My original ambitions were, in fact, theatrical. I longed to be an actress or a drama critic. I didn't mind which; I simply wanted to be able to be in the theater every night of my life. This was odd, as my family rarely went to the theater, and the only plays I saw when I was young were school productions of the classics or Christmas pantomimes at the Sheffield Lyceum. But as it happened, those school productions were enough to enthuse anyone. The first memorable one was a production of *The Tempest,* in which Judi Dench played Ariel. The second was a production of *A Midsummer Night's Dream,* in which Judi played Titania and I played a fairy. Both productions were magical, to me, and I fell in love with the magical Judi and with Shakespeare and started to read my way

through the canon, play after play, in tiny double column print in my
mother's old cloth-bound Collected Works (Craig's edition). I was
bewitched. I thought then, as I think now, that the greatness of these
works is some kind of testimony to the possibilities of the human spirit,
possibilities that most of us daily deny. They became, and remain, what
Matthew Arnold would call a touchstone, and even in these days of
relativism and deconstruction I still find myself late at night with friends
after a bottle or two of wine returning to that question which we used to
debate so repetitively at Cambridge: how is it that we *know* that Shakespeare is better than Swinburne? This seemed to me then and seems to me
now one of the key unanswerable questions of aesthetics. You see how
little I have progressed in critical theory since the 1960s.

For, after this taste of the theater at a curiously drama-enlightened
Quaker school, I then went on to study, not drama or acting, but literature,
in the Cambridge of the 1960s. This was very much the Cambridge of the
great late Dr. Leavis. The spirit and standards of Leavis ruled the English
school, and he was no mean performer himself, a master of the lowered
voice, the cutting aside, the sudden unexpected song of praise. But it has
to be said that he did not encourage creative writing. In literary terms, the
Cambridge of my day was arid. Ted Hughes and Sylvia Plath had vanished,
leaving no perceptible trace. *Granta* was then a fairly dull little magazine,
which rejected my poems and stories even when I was its assistant editor.
There were one or two aspiring writers who met to read one another their
poems, but the analytic training and adversarial, combative tone of the
Leavises had so sharpened their wits and their tongues that they made
mincemeat of one another, and hardly any lived to tell the tale. It was not
a time for minor writers, for experimentalists, for novices. Either you
made it straight into the Great Tradition, or you kept quiet and taught it.
And of course most had no choice but the latter.

Except, of course, for those who chose the theater. Looking back, with
the benefit of hindsight, it seems likely that the extraordinary theatrical
creativity of that period did in some way connect with the vacuum left in
the creative world by the rigour and pressure of the Leavisite literary
orthodoxy. Energy and experiment were squeezed out of literature and
into drama. For Cambridge of the late 1950s and 1960s was not only the
Cambridge of Leavis; it was also the Cambridge of Peter Hall and Peter
Wood and Peter Woodthorpe, of John Barton and Jonathan Miller and
Toby Robertson and Tony Church and Peter Jeffrey, of Ian McKellen and
Derek Jacobi and Eleanor Bron and Clive Swift and Joe Melia and David
Buck and Trevor Nunn and Waris Hussein and Corin Redgrave and John
Tydeman and Richard Marquand and Tom Kempinski, and of a host of
others whose productions and performances linger in the memory, and

who still rejoice us on stage, in opera, on the radio, in television and film. They were and are an extremely gifted generation, and the connections of many of them with Stratford and the RSC have been close. It was a director's and actor's era, not a writer's, and, significantly, the name of Tom Kempinski, author of *Duet for One* and *Separation,* has taken much longer to reach the roll call of honor.

Bliss was it in that dawn to be alive, and wonderful were the plays we put on. Discounting the nostalgia factor, I do think some of them *were* wonderful, and it was a privilege to be around when such a spirit was in the air. This was the era of the new, Peter Hall–approved verse speaking, over which the influence of George Rylands (Dadie, to everyone who knew him) hovered benignly. I recall fine productions of *King John*, of the *Henry the Fourths*, of Marlowe's *Edward the Second*, of *Twelfth Night*. There were also fine versions of prose classics by Chekhov, Ibsen, Sartre, Tennessee Williams, Pirandello, Arthur Miller, Anouilh. . . . The directors were in training for the classical repertory that many hoped to see from a National Theatre, and which in fact slightly preceded the opening of the National Theatre in the early diversified work of the RSC at the Aldwych. To those of us studying English Literature—as most of us were—the ADC, the Mummers and the Marlowe Society, as well as many other independent productions, offered an opportunity to see a living theater, a theater off the page, and to see it in a new nonacademic light.

I well remember, during this period, the stimulating conflict of impressions that arose from writing an essay upon a Shakespeare text, discussing its textual cruces or its moral ambiguity, and the totally different experience of working on a play for performance, of trying to make it work on stage, for an audience. My time was divided rather unevenly between the two. I spent most of my Cambridge days in rehearsal, and read my texts and wrote my essays during the vacation. And I greatly enjoyed both sides of my life. I was thoroughly and happily split. The University did not frown too much on the acting community, partly, perhaps, because Peter Hall had already acquired distinction and power on a national stage (if not yet *the* National stage), and I do not remember ever being discouraged from spending my time with the strolling players. So any sense of division, of competing loyalties or ambitions, was internalized. But I do recall becoming vaguely aware, during my last year in Cambridge, that there was some real dichotomy between Shakespeare-on-the-stage and Shakespeare-on-the-page. There were even hints of a power struggle between the two—a power struggle which was to surface here in Stratford with John Barton's production of the *Shrew* which I saw on my wedding night. Many still remember the open war waged between the Don and the Actors, between Cambridge and Comedy.

These questions crystallized for me around a Marlowe Society production of *Cymbeline,* in which I had the good fortune to be cast as Imogen. I
wanted this part for the reasons that almost every actress wants it—because
it is sympathetic, varied, showy, tragic, romantic, moving, and because
Imogen has some wonderful verse. Little did I realize when I took it on
that the play itself presents almost insuperable difficulties of tone and
style, and that on stage its implausibilities are grotesque. Indeed, my
mother, who was dragged unwillingly to the Cambridge Arts Theatre to
watch this, the only performance she ever saw me give, was heard
to remark loudly at the end "What a ridiculous play, I could write a better
one myself!" I was too wrapped up in my own role to worry about that
kind of thing, though I suspect (a suspicion confirmed in recent conversation with Ian McKellen, who played Posthumus) that our production was
found comic by more spectators than my mother. Indeed, to compound
my humiliation, I discover that Argo Recordings have recently reissued as
a tape the recording we made of the play, and have named me as the
perpetrator of the role of Imogen, a naming that contravenes, I may say,
the anonymous tradition of the Marlowe Society. I have not dared to
listen to much of this but when I asked my son, himself something of an
actor in his university days, and a campaigning President of Oxford
University Dramatic Society, what it sounded like, he responded dis-
appointingly with his round, loud laugh, and said, "Well, Mum, it's
terribly funny!" "Funny?" I echoed, feebly. "Yes, funny," he said, veering
towards apology, "you know, all that elocution, all that verse speaking,
it's all a bit—well, *dated,* you know. A bit sixties. *You* know." In self-
defense, I must point out that even while rehearsing for the role of
Imogen, and writhing in despair by an imaginary headless corpse on
Dadie Ryland's carpet in front of a painted fireplace that I now know to be
the work of Carrington, even then, I was aware that the plot of *Cymbeline*
was a bit odd. My brain told me what my actress-self could not afford to
know. And, as brains do, it got to work on it.

In our final year, we scholars of English had the option of writing an
Original Composition for Part Two of the English Tripos, an opportunity
declined by many of my friends—though I believe David Buck wrote an
impressive piece on the Elizabethan Theater and the composition of
Shakespeare's company. I chose as my title "The Unheroic Mode," and
produced a seventeen-page piece on *Cymbeline,* Euripides, Ingmar Bergman,
and Pirandello. I have the piece still, and on re-reading it recently, wondering
if there was anything in it that would inspire me to more original thoughts
for this essay, I discovered to my astonishment that it is in fact a very early,
indeed a pioneer essay in deconstruction. I take as my theme the curious
impulse on the part of Euripides and late Shakespeare to play games with

their own plots, and ask what these writers, who could write realistically and not fantastically when they chose, thought they were playing at? The games of illusion and deception and mistaking in late Shakespeare are extraordinary, and I think I was rebelling against the prevailing view that the oddities of the plots (oddities that so amused my mother) could be resolved or explained or, let us be frank, excused in terms of "poetic structure" or "the meaning of the verse."

Verse drama was still in vogue in the sixties, and we still admired Christopher Fry and T. S. Eliot's neoclassical cocktail tragedies; in fact Fry's *Curtmantle* was one of the first plays put on by the new Royal Shakespeare Company. But even then, I found something unsatisfactory about the emphasis on verse at the expense of drama. I was puzzled by some of Eliot's highly influential remarks on the drama, and here I may quote myself of thirty years ago with approval, for I think my comments are still apposite: "In his essay on the Elizabethan theater T. S. Eliot remarks that the only English play to remain within the limits of art is *Everyman*. *Everyman* is an allegorical play; the audience is never asked to believe that a real particular man imaginatively identifiable with a real particular actor is living through a real situation. Thus the element of illusion and deception is removed, and the drama becomes, as Eliot would have it be, a pure form. However, there is something lacking in a definition of the drama that admits only one artistic success. The drama is basically an impure form; it does not merely have to put up with illusion, with the undefined effect of the sense of stage, set, and acting, but it depends upon them. The relationship of confidence between the audience and the play on the stage is the source of dramatic experience, and it is what distinguishes drama as a form from any other type of literature." I continue, "The sense of illusion may be created by deception as well as by confidence voluntarily given" and suggest that the late Shakespeare, Euripides, etc. all "sense an element of gross, vulgar deception involved in the theatrical art.... they realize they are juggling with sham materials, with an imposition on the vulgar by vulgar means not far removed from optical illusions and conjuring tricks." I continue to discuss the role of papier mâché severed heads and glass diamonds and headless corpses and false beards, that part of theater that Aristotle called spectacle, and go on to conclude that in *Cymbeline* Shakespeare was, effectively, in a deliberate postmodernist manner, deconstructing his own text, exposing his own stage devices to our incredulity, and inviting a very complex response, a response which embraces both that of my mother and the remarkably similar response of Bernard Shaw, the more reverent response of Tennyson, who, you will recall, asked for a copy of the play to read upon his deathbed, and the eagerness of actresses from Ellen Terry to Vanessa

Redgrave and to Harriet Walter to risk making fools of themselves in an unplayable role.

I accepted then, and I accept now, that it is perfectly possible to make out a case for *Cymbeline*—or, come to that, *The Winter's Tale* or *The Tempest* or *Pericles*—as poetic texts on regeneration and symbolic rebirth. But what about "Exit, pursued by a Bear"? Or the headless Cloten? Or the strange parody of Othello's jealousy in Posthumus's "I will go there and do't, i' the court, before Her father. I'll do something"? What about the gods from the machine—Euripidean, mocking gods, I would argue—who seem almost to laugh at the dénouements over which they preside? Has Shakespeare *forgotten* how to write a plausible narrative, or is he up to something quite different? I argued then that he was, and would argue the case more boldly now, were that my theme. Why is the text of *Cymbeline* littered with sardonic reflections on its own improbability? In the very first scene, the first gentleman, in a stunningly inelegant recap of the pre-ceding pre-play action, tells us of the loss of the two little princes as babes—princes who, you may or may not recall, turn out to be Imogen's long-lost brothers—and defends it in these words: "Howsoe'er 'tis strange, / Or that the negligence may well be laughed at, / Yet is it true, sir." Are we not here more in the realm of Oscar Wilde than of *King Lear*, or even of *As You Like It?*

And so the play continues, bathos heaped on bathos, implausibility upon implausibility, and not concealed, not mitigated, but almost, as it were, flaunted. When Posthumus, later in the play, gives his glowing account of the fine swordsmanship of these same two princes, a casual bystanding lord comments, as might my mother, "This was strange chance: A narrow lane, an old man, and two boys!" Add to these com-ments the other implausibilities—the Iachimo bedtrick, when he observes Imogen's breast and counts the spots of her mole after leaping like a pantomime villain out of a trunk, the impossibly mistaken identity of Cloten-dressed-as-Posthumus and conveniently, unidentifiably headless—and we find ourselves in a very strange realm. Shakespeare is not incompetent, he is not trying and failing to write a romance, he is not making his debut as a Beaumont-and-Fletcher manqué any more than David Lodge in *Small World* is trying to rewrite Ariosto or Sidney's *Arcadia* or Greene's *Menaphon* (wherein you may recall, according to one of my favourite sentences in the *Oxford Companion to English Literature,* "the convention of impenetrable disguise is taken to ridiculous lengths as Sephestia, disguised as Samela, is wooed simultaneously by her father and her teenage son, while herself carrying on a love affair with her (disguised) husband"). No, both Shakespeare and David Lodge here are postmodernist (arguably Greene was too, of course) and Shakespeare in *Cymbeline* is doing something quite other than trying and failing to write an orthodox romance. He is, I submit, commenting on the very nature of the theatrical materials he has used all his life, and perhaps, like Euripides, like Pirandello, like Prospero himself, he is attempting some kind of apologia for the use and misuse of power. For within the implausibilities, ordinary, unheroic reality rings out. Imogen does not kill herself on the supposed corpse of her headless husband as Juliet would have done; she literally soldiers on. We have left heroics and tragedies behind. We are in the realm of bathos and survival.

This, with some embellishment and update, was the gist of my rethink of *Cymbeline* in 1960. It was an attempt to make sense of the dual nature of my experience of Shakespeare from back stage and on the page, and I now see that I hadn't yet admitted into it some of the other doubts about the play that had already, as I recall, begun to perplex me. The key text here is the lines spoken about Imogen, or Imogen-as-Fidele, by her disguised and as-yet-unrecognized brothers, Guiderius and Arviragus, and by their adoptive father, Belarius:

> *Belarius*
> This youth, howe'er distressed, appears he hath had
> Good ancestors.
> *Arviragus*
> How angel-like he sings!
> *Guiderius*
> But his neat cookery! he cut our roots in characters,
> And sauced our broths, as Juno had been sick,
> And he her dieter.

For some reason, I found these lines peculiarly irritating, and it took me some time to admit that they annoyed me because of their references to Imogen's culinary skills. We come back, by a biographical loop, to the Brussels sprouts and Stratford, and leap on, by another biographical loop, to Bernard Shaw. Shaw, decades ago, had the wit to note, good protofeminist that he was, that there was absolutely no dramatic need at all for Shakespeare to portray Imogen as, of all things, a good cook. Why on earth should she, a royal princess, be able to cook at all? And why, disguised as a boy, should she immediately risk revealing her identity by getting down to the cave housework? Surely here was her chance to slack, even if she did spend all her time back at the palace cooking broths and baking dainties! Shaw writes to Ellen Terry, while she was rehearsing the role, in September 1896;

> I really dont know what to say about this silly old Cymbeline, except that it can be done delightfully in a village schoolroom and

cant be done at the Lyceum at all, on any terms. . . . All I can extract from the artificialities of the play is a double image—a real woman divined by Shakespear without his knowing it clearly, a natural aristocrat with a high temper and perfect courage, with two moods—a childlike affection and wounded rage; and an idiotic paragon of virtue produced by Shakespear's *views* of what a woman ought to be, a person who sews and cooks and reads improving books until midnight and "always reserves her holy duty", and is anxious to assure people that they may trust her implicitly with their spoons and forks, and is in a chronic state of suspicion of improper behaviour on the part of other people (especially her husband) with abandoned females. If I were you I should cut the part so as to leave the paragon out and the woman in; and I should write to The Times explaining the lines of the operation.

Shaw continues, in a lengthy, witty, and thoughtful correspondence, to advise and sympathize with Ellen Terry and to comment on the play's beauties and idiocies. When the play opened at the Lyceum he gave it what can only be called a mixed notice in the *Saturday Review* (26 September 1896) entitled "Blaming the Bard," in which he describes the play as "for the most part stagey trash of the lowest melodramatic order" and continues "There are moments when one asks despairingly why our stage should ever have been cursed with this 'immortal' pilferer of other men's stories and ideas, with his monstrous rhetorical fustian, his unbearable platitudes, his pretentious reduction of the subtlest problems of life to commonplaces against which a Polytechnic debating club would revolt, his incredible unsuggestiveness. . . . With the single exception of Homer, there is no eminent writer, not even Sir Walter Scott, whom I can despise so entirely as I despise Shakespeare" and goes on, when reviewing the actual production, to praise Ellen Terry's "infinite charm and delicacy of appeal" and to congratulate her, with characteristic impudence, for cutting her own part so skilfully that the "Mrs Grundyish Imogen" had been dissected out of it.

And this was not the end of his relationship with *Cymbeline,* as we know. Many years later, half a lifetime later, he wrote his own version of the last act, *Cymbeline Refinished* (1936), which begins rather brilliantly with the Captain shouting up to Philario in armor standing on a tall rock ("Ho there, signor! You are in danger there. You can be seen a mile off.") and continues in a racy pastiche which includes an invective against the monarchy from young Guiderius, furious to discover he is by birth a prince. It ends, "I abdicate, and pass the throne to Polydore," to which Polydore replies, "Do you, by heavens? Thank you for nothing, brother."

Posthumus's penitent speech, "Yea, bloody cloth, I'll keep thee," is left entire, on the grounds that it anticipates Ibsen's criticism, through Mrs. Alving in *Ghosts*, of "the slavery to an inhuman ideal of marital fidelity which leads him to the villainous extremity" of ordering his wife to be murdered.

Well, here is pioneer deconstruction and reconstruction work more bold than most dare undertake, and I have to admit that I used to find Shaw's attacks on Shakespeare more than faintly shocking. But, shocking though they were, I continued in my heart to agree, as I struggled with carrots and sprouts and stubbornly unboilable potatoes, that it was a pity that Imogen had been portrayed as a Good Cook. Where, I wondered, was I to find other, positive images of womanhood, of the wife's role? No, I did not like the *Shrew* as a play then, and I do not like it now. But then, in 1960, the feminist lobby had hardly got off the ground. Shaw's voice was a forgotten wail in the wilderness, and we were all merry little actresses and housewives and housewife-actresses trying to cook nice little meals and look after our babies and learn our lines and clean our silver and please everybody—trying, in short, to be paragons, with hardly a murmur of protest.

As chance would have it, in my second year in Stratford, two of the plays in repertory were *Cymbeline* and the *Shrew*, and I found myself night after night as lady-in-waiting in the first and as serving-girl in the second watching the humbling of Vanessa Redgrave, and puzzling over the fate of the high-spirited wife and the Bad Cook. Night after night, as I heard Maroussia Frank as the widow in the last act of the *Shrew*, after watching Katharine debase herself, deliver the lines "Lord, let me never have a cause to sigh, Till I be brought to such a silly pass," I thought "that's right, spot on, go for it," and hoped that somehow the play would end differently tonight. But it never did. Of course, I should have taken a leaf out of Shaw's book and written my own ending. Directors in the last twenty years have tried many ingenious ways of making the play more sympathetic to a postfeminist audience but the text remains stubborn, intended, appalling. (I was delighted to discover years later during my *Oxford Companion* research that John Fletcher had in fact, in 1604 or thereabouts, written a riposte called *The Woman's Prize, or the Tamer Tamed*, showing the second marriage of Petruchio. Katharine is dead, and Petruchio marries Maria, who locks him out of his house on his wedding night and thoroughly subdues him.)

But back in the 1960s, what happened was that I came to recognize that there was no place for a person like me *either* in the theater *or* as a housewife in Stratford. Neither role would work. So I settled down to write the novels that eventually brought me a degree of autonomy and allowed me to laugh at the Brussels sprouts. I would like to say a few words about the difficulties of living in Stratford as a theater wife. Maybe things are different now, but in those days, there was much emphasis from the management on the virtues of company spirit and team spirit and togetherness. The first long-term contracts for actors were offered, in an attempt to provide security and ensure continuity. Husbands and wives congregated, theater babies were born, prams clustered and jostled in the streets of Stratford. In very early days here I used to look forward to babysitting for Tony and Margaret Church, because I knew that they would leave me a well-cooked meal in the oven, and I hoped that if I studied it hard enough I might one day learn how to emulate Imogen and cook such a wondrous casserole myself. But it was not easy, being a half-participant, being a sort of intermediate creature, neither part of nor yet quite exiled from the charmed world of starry glamour. I loved and hated it. And I was not the only wife in Britain to feel the stirrings of revolt. When I published my second novel, *The Garrick Year,* which is set in a thinly disguised Stratford—I hasten to say all the characters and incidents are entirely fictional—I found I had unwittingly tuned into a mood that was spreading through the country. Far from being isolated, I was part of a movement. The time was right. The times were changing. The captive housewife spoke, the Housebound Housewive's Register was founded, Mary Stott gave space and encouragement.in other pages of the *Guardian* to a new breed of feminism. The Shrew began to see how to rewrite the last act.

NOTE

This essay is a slightly cut version of the Gareth Lloyd Evans Celebration Lecture, delivered at Stratford-upon-Avon on 2 April 1988.

MALIN LAVON WALTHER

Toni Morrison's *Tar Baby:* Re-Figuring the Colonizer's Aesthetics

Literary criticism has produced two distinct readings of *The Tempest,* as Meredith Anne Skura has argued: one, which she terms "idealist," constituted the dominant interpretation until the second, which she labels "revisionist," critiqued the ahistoricism of traditional interpretations and focused on *The Tempest* as a text of English colonialism.[1] Colonialist interpretations of *The Tempest,* however, have not been limited to literary criticism. As Thomas Cartelli points out, there exists a "nonwestern interpretive community for whom *The Tempest* has long served as the embodiment of colonial presumption."[2] While he cites African and West Indian literatures as expressions of this interpretive community, the same could be said of African-American literature or the literature of any cultural group that has experienced a master/slave relationship.

Cartelli's analysis of fictional rewritings of Shakespeare by the colonized offers an illuminating context for the work of Toni Morrison, who has recently outlined a prospective critical reading practice for American literature. In "Unspeakable Things Unspoken: The Afro-American Presence in American Literature," Morrison suggests rereading canonical American works, usually written by white male authors, to elucidate racial themes, or the "unspeakable unspoken."[3] She believes that the "re-examination of founding literature of the United States for the unspeakable unspoken may reveal those texts to have deeper and other meanings, deeper and other power, deeper and other significances" (14).

Morrison's own fiction has been involved in this critical project from the beginning and has not limited itself to the founding literature of the American literary canon. Her trademark juxtaposition of African-American texts with Euro-American texts suggests an ongoing dialogue with American Eurocentrism, in which African-American texts critique and reconstruct the assumptions, practices, and critical interpretations of Euro-American texts. In her novel *Tar Baby,* Morrison places the tar-baby text in corrective counterpoint to Shakespeare's *Tempest.*[4] Just as Morrison interrogates the fictional family of the Dick-and-Jane reader in *The Bluest Eye*[5] and exposes the assumptions and limitations of the bildungsroman in *Song of Solomon,*[6] so too in *Tar Baby* Morrison re-figures what she sees as the hierarchical and binary foundations of Eurocentric aesthetics—the hegemonic standards of beauty and value in art and life.[7] In so doing, Morrison targets colonialism as the root of aesthetic hegemony, revealing art's inherent politics.

Morrison's reading of *The Tempest* in *Tar Baby* draws upon both of the interpretive schools outlined by Skura, the idealist and the revisionist, using the ideological awareness of the latter to critique the aesthetic assumptions of the former.[8] *Tar Baby* confronts idealist readings of *The Tempest* in which the play functions as a tool in legitimating the Western discourse of power. Such conventional readings of *The Tempest,* as Peter Hulme succinctly notes, view it as "a pastoral tragi-comedy with the themes of nature and art at its centre."[9] Viewed from this perspective, the narrative pursues a proper balance between nature and art,[10] embodying the hierarchical and binary aesthetics typical of the Renaissance. The characters constitute a vertical continuum,[11] from those associated with spirit, intellect, and art at the top, to those reflecting nature, earthly passions, and life at the bottom. The island community is headed by Prospero, a magus who controls the forces of nature for his own cultural purposes. His main assistant in this is the sprite Ariel, an otherworldly being associated with creative forces. Under Prospero's control, but still on a pedestal, is his beautiful daughter Miranda, who, as "pure maiden," lacks her father's educated intellect yet controls her physicality, thereby remaining above earthly passion. The lowest figure in the island hierarchy is Caliban, whose ugliness, lack of intellect, and base passions place him under Prospero's domination. In this hierarchical vision of the ordered society, the "Big Dichotomies" of Western culture are apparent: Prospero's civilization opposes Caliban's nature; Prospero's mind controls Miranda and Caliban's bodies; Miranda's beauty contrasts Caliban's ugliness; and Prospero's artifice, with Ariel's creative agency, shapes the island's life.

This idealist reading of *The Tempest* promulgates an aesthetic in which Art holds a mirror up to Nature.[12] Prospero's "magic" or art, in shaping and controlling not only the native spirits on the island but also its visitors, is seen as enabling everyone's redemption and creating a "harmoniously reconciled new world" (Skura 42). This aesthetic is both hierarchical—in its positive valuation of Prospero's controlling artifice—and binary—in its separation and opposition of art and nature. As an allegory about, among other things, "the nature of art,"[13] *The Tempest* has constituted a touchstone for several twentieth-century author's statements on literary aesthetics. From T. S. Eliot, whose allusions to *The*

Tempest throughout *The Waste Land* reflect his reconstructive modernist project, to Sylvia Plath, whose posthumous collection *Ariel* and its title poem signal her poetry's central confessionalist tension between art and life, these authors' readings and rereadings of *The Tempest* mark their definitive positions on their own aesthetic projects. For example, W. H. Auden, in "The Sea and the Mirror—A Commentary on Shakespeare's *The Tempest,*" uses Caliban as a spokesman for the poet's aesthetic positions. This refiguring of the natural Caliban into an aesthetic spokesman may reflect Auden's critique of the assumptions he sees underlying the aesthetics of *The Tempest;* however, others, such as Stephen Orgel, read Auden's poem as a sentimental attempt to domesticate Caliban.[14] Authors in this idealist tradition of reading *The Tempest* focus on the themes of art and nature within the play in order to make their own aesthetic statements.

In contrast to placing *The Tempest* at the center of twentieth-century aesthetic discourse, revisionist readings of the play situate it within the context of colonialist discourse. These readings are of two types: works of literary criticism that apply postcolonial theory to the text, and literature of the colonized which critiques colonialism. Among writers of the former group, critics like Peter Hulme see *The Tempest* as "emblematic of the founding years of English colonialism" (90) and focus on how the hierarchical and binary grid of the play reflects the workings of colonial ideology. A central unresolved question among this group is to what extent the play is for or against colonialism (Skura 49).

However, among the latter group—literature of the colonized—revisionist readings of *The Tempest* do not debate the text's colonialism; instead, Cartelli argues, they recuperate the "master/slave configuration, thus making it appear to function as a foundational paradigm in the history of European colonialism" (101). Cartelli's discussion of the Kenyan writer Ngugi wa Thiong'o asserts that, in his *Grain of Wheat,* Ngugi advances a reading of Shakespeare in which Shakespeare represents the assumptions of European superiority and its effects on the culturally dispossessed (105). If writers such as Ngugi and the West Indian George Lamming "misread" Shakespeare's text, Cartelli argues, "they do so in consistency with the way colonial history has inscribed itself on colonizer and colonized alike" (105). These writers use *The Tempest* not to make aesthetic statements as much as to discuss issues of race, culture, and ideology. While Cartelli also mentions Derek Walcott's play *Pantomime* as within this revisionist reading community, his argument could profitably be expanded to include African-American writers, such as John Edgar Wideman, who have appropriated Caliban from *The Tempest.* As Leslie Fiedler notes, black American writers have used Caliban as "a central symbol both for their old indignities and the possibility of revolt against them."[15] Just as Ngugi uses Shakespeare's text to critique the effects of Europe's cultural colonialism, so might African-American writers employ the idealist interpretation of *The Tempest* to analyze Eurocentric discourse in America. In light of the historical parallels between the settlement of America and the composition of the play, African-American, and, for that matter, American Indian, literary revisionist readings of *The Tempest* may prove particularly illuminating.

Morrison positions *Tar Baby* at the intersection of these idealist and revisionist readings of *The Tempest*. *Tar Baby* takes a revisionist stance towards idealist readings of Shakespeare, critiquing the play's role in colonialist ideology; yet, unlike Walcott or Wideman, Morrison's central figure of appropriation is not Caliban. Instead, signaling a feminist project, Morrison makes the beautiful Miranda her key figure.[16] Morrison uses this revisionist reading to unhinge the Eurocentric aesthetics underlying the play's idealist interpretation. Like Ngugi and Lamming, Morrison "misreads" Shakespeare's text, focusing on its position in traditional readings as a tool of the colonizer's aesthetic discourse. As a result, *Tar Baby* reveals aesthetic standards to be an arm of colonialist ideology; art and politics do, indeed, belong together.[17]

Morrison constructs the setting and themes of *Tar Baby* to suggest an intertextual parallel with *The Tempest*. In placing most of the action on a Caribbean island, Morrison not only parallels the "uninhabited isle" of *The Tempest* but also thus enters the discourse of colonialism, for, as Hulme argues about *The Tempest*, "discursively the Caribbean is a special place, partly because of its primacy in the encounter between Europe and America, civilization and savagery" (3). Thus, in her choice of setting, Morrison situates *Tar Baby* squarely within colonialist dynamics.[18]

Tar Baby's characters also echo those of *The Tempest* and particularly exemplify the issues of colonialism and aesthetics. At the beginning of the novel, the head of the island household, Valerian, is like Prospero, an "exile" from civilization (12). He controls, by intellect and power, the rest of the characters. Morrison evokes Shakespeare's Prospero when she specifically associates Valerian with the artifice of his greenhouse, "a place of controlled ever-flowing life" (45), where he can magically "conjure . . . up old friends and childhood playmates" (123). Thus, like Prospero, Valerian controls nature and dominates the other characters; Morrison's characterization of Valerian emphasizes a reading of Prospero which critiques his use of magic for power. In his role as civilizing "emperor" of the island household (126), Valerian is presented as the locus of Eurocentrism and its aesthetic standards.

Jadine, the niece of Valerian's employees Ondine and Sydney Childs, echoes the role of Miranda in her relationship with Valerian. As an orphan, she, like Miranda, is motherless, and has been raised not only by her aunt and uncle but also under Valerian's patronage. As such, Morrison situates her as enmeshed in the hierarchical and binary practices of Eurocentric aesthetics.[19] Owing her formal education to Valerian, she has incorporated many of his values and ideals, as reflected in her comment to him: "Picasso *is* better than an Itumba mask. The fact that he was intrigued by them is proof of *his* genius, not the mask-makers' " (62).

Disrupting this aesthetic hierarchy is Son, whom Morrison connects with "that great underclass of undocumented men. . . . Some were Huck Finns; some Nigger Jims. Others were Calibans" (142–43). As a Caliban figure, Son reintroduces the principles of nature, physicality, and the folk life repressed, denied, and devalued in Eurocentric aesthetics. His relationship with Jadine initially recapitulates that of Caliban and Miranda in *The Tempest*. Fearing he will rape her, a repeated concern in *The Tempest*, Jadine tells Son, "You rape me and they'll feed you to the alligators" (103). She then rejects him, as Miranda rejects Caliban in *The Tempest*, as an "ugly barefoot baboon!" (104). Continuing, Jadine evokes the whole of *The Tempest*'s hierarchy: "A white man thought you were a human being and should be treated like one. He's civilized and made the mistake of thinking you might be too. That's because he didn't smell you. But I did and I know you're an animal" (104). Morrison echoes Prospero and Miranda's disgust at Caliban's supposed animal passions and his failure to adhere to their teachings. Furthermore, Jadine's speech reflects her belief in two binary oppositions: white/black and civilized/animal.

Revisionist readings of *The Tempest*, such as Stephen Orgel's, suggest that the fear of Miranda's rape in the play arises from "sexual imperialism" implicit in the play (40). Orgel points out that, actually, "Miranda has two royal suitors, and Caliban is one of them" (55). Thus, in this reading the accusation of rape becomes a tool to delegitimate Caliban as a suitor in favor of Ferdinand. That Son in *Tar Baby* is repeatedly accused of the desire to sexually assault Margaret and Jadine revoices these concerns in an American frame, in which black men serve as a projection screen for fears of miscegenation and sexual prowess. Morrison emphatically critiques these dynamics of sexual imperialism in a long passage which repeats "he had not followed the women" seven times (114–18). Thus, Morrison's initial presentation of the main characters Valerian, Jadine, and Son evokes the hierarchical and binary order of idealist readings of *The Tempest* and presents Jadine as the central figure of negotiation.

Morrison interrogates Jadine's Eurocentric standards through two key binaries of the general Nature/Culture dualism which undergirds the aesthetics inherent in idealist readings of *The Tempest*: Art versus Life and

Beauty versus Ugliness.[20] In the course of the novel, these oppositions are discovered to be untenable and Morrison's own aesthetic assumptions are revealed.

Jadine stands at the center of both these re-figurations. Not only is she a beautiful model, but she has also passed prelims for her art history Ph.D. Throughout *Tar Baby,* Jadine repeatedly attempts to make distinctions between art and life. She feels she is "lucky to know it, to know the difference between the fine and the mediocre, so she'd put that instinct to work and studied art history—there she was never wrong" (155). As we have seen, she sees Picasso's use of African masks as a higher art than the masks themselves, created by the Itumba as part of their religious practice. This aesthetic of distance from nature and lived experience as essential to high art is evoked repeatedly in scenes with Jadine in which photography or drawing figure prominently. In one scene, Jadine shows Son her magazine layout. In response, Son can only whisper, "Goddamn" (99). Mesmerized by the photographs, Son becomes distanced from reality, repeatedly "fingering the photograph" as a substitute for fingering Jadine herself, who is sitting next to him (101). Then, with a great twist of irony, Morrison reveals the ramifications of art's alienation:

> "Why don't you look at me?" [Jadine] asked him.
> "I can't," he said.
> "Why can't you?"
> "The pictures are easier. They don't move."
> Jadine felt a flash of pity. "You want me to be still? Will you look at me if I'm still?"
> He didn't answer.
> "Look." she said. "I'm still. Very still."
> He lifted his head and looked at her. Her eyes were mink-colored just like in the pictures, and her lips were like the pictures too. (101–2)

Here Son and Jadine try to make life imitate art. Son is just as stuck on this aesthetic tar baby as Jadine is. This scene reveals how an aesthetic that privileges artistic expressions detached from life ultimately alienates us from lived experience.

Jadine's art-centered European worldview also leads her to use her own productions of photography and drawing as a means of distancing herself from reality through the objectification of artistic representation. When Jadine visits Son's community, Eloe, she "remembered her camera just before she thought she would go nuts, trying to keep a conversation going" (215). Jadine scrambles to objectify the experience through photography. Jadine also uses drawing as an art form to keep life at bay.

She wants "to sketch [Son] and get it over with" (135). Because his sexual attractiveness disturbs her, she wants to distance herself from him via art. Her reaction to Alma, an island woman, is also to want to draw her rather than engage her directly (249). As Morrison summarizes, "she saw planes and angles and missed character" (135).

Interwoven with Jadine's Eurocentric division of art and life is her repeated distinction between beauty and ugliness, an issue for Miranda in *The Tempest*. Repeatedly in *The Tempest,* Miranda's first comments about other characters are based on physical appearance. About Caliban, she states he is "a villain, sir, / I do not love to look on" (1.2.308-9). Her response to her first sight of Ferdinand focuses on his "brave form" (1.2.413). When Miranda sees all the shipwrecked men together, she exclaims, "How beauteous mankind is!" (5.1.182). Furthermore, Miranda relies on these aesthetic judgments to ascertain character: when Prospero accuses Ferdinand of usurpation, Miranda defends him, saying, "There's nothing ill can grow in such a temple. / If the ill spirit have so fair a house, / Good things will strive to dwell with't" (1.2.459-61). In *Tar Baby,* Jadine, as an art historian and model, adheres to the belief that aesthetic evaluations can be objectively determined; beyond that, she, like Miranda, believes that what is judged beautiful has more value. For example, when Son first intrudes upon the household, Jadine dismisses him as "ugly" (104), just as Miranda rejects Caliban. Yet the next day, after Son's shower, haircut, and change of clothes, Jadine determines Son is "gorgeous" (134). And this makes him matter, a lot, "for she was more frightened of his good looks than she had been by his ugliness the day before" (135). In this scene Morrison allows her Caliban to transform into a Ferdinand to reveal the standards of beauty and value under which Jadine has been operating. As an attractive man, Son becomes a sexual possibility, a possibility Jadine is trying to control, as suggested by the repeated image "she was holding tight to the reins of dark dogs with silver feet." (135).

Tar Baby challenges Jadine's traditional European aesthetics in several ways. Morrison re-figures beauty and art through Jadine's confrontations with a black female character and the natural world of the island landscape. At the beginning of the novel, we find that Jadine has come to the island to escape the woman in yellow, who she feels has "run her out of Paris" (40). This woman, Jadine recalls, "was . . . much too tall. Under her long canary yellow dress Jadine knew there was too much hip, too much bust. The agency would laugh her out of the lobby, so why was she and everybody else in the store transfixed? The height? The skin like tar against the canary yellow dress?" (38). This woman explodes Eurocentric determinations of beauty by having "too much hip, too much bust." She even has, Jadine notices, "eyes too beautiful for eyelashes" (39). And

Morrison grounds this re-figured aesthetic in racial specificity; the woman's "skin like tar" may be the very source of her beauty. In this depiction, Morrison also counters the apprehension of this woman as an art object, noting her "unphotographable beauty" (39). Jadine's early encounter with this woman in yellow follows her throughout *Tar Baby* as an emblem of her struggle with Eurocentric aesthetics, reappearing in her dreams and thoughts.

Although Jadine tries to escape this aesthetic challenge on the island, paralleling Prospero and Miranda's self-protective exile in *The Tempest,* the island landscape itself subverts her aesthetic frame. Echoing the woman in yellow's "too much hip, too much bust," the "island exaggerated everything. Too much light. Too much shadow. Too much rain. Too much foliage and much too much sleep" (57). The island exceeds Jadine's Eurocentric standards of beauty, and she cannot value it. Like Valerian, Jadine seems unable to appreciate nature unless it has been artificially cultivated. Out on a drive with Son, Jadine confronts what she feels is "the ugly part of Isle des Chevaliers—the part she averted her eyes from whenever she drove past" (155). Despite her dismissal, the landscape has other plans for her. Walking toward the trees, she discovers that "the trees were not as close together as she'd thought" (156). Stepping into the forest,

> she almost laughed at what she saw. Young trees ringed and soared above the wavy mossy floor. There was hardly any color; just greens and browns because there was hardly any light and what light there was—a sentimental shaft of sunlight to the left—bunched the brown into deeper shadow. In the center under a roof of green was a lawn of the same dark green the Dutchmen loved to use. . . . Jadine tucked her [drawing] pad under her arm and clenched the charcoal stick. It was amazing; the place looked like something by Bruce White or Fazetta—an elegant comic book illustration. (156)

In this scene Jadine reads the forests through the European-trained eyes of an art historian, for whom this landscape is a "sentimental" and "comic" illustration. But Morrison challenges Jadine's assumptions when she literally has the floor drop out from under them: "The lawn, the center of the place began only a couple of yards ahead. She walked toward it and sank up to her knees" (156). The landscape, Jadine discovers, is not an art illustration; instead, it is almost alive: "The women hanging from the trees were quiet now, but arrogant—mindful as they were of their value, their exceptional femaleness" (157). Here, as throughout *Tar Baby,* Morrison animates the landscape, personifying it, filling it with magical properties.[21] In this "magic realism," art and life, beauty and ugliness, are not mutually exclusive categories and are, in fact, intermixed.[22] Jadine's "desperate struggle . . . to be free" of the swampy forest (157) enacts the struggle that is the black female subject's negotiation of aesthetics.

The novel's final aesthetic is summarized when Morrison writes,

> At some point in life the world's beauty becomes enough. You don't need to photograph, paint or even remember it. It is enough. . . . A dead hydrangea is as intricate and lovely as one in bloom. Bleak sky is as seductive as sunshine, miniature orange trees without blossom or fruit are not defective; they are that. So the windows of the greenhouse can be opened and the weather let in. The latch on the door can be left unhooked, the muslin removed, for the soldier ants are beautiful too. (208)

Morrison here affirms an inclusive aesthetic grounded in the beauty of the natural world—things as they are.[23] Morrison rejects the view that art must be separated from life, that one must "photograph" or "paint" nature for it to be transformed into art. Furthermore, she dismisses the binary categorization of nature into the beautiful and the ugly, intermixing the two by allowing the soldier ants into the greenhouse.

While the aesthetics imposed on the island have been re-figured, as Jadine leaves the island her own struggle remains incomplete. The island has not resolved her conflicts. She "would go back to Paris and begin at Go. Let loose the dogs, tangle with the woman in yellow" (250). According to idealist readings, Shakespeare's island paradise offers an artificial realm to restore an order that the characters then take back to society, but Morrison's island functions as a touchstone for interrogating various cultural orders. Jadine is going back to Europe but not necessarily capitulating to it; the island has begun a process in her. That Jadine does not return to society with a new vision of order reflects Morrison's skepticism toward the easy answers order provides. Furthermore, the open-endedness of Jadine's story suggests the necessity for a dialogue between the island and society. Some interpretations suggest that Shakespeare's ideal order is spawned by Prospero's isolation; Morrison's realistic disorder functions in a call-response relationship with the society it reflects.[24] At the end of *Tar Baby,* Jadine has heard the call and, in her European context, will shape her response.

Jadine's resolve to interrogate her own assumptions is followed by Morrison's allegory of *The Tempest,* re-figured from the perspective of the queen of the soldier ants (250–51). In the figure of the ant queen, Morrison presents a female Prospero, heiress to "some four-million-year-old magic," who, "just before a summer storm [a tempest?]," remembers the moment she "trembled in the air waiting for a male to mount her"

(250). This "one, first and last copulation" is central for two reasons: one, it enables her, during a self-imposed exile "from all society," to produce all the necessary larvae "to build her kingdom"; two, it provides her with her one transcendent dream (251). Morrison writes,

> No time for dreaming, although sometimes, late in life . . . she might get wind of a summer storm one day. The scent of it will invade her palace and she will recall the rush of wind on her belly—the stretch of fresh wings, the blinding anticipation and herself, there, airborne, suspended, open, trusting, frightened, determined, vulnerable—girlish, even, for an entire second and then another and another. She may lift her head then, and point her wands toward the place where the summer storm is entering her palace and in the weariness that ruling queens alone know, she may wonder whether his death was sudden. Or did he languish? And if so, if there was a bit of time left, did he think how mean the world was, or did he fill that space of time thinking of her? But soldier ants do not have time for dreaming. They are women and have much to do. Still it would be hard. So very hard to forget the man who fucked like a star. (251)

Despite the repeated insistence in the lines preceding this passage that the ants have "no time for dreaming" because "the work is literally endless," the queen of the soldier ants has her dream, the memory of which is prompted by the tempest (250). Morrison thus presents in this Prospero figure an aesthetic in which labor and art, nature and art, are not necessarily alienated. Furthermore, instead of art standing apart, holding a mirror to nature, the two are momentarily intertwined. *Tar Baby* as a whole has moved away from a standard of beauty and value in which the soldier ants are kept out of the greenhouse with muslin and mirrors (127), to a magic realism that intermixes nature and culture, art and life.

Interestingly, however much Morrison critiques the aesthetic assumptions underlying the old critical discourse surrounding *The Tempest,* she shares with Shakespeare a tone of farewell. Commonly, *The Tempest* has been read as Shakespeare's farewell to his art; when Prospero renounces his magic at the end of the play, traditional critics felt Shakespeare had done so too (Frye 1371). There is something of that farewell to artifice in Jadine's flight from the island and Morrison's allegory of the ant queen. Having critiqued Eurocentric aesthetics in the figure of Jadine, it is as if Morrison bids farewell to those issues as Jadine's plane takes off. Instead of following Jadine, the narrative turns to follow the daily lives of the soldier ants.

Tar Baby thus voices a shift in Morrison's oeuvre. *Beloved* and *Jazz* do not engage Eurocentric aesthetics to the same extent as *The Bluest Eye,*

Song of Solomon, or *Tar Baby.* Through the vehicle of *Tar Baby,* perhaps Morrison has bid a textual farewell to such standards of beauty and value in her fiction; her article "Unspeakable Things Unspoken" hands the reins over to the critics. This literary escape into the briar patch of magic realism suggests that perhaps for Morrison Eurocentric aesthetics was the tar baby.[25]

NOTES

1. Meredith Anne Skura, "Discourse and the Individual: The Case of Colonialism and *The Tempest,*" *Shakespeare Quarterly* 40 (Spring 1989): 42–69. Skura's article provides an excellent overview and analysis of the revisionist debate.

2. Thomas Cartelli, "Prospero in Africa: *The Tempest* as Colonialist Text and Pretext," in *Shakespeare Reproduced: The Text in History and Ideology,* ed. Jean E. Howard and Marion F. O'Connor (New York: Methuen, 1987), 99–115.

3. Toni Morrison, "Unspeakable Things Unspoken: The Afro-American Presence in American Literature," *Michigan Quarterly Review* 28 (Winter 1989): 1–34. Morrison extends and elaborates upon her critical agenda in *Playing in the Dark: Whiteness and the Literary Imagination* (Cambridge, Mass.: Harvard University Press, 1992), where she proposes a study of "American Africanism" (6). Unlike Afrocentric theories, which she cautions against as "totalizing" (8), her study investigates "the entire range of views, assumptions, readings, and misreadings that accompany Eurocentric learning about" African peoples (6).

4. Toni Morrison, *Tar Baby* (New York: Signet, 1981); and *The Tempest,* in *William Shakespeare: The Complete Works,* ed. Alfred Harbage (New York: The Viking Press, 1969), 1373–98.

5. See Phyllis R. Klotman, "Dick-and-Jane and the Shirley Temple Sensibility in *The Bluest Eye,*" *Black American Literature Forum* 13 (Winter 1979): 123–25, on Morrison's juxtaposition of the white fiction of the Dick-and-Jane reader to the reality of black children's lives.

6. See Gerry Brenner, "*Song of Solomon:* Morrison's Rejection of Rank's Monomyth and Feminism," *Studies in American Fiction* 15 (Spring 1987): 13–24, for Morrison's satiric use of the monomyth as a "universal" mythic pattern.

7. For a discussion of Morrison's use of the tar-baby folktale, see Barbara Christian, "Testing the Strength of the Black Cultural Bond: Review of Toni Morrison's *Tar Baby,*" in *Black Feminist Criticism* (Elmsford, N.Y.: Pergamon Press, 1985), 65–70; Robert G. O'Meally, "Tar Baby, She Don' Say Nothin'," *Callaloo* 1–3 (Feb.–Oct. 1981): 193–98; and Eleanor W. Traylor, "The Fabulous World of Toni Morrison: *Tar Baby,*" in *Confirmation: An Anthology of African American Women,* ed. Amiri and Amina Baraka (New York: Quill, 1983), 333–52.

8. Skura's article and the work she cites helped shape this summary.

9. Peter Hulme, *Colonial Encounters: Europe and the Native Caribbean, 1492–1797* (London: Methuen, 1986), 105.

10. Leo Marx, *The Machine in the Garden: Technology and the Pastoral Ideal in America* (London: Oxford University Press, 1964), 65.

11. Feminist criticism of *The Tempest* has emphasized the racism and sexism inherent in the hierarchical valuation of the characters. See Lorie Jerrell Leininger, "The Miranda Trap: Sexism and Racism in Shakespeare's *Tempest,*" in *The Woman's Part: Feminist Criticism of Shakespeare,* ed. Carolyn Ruth Swift Lenz, Gayle Greene, and Carol Thomas Neely (Urbana: University of Illinois Press, 1980), 285–94; and Gayle Greene, "Women on Trial in Shakespeare and Webster," in *The Elizabethan Woman,* special issue of *Topic* 36 (1982): 10–11.

12. See, for example, Northrop Frye's introduction to *The Tempest,* in which he asserts that Prospero "has done what his art can do; he has held the mirror up to nature" (*William Shakespeare: The Collected Works,* ed. Harbage, 1371).

13. Philip Brockbank, "*The Tempest:* Conventions of Art and Empire," in *Later Shakespeare* (New York: St. Martin's Press, 1967), 183–84.

14. Stephen Orgel, "Shakespeare and the Cannibals," in *Cannibals, Witches, and Divorce: Estranging the Renaissance,* ed. Marjorie Garber (Baltimore: Johns Hopkins University Press, 1987), 57.

15. Leslie Fiedler, *The Stranger in Shakespeare* (New York: Stein and Day, 1972), 248.

16. For an analysis of Morrison's revision of hegemonic standards of female beauty in *Tar Baby,* as well as *The Bluest Eye* and *Song of Solomon,* see Malin LaVon Walther, "Out of Sight: Toni Morrison's Revision of Beauty," *Black American Literature Forum* 24, no. 4 (Winter 1990): 775–90.

17. By Eurocentrism I mean the centralizing cultural discourse of Europe and America, as perceived by peoples of "other" cultural frames, such as the colonized. Whether or not there exist verifiable characteristics of Eurocentrism, such as oppositionalism or false universalism, is still under debate. Yet Eurocentrism functions as a perceived reality in African-American discourse, signifying the hegemony of European culture in American life and the consequent marginalization of African Americans. See Molefi Kete Asante, *The Afrocentric Idea* (Philadelphia: Temple University Press, 1987), 3–16; and Patricia Hill Collins, *Black Feminist Thought: Knowledge, Consciousness, and the Politics of Empowerment* (Boston: Unwin Hyman, 1990), 70.

18. Evelyn Hawthorne, "On Gaining the Double-Vision: *Tar Baby* as Diasporean Novel," *Black American Literature Forum* 22, no. 1 (Spring 1988): 97–107, makes a different, yet related point about the politics of setting. She suggests that Morrison's use of the West Indies as a setting in *Tar Baby* allows a detached vantage point for observing Western culture in America.

19. See Marilyn E. Mobley, "Narrative Dilemma: Jadine as Cultural Orphan in Toni Morrison's *Tar Baby,*" *The Southern Review* 23 (October 1987): 761–70, for a discussion of Jadine's refusal of her cultural past.

20. Lauren Lepow, "Paradise Lost and Found: Dualism and Edenic Myth in Toni Morrison's *Tar Baby,*" *Contemporary Literature* 28, no. 3 (Fall 1987): 363–77. Lepow discusses dualism as symptomatic of a Christian worldview which Morrison critiques.

21. The landscape of *The Tempest,* too, is magical; however, Morrison critiques Prospero's control of it, paralleling Leslie Fiedler's characterization of how "Prospero thinks of his island kingdom as a place to be subdued, hewed, trimmed, and ordered. . . . But Caliban remembers a world of unprofaned magic, a living nature" (235–36). Like other African-American writers, Morrison takes Caliban's view.

22. For a discussion of Morrison's use of "magic realism," see Sanford Pinsker, "Magic Realism, Historical Truth, and the Quest for a Liberating Identity: Reflections on Alex Haley's *Roots* and Toni Morrison's *Song of Solomon,*" *Studies in Black American Literature* 1 (1984): 183–97; and Craig Werner, "Homer's Joyce: John Updike, Ronald Sukenick, Robert Coover, Toni Morrison," in *Paradoxical Resolutions: American Fiction Since James Joyce* (Urbana: University of Illinois Press, 1982), 68–96. For a particularly harsh critique of Morrison's use of "magic realism" as compared to that of Marquez, see Martha Bayles, "Special Effects, Special Pleading," *The New Criterion* 6, no. 5 (Jan. 1988): 34–40.

23. Morrison obliquely articulates these aesthetic principles in two essays: "What the Black Woman Thinks About Women's Lib," *New York Times Magazine,* 22 Aug. 1971: 14–15, 63–66; and "Behind the Making of the *Black Book,*" *Black World,* Feb. 1974: 86–90. For an analysis of how the aesthetics of art by women of color offer a "deaesthetic" sorely needed in the feminist project of reconceiving aesthetics and formal knowledge, see Teresa de Lauretis, *Technologies of Gender: Essays on Theory, Film, and Fiction* (Bloomington: Indiana University Press, 1987).

24. I am indebted to Craig Werner for pointing out this call-response parallel. His essay, "The Briar Patch as Modernist Myth: Morrison, Barthes and *Tar Baby* As-Is," in *Critical Essays on Toni Morrison,* ed. Nellie McKay (Boston: G. K. Hall & Co., 1988), 150–67, offers a powerful analysis of Morrison's apprehension of myth as a tool of Euro-American power and a reservoir of historical knowledge capable of resisting that power.

25. Earlier versions of this essay received helpful readings from Craig Werner, Standish Henning, Marianne Novy, and several anonymous readers.

VALERIE TRAUB

Rainbows of Darkness:
Deconstructing Shakespeare in the Work of
Gloria Naylor and Zora Neale Hurston

This essay was conceived in a moment of intellectual distress. While presenting a feminist analysis of Zora Neale Hurston's short story "Spunk," I was interrupted by a male colleague. How had I failed to notice, he asked, that the allusion in the story to "funeral baked meats" obviously referred to the moment in *Hamlet* when the young prince shares with Horatio his anguish over Gertrude's marriage? Couldn't I see that by means of this allusion, "Spunk" reproduces the patriarchal bias of Shakespeare's tragedy?

This interaction rankled. Not merely as an uncomfortable instance of more-feminist-than-thou-ness, but more importantly as a question of intertextuality. Is to invoke Shakespearean drama always to reproduce Shakespearean ideology? Is the ideology of Shakespearean texts so self-evident as to admit no room for alternative response, interpretative negotiation? Is the cultural power of the bard so absolute as to obviate all revision, all subversion? To my mind, my interrogator's interpretation too quickly closed the gap between the Harlem and English "Renaissances"[1] by erasing the possibility of African-American intervention in an over-determined cultural field.

My essay attempts to redress that erasure by using Gloria Naylor's revision of Shakespeare in her 1988 novel *Mama Day* as a test case by which to explore the particular exigencies within which African-American cultural expression occurs. The case of Shakespeare palpably raises the question: how do African-American authors negotiate the plots, conventions, and politics of Anglo-European cultural traditions? I use the term "intertextuality" rather than "influence" to imply that there is far more at stake in Naylor's relationship to Shakespeare than a mapping of "sources."[2] Because Shakespearean drama holds pride of place within the dominant cultural field and is enlisted consistently by politicians, advertisers, and academics for the promotion and defense of Anglo-European standards of aesthetic value, African-American writers' responses to Shakespeare would seem to be paradigmatic of the larger issue of the intertextuality of *cultures*.[3] Insofar as "Shakespeare" remains in both popular and academic circles the aesthetic yardstick—I would, following Marjorie Garber, say, the "fetish"[4]—against which cultural production is measured, the institutional, regulative function of Shakespeare's name summons up the problematic of what I have come to call the cultural paradox of Caliban's curse.

Caliban's speech to Prospero, "You taught me language, and my profit on't / Is, I know how to curse. The red-plague rid you / For learning me your language!" (*Tempest* 1.2.365–67), has figured prominently in recent African-American and early modern literary criticism.[5] Caliban's yoking of the ambivalent powers of language—the constraints and possibilities it affords to speaking subjects positioned within a symbolic order permeated with racial, gender, and class hierarchies—seems to articulate rather handily the position of African-American writers working in relation to Anglo-American traditions. If the question facing African-American writers is how, in the words of Henry Louis Gates, Jr., to "posit a full and sufficient self in a language in which blackness is a sign of absence,"[6] then the question facing black women writers is doubly problematic: how to negotiate a relationship to an Anglo-European language and tradition that doubly defines them as absence and lack—as black and as women.

Houston Baker describes one possible response to this problematic as the "deformation of mastery," by which he means a strategy for self-representation in a hostile structural field, wherein texts of the dominant culture are read and *re*read, invoked and reworked to undermine their pretensions to universality and transcendence.[7] Repetition for the purpose of undoing, or "repetition/mimicry and difference," to use the phrase suggested to me by Jyotsna Singh's analysis of Indian appropriations of Shakespeare, becomes a crucial critical strategy.[8] Indeed, Baker figures this strategy within the terms provided by *The Tempest*: "The Afro-American spokesperson who would perform a deformation of mastery shares the task of Sycorax's son insofar as he or she must transform an obscene situation . . . into a signal self/cultural expression."[9]

Baker's notion of the deformation of mastery derives from a powerful African-American tradition of "speaking in tongues," of voicing on multiple registers at once in order to negotiate between a dual heritage of enslavement and resistance. In linguistic terms, this dual heritage asserts the necessity of drawing on the black idiom or vernacular and Anglo-European signifying traditions to create a "two-toned" or "double-voiced" expressive culture.[10] Such doubling has functioned historically as a means of preserving psychic and cultural health: while posing as a compliant "minstrel" story or song for the dominant culture, expressive traditions have employed a complex system of codes to relay aesthetic and political messages throughout African-American communities.

Within this context, African-American women writers' return to Shakespearean drama is hardly surprising, for what more obviously statusstudded example of Anglo-European patriarchal culture exists to "signify" or "trope" upon? I will first briefly discuss the way in which Hurston's short story "Spunk" rewrites, by means of a few words, Gertrude's marriage to Hamlet's uncle, transforming an action that in Hamlet's mind is equated with adultery and incest into the personal prerogative of any woman who finds herself defined as an object of property. I will then turn in considerably more detail to Gloria Naylor's complex, ambivalent relationship to Shakespeare, and her attempt in *Mama Day* to voice African-American subjectivities within the problematic described and enacted by Caliban.

"Thass mah house," Lena speaks up. "Papa gimme that."
"Well," says Spunk, "doan give up whut's yours, but when youse inside don't forgit youse mine, an' let no other man git outa his place wid you!"(107)[11]

"Spunk" depicts a struggle among men over "woman-as-property" that continues even after the men's deaths. "Cuckolded" and eventually killed by his wife's lover, Joe returns from the grave for revenge: he pushes his usurper, Spunk, into the blades of a massive saw at the community lumber mill. Yet, inserted within this narrative, working *within* the logic of patriarchal discourse to subvert it, is an unnamed force, conjured up in the final sentences of the story: "The women ate heartily of the funeral baked meats and wondered who would be Lena's next. The men whispered coarse conjectures between guzzles of whiskey" (111). Women heartily consuming funeral baked meats—meats prepared in remembrance of the dismembered Spunk—extends Lena's individual erotic power to a community of women: they too are metaphorically figured as powerfully devouring erotic agents.

In this light, Lena's earlier assertion of property rights, "thass mah house"—although immediately assimilated by Spunk into his own logic of patriarchal possession ("when youse inside don't forgit youse mine")— *prefigures* the subversion of the meaning of property and possession by precisely the female erotic power that such symbolic enclosures are meant to contain. Having moved in to Spunk's house after Joe's death, Lena is, at Spunk's death, possessed of house and of herself as sexual subject. The trajectory of erotic power within the narrative transforms Lena from male-possessed object to self-possessed subject. By the end of the story, the meaning of the title "Spunk" has been transferred and transfigured from male patronymic to Lena's "spunky" assertion of erotic power.

The sly reference in "Spunk" to funeral baked meats echoes Hamlet's cynical retort to Horatio's admission that the queen's marriage "followed hard upon" the king's funeral: "Thrift, thrift, Horatio! The funeral bak'd meats / Did coldly furnish forth the marriage tables" (*Hamlet* 1.2.80–81). Why does "Spunk" invoke, through this reference, Shakespeare's play? To call attention, I would argue, to its implicit revision of *Hamlet*'s vilification of female desire. Gertrude's "adulterous" marriage becomes newly figured as an exchange fatal to any man who treats woman as his object of property. As in *Hamlet,* the men in *Spunk* violently destroy each other, with women's bodies serving as the psychic battleground upon which masculine subjectivity asserts itself or founders; but unlike Gertrude or Ophelia (the woman upon whom Hamlet's anxieties about his mother are projected), Lena is not positioned as the sacrificial victim to male heroism— instead, possessed of self and property, a heroic figure in her own right, she moves on. Even as the men seek to contain Lena's "predatory" sexuality between their "guzzles of whiskey," it has, by means of their "coarse conjectures" and the women's silent musings, already slipped off the page. Already presumed to be elsewhere, Lena's erotic agency is in excess of what can be said or contained within a patriarchal frame.

If "Spunk" 's intertextual debt to *Hamlet* is limited to a few well-chosen words, and if Hurston's revisionary relation to Shakespeare's text is unequivocal, Naylor's *Mama Day* ranges over the Shakespearean canon and embodies a far greater tension between adulatory and deconstructive impulses.[12] Naylor's project of repetition/mimicry/difference is marked by contradiction. At times, *Mama Day* would seem to celebrate "Shakespearean humanism," as two of the main characters engage in a putatively transhistorical process of reading Shakespearean character through their own psychic identifications. This popular reading practice, in which aesthetic pleasure and value depend on the reader's feeling of access into the "emotional reality" and "lived experience" of dramatic character, assumes and reproduces the universal pretensions of Shakespeare's exploration of "human nature." Whereas there may be some radical import to having black characters lay claim to the experience of Lear, Hamlet, or Juliet, this subversiveness is moderated by the extent to which it takes place within, and reproduces, the terms and logic of bardolatry.

This impulse toward universalization, however, is contested by the novel's investment in revising the patriarchal and racist ideologies that often inform Shakespeare's plays. If Naylor's *characters* uphold *King Lear* as proof of a transcendent human nature, the novel itself employs *The Tempest* to assert the irreducible fact of historical and political difference. Although no character based on Caliban animates *Mama Day,* the entire novel enacts the *desire* of Caliban who, in the words of Baker, "would have the isle wisely pre-Prosperian, revising or deforming the contraries of Western civilization in order to return to a 'natural' signification. Such a world would witness Caliban not as a student of 'culture as a foreign language' (CFL, as it were), but rather as an instructor in a first voice, resonant with 'a thousand twangling instruments' *in* nature."[13]

Naylor's novel needs no cursing Caliban, for the natural world of Willow Springs (contrasted throughout to New York City) invokes and instructs us in a "first voice," a voice replete with magical significations, a voice speaking not only the horrors of slavery but the powers of resistance. The deliberate erasure of Caliban may have to do, as well, with the decreasing attraction of the specifically *male* nationalism he has come to figure, a male self-assertion that can coexist comfortably with sexism and even rape.[14] Indeed, in his analysis of African and Caribbean appropriations of the play, Rob Nixon spells out "the difficulty of wresting from [*The Tempest*] any role for female defiance or leadership in a period when protest is coming increasingly from that quarter. Given that Caliban is without a female counterpart in his oppression and rebellion, and given the largely autobiographical cast of African and Caribbean appropriations of the play, it follows that all the writers who quarried from *The Tempest* an expression of their lot should have been men."[15] In Naylor's work, the tension between feminist and anticolonialist politics inhering in Caliban's figure is elided in favor of a matriarchal, female-centered, postcolonial scene.

Like many other novels by African-American women, *Mama Day* is a narrative of return.[16] A return for Ophelia to Willow Springs, the all-black island of her birth and upbringing before going "mainland" to college and New York City. A return for George, an orphan-turned-engineer, to a place of (black) magic he never dreamed existed. A return to an island just off the Atlantic coast, halfway between South Carolina and Georgia—claimed by neither state and thus legally "nowhere." Linked to the mainland only by a bridge that periodically blows down during hurricanes, Willow Springs deliberately invites associations with other isolated isles inhabited by conjurers, where dramas of reconciliation and redemption are ambivalently orchestrated.[17]

In contrast to *The Tempest*'s implicit colonialist intertext, however, in Willow Springs, colonialism and slavery were extradited in 1823 when "real history" began: the slave woman Sapphira (Ophelia's great-great-

great-grandmother) walked away from the white slave-owner Bascombe Wade, but only *after* she conjured him to deed all of his lands to his slaves, and only *after* she had smothered, stabbed, or poisoned him—no one knows quite which. Sapphira not only invokes but newly configures Caliban's mother, Sycorax, the original mother and conjurer of the uncharted island usurped by Prospero.

Contrary to the effaced prehistory of Sycorax's island, the prehistory of Willow Springs is intact, if ambiguously heterogenous, in the minds and mouths of the people who live there, where the conjure woman, now in the living form of Sapphira's great-grandaughter Miranda, still practices the hereditary healing arts.[18] The displacement of the usurping patriarchal magician and slaveholder, Prospero, by Sapphira's lineage of maternal conjurers reasserts the creative properties of the island: in these women's hands, magic does not wreak vengeance but maintains and restores health.

In a world where names such as Grace, Peace, Hope, Buzzard, and Ambush (not to mention Matthew, Mark, Luke, Timothy, James, John, and John-Paul) hold signifying power, the names Miranda and Ophelia deliberately image forth a Shakespearean genealogy. As neither woman goes by her given name—Miranda is better known as Mama Day and Ophelia prefers Cocoa—the deliberate invocation of *and distancing from* Shakespearean characters registers an unsettling echo: will Naylor's characters reenact or reenvision the fates of Miranda and Ophelia? Insofar as the desire of Prospero's daughter is encoded as the desire of the father—her marriage to Ferdinand a part of Prospero's grand scheme to "benevolently" transfer patriarchal power through his daughter's body—and insofar as Ophelia's suicidal madness is born of the indifference of *Hamlet*'s plot to represent women as autonomously desiring subjects, both textual heritages can be claimed by women only with deep ambivalence.[19] Indeed, such ambivalence fractures male-female relationships in *Mama Day* precisely along the faultlines of revenge and betrayal.

The three epigraphs to the novel—a bill of sale for Sapphira to Bascombe Wade; Sapphira's flourishing family tree of descendents; and the pseudo-biblical phrase, " 'God rested on the seventh day and so would she.' Hence, the family's last name"—position the branching of the family of Days as an antidote to and exorcism of that initial sale of human flesh as property. Not that the post-slave history of the Days on this island of "nowhere" is exactly utopian; indeed, the very name Ophelia carries with it a history of male betrayal and female vengeance. Ophelia's mother, Grace, named her daughter out of spite, reaching back two generations to repersonify the name of her own abandoned yet powerful grandmother. Here, Ophelia imagines/hears her mother, Grace, speaking: "I gave the first and only baby my grandmother's name. Ophelia. I did it out of vengeance. Let this be another one, I told God, who could break a man's heart. Didn't women suffer enough? Eight months heavy with his child and he went off to chase horizons. I hoped he'd find them in hell. If I had known then what I was knowing all along, I woulda named her something else. Sapphira. My grandmother [Ophelia] only softly broke a heart. My great-great-grandmother [Sapphira] tore one wide open" (151).

Significantly, only George prefers Ophelia's Shakespearean name; he naively calls it "a lyrical name, pleasant to say because my tongue had to caress the roof of my mouth to get it out" (63). Her own preference for the "pet name" Cocoa (which was given to her to "put color on her somewhere" [39–40]) signals a desire to move beyond Shakespeare's plot of female victimization and, within the novel, Cocoa and her relatives' desire to escape her own bitter family history. Indeed, *Mama Day* details the attempt to redeem this troubled past through the "new day" marriage of Cocoa and George. The attempt fails. George, the Ferdinand-figure who arrives on the island for maternal (rather than paternal) blessing, falters in his appointed "tasks." Orphaned from his spiritual ancestry, he shirks from performing the acts of faith—more meaningless to him than Ferdinand's repetitious bearing of wood—demanded of him by the island's heritage. Part of that heritage is the danger represented by Ruby, an inverted Prospero figure who, out of foolish jealousy of Cocoa, attempts to kill her by magical means. The show-down between the two conjurers' opposed uses of the island's natural properties eventually draws in George, whose reliance on Western empirical resistance to the supernatural comes to figure the final conflict of the novel.

As we are reminded countless times, George has an "injured heart," and his inability to perform the labors deemed necessary to save Cocoa stem from this symbolic congenital defect—a possible reenactment of Hamlet's fatal flaw, the "stamp of one defect" that, in the dominant reading of Shakespeare's play, is presumed to lead to indecision and a vacillating will.[20] If Cocoa's female ancestors routinely broke men's hearts, George's heart is faulty from birth, and it finally explodes when placed under the stress of conflicting conceptual, emotional, and spiritual paradigms. Yet, despite George's sacrificial death, Cocoa and Mama Day retain the hope of *The Tempest*'s Miranda who exclaims: "O wonder! / How many goodly creatures are there here! / How beauteous mankind is! O brave new world, / That has such people in 't!" (5.1.183–86). Prospero's cynical retort, " 'Tis new to thee," has no place on this postcolonial island; death does not foreclose the wonder of those who see in each coming generation a "brave new world."

Whereas *The Tempest*'s Miranda is isolated from women—"I do not know / One of my sex; no woman's face remember" (3.1.49–50)–Naylor's Miranda becomes the head of a female family and community, the name displaced generationally upward from the adolescent on the brink of marriage to the wise woman pushing one hundred. Miranda's chosen name, Mama Day, implies the maternal act of creation as each new day is gloriously or painfully brought forth—just as Ophelia's "crib name" of Baby Girl lays claim to Miranda's youthful innocence.

Shakespearean allusions are scattered throughout the novel. George describes his relationship to Cocoa as "star-crossed" (129) and compares the magical events on Willow Springs to those described in Prospero's "revels" speech—"No, this was the stuff of dreams" (258). Indeed, his penchant for Shakespearean references position him as arbiter of cultural taste. Here is how George puts it to himself during his first date with Cocoa: "You were Harold Robbins in general and James Michener when you wanted to get deep. I hadn't read any fiction more recent than Ernest Hemingway and Ralph Ellison, remembering with a sinking heart the worn copy of *King Lear* I could have been spending my evening with. . . . I'd gone through *Lear* uncountable times. It had a special poignancy for me, reading about the rage of a bastard son, my own father having disappeared long before I was born" (60, 106).

The special poignancy George feels for Edmund is a symptom of his reading strategy: he searches for those characters who, despite historical, social, and racial differences, represent his own experience. Refocusing the play on the character who is not only a bastard, but also marginalized by the reigning political hierarchy, George places himself at the center of the fictional world. Such readerly identification, of course, is one of the primary pleasures of the text; without such pleasures, it is questionable whether many people would read at all. It is also, as in George's case (and, as I shall show, in Cocoa's case as well), a primary method of access into alternative, even subversive, interpretations. Yet the belief that characters act as real people can be misleading. Reading through identification does not, for instance, encourage George to interrogate how Edmund's "villainy" is constructed and naturalized by virtue of his bastardy; it does not push him to question what "stars" might be "crossing" his marriage to Cocoa, a question that might lead him directly into a new (black) spiritual universe. Perhaps because George's fixation on Edmund reminds me of my father's use of *King Lear* to school his three daughters in proper filial obedience— citing "How sharper than a serpent's tooth it is / to have a thankless child!" (1.4.285–86)–I suspect that reading-as-identification can often lead to ideological mystification, or, more precisely, mimetic *mis*identification. And, if the conclusion of the novel is any indication, it is precisely George and Cocoa's tendency to read themselves into Shakespearean plots—specifically those narratives of victimization, betrayal, and disintegration represented by *Hamlet* and *Lear*—that results in *Mama Day*'s tragic outcome of misunderstanding, death, and loss.

Mimetic misidentification continues in the fact that *King Lear*—a play obsessed with the disintegration of filial ties—acts as an index of Cocoa and George's evolving relationship, as they eventually move toward a love affair and marriage. After having made the decision never to see Cocoa again, George changes his mind when she unexpectedly pulls out a copy of *King Lear*. Their first communal reading of the play is also their first seduction, after which George says,

> It came as a shock when you opened up and told me that you cried when you first read through the play. It seemed that although your parents were married, your father had taken off before you were born, too. And you were so glad I'd turned you on to this. It showed you how hard the playwright tried to convey that men had the same feelings as women. No, that was not true. No way. Along with *The Taming of the Shrew,* this had to be Shakespeare's most sexist treatment of women—but far be it from me to contradict anything you had to say. (106)

The implied if unspoken dialogue between George and Cocoa regarding Shakespeare's "treatment of women" gestures toward feminist debates over the (im)possibility of a "feminist Shakespeare." George's position—that despite whatever feminine values the play instances (in, for example, Lear's admission that he too possesses feelings he deems appropriate only to women), the representation of women is still "sexist"—is narratively privileged; we aren't offered access to Cocoa's possible rejoinder. Yet, despite their different readings of the gender politics of the play, Cocoa joins George in reading-as-identification, as her familial past is made palpably present—and shareable—through the representation of Edmund's bastardy. Indeed, Cocoa joins George and "Edmund" in a collectivity of father-deserted children; their mutual identification with the Shakespearean bastard dissolves their personal differences, and a unified aesthetic response literally leads to sexual union.

Yet before George "turned her on" to Shakespeare (the erotic metaphor is significant insofar as reading and sexuality become homologous), the poet was for Cocoa a resented icon of "high culture" that excludes her black presence. Whereas Cocoa's past response was a reaction against her *lack* of identification with Shakespeare's drama—a lack now replayed as a misinterpretation based on unfamiliarity—Naylor's response is more complex, for Cocoa's meditation on Shakespeare marks the moment when Naylor most successfully subverts the bard's authorizing presence.

When George asks Cocoa to go out with him again after the end of a truly rotten evening together, her response is

Surely, he jests. I swear, that's the first thing that popped into my head when you asked me out again. I don't know where that phrase came from—had to be something from my high school Shakespeare and you had been going on and on about him earlier in the evening. Just proves that Shakespeare didn't have a bit of soul—I don't care if he did write about Othello, Cleopatra, and some slave on a Caribbean island. If he had been in touch with our culture, he would have written somewhere, "Nigger, are you out of your mind?" Because that's what I really meant to think. (64)

The fact that the phrase, "Surely, he jests" is *not* something from her "high school Shakespeare," that *The Complete Concordance to Shakespeare* lists 115 references to *jest* (not to mention *jested, jester,* and *jesting*) without identifying this quotation, that this phrase *sounds* like Shakespeare but apparently was not *penned* by Shakespeare (or even by what some critics might call the author-function of Shakespeare), registers simultaneously how omnipresent *and how dispersed* a figure of cultural authority "Shakespeare" has become.[21] Both George and Cocoa "think through" Shakespearean texts, but whereas George thinks through a fiction, Cocoa thinks through a fiction of a fiction. Through this displacement of origin and authorship, the reader is encouraged to recognize Cocoa's "Shakespeare" as a fetish—that is, as a stand-in for an irrecoverably lost object of cultural desire.

At the same time, however, Cocoa's interpretative stance potentially de-fetishizes Shakespeare, toppling the icon from his pedestal, as her misattribution inadvertently refigures the Shakespearean corpus. It is here that Cocoa's reading-as-identification takes a subtly subversive turn. Just as George re-centers *Lear* on the bastard son rather than the misused father, Cocoa deftly (if not quite consciously) rewrites the significations of Othello, Cleopatra, and Caliban. All three are unified, in Cocoa's mind, as black: the moor, the Egyptian queen, the slave. By reading through *her* identifications, she creates a black community of Shakespearean characters, transforming the way they are traditionally viewed as isolated, anomalous, and, in Caliban's case, peripheral. Her interpretative gesture enacts a strategy of reading across plays, across genre, with an eye toward transcultural connection, on the basis of a shared history of conflictual relations to white Western cultures. In addition, her community-building harbors within it the implicit gesture of specifying and differentiating the diverse histories of Moors, Egyptians, and Africans; soldiers, queens, and slaves.

Reading-through-identification, then, can either uphold conventional interpretations or subvert aesthetic and political constraints. The significant difference between Cocoa and George is less their reading *strategies* than the *effects* their readings occasion. In the novel and in the world at this time, blackness has a political existence as a basis for oppression, resistance, and community in a way that being a father-rejected child does not. In the end, George's internalization of Shakespearean roles is rejected by the text; his reading strategy doesn't provide him with the materials which would enable him to read *differently*—that is, to read outside of his victimization as a bastard and *inside* the world of Willow Springs where individual agency, with the help of the natural world, can give birth to *new* narratives. It is precisely Cocoa's ability to connect different cultures— Willow Springs and the mainland, city and country, supernatural belief and empiricist disbelief, Shakespeare and African-American traditions— that ensures her survival.

Cocoa's ability to forge cultural connections through a refusal of strict and mutually exclusive polarities is reminiscent of the interpretative strategy enacted by Toni Morrison's Pilate, who in *Song of Solomon* teaches her nephew, Milkman:

> You think dark is just one color, but it ain't. There're five or six kinds of black. Some silky, some woolly. Some just empty. Some like fingers. And it don't stay still. It moves and changes from one kind of black to another. Saying something is pitch black is like saying something is green. What kind of green? Green like my bottles? Green like a grasshopper? Green like a cucumber, lettuce, or green like the sky is just before it breaks loose to storm? Well, night black is the same way. May as well be a rainbow.[22]

To read Shakespeare through the eyes of Pilate is not only to refuse the totalization of "black" as a single, ontological category, but also to recognize "black" itself as a constitutive fantasy, a projection, of white Western minds. To read Shakespeare through the eyes of Cocoa is to see the spiritual and political connectedness *and* the cultural differences of much of the world's "black" population. Consciously or unconsciously, Pilate and Cocoa together momentarily shatter Western fantasies; through their collective vision, the alleged void of blackness is transmogrified into that paradoxical presence of a rainbow of darkness. If Shakespearean drama names and fixes "black" characters from the outside, *Mama Day* reconstitutes them in the name of a diverse African-American subjectivity. In *Mama Day,* every character has many names, drawn from both Anglo- and African-American heritages; each name carries its own history, and their stories are always in the process of being told. There is, as Cocoa finally says, "just too many sides to the whole story" for one story to tell them all (311).

If we put Cocoa's criticism of Shakespeare's lack of "soul" in the context of Baker's suggestion that a cultural education in "soul" is the essential requirement for the critic of African-American expressive culture, perhaps we will think more critically about Shakespeare's possible "lack" and explore more thoroughly than I have done here the possibilities of reading Shakespeare from a "soulful" perspective.[23] The way Cocoa frames her criticism—"If he had been in touch with our culture, he would have written somewhere, 'Nigger, are you out of your mind?' "—usefully reminds us that Anglo-Americans *can* all be "in touch" with African cultural heritages if we make the necessary efforts. That does not mean that everyone will speak the same language—indeed, Cocoa's word "nigger" signifies rather differently depending on who is saying it and in what tone—but we can all labor to hear the differences in nuance, tone, and meaning that various cultural traditions work upon our common inheritance of the English tongue. For it is precisely the gap between "Surely, he jests" and "Nigger, are you out of your mind?" that constitutes a fecund space of new cultural expression grounded in intercultural tensions and dialogue.

It is by virtue of our different relationships to "soul" that we are all "raced"—not only positioned in terms of privilege and power by virtue of our putative skin color, but inheritors of complex, different cultural heritages. Such differences are not only oppressive but fertile as well; not merely tragic in the effects of systematic inequalities in the distribution of goods, jobs, services, and opportunities, but also comedic in the Shakespearean sense of spawning imaginative visions of social reconstitution and regeneration.

If Shakespearean plots, characters, and language provide Naylor with a productive aesthetic framework which she then stretches and molds to her own design, it is not only Shakespeare who is transfigured, but all of those readers who thereafter use her Shakespeare as a lens from which to re-read their own. For, as much as Naylor's characters posit a transhistorical reading strategy (represented by their reading of *King Lear*) that occludes even as it inserts racial difference, the novel's overall project (represented by the structural and thematic revision of *The Tempest*) is to educate us in reading for a diversity of historical and racial pasts. The structural ambivalence with which Naylor relates to the Shakespearean repertoire—the mixture of admiration and resentment her novel reveals—maps the outlines of one possible strategy for negotiating the field of white Western aesthetic production. Each subsequent work that enters the Anglo-African intertext will no doubt follow its own compass. But I would suggest that we are drawn to deconstruct only that which also speaks *to* us—but with a difference.

NOTES

1. I put quotation marks around "Renaissance" in order to call into question its status as a unified phenomenon, transcending rank, gender, and racial lines.

2. For a useful introduction to the history and use of the concept of inter-textuality, see Jay Clayton and Eric Rothstein, "Figures in the Corpus: Theories of Influence and Intertextuality," in *Influence and Intertextuality in Literary History,* ed. Jay Clayton and Eric Rothstein (Madison: University of Wisconsin Press, 1991), 3–36.

3. Two recent books that address Shakespeare's status in Anglo-American culture are Michael Bristol, *Shakespeare's America, America's Shakespeare* (New York: Routledge, 1990), and Gary Taylor, *Reinventing Shakespeare: A Cultural History from the Restoration to the Present* (New York: Oxford University Press, 1989). For two particularly astute analyses of the use of canonized authors, including Shakespeare, in the discourse of the law, see Mark Schoenfield, "Deposing Literature: Robert Bork, Richard Posner, and the Uses of the Literary Canon," talk given at the American Studies Association Conference, Nov. 7, 1992, Costa Mesa, Calif.; and Patricia Williams, *The Alchemy of Race and Rights* (Cambridge: Harvard University Press, 1991), 80–97.

4. See Marjorie Garber, "Shakespeare as Fetish," *Shakespeare Quarterly* 41, no. 2 (Summer 1990): 242–50. See also Garber's *Shakespeare's Ghost Writers: Literature as Uncanny Causality* (New York: Methuen, 1987).

5. All references to Shakespeare are from *The Complete Works of Shakespeare,* 3d ed., ed. David Bevington (Glenview: Scott, Foresman, & Co., 1980) and hereafter cited parenthetically in the text. For criticism focusing on Caliban and the discourse of colonialism see, in particular, Paul Brown, " 'This thing of darkness I acknowledge mine': *The Tempest* and the Discourse of Colonialism," in *Political Shakespeare,* ed. Jonathan Dollimore and Alan Sinfield (Manchester: Manchester University Press, 1985), 48–71; Francis Barker and Peter Hulme, "Nymphs and Reapers Heavily Vanish: The Discursive Con-texts of *The Tempest,*" in *Alternative Shakespeares,* ed. John Drakakis (London: Methuen, 1985), 191–205; Stephen Greenblatt, "Learning to Curse: Aspects of Linguistic Colonialism in the Sixteenth Century," in his *Learning to Curse: Essays in Early Modern Culture* (New York: Routledge, 1990), 16–39; and Meredith Anne Skura, "Discourse and the Individual: The Case of Colonialism in *The Tempest,*" *Shakespeare Quarterly* 40, no. 1 (Spring 1989): 42–69. For a review of British, French, and West Indian responses to Caliban, see Chantal Zabus, "A Calibanic Tempest in Anglophone and Francophone New World Writing," *Canadian Literature* 104 (Spring 1985): 35–50. For African-American appropriations, see Rob Nixon, "Caribbean and African Appropriations of *The Tempest,*" *Critical Inquiry* 13 (Spring 1987): 557–78; George Lamming, *The Pleasures of Exile* (London: Allison and Busby,

1984); and Houston Baker, "Caliban's Triple Play," *Critical Inquiry* 13 (Autumn 1986): 182–96.

6. Henry Louis Gates, Jr., "Editor's Introduction: Writing 'Race' and the Difference it Makes," *Critical Inquiry* 12 (Autumn 1985): 12.

7. Baker, "Caliban's Triple Play," 190.

8. Jyotsna Singh, "Different Shakespeares: The Bard in Colonial/Postcolonial India," *Theatre Journal* 41, no. 4 (Dec. 1989): 445–58.

9. Baker, "Caliban's Triple Play," 194.

10. See Houston Baker, *Blues, Ideology, and Afro-American Literature: A Vernacular Theory* (Chicago: University of Chicago Press, 1984), and Henry Louis Gates, Jr., "Criticism in the Jungle," in *Black Literature and Literary Theory*, ed. Gates (London: Methuen, 1984), 3.

11. Zora Neale Hurston, "Spunk," in *The New Negro*, ed. Alain Locke (New York: Atheneum, 1986), 105–11. "Spunk" was awarded second prize in the 1925 *Opportunity* competition.

12. I have benefitted greatly from Peter Erickson's "The Role of Shakespeare in the Novels of Gloria Naylor," in *Rewriting Shakespeare, Rewriting Ourselves* (Berkeley: University of California Press, 1991), which concurs with this assessment of Naylor's relationship to Shakespeare.

13. Baker, "Caliban's Triple Play," 193.

14. See Ania Loomba's analysis of "the black rapist" in her discussion of Caliban in *Gender, Race, Renaissance Drama* (Manchester: Manchester University Press, 1989), 148–53. In Naylor's first novel, *The Women of Brewster Place* (New York: Viking, 1982), a lesbian is brutally raped by a group of young men. Although uncompromising in its condemnation of sexist violence, *The Women of Brewster Place* does not let the reader forget the social conditions that contribute to such defensive modes of masculine self-assertion: poverty, unemployment, and urban disenfranchisement.

15. Nixon, "Caribbean and African Appropriations," 577.

16. See Toni Morrison, *Song of Solomon* (New York: New American Library, 1977) and *Tar Baby* (New York: New American Library, 1981); Paule Marshall, *Praisesong for the Widow* (New York: E. P. Dutton, 1983) and *The Chosen Place, the Timeless People* (New York: Vintage, 1969); and Alice Walker, *The Color Purple* (New York: Washington Square Press, 1982).

17. For a brief analysis of the Shakespearean allusions in *Mama Day,* see Bharati Mukherjee, "There are Four Sides to Everything," *New York Times Book Review,* 21 Feb. 1988. For readings of *The Tempest* as a drama of reconciliation, see the essays in *Representing Shakespeare: New Psychoanalytic Essays,* ed. Murray Schwartz and Coppélia Kahn (Baltimore: Johns Hopkins University Press, 1980).

18. On the "conjure woman," obvious comparisons can be made to Toni Morrison's Pilate in *Song of Solomon* and Thérèse in *Tar Baby.*

19. For an analysis of *Hamlet* along these lines, see Valerie Traub, "Jewels, Statues, and Corpses: Containment of Female Erotic Power," in *Desire and Anxiety: Circulations of Sexuality in Shakespearean Drama* (London: Routledge, 1992). For a discussion of Prospero's fantasy of paternal power, see Stephen Orgel, "Prospero's

Wife," in *Rewriting the Renaissance,* ed. Margaret Ferguson, Maureen Quilligan, and Nancy Vickers (Chicago: University of Chicago Press, 1986), 50–64.

20. I am indebted to Marianne Novy for noting the connection between Hamlet and George. George first discusses his injured heart with Cocoa, however, in the context of *Lear:* "None but the fool who labors to outjest his heart-struck injuries" (106).

21. *The Harvard Concordance to Shakespeare* lists only 109 references to *jest.* I am indebted to Marianne Novy for alerting me to the possible significance of this misquotation, and to the later political distinction between being black and being orphaned.

22. Morrison, *Song of Solomon,* 40. Naylor's general indebtedness to Morrison is mentioned by Erickson.

23. See Houston Baker, *Afro-American Poetics: Revisions of Harlem and the Black Aesthetic* (Madison: University of Wisconsin Press, 1988).

DIANA BRYDON

Sister Letters:
Miranda's *Tempest* in Canada

when did we lose
our sense of moment
how did we allow
those raw Ferdinands to enter
and become our new brave worlds
. . . .
Canada my husband is an idiot

Jan Horner, "Sister Letters"

What happens at the historical moment when the voiceless and
powerless seek to unravel their riddle? (For Caliban does seize his
voice, reject the magician of civilization in Césaire's writing of
Shakespeare's *Tempest*) ANS.: We are cutting into the deep heart,
the deepest heart of cultural compacts. They have already lost our
allegiance. Something is finished.

Rachel Blau DuPlessis, "For the Etruscans"

These two epigraphs, with their differently posed questions, frame my
essay. In speaking of loss and of allowing others to determine the future,
the first implies victimization and complicity. In imagining the seizing of
agency, the second questions the historical forces that, in theorizing
civilization and its others, have enabled imperialism. The first takes the
form of a letter addressed to a sister; the second, of a feminist meditation
addressed to the sisterhood of women. Each is concerned with historical
moments of choice for women involving identification and disaffiliation,
and each chooses illustrative instances (Miranda's choice of husband,
Caliban's choice of rebellion) from Shakespeare's play *The Tempest* to
focus their questioning. My argument begins with the intersections between
these two lines of questioning, in the hope of initiating a dialogue between
them. This essay examines some Canadian reimaginings of Miranda's
motivations and her options, shifting attemtion temporarily from those
postcolonial readings of *The Tempest* that privilege the Prospero-Caliban

dialectic and Third World fictions, toward rethinking the possibilities of Miranda's story in rewritings that emerge from settler-invader societies such as Canada.

Although there is a long tradition of Canadian rewritings that privilege Miranda's perspective, such re-visions are not unique to Canada, as Elaine Showalter points out in arguing for Miranda's "long and significant history in American women's writing."[1] Showalter concentrates on the implications of the Miranda figure for contemporary feminism, concluding that white feminists must ultimately abandon identification with the only woman on the island to acknowledge that many different women inhabit the world. Although we agree in our conclusions, my argument takes a different route. I hope to use the ambivalences of the Miranda figure to suggest some of the ways in which postcolonial and feminist critiques overlap, differ, and may inform one another. The Miranda figure is as useful in dramatizing the limits of certain kinds of African-nationalist postcolonial readings as it is in testing the limits of international white feminisms. The ways in which creative writers have tested these limits may direct us toward creative renegotiation of our cultural compacts. Without wishing to downplay the importance of gender, I believe that Miranda's position is particularly appropriate for exploring the ambivalences of a settler-colony culture, attempting to create a neo-Europe in an invaded land, torn between Old World fathers and suitors while unable to ignore the just grievances of those whose culture hers is displacing. Recognizing this ambivalence, the New Zealand writer Ian Wedde notes the necessity, for countries like Canada and New Zealand, who have rejected the revolutionary solution established by the United States model, of balancing what we can learn from "the ruling Prosperos with institutionalised magic and language on their side" against "the talking-back of the 'innocent' Mirandas and 'primitive' Calibans."[2] My focus falls on the discussions among these three voices and on the power relations they reveal at work within the *Tempest* paradigm, to see if nonrepressive alternatives can be developed beyond its models for human relationships.

From the time of Sir Charles G. D. Roberts's fable *The Heart of the Ancient Wood* (1900),[3] Canadian rewritings have recognized that Miranda cannot "seize her voice" as Caliban does in the play by Aimé Césaire invoked by Blau DuPlessis.[4] She cannot make a revolution in the same confrontational style because to a certain extent her enemy is part of herself, part of her socialization as dutiful daughter of Empire and part of her acquiescence in Caliban's oppression, whether Caliban be read as First Nations indigene, Québécois, or Third World radical. Denied the luxury of outright rebellion, Miranda must ask how she allowed the utopian dream of a brave new world to degenerate into a repetition of Old World usurpations. Her story invites consideration of modes of domination that depend more on the manufacture of consent than on violent suppression. When Rob Nixon claims that it is difficult to wrest "any role for female defiance or leadership" from this play, he derives his conclusion from reading African and Caribbean texts responding to violent conquest and racism.[5] This focus causes him to miss the significance of Miranda as in some ways a "female counterpart" to Caliban. By ignoring Canadian appropriations of The Tempest, and models of defiance and leadership that may not take the form of outright rebellion or violent retaliation, he ignores an important dimension of postcolonial revisions of The Tempest.

Other commentators have also stressed the negative potential of Miranda in opposition to the rich inspiration that Caliban appears to offer.[6] Lori Leininger calls for the kind of revision that Rob Nixon thought impossible, apparently unaware that Canadian appropriators of The Tempest, both male and female, have anticipated her challenge to spring what she terms "the Miranda trap." They have invented the "modern Miranda" she calls for and they have permitted her to speak new epilogues.[7] But the trap has proved more dangerous than Leininger anticipated. Laura Donaldson goes beyond the call for feminist self-assertion to follow Gayatri Spivak's lead in considering the ways in which white women's self-consolidation depends on the silencing and victimization of women of color. Ironically, Donaldson's article "The Miranda Complex" exemplifies the very problem her article identifies so cogently. She asks why Miranda and Caliban, "these two victims of colonialist Prosperity cannot 'see' each other,"[8] yet her own work is blind to the postcolonial examinations of the Caliban-Miranda relationship undertaken by African, Canadian, and Caribbean writers, most extensively since the 1950s. She argues that "the relationship between Miranda and Caliban has been virtually ignored" (68), but seems to be referring to mainstream criticism rather than to the creative work of postcolonial writers. Certainly work by postcolonial writers such as George Lamming, Lemuel Johnson, David Dabydeen, Audrey Thomas, and Margaret Laurence has interrogated this relationship from a variety of perspectives. Although Donaldson is correct in identifying Miranda's role as pivotal in evading the Manichean dualities of a colonialist discourse, her argument suffers by its silence in relation to much of the creative fiction pioneering this movement beyond the old binarisms of master and slave. Ann Thompson repeats this now familiar gesture, when she concludes her survey of Tempest criticism with the question, "what kind of pleasure can a woman and a feminist take in this text beyond the rather grim one of mapping its various patterns of exploitation?"[9] Let us see.

The Canadian Mirandas do not always "talk back" as a contemporary feminist might wish. Alternative patterns of ambivalence, complicity, and resistance emerge in Canadian women's re-visionings of *The Tempest.* Like Miranda, Canada is the daughter of Empire. The Canadian Miranda may opt either to assume Prospero's power as his heir or to continue to manifest his power through her assumed innocence. But both are dangers she must avoid if she is to find her brave new world of transformed possibilities. Some critics may be tempted to follow Tim Brennan's lead in dismissing the differences of this kind of writing as "too much like the fictional 'us' of the so-called mainstream, on the inside looking out."[10] But that would be comparable to equating Miranda's "inside" position with Prospero's. We need to move beyond thinking solely in terms of insiders versus outsiders if we are to understand the complexities of colonial and postcolonial discursive systems. While the construction of white femininity "can play a pivotal role in negotiating and maintaining concepts of racial and cultural difference,"[11] it performs a role very different to Prospero's. We need to attend to these differences if we are to escape the unproductive repetitions of what Edward Said has termed a "politics of blame."[12]

A focus on Miranda in Canada reveals diverse responses, often articulated through an irony so understated it seems to invite easy dismissal and misunderstanding. Constance Beresford-Howe, in *Prospero's Daughter* (1988), locates her Canadian Prospero with his two daughters in a country home in England. She explores the dilemma of Miranda as dutiful daughter through these two sisters, one of whom becomes an actor on the stage and learns to speak for herself and, more problematically, for her sister. The silent sister's rebellion is both more conventional and more radical. Apparently little more than a simple and obedient servant who cooks and cleans for her father, she disappears completely from her family's life (and from the text) after her father's efforts to set her up with a suitable mate have failed. She chooses silence and absence, which her family interpret as loss and death, yet which hint at initiative in forging her own rebellion, writing herself an unscripted exit from the scene devised for her by her manipulative writer-father.

Elizabeth Brewster, in a short poem called "Prospero in the Twenty-First Century" (1988), shows Miranda blandly assuming Prospero's imperialist role, dominating Caliban through the love she inspires in him rather than through fear, but dominating nonetheless: "The native boy is civilized / Miranda's favourite servant, / walks two steps behind her always / glowering / at her enemies."[13] Although this could perhaps be read at face value, the juxtapositions of "civilized" and "glowering" seem to imply an ironic questioning of imperialist assumptions of racial superiority. Marjorie Pickthall, an early twentieth-century sentimental poet, once popular and now neglected, also imagined Miranda inspiring undying loyalty, but after her death, and from Ariel. Ominously entitled "Miranda's Tomb" (1917), Pickthall's poem seems to imply, to the contemporary reader at least, the price women must pay if they are to emulate the ideal set by Shakespeare's Miranda.[14] That sickly embracing of death and idealizing an impossible love seem to be satirized in Brewster's poem, with its anachronistic images projected into the twenty-first century, but it is impossible to tell for sure. Writing such as Beresford-Howe's and Brewster's works within the limits of the traditional view of Miranda's role in *The Tempest*, challenging it slyly and obliquely through an understated irony that destabilizes any attempt at fixing meaning.

Other writers more radically reconceive Miranda's role to encompass agency. Suniti Namjoshi and Sarah Murphy reinscribe *The Tempest* as immigrants to Canada, Namjoshi from India and Murphy from the United States. They represent the different sources of Canada's largely immigrant population, which continues to draw on Prospero's and Caliban's children. Although Namjoshi has left Canada for England, she wrote and published "Snapshots of Caliban" in Canada, so it seems legitimate to read the work as at least partly in dialogue with Canadian concerns, although the focus of the book as a whole is on larger patterns of misogyny within the literatures and myths of many cultures, written from what Namjoshi has identified as an Asian and lesbian perspective.[15] Namjoshi's female Caliban finds sisters among Baby F (as female and Frankenstein), Rose Green, and a reformed Antigone—a revisioned sisterhood of rebellious, monstrous women. In a poem relevant to her radical rereading of Miranda, one of her women's voices rejects the "female protagonist / straight out of James" because there is no place for the speaker in James's "portrait of a lady." She insists on her difference: "I don't shut up, / And I am not dead."[16]

Namjoshi's long poem sequence "Snapshots of Caliban" in *The Bedside Book of Nightmares* (1984) explores Miranda's repressed and violent desire for the other and shows her developing an alliance with a female Caliban that eventually excludes Prospero.[17] Her focus is on sexual politics; her critique is of the patriarchy and the heterosexuality it enforces. The book as a whole contextualizes Caliban as part of a larger project of feminist re-revisioning.[18] Sarah Murphy's novel *The Measure of Miranda* (1987) deconstructs Miranda's innocence as manifestation of Prospero's power and explores the motivations of Miranda's white liberal guilt.[19] Her focus is on Canada's participation in international capitalism and the ways in which women's oppression serves to maintain this inequitable system.

Each of these directions is implicit in Margaret Laurence's earlier experiments with the potential of the Miranda figure. In *The Diviners* (1974), Laurence's last novel, Morag's infatuation with Brooke, her English professor and then her husband, later rewritten in Morag's novel *Prospero's Child*, explores Canada's colonial mentality in terms of sexual power relations. Her marriage to Brooke reflects her love for British literature and her dependence on English cultural tradition, as well as her need to make Prospero's creative power her own. Morag's lifelong love affair with the Métis Jules Tonnerre explores Miranda's desire for the native other and the possibility of an alliance between Native American and white Canadians.[20] Morag is a Miranda who uses her affinities with Prospero and with Caliban to "talk back" against what would silence her, and to enter into dialogue with the various traditions that compose her multicultural heritage.[21]

Laurence's first novel, *This Side Jordan* (1960), tentatively explores what Sarah Murphy explicitly theorizes—Miranda's potential as symbolic white liberal, in both cases through a character deliberately named Miranda. But Laurence blurs the implications for understanding Canadian culture by making her Miranda an Englishwoman. Jane Leney sees Laurence's Miranda in *This Side Jordan* as "the white liberal carried to extremes."[22] "Affectionate, well-mannered Miranda" (*This Side Jordan* 8), she reaches out to Africans but cannot comprehend, or chooses to ignore, the power relations that make nonrepressive intercultural relationships of the kind she seeks almost impossible. She is Prospero's privileged daughter, but her husband Johnny Kestoe is no Ferdinand. He is a working-class Caliban figure in Prospero's employ, wielding Prospero's discarded wand, but suspicious of his new authority. Whereas Miranda's class privilege is compromised by her gender, Johnny's gender privilege is crippled by his class. Their alliance suggests their affinities. Nathaniel Amegbe is presented as an African Caliban seeking to master Prospero's books to help his family and his people. Through her attempts to mediate between these two Calibans in their grasping at Prospero's power, Miranda comes to recognize her own responsibility for what happens, moving beyond the original play's insistence on Miranda's unassailable innocence and passivity, to adult stature. From the failure of her scheme to promote Africanization, Laurence's Miranda concludes, "So who's really responsible for what happened? Perhaps we all are" (17). She can no longer claim an absolving innocence and good intentions. They are not enough. But this Miranda has nowhere else to go. She is still the white woman alone on her island, deprived of female companionship and the notion of sisterhood.

Although perhaps in part an ironic self-portrait of Laurence's younger self on her first arrival in Africa, *This Side Jordan*'s Miranda is spared the further complications of a Canadian nationality. Sarah Murphy's *Measure of Miranda* explores similar dynamics in a novel in which Miranda is self-consciously presented as "Miss Canada" (158), the ironically bestowed nickname she has earned from the more streetwise women at the shelter where she works. She so immaculately embodies the dominant ideal of female perfection (antiseptic, innocent, and concerned) that the women she works with joke about whether "her shit smells like everyone else's" (158). She seems too good to be true.

But we learn this in retrospect, for Murphy's Miranda is already dead when the story that takes her measure begins. Amparo, her Chilean house-mate, had shown her some photographs of Central American torture victims. Traumatized by this discovery, Miranda, the "sweet Canadian,"23 decides that she must act. Her sacrifice of her own life and her father's in order to blow up a Central American major who is responsible for many of these atrocities rewrites *The Tempest*'s marriage masque as a consummation with death.

Miranda dresses carefully for the assassination. She embroiders her dress of white Oaxacan cotton, "traditional as hell, from one particular village in the mountains, but so popular that it is found world-wide now (112)," with additional images of her own: flowers "for the dead of the villages" and "corn for lord Xipe Totec, the god of spring and rebirth" (113). On her head she wears a bead belt headband with a Cree floral pattern. Dressed as a bride in this composite costume, she seems to be trying to reclaim the commodified and exoticized Native American cultures as a source of power for her resistance. Although she means the gesture to signify good will, her own position as descendent of white invaders inevitably marks the gesture as appropriative. The symbolism of her dress transforms *The Tempest*'s Eurocentric marriage masque motifs of Ceres into a tribute to the oppressed indigenous cultures of America, but a tribute that ironically marks their continuing exploitation. Wearing this dress, Miranda approaches her transformed Ferdinand, the Major, and consummates a marriage with death, as if through this human sacrifice she might redeem five hundred years of violent history "on the usurped lands" of North and South America (124–25).

Born and partly educated in the United States, Sarah Murphy brings an outsider's perspective to her depiction of the Canadian Miranda. This perspective takes shape in the form of the text itself. An elegiac romance, *The Measure of Miranda* has a double focus. Although it appears to be about the dead Miranda, the novel increasingly reveals itself as at least as much about its narrator, her surviving friend Susan, who despite her best efforts to wish her text into dialogue finds herself trapped in monologue (132). Susan takes Miranda's measure and explores Miranda's taking of her parents', her friends', and her society's measure. The book is Susan's assessment of exactly where Miranda has left her, with the unanswerable question: why? Susan's reconstruction of Miranda's life from the fragments Miranda has left and from what Susan herself remembers mirrors Miranda's earlier attempts to reconstruct the life of the photographic image that she has named "Maria de la Dignidad," a Central American torture victim.

Susan ends where she began, repeating her initial formulation of Miranda's quest in mathematical terms as a driving need to understand "where it was exactly that she fit in. The exact position occupied by that individual function that was herself, another innocent Canadian integral in the calculus of all pain" (9, 238). In Susan's account, Miranda experiences "her own mini heart of darkness" (35) through her encounter with Central America: that is, with an alternative, resistant culture, with poverty, and with torture. Miranda's professor and lover Jim (a Prospero figure and father substitute) is writing his own book about her life, in Susan's view a "soft focus adventure" which canonizes her as "St. Miranda of the Locket," in what sounds like (on Jim's part) an unintentional parody of Love Story. Susan makes the parody explicit, caricaturing his attitude, "What can you say about a twenty-one year old who dies?" To this Susan responds, "that always makes me want to shout—Who blew herself up Jim, who blew herself up. And everything else within fifty feet" (233). In these competing interpretations of Miranda's death, the issue of agency emerges as crucial. Miranda's uniqueness as a person is constantly put into question by the intertextual webs through which her story is told. Yet their very proliferation prevents oversimplification. The novel's mixing of the languages of mathematics and sentimental romance and its interweaving of intertextual references from contemporary popular fiction to Conrad and Shakespeare mark its complications of what Coral Ann Howells terms, echoing Lyotard, "the metanarratives of imperialism."[24]

This Miranda has "talked back" in the only way she could imagine. Her enigmatic gesture puzzles those who attempt to "read" the meaning of her action and so becomes a potent reminder of injustice and our own roles in relation to it. The horror and the futility fused in that image of destruction remain to haunt us just as the photographs of torture victims had haunted Miranda herself. We can never finally decide whether Miranda's gesture was heroic or foolish, but the process our questioning involves us in forces us to reconsider our values. Timothy Findley's celebrated Canadian novel The Wars (1977) gives us the male version of this futile gesture.[25] Robert Ross defies gender stereotyping and social norms, disobeying and killing a superior officer in order to rescue a barnful of horses from the general slaughter. No one knows what to make of his action. Similarly, Murphy's Miranda defies gender stereotyping to assume the role of terrorist. In both instances, the fundamentally ambiguous gesture freezes their protests into emblematic images that challenge our assumptions about right and wrong, about how to act to challenge oppression.

In *The Measure of Miranda,* Susan the survivor, a lawyer and would-be municipal politician, rejects the revolutionary route, but Susan also feels that Miranda's friends—her chosen community—have failed her. The book expresses white English Canada's collective "survivor's guilt," guilt that we have profited from genocide, from the invasion and settlement of First Nations territory, and that we continue to profit from their marginalization and from Third World oppression. With Miranda, Susan believes that "we don't have to live by eating each other" (232), but the communal alternative to emotional cannibalism that they try to establish in their Canadian group house fails. In Murphy's text cannibalism becomes the sign of consumer capitalism; the old distinctions between barbarism and civilization have been collapsed.

Miranda's Canadian house-mates have been unable to provide the alternative vision of a creative cultural compact that Miranda required and romantically believed could be found in the solidarity of a Latin American resistance movement, a movement in which she could find no place as a privileged white woman. To Miranda, Amparo represents the Third World, which she both fears and longs to join. To Susan, Amparo is a more complex individual who moves in and out of several worlds, self-consciously assuming "her role as symbolic representative of the Third World" (80) when necessary. In the novel's play with Shakespeare, Amparo is in part a female Caliban figure, but reimagined as possessing the dignity, integrity, and the warmth that Miranda desires. Susan and Amparo see the danger in this idealization. It comes close to the fascination that Miranda's father Wayne feels for Amparo, who is his Spanish-language teacher as well as Miranda's house-mate: "he seemed to love the fact that she considered herself a Marxist-Leninist, it was such an authentic thing to be if you were from down there that it made him feel like Columbus discovering the same new world (the third one). Which made him bait her more" (89). Amparo wishes to be seen for herself and not as a projection of Wayne's need for an adversary or Miranda's need for a model of resistance to Wayne. Significantly, Miranda turns from Amparo, the real woman who cannot satisfy her need, to her fantasy of the dead Maria, the violated victim, whose photograph is safely enclosed in Miranda's locket.

Thinking back, Susan realizes that she had noticed that Miranda's stuttering "bbb.ut" (127)—her questioning of the world's lies and her father's rules—"had become—Ssp.eak" (128)—a command to choose and to act. Miranda, like Findley's Robert Ross, presumably stutters because she is choking on the lies of her civilization, because the smooth master narratives do not correspond to the experience she struggles to articulate.

Their stuttering links them to Caliban, the only character in Shakespeare's text to stutter. Just as Caliban sings a stuttering song in anticipation of a successful revolution overturning Prospero's power, so Miranda mangles Prospero's language in her quest for an alternative speech. (And so Amparo and her fellow Spanish teachers rejoice, silently, in the comic misspeakings and misunderstandings of their pupils, misunderstandings that give back, if only symbolically, the power they have lost to their Anglophone student-masters.)

But Susan can only hear this change in the meaning of Miranda's consistent stutter in retrospect. She was not listening carefully enough at the time. Susan laments her inability to respond to Miranda's indirect pleas for guidance: "all I did was grin and blow a kiss. Blow you my own Judas kiss of self-betrayal" (130). North American individualism, she implies, inhibits the "birthing each other" (232) that accomplishes genuine social change. As in Shakespeare's *Tempest,* this is still a world of absent mothers.

Susan thinks that "in a world where taking responsibility for yourself just means for your debts and your purchases, never who they are to or where they come from . . . if you stray it can never be into significance . . . or even tragedy . . . but only into madness . . . a place from which no meaningful statement . . . can emerge" (204).

The media coverage of Miranda's straying gesture proves Susan's analysis right. Miranda remains enigmatic; her action is interpreted as a mad and meaningless aberration. Susan's book, in contrast, reinterprets Miranda's act into a convoluted search for meaning (hard to quote briefly without substituting ellipses as I have done above). The convolutions refuse to sacrifice complexity and contradiction to clarity. The method is the meaning, yet paradoxically, then, Susan's Miranda also remains finally elusive, a mystery to be probed, defying summation, a self in the process of making rather than an achieved identity.

In her search for "the story that makes us human" (206), Susan shows us multiple Mirandas, characterized inhumanly as if Miranda were a logarithm to be calculated. Each chapter heading presents her as part of an indefinite set. $Miranda_1$ has three subsets: Sugar, Honey, Fairy. The text moves through $Miranda_2$ (Sorry, Princess, But) to $Miranda_3$ (Thank You, Please, No) to $Miranda_n$ (Ever). The use of the n as the concluding member of the set indicates that the final number is unknown. Murphy's parody of Robinson Crusoe's mathematical accounting of a life releases the "measure of Miranda" from her definition as exchange commodity and visible sign of her father's power into a multiplying and expanding definition of Miranda derivatives, moving through a series of metamorphoses beyond such containment. Her father's My Randa becomes in

Susan's text Our My Randa (225). (George Lamming also deconstructs the name in *Water with Berries*, creating a white prostitute-daughter in Myra and a black wife, who is unfaithful in order to be faithful, in Randa.[26])

Susan's Miranda is both dutiful and "prodigal daughter" (160). The "perfection of her innocence" seems to be an ultimate proof of her father's power (207), yet she learns to insist on "her vision of the world," to say, "Daddy, your world is a lie" (193). The only way she finds of integrating the circuit of her various selves brings about her death but affirms her dignity and integrity as an adult who has sought to challenge hypocrisy, albeit in a way that reinforces rather than challenges the fundamental violence of her culture. She deliberately kills her adversary, the Major; she accidently kills her father, who is described by Amparo as "the best of them" (86), but who the text implies must die as symbol of patriarchal culture in general; and she inevitably kills herself, as the price willingly paid for a successful assassination. She leaves the reader, with Susan's guidance, to reassemble the pieces.

Susan ponders the events leading up to Miranda's death and the records Miranda left her: photographs of Central American torture victims; Miranda's family heirloom locket, a gold heart engraved with an *M,* passed down through the women in her family and now containing carefully selected fragments from photographs of one of those victims, pasted in by Miranda on top of a picture of Miranda and her family; pornographic pictures Miranda had found by the river; and Miranda's journal: a collage uniting the disparate parts of her experience (the violences against women in North American society—through advertising, pornography, family politics, and wife-battering—with the violences practiced in Central and South America by repressive regimes). Here again Miranda's practice becomes a legacy to be interrogated by Susan.

Miranda takes the anonymous torture victim's photograph literally to heart by encapsulating it in her locket. She means this as a gesture of solidarity, as a reminder to herself not to forget the violences on which her privilege is founded, and as a spur to action to right the wrongs of her world. Nonetheless, the gesture can be seen as appropriative. The picture is subsumed within Miranda's enclosing perspective; the victim is named by her. Murphy seems to be suggesting that Miranda and Maria are linked as oppressive ideals for female behavior, but her Miranda belies the passivity of the ideal, for she cannot escape her own will to power, even in her search for a sister.

Whereas the locket holds close an unspeakable violation, Miranda's collage journal speaks "a concrete testimony." Josh, the ceramist, swears that the journal is "a work of art . . . [a] masterpiece, the way [Miranda] placed them all together" (174). Josh responds to the journal as men had always responded to Miranda: in admiration at a perfectly achieved work of art. But Susan reads the same journal as a challenge to her own understandings of the world. The journal's collage of images depicting advertising, pornography, and torture encourages Susan to draw the missing connections between circuits of power, between the oppression of women in capitalist societies and the continuing violence of neocolonialism. Miranda's journal leads Susan to see the construction of Miranda's innocence as "an ultimate proof of power . . . the most important gift power can give itself. . . . The sullying of alien dignity and thus one's own countered only by the knowledge that there is one at home who is unsoiled by such blood or offal or excrement" (207).

Miranda is the ultimate "example of what makes us believe we are the very best of cultures: our ability to protect more people and keep them that much blinder (more innocent more bystander) than was hitherto possible thanks to technology and distance" (207). All the incentives were there for this Miranda to continue in her role as innocent bystander, but her "terrible need to know" (9) led her to reconnect the circuits of her character—the capacity for wonder, the desire for a brave new world—in order to question rather than affirm the fantasy that her father—our patriarchal culture as imaged in Prospero—had fashioned for her. She uses his art—dynamite—to blast away forever the Miranda who as "quiescent pet" (202) served as ultimate proof of his power.

For Murphy's Miranda, violent rebellion must entail self-destruction, because she is part of the system she rejects. Her assumption of Prospero's technological art fails her because she adopts it without transforming it. In contrast, her journal takes artifacts from a male-dominated society and recombines them into a new creation that transforms them, extracting them from their original exploitative contexts and reinserting them in her own design to reveal their effects and to insist on the validity of her own perspective.

If Miranda's legacy seems to be two kinds of ambiguous failures, Susan's attempt to work within the system, running for local election, also fails, as do Amparo's attempts to continue work for her people in Canada. We do not know what to make of Amparo's decision to return to Chile. Yet the story that Amparo tells of her pre-Canadian life, a story embedded in Susan's account of Miranda's life, affirms Amparo's belief that power can be shared. The moral she draws from her story, that we must focus on what is useful rather than try to measure importance, reminds the reader not to discount such small, seemingly fruitless, efforts for change. Through storytelling, through remembering, through struggling, alternatives survive. Like the sisterhood of ordinary women in Amparo's jail, these underestimated attempts at keeping our story human are where the real alternative sources of power lie.

The Measure of Miranda moves Canadian women "beyond Miranda's meanings," as analyzed by the Caribbean writer Sylvia Wynter.[27] Wynter argues,

> Nowhere is the mutational shift from the primacy of the anatomical model of sexual difference as the referential model of mimetic ordering, to that of the physiognomic model of racial/cultural difference, more powerfully enacted than in Shakespeare's play *The Tempest,* one of the foundational endowing texts both of Western Europe's dazzling rise to global hegemony, and, at the level of human "life," in general, of the mutation from primarily religiously defined modes of human being to the first, partly secularizing ones. ... That is, in the relations of enforced dominance and subordination between Miranda, though 'female', and Caliban, though 'male'; relations in which sex-gender attributes are no longer the primary index of 'deferent difference'. (358)

She argues that Miranda, as the only woman in the play, becomes the idealized and sole object of male desire for all classes and races, in her very being playing her part in the systemic silencing of the "native" woman, Caliban's woman.

The Measure of Miranda comes to similar conclusions, exploding the myth of "Miranda" as cultural ideal to celebrate a community of women as differentiated individuals, each seeking to reconnect the circuits of power in a new way. In this community of women, the Third World woman is not presented as "Caliban's woman," however, but as a Caliban figure herself. She stands alone, having been betrayed by her Chilean lover, a man who betrayed himself and her through believing he alone knew what was truly important in their struggle. Amparo presents herself in Canada as "indigestible. Maybe even poisonous. Not any kind of article of consumption at all" (138). In prison in Chile, she appeared to her torturers as a kind of Sycorax, covered with the blood of her miscarried child: "how she must have seemed the witch of every witch hunter's nightmares, covered with the blood of sacrifice, the child's blood (the scream and the scream within the scream) and her own, with a face (a laughing, a smiling face, she has joined the Cihuateteo with her death head warrior birthing mother's face) turned to stone" (146).

Amparo's power comes from having endured such torture and survived. She survives through holding on to her connections to other human beings, through her love for her companions and her hatred for her torturers. Her incessant knitting represents this weaving of connections

through a valuing of the underestimated, often forgotten work necessary
for daily survival.

Suniti Namjoshi's "Snapshots of Caliban" also moves "beyond Miranda's
meanings" by turning her attention to a re-visioned Caliban as her own
woman, rather than as male figure requiring a mate. In her retelling, as in
Murphy's, it is Miranda who is fascinated by Caliban, not Caliban by
Miranda. Her Miranda too is tempted by violent solutions, but whereas
Murphy's Miranda is motivated by the conflicts she experiences between
her desire to please Prospero and his representatives and her longing for a
brave new world, Namjoshi's Miranda acts out of a confused desire and
rage. She tries twice, unsuccessfully, to murder Caliban, yet recognizes
that Caliban's death is not the solution she seeks. The affinities between
Miranda and Caliban as both subject, although in different ways, to
Prospero's rule are highlighted by Namjoshi's decision to make her
Caliban female. And as in Murphy's novel, Namjoshi's Miranda explores
her mixed feelings through a journal:

> Caliban, this is a hate poem.
> You are squat and ugly.
> You are not the noble,
> the beautiful other.
> You are part of me.
> But that's wrong, very wrong. Not what I intended to write at all.
> I shall cross it out. (Namjoshi 61)

The slash across the page puts this knowledge under erasure. Miranda
must deny the affinity with Caliban if she is to realize the "pretty dreams"
(61) constructed for her by Prospero and Ferdinand. Yet listening to their
talk of her birthright as a lady she understands clearly that "in myself I was
nothing" (64). Their dream-Miranda is so adaptable and so attenuated
that she is in danger of losing her own sense of self. She thinks,

> Sometimes the airy substance of Miranda
> is beaten so fine . . .
> I am so pure . . . I can take
> any colour, fit any mould. . . .
> And then I know that it is my soul
> and not my body that is stretched so thin. (68)

Again, as in Murphy, the temptation for Miranda to be "beautiful" in
Prospero's terms seems superficially rewarding yet must lead to the death
of her own selfhood.

This realization prompts a confession to Caliban, who responds with a
confession of her own. Anger turns to laughter as the two women share a

moment of recognition. Caliban concludes, "M said she had not intended to kill me entirely, she had just wanted to make me sick. (I am learning irony.) I thanked her for it. She then explained why she was angry. P overheard us, but we were not able to explain it to him" (69). Miranda and Caliban have negotiated a new cultural compact, based on the mutual recognition of a complexity denied them by Prospero's naming. This compact inadvertently but necessarily excludes Prospero. He had named them "Maiden and monster / and then disdained them" (70). They have escaped this stereotyping with much difficulty. The sequence concludes with a reversal of Shakespeare's ending, when Prospero admits, "I dare not claim them" (70). Namjoshi reveals the maiden in the monster and the monster in the maiden. Prospero's naming is superseded by the "talking back" of Miranda and Caliban. They people the island with their own words, transforming the original *Tempest*'s obsession with biological procreation into literary re-creation, and a new story emerges.

In "Snapshots of Caliban," this new story emerges through the dialogue among the three voices, maybe more. Caliban writes a Notebook and a Journal. Miranda writes a Journal. Prospero no longer holds the monopoly on creativity. The remainder of the poems are not explicitly signed. Because the speaking voice is not identified, the reader is compelled to reexamine stereotypical gender expectations and assumptions about power relations to guess who might be speaking. This process encourages us to consider the ways in which the speakers' concerns, particularly with power, overlap. As in Murphy's novel, authority is dispersed. The texts provide competing interpretations of actions that remain elusive; the reader is invited to form her own conclusions or allowed to hold her judgments in abeyance, as she pleases.

Namjoshi's Caliban is female. The feminization of Caliban highlights the overlapping structures of patriarchal and imperialist domination and exposes the social construction of heterosexual identity, femininity, and ethnic otherness as interrelated. The shock of a female Caliban exposes the limitations of a postcolonial resistance literature that excluded black women. The friendships among women renew Miranda's utopian vision of a brave new world, retrieving it from her mistaken application to *The Tempest*'s male shipwrecked conspirators to reaffirm its positive grounding in women's experiences of friendship. Just as Amparo, Susan, and Miranda represent the potential for social change in *The Measure of Miranda,* so the female Caliban and Miranda come to recognize their common interests in Namjoshi's long poem. There is still sexual attraction between these two figures, but the relation is no longer one of violent subordination of female to male. Rape fantasies have yielded to relations of equal exchange. The resolution is far from utopian, nor is it final. Namjoshi's women learn to laugh together, but they retain their differences.

Namjoshi's and Murphy's Mirandas both "talk back" against their silencing, through misguided attempts at violent action, and more successfully, through writing their journals. But their real success comes through forging alliances with other women, particularly alliances between the privileged and the oppressed. Ferdinand and Prospero are left behind. In Blau DuPlessis's words, they represent the old cultural compacts that have lost women's allegiance. "Those raw Ferdinands" from Jan Horner's "Sister Letters" are no longer "our new brave worlds." Prospero's play yields to "Sister Letters." Miranda discovers her sister in Caliban. Something is finished. Further sea-changes are on the way.

Both texts show a daughter growing beyond her father's control and challenging his version of reality. Miranda's very attentiveness and relative silence in the source play become the focus of these rewritings, which reveal the heavy psychological cost of such repression. In contrast, David Dabydeen's contemporary Caribbean version of Miranda in *Coolie Odyssey* (1988) continues to cast her as the silent object of the male gaze. His Caliban longs for alliance, but only on his terms. He fantasizes speech for Miranda, but in such a way as to repeat the original play's obsession with her sexuality as a male possession and with her body as the site of a battlefield between black and white races.[28] These Canadian texts enact a more radical rewriting, imagining a post-*Tempest* future in which Miranda seizes the initiative to work for change and then surrenders her control to make room for others, so that power can be shared rather than contested. Compulsory heterosexuality is replaced by female friendships in Murphy's text and radically challenged by lesbian alliances in Namjoshi's poetry.

Not only have these women writers found a role for female resistance and leadership in *The Tempest*, but they have also reinterpreted it in a Canadian way, exploring the potential of the play's quietest and apparently most innocuous character for shifting the balance of power away from a dialogue between oppressor and oppressed and toward an exchange of equals. David Sundelson describes *The Tempest* as a play where "middle ground scarcely exists."[29] In typically English-Canadian fashion, these writers imagine that absent middle ground into existence. Here is the kind of writing we might expect from a country that has never experienced a successful revolution seeking independence from imperialist rule—a literature of the middle ground, but the middle ground itself redefined, not in compromise so much as through endless negotiation. The model for the shift from father to sister, enacted in *The Measure of Miranda* and "Snapshots of Caliban," occurs as well in Jan Horner's poem "Sister Letters," from which I have borrowed my title.[30] Like Murphy, Horner puns (like Shakespeare before her) on Miranda as wonder and the Miranda who wonders, taking her Miranda from noun to verb, from passivity to activity. Wondering about "her classic choice: Wildman or exotic prince" (58), she turns from it toward the exchange of "dreams and stories" in letters to and from her sister. Writing in rebellion against the lines women have bought or swallowed from men, Horner questions both the old male stories and women's complicity in maintaining them.

Like their postcolonial counterparts elsewhere, English-Canadian writers read and rewrite *The Tempest* as political allegory. The family drama of father and daughter may be more fraught with ambivalence than that of colonizer and colonized, but it is shown to be no less political, in its dramatization of "the contradictory position occupied by white women in the colonial adventure."[31] The father is killed in Murphy's text and ostracized in Namjoshi's—in each instance, inadvertently rather than by design, as the result of Miranda's concentrating on objectives she has chosen for herself. Namjoshi and Murphy show Miranda welcoming her new alignment with her sister Caliban, abandoning her role as teacher and starting to learn, as Prospero could not, from his former slave. The silence that is seen as crippling—when seizing one's voice is the model for resistance—can be revisioned as enabling when listening to Caliban, rather than solely to Prospero, becomes a priority. The parent/child deadlock is broken when the rest of the world enters the dialogue. These texts demonstrate that springing "the Miranda trap" is a complex and protracted undertaking, demanding flexibility, patience, and humor, and they insist that for those of us with an investment in Miranda's meanings, to move beyond them will require what Gayatri Spivak describes as the process of "un-learning our privilege as our loss."[32]

NOTES

I am extremely grateful to Marianne Novy for her advice and encouragement, and to the anonymous readers whose suggestions helped clarify my argument.

1. Elaine Showalter, "Miranda's Story," in *Sister's Choice: Tradition and Change in American Women's Writing* (Oxford: Clarendon, 1991), 40.

2. Ian Wedde, "Checking Out the Foundations: Editing the *Penguin Anthology of New Zealand Verse*," *Meanjin* 44, no. 3 (Sept. 1985): 347.

3. Sir Charles G. D. Roberts, *The Heart of the Ancient Wood* (1900; rpt. Toronto: McClelland and Stewart, 1974). For thematic readings of the tradition Roberts inaugurated, see Diana Brydon, "Re-Writing *The Tempest*," *World Literature Written in English* 23, no. 1 (1984): 75–88; and Chantal Zabus, "A Calibanic Tempest in Anglophone and Francophone New World Writing," *Canadian Literature* 104 (Spring 1985): 35–50. Despite this early beginning, both articles show

that rewriting *The Tempest* became a matter of cultural urgency, in Canada as elsewhere, in the late 1960s and 1970s. Whereas English-Canadian rewritings identified Canada with Miranda, Quebec writers saw Quebec as Caliban. See Max Dorsinville, *Caliban Without Prospero* (Erin: Porcepic, 1974), for the affinity between Québécois writers and Caliban. In this essay, I focus only on English Canada.

4. Aimé Césaire, *Une Tempête* (Paris: Seuil, 1969). Rachel Blau DuPlessis, "For the Etruscans," in *The New Feminist Criticism: Essays on Women, Literature and Theory,* ed. Elaine Showalter (New York: Pantheon, 1985), 171–91.

5. Rob Nixon, "Caribbean and African Appropriations of *The Tempest,*" *Critical Inquiry* 13, no. 3 (Spring 1987): 577. George Lamming, one of the writers Nixon discusses, considers the affinities between Miranda and Caliban in *The Pleasures of Exile* (London: Michael Joseph, 1960), 15.

6. For an account of the voluminous literature Caliban has inspired, see Alden T. Vaughan and Virginia Mason Vaughan, *Shakespeare's Caliban: A Cultural History* (Cambridge: Cambridge University Press, 1991).

7. Lorie Jerrell Leininger, "The Miranda Trap: Sexism and Racism in Shakespeare's *Tempest,*" in *The Woman's Part: Feminist Criticism of Shakespeare,* ed. Carolyn Ruth Swift Lenz, Gayle Greene, and Carol Thomas Neely (Urbana: University of Illinois Press, 1980): 291.

8. Laura Donaldson, "The Miranda Complex: Colonialism and the Question of Feminist Reading," *Diacritics* 18, no. 3 (Fall 1988): 68.

9. Ann Thompson, " 'Miranda, Where's Your Sister?' Reading Shakespeare's *The Tempest,*" *Feminist Criticism: Theory and Practice,* ed. Susan Sellers (Toronto: University of Toronto Press, 1991), 54.

10. Tim Brennan, "Cosmopolitans and Celebrities," *Race and Class* 31, no. 1 (1989): 8.

11. Vron Ware, *Beyond the Pale: White Women, Racism and History* (London: Verso, 1992), 4.

12. Edward Said, "Intellectuals in the Post-Colonial World," *Salmagundi* no. 70–71 (Spring–Summer 1986): 46.

13. Elizabeth Brewster, *Entertaining Angels* (Toronto: Oberon, 1988): 48.

14. Marjorie Pickthall, "Miranda's Tomb," *University Magazine* 16, no. 4 (December 1917): 508.

15. Suniti Namjoshi, *Because of India: Selected Poems and Fables.* (London: OnlyWomen, 1989), 22.

16. Suniti Namjoshi, "For the Student of Literature," in *The Bedside Book of Nightmares* (Fredericton: Fiddlehead and Goose Lane, 1984), 35.

17. Namjoshi, "Snapshots of Caliban," in *The Bedside Book of Nightmares,* 51–70.

18. In *Because of India,* Namjoshi writes, "In 'Snapshots of Caliban' I tried to create a female Caliban, with a strong ego and a healthy appetite, who just wanted what she wanted. My conscious intention at the outset was to kill her off. But I couldn't. Perhaps no poet can. And I found that though its manifestation differed, egoism itself was as central to the voices of Miranda and Prospero as it was to

Caliban's. I had known for some time that identity isn't only a matter of self-definition. It also depends on the identity that other people attribute to one" (83–84).

19. Sarah Murphy, *The Measure of Miranda* (Edmonton: Newest, 1987).

20. "Métis" now means "any person of mixed Indian-white ancestry who identified him- or herself and was identified by others as neither Indian nor white," according to the introduction to *The New Peoples: Being and Becoming Métis in North America,* ed. Jacqueline Peterson and Jennifer S. H. Brown (Winnipeg: The University of Manitoba Press, 1985), 5. In Canada, the term was originally applied to the French- and Cree-speaking descendants of the Red River Métis who took part in the North West Rebellion. This is Jules's heritage.

21. My emphasis differs from that developed by Gayle Greene in "Margaret Laurence's *Diviners* and Shakespeare's *Tempest:* The Uses of the Past," in *Women's Re-Visions of Shakespeare,* ed. Marianne Novy (Urbana: University of Illinois Press, 1990): 165–82. My position is more fully articulated in "Re-Writing *The Tempest.*" Basically, I see Morag (and Laurence) as much more critical of Prospero's power, not just as imperialist but also as artist. Whereas Prospero used Ariel, Caliban, and Miranda to create his Art, Morag identifies with their subjected and daughter positions. Indeed, she has lived them and knows them first-hand. Her art is a more tentative, explorative creation. As artist, she is a humbler figure, respectful of the natural environment and the integrity of others. Her imaginative power comes from dispossession; her project is to affirm the dignity of the dispossessed. Therefore, I would argue that far from "maturing . . . into the powers of Prospero himself" (165), as Greene argues, Morag transforms Prospero's very definition of artist and art and never assumes that the power she wields for a time is hers, but always sees it as a gift that entails a responsibility for the stewardship of the earth and the well-being of the human community. Far from assuming "the male part" (Greene 177), Morag, as Prospero's daughter, grows into a very different kind of artist, learning from those around her and acting as a nurturing rather than an authoritative power. Laurence saw Prospero as a symbol of the British administrator in Africa and claimed, "To me, Prospero is a very sinister character" (Rosemary Sullivan, "An Interview with Margaret Laurence," in *A Place to Stand On: Essays by and about Margaret Laurence,* ed. George Woodcock [Edmonton: Newest, 1983], 67).

22. Jane Leney, "Prospero and Caliban in Laurence's African Fiction," *Journal of Canadian Fiction* 27 (1980): 68.

23. See Dr. Minnow's characterization of the "sweet Canadian" in Margaret Atwood's *Bodily Harm* (Toronto: McClelland and Stewart, 1981), 29. Miranda is teased in Murphy's novel for being "the sweet protected Canadian" (41). These books form part of a tradition of guilty but fascinated Canadian encounters with the horrors of other places.

24. Coral Ann Howells, "Free-dom, Telling, Dignidad: Margaret Laurence, 'A Gourdful of Glory,' Margaret Atwood, *The Handmaid's Tale,* Sarah Murphy, *The Measure of Miranda,*" *Commonwealth* 12, no. 1 (Autumn 1989): 39.

25. Timothy Findley, *The Wars* (Harmondsworth: Penguin, 1977).

26. George Lamming, *Water With Berries* (London: Longman, 1973).

27. Sylvia Wynter, "Afterword; Beyond Miranda's Meanings: Un/Silencing the 'Demonic Ground' of Caliban's 'Woman,'" in *Out of the Kumbla: Caribbean Women and Literature,* ed. Carole Boyce Davies and Elaine Savory Fido (Trenton, N.J.: Africa World Press, 1990), 366.

28. David Dabydeen, *Coolie Odyssey* (Coventry: Hansib and Dangaroo, 1988). See Dabydeen's interview with Wolfgang Binder for his own understanding of his rewriting of the Caliban/Miranda relationship ("David Dabydeen," *Journal of West Indian Literature* 3, no. 2 [Sept. 1989]: 78–79). He suggests, "So it may be that Miranda becomes a whore, or else she becomes the virgin who lusts after our dark skins and tropical experiences, or whatever" (78). "In other words, it is not sufficient to rape Miranda, because rape is destructive. It is better to love her, the sexual romance peopling the isles with new Prosperos" (79).

29. David Sundelson, "So Rare a Wonder'd Father: Prospero's Tempest," in *Representing Shakespeare: New Psychoanalytic Essays,* ed. Murray M. Schwartz and Coppelia Kahn (Baltimore: Johns Hopkins University Press, 1980), 33.

30. Jan Horner, "Sister Letters," *Recent Mistakes* (Winnipeg: Turnstone, 1988), 58–62.

31 Ania Loomba, *Gender, Race, Renaissance Drama* (Manchester: Manchester University Press, 1989), 153.

32 Gayatri Chakravorty Spivak, "Criticism, Feminism, and the Institution," in *The Post-Colonial Critic: Interviews, Strategies, Dialogues,* ed. Sarah Harasym (New York: Routledge, 1990), 9.

JOYCE GREEN MACDONALD

Women and Theatrical Authority: Deborah Warner's *Titus Andronicus*

What difference do women make to Shakespearean production? Much previous feminist attention to this question has concentrated on the presence of women in roles originally written for boys, suggesting optimistically that women performers can create and deliver theatrical meanings unavailable to audiences when women were forbidden the stage. More radical critiques assert that the persisting effects of male authorship and male performance define the roles beyond the power of mere female substitution to recover or possess them in any lastingly meaningful way.[1] If, in fact, dramatic narrative is in many cases designed to contain Woman as a category of social value, it cannot be wholly undone through the relatively simple expedient of exchanging woman for boy; Woman as sign still remains.

Setting aside absolutist arguments about women's innate powers to transcend the limitations of intractable material, or about the imperviousness of dramatic narrative to strategic intervention, both of which slight institutional circumstances, this essay addresses another instance of women's employment in roles traditionally reserved for men. In the dominant British theater, the hierarchy which oversees the theatrical construction and presentation of those classical narratives of social and sexual value is top-heavy with men. As the following discussion of the three Royal Shakespeare Company productions of *Titus Andronicus*[2] will suggest, just as dramatic narrative constructs male and female according to particular definitions, so too does the structure of theatrical enterprise invest male and female, director and actor, performer and audience, with certain preexisting definitions of authority and passivity.[3] The literal authority of male directors over the means of production reproduces in administrative terms the androcentric bias of Shakespeare's theatrical culture, as well as that of contemporary societies. In confronting the problem of distance between Renaissance culture's versions of sexual politics and their own, two RSC directors of *Titus* performed a naturalization of the text's conflicts that tended to mute and de-spectacularize them, removing them from specifically sixteenth-century frames of visual and historical reference while identifying their own views of historical and political conflict with Shakespearean values. The work they did on *Titus Andronicus,* and the kinds of relationships with the company that made it possible, exemplified the authority of the director under previous RSC hierarchies.

I hesitate to argue that the differences between Deborah Warner's *Titus Andronicus* and the two earlier RSC productions primarily stem from her gender, although it is certainly noteworthy that her 1987 *Titus* was the first time a woman had directed an RSC Shakespeare since Buzz Goodbody's *Hamlet* at The Other Place in 1975.[4] What seems far more significant about her *Titus,* the first time that the Royal Shakespeare Company had produced an uncut version of the play, are the differences between her uses of directorial authority and those of the earlier *Titus* directors. In effect, her production re-viewed the sources and nature of theatrical power, a Shakespearean revision that was the product not solely of gender difference but more deeply of the differences between Warner's training and experience and those of the "typical" RSC assistant director. As a woman coming to the RSC with experience in independent theatrical production, Warner performed a revision of company formulations of the politics of Shakespearean texts and Shakespearean production. She created a *Titus* which foregrounded the bonds between family, gender, and imperial dominion that the two earlier RSC productions obscured. It accomplished this reorientation through Warner's retreat from illusionistic practice and through the consequent freedom to expose and explore the material bases of *Titus*'s representations of political authority and its abuse in the patriarchal Roman family. Shaped in rehearsal by an unusually collective decision-making process, and performed by a company in the midst of asserting its own voice in the perpetual controversies that seem to dominate RSC relations with its patrons, her production represented a new attempt on the company's part to redefine the politics of Shakespearean production.

The case of *Titus Andronicus* illustrates the contingency of the reputations of individual Shakespeare plays, their repeated textual production not by a static audience's unvariegated receptivity but rather by shifting literary and social events. *Titus,* with its murders, gang rape, mutilation, and cannibalism, is an undeniably strange and savage work. While it may have exercised a certain kind of fascination on an elite segment of its original audience (as suggested by the existence of the so-called "Peacham drawing" of several of the characters captioned by three passages from the text), its apparent "delight in tragedies" (4.1.60)[5] no doubt contributed to its lack of performance between its 1594 premiere and the Restoration and served as Thomas Ravenscroft's rationale for his 1678 adaptation: "'tis the most incorrect and undigested piece in all his works. It seems rather a heap of rubbish than a structure."[6] Ravenscroft set about correcting Shakespeare's play by strengthening its characters' revenge motives and adding prominence to the role of Aaron the Moor, a simplification which, while ignoring the original's imperial concerns, more clearly forced spectator and reader identification with dominant perspectives on cultural value: male instead of female, white instead of black.[7] The play's eighteenth- and nineteenth-century performances indicate an incorporation of bits of other plays about vengeful yet heroic Moors, further unifying what remained of Shakespeare's original conception around the role of Aaron, but once the days of Quin, Kean, and Aldridge had passed, the play again receded into oblivion.[8]

The Royal Shakespeare Company, then known as the Shakespeare Memorial Theatre, did not perform *Titus* until 1955, by which time it had produced every other play in the canon. Director Peter Brook spent nearly a year's preliminary work cutting some 650 lines from the play, designing its costumes and sets, and composing a musical score. He aimed his efforts at what remained immanent, yet imperfectly expressed, in *Titus:* "In *Titus Andronicus,* the whole work was to take the hints and hidden strands of the play and wring the most from them, take what was embryonic perhaps, and bring it out. But if it isn't there to begin with it can't be done."[9] His vision of the "dark flowing current" contained within the text that shaped it as "a powerful and eventually beautiful barbaric ritual"[10] in effect superimposed his own narrative notion of tragic significance over the text. Thus he turned the tragedy of Aaron into the tragedy of Titus Andronicus, his excavation of the role being inestimably aided by the passionately committed performance of Laurence Olivier.[11] His rewriting of *Titus* centered on the anguished coming to consciousness of a great man and the circumstances of his fall.

That the "powerful and . . . beautiful barbaric ritual" Brook claimed to have discovered at the heart of *Titus Andronicus* affirmed the androcentric nature of narrativity in the dominant cultures is suggested by the relative disappearance of the role of Lavinia in his production. Lavinia's rape and mutilation lies near the center of Shakespeare's text, where its horror is insistently pointed by the forty-seven-line Ovidian soliloquy her uncle Marcus delivers as he tries to understand what could possibly have happened to her. The scene's stage directions are brutally and impossibly explicit: "Enter the Empress' sons, with Lavinia, her hands cut off, and her tongue cut out, and ravish'd" (2.4). The relentless spectacle that the text makes of Lavinia's degradation and silencing, which there adds to Titus's bitterness at Rome's treatment of his family, was entirely absent from Brook's version. He cut the soliloquy and, instead of following the text's specificity about Lavinia's appearance, presented Vivien Leigh in the role with red streamers tied to her wrists and held in her mouth. While critical comment on Brook's production was virtually unanimous in its acceptance that his abstract, distanced style was necessary to make tolerable the play's sensational violence, some reviewers seemed especially to regret his disinterest in spectacularizing rape and mutilation: "a few more hairs might credibly have been misplaced after her morning in the wood."[12] Kenneth Tynan, whose opinion of Leigh's stage work was generally poor, managed to combine regret at foregone opportunity for voyeuristic pleasure with an acknowledgement of the precise effect its treatment had on the connection the text establishes between Lavinia's suffering and Titus's outraged patriarchal pride. He remarked that Leigh as Lavinia "receives the news that she is about to be ravished on her husband's corpse with little more than the mild annoyance of one who would have preferred foam rubber. Otherwise, the *minor* parts are played to the hilt."[13]

Before Warner, the RSC had last performed *Titus Andronicus* in the 1972 season as part of "The Romans," the first company presentation of *Coriolanus, Julius Caesar, Antony and Cleopatra,* and *Titus* as a group. Although artistic director Trevor Nunn denied the intention to extract a consistent unity from the four plays apart from the opportunity the project offered to view Shakespeare's portrayal of Rome as it changed through his career, he did indeed impose a narrative structure on the season, outdoing Brook's comparatively more modest accomplishment. Nunn was the first British director to perceive *Titus's* historical and political concerns,[14] but his production of its history and politics demonstrated a radical skepticism about the possibility of political change and an anxiety to reaffirm the status quo more resembling Brook's abstract and apolitical modernism than the product of the "basically left wing organization" he asserted the company had become by 1972.[15]

Named to succeed Peter Hall as artistic director in 1968, Nunn took control of the company during a period of intense internal change. Junior members were expressing the desire for greater control over the conditions under which they worked, seeking out opportunities for more studio performance and more direct participation in the selection and adaptation of performance texts. With the strong participation of Buzz Goodbody (whose feminism and love for theater found joint expression in her performances with the London Women's Theatre Group and who became the founding director of RSC's The Other Place), the RSC imported some of the confrontational, direct style of the so-called "Fringe" of the country's growing political theater movement. Yet, while creating regulated spaces for more intimate and direct theater than was always possible in the main house, and while serving as an artistic home for many sympathetic individuals, the company institutionally resisted the kind of transformation of theater into a cultural tool for intervention that the alternative theater prized.[16] In 1970, noting that the company had accomplished a great deal of politically conscious production under the previous directorship of Peter Hall, Nunn remarked that the RSC was now more interested in exploring "the human personalities of a king or queen, rather than . . . their public roles."[17] His *Titus* was to demonstrate precisely this separation between characterization of the persons in whom authority is vested and the exercise of that authority.

Nunn produced his *Titus Andronicus* in the Royal Shakespeare Theatre, as had Brook, but under his administration that theater's stage had undergone major renovations; "The Romans" were to constitute its first public test. Aimed at increasing the versatility of the main stage, which was thrust farther out into the auditorium to lessen the distance between stage and audience and divided into sections equipped with individual hydraulic lifts,[18] the mechanical changes perhaps had the ultimate effect of facilitating the large-scale, self-consciously theatrical style which has since become a Nunn trademark. Designed to distract spectators from the unbridgeable space built between them and the main stage, the renovations also succeeded in inscribing the separation into the experience of watching a play in the Royal Shakespeare Theatre. Although it was increasingly to be used to create effects of great sophistication and power, the company's main house became a physical representation of the enforced passivity of spectatorship in the realist theater: meanings enacted upon it were delivered to audiences whose only role became to submit to them.[19]

The four productions sometimes presented their assumed correspondence between Shakespearean politics and contemporary institutions in strikingly concrete and imaginative ways—perhaps most notably in its portrayal of *Coriolanus*'s quarrel between patricians and plebeians as a contest between labor and capital, with the plebeians' complaints about the falsely-engineered food shortage and the creation of punitive new laws designed to "chain up and restrain the poor" (1.1.84–85) turned into the occasion for a wildcat strike.[20] But, true to the apocalyptic tone of Nunn's program notes—"Shakespeare's Elizabethan nightmare" of blood and state violence "has become ours. . . . have we time for answers, or are we already in the convulsion which heralds a fall greater than Rome's?"—the productions most often seemed to settle for emphasizing the workings of a monolithic Roman state as it crushed and devoured its citizens, rather than the responses of Shakespeare's characters as they confronted and attempted to define themselves in relation to state power.

The 1972 *Titus* exemplified Nunn's lack of nuance. In deliberate contrast to Peter Brook, Nunn chose realistic detail, with accurate models of Chiron and Demetrius's severed heads and the sound of a saw cutting through bone when Titus severs his hand in 3.1. The production also declined to take advantage of the technical possibilities created by the newly-mobile stage, being played almost wholly on the thrust. Despite such specificity and relative simplicity of staging, however, the production was more interested in presenting *Titus* as a spectacle of Rome in decadence than it was to exploring the text's treatment of the empire's political and social institutions.[21] Having "explained" Rome's transformation into a "wilderness of tigers" (3.1.54) through his stylized portrayal of the (energetic and entertaining) corruption of its imperial court, Nunn concluded his narrative of *Titus*'s politics by offering an explicitly Christian hope of renewal: his Lucius (Ian Hogg) accepted bread and wine as he assumed the political authority that had descended on him by default.

Even critics who recognized the reactionary potential of Nunn's conception of "degeneracy as an historical pressure" had trouble accepting his original proposition that *Titus* did indeed display a political self-consciousness. More familiar with reports of Brook's ritualistic production of seventeen years before than with the text, which was hardly required reading in schools or universities, one critic exclaimed impatiently that "*Titus Andronicus* is no more a play about history or politics than *Measure for Measure* is a play about Vienna."[22] The remark suggests the extent of the theatrical neglect that the play had suffered, a process of marginalization which simultaneously delivered it more directly to directorial fiddling and distanced it from the Roman group's ideas about the connection between public and private, the desires of the individual and the demands of the state, the process and cost of fashioning oneself into a citizen of Rome.[23]

Observers of Nunn's *Titus* were not aided in this reintegration of the play into the canon by the cuts he made in the text, the prominence he and Wood gave to the role of Saturninus, or by the stylistic discontinuity between the lavish excess of his Roman orgies and his comparatively "realistic" treatment of the play's violence, a discontinuity which disrupted an important opportunity for visually establishing the contexts for the savageries the characters perform upon one another. Nunn's *Titus* in fact foreshadowed the atomized and disengaged mainstream British theater of the late 1970s and the 1980s, a spectacular theater of which he was to become one of the leading impresarios: " 'Evil' or 'dark' forces are experienced as located outside the self—and thus the individual feels unable to control those forces."[24] He produced his witty, energetic, detached *Titus* during a period of high unemployment, industrial decline, violent strikes, and increasing class polarization, when the authority of the British left was eroding. The Labour Party's decisive electoral defeats in the early 1970s presaged the public shift toward the law and order platform of the Conservative Party. With the range it allowed its director's exercise of authority, and its enshrinement of social decadence as a historical explanation of moral decay, the 1972 *Titus* did achieve a kind of political topicality—although not, perhaps, the kind Nunn originally envisioned.

Neither wholly the "basically left-wing organization" Nunn felt an accurate description of the company in 1972, nor wholly internally comfortable with its status as the most revered arts organization in the country, the RSC almost necessarily encountered contradictions when it came to producing the politics it was coming officially to insist inhered in Shakespearean texts. Some of these contradictions were the result of life under government subsidy, whose administrators in the increasingly conservative mood of the early 1970s were more likely to state openly the belief that it was "wholly improper that an artistic organization receiving a very large subsidy from the taxpayers should be run by people who boast of using this subsidy for political purposes."[25] Others, however, were the result of the degree to which the company as an institution had internalized the conservative social values that some of its members individually opposed. Cast in the role of wise father, Nunn fashioned a *Titus* which unquestioningly reproduced patriarchal perspective: one which allowed great theatrical presence to the head of the macrocosmic state, one whose primary notion of political change was the decay and renewal of hierarchical authority, one whose very stage worked to limit audience response to its representation of the relentless victimization of individuals by the omnipresent yet mysteriously nonmaterial power of the state ("degeneracy as an historical pressure").

Prevented by her theatrical training and experience from replicating Nunn's patriarchal control over the apparatus of production, Deborah Warner produced a *Titus* which declined to replicate its text's patriarchal politics as an unproblematical Shakespearean given. She could portray the material bases of the play's conception of Roman politics in the family of its hero because of her focus on the conditions necessary to theatrical production, on textual and narrative integrity, and on the bond between stage and spectator. She succeeded for the first time in revealing *Titus*'s stature as a play inescapably about Shakespearean politics and history, and about the use of patriarchal families as the instrument through which political order is maintained or shattered.[26]

A graduate of London's Central School of Speech and Drama rather than Oxford or Cambridge,[27] Warner developed her directorial style primarily through work with a theater group she founded after leaving school instead of through apprenticeship with an established company.[28] The hallmarks of her Kick Theatre Company, which she founded in 1980, were its emphasis on ensemble work and intensive rehearsals, small casts, close attention to uncut texts (primarily though not exclusively Shakespeare), and minimal reliance on elaborate props, sets, or costumes. Kick's small scale—it performed an uncut *King Lear* with a cast of ten at the 1985 Edinburgh Fringe—enabled it to become a kind of permanent theater workshop, attracting a committed core of actors who returned from other jobs to help develop its annual productions despite the fact that most of the time there was no company money to pay them. She believed that "actors want to work with Kick because we offer them for some unknown reason something which is not being offered elsewhere. We offer them a chance to be fully creative in the rehearsal room."[29] The kind of creativity Warner elicited from her actors was based on careful group attention to detail throughout extended rehearsal periods; the six-hour nightly call for Kick's 1986 *Coriolanus* (performed in London by a cast of twelve) included two hours of warming-up exercises in addition to the four-hour performance.

Despite the acclaim its work received, Kick remained more interested in arriving as a group at a way of doing a particular play designed for a particular venue rather than making its "house style" unevenly available under touring conditions; in 1986, the company lost its Arts Council grant precisely because it declined to undertake the extensive tours which are one of the prerequisites for British theater subsidy. This insistence on collaborative closeness extended to the ways in which the company delegated authority. It operated collectively, with Warner's voice one of a dozen equal voices making decisions about meanings of words or scenes: "I have to admit I go into rehearsal knowing as little about the play as the actors and we discover it together—which all sounds very Utopian and merry, but its actually true. . . . Creating the right environment for the right group of people is the most important thing of all, so people will feel happy to suggest ideas and play about and make absolute fools of themselves. That, I think, is the director's job."[30] The closeness guaranteed by the company's small size and by its development of a core of returning actors facilitated its commitment to what Warner described as "textual theatre," a style of production which subordinated theatrical realism to manifesting the company's discoveries about Shakespeare's language: "It's much more exciting to try and get the actors to do everything, to get them to create the storm scene in *The Tempest* themselves, as I did, rather than use a tape. I think you'll find far more imaginative ways if you don't allow yourself an easy option, if you don't allow yourself a tape recorder or a set."[31] She suggested that Kick's minimalism could be more effective as a means of producing *Coriolanus* than the "exclusively epic approach to production" that had "drowned" that play in the past, describing her task as telling its story "excitingly" instead of "trying to recreate a place called Rome." Her interest remained in finding imaginative ways of reaching spectators: "lose contact between performer and audience and then theatre is the dullest thing in the world."[32]

Warner's reliance on her actors' abilities, her trust of Shakespearean texts, and her antirealistic theatrical bent—"I loathe plays with a lot of furniture or stage directions"[33]—directly opposed themselves to the highly designed productions which had come to dominate RSC programs in the late 1980s. The structure of the Royal Shakespeare Theatre stage itself, whose proscenium arch was literally a weight-bearing part of the structure and so could not be knocked down without endangering the entire building,[34] designated it as a picture frame whose borders constitutionally resisted resizing. The mobile stage installed under Nunn's guidance was intended to increase the versatility of the stage space, and it did so. Yet while company directors and designers have learned to exploit to the fullest its spectacular possibilities, actors have sometimes felt themselves and the words they speak to be smothered in the process: "Some directors and designers habitually contrive spectacular moments that simply collapse when the actors open their mouths. They create productions where what looks worst, and weakest, and least fulfilled, are the actors."[35] Partially in response to the limitations of the Royal Shakespeare Theatre stage and the limitations it imposed on casts and crews,[36] the company received in 1986 a one-million-pound gift from an anonymous contributor which enabled it to commission a new Stratford auditorium. The Swan Theatre, a contemporary approximation of a late Renaissance playhouse dedicated to performing forgotten plays of the period between 1570 and 1750, was the site of Warner's *Titus Andronicus* and contributed greatly to its impact.

The Swan is a semicircular structure, built within the walls of the first Shakespeare theater in Stratford; including upstairs an elevator, a large new rehearsal room, and office space, it tended to long-standing company administrative needs as well as to the need for a new kind of playing space. Its stage is a rough rectangle about twenty feet wide by about forty feet deep, thrusting out to about chest-height of spectators sitting in the first row of seats. Three levels of seats rise on three sides of the stage, with the top level running all the way around and reserved as an extra gallery for actors or musicians. It seats fewer than 500 spectators, with most seats ten meters or closer to the stage, and the house lights cannot be completely dimmed.[37] Inside the theater, actors and audience are both exposed, completely visible to each other, thrown into an unusually intimate spatial relationship. Spectators can see actors' facial expressions and the details of their movements in new detail, and audience members also remain aware of each other as they sit closely together, watching. Actors and directors accustomed to the vast stage of the Royal Shakespeare Theatre and its separation from the audience must learn different methods of communicating with a house seated so near as virtually to become collaborators in the creation of new theatrical tensions.[38]

Produced in the Swan's second season, Deborah Warner's *Titus Andronicus* demonstrated a greater sensitivity to the space, a sensitivity originating in her work for Kick, which was always carefully tailored to specific stages at Edinburgh or at London's Almeida Theatre. Her production was not as vividly and insistently designed as those from the theater's first season, nor was its set the product of the constrained time schedule of the company workshops. Designer Isabella Bywater was present from the first cast meeting and made sketches on the spot as Warner and her actors worked on the script scene by scene.[39] This collaborative discovery of meaning resulted in a very simple set design which covered the stage with plain scrubbed wooden boards.[40] While some characters wore togas and classical armor, many of the costumes were not recognizably "Roman" at all, Chiron and Demetrius for example wearing leather boots with attached spur-like metal rowels.

Visually, as Warner remarked about her Kick *Coriolanus* of the previous year, the play was not interested in "trying to recreate a place called Rome." Rather than overwhelming the stage with props which would realistically depict the play's interiors, she and Bywater chose only a few deliberately unclassical objects—an aluminum ladder, an electric light bulb, a white chef's toque—and used them tellingly. Bywater's austere work responded to the theater's insistent physical exposure of actors and their playing to their audience in its refusal to erect distracting barriers between text and performance. In contrast to the sumptuous detail of Nunn's *Titus* and the design of the initial season's work at the Swan, Warner's *Titus Andronicus* declined the opportunity to write a naturalizing visual narrative for its text (which, except for its translation of *"Terras Astraea reliquit"* into English, was unaltered from J. C. Maxwell's Arden edition). From its opening scene, in which Saturninus and Bassianus hurried onstage to address their arguments about the descent of the Roman empery to the assembled audience, spectators were urgently drawn into the play's presentation of the origins and nature of Roman political authority. Its visual restraint allowed Warner the liberty of dramatizing that location in its construction of difference: between Romans and foreigners, men and women, parents and children.

After establishing a mood of political inquiry with its opening direct addresses, Warner's *Titus* played its first scene with careful attention to how Shakespeare's early vision of Roman politics might look onstage. A grizzled and battered Titus entered sitting atop an aluminum ladder carried on the shoulders of Aaron and Tamora's sons, all bound at the wrists, in a striking visualization of Titus' status as a warrior and of Rome's military dominion over its enemies. Dismounting, he led Tamora in at the end of a dog's leash attached to a leather collar around her neck. Brian Cox's performance as Titus suggested that the hero's exercise of supreme military and imperial authority existed alongside other, contradictory strains in his character. Dirty-faced, wearing a battered and stained metal breastplate with laced and buckled boots, an old knitted cloak, and a crown of laurel leaves, he projected a kind of obdurate, self-centered complacency as well as age and weariness. When Marcus attempted to argue Titus out of his refusal to bury Mutius in the family tomb, for example, Cox as Titus ignored him by putting two fingers in his ears and humming loudly like a child resisting a parent's discipline. This Titus was distracted enough from the public rhetorical purpose of his own first speech in 1.1 to fondle Tamora absently at the line "Here, Goths have given me leave to sheathe my sword" (1.1.85); when Lucius whispered a reminder to him, he slapped his head in exasperation and proceeded with the rest of the speech. And yet, when challenged, this Titus became as blind, brutal, and dedicated to the humiliation of his enemies as the Rome his military triumphs served. Cox established a daring equilibrium between humor and enormity, creating a character which could move from childishly stopping his ears to murdering his son, and root both actions in the egotism and rigidity nourished by a life devoted to administering the will of Rome. In the close confines of the Swan, the disorientation caused by Cox's blending of horror and burlesque was jarring and inescapable, and helped immeasurably to reveal the play as a text about the abuses of power.

The eccentricities of this Titus threw into sharper relief the fact that, despite them, he still wielded enormous authority in Rome. In Warner's production, individuals became the instruments and not the creators of the dehumanized, corporate values of Roman culture. Rather than drawing, as Nunn did, on the sensationalized general outlines of "a place called Rome," Warner and Cox instead used their Titus as a means of describing their production's distance from more conventionally recognizable depictions of Rome or Roman warriors—ones centering on the marmoreal implacability of a virtuous republican hero or obscuring the connection between the demands of *imperium* and the lives of those citizens living under its sway. This deliberate undercutting of preexisting familiarity with Shakespeare's Rome or the nature of the characters in whom Shakespeare invests political authority participated in the kind of theatrical historicization familiar from the theoretical writings of Bertolt Brecht, whose work has been much more influential in Britain than in the United States, and was central to British alternative political theater. The Brechtian conceptions of alienation and the social gest were formulated to reveal how social relationship works as the material manifestation of ideology, of how individual behavior is inscribed with class, gender, and historical determinants.[41] This materialist practice was perhaps particularly well-suited to a production of *Titus Andronicus,* a text whose examples of extreme physical violence plainly depict the appropriation of its characters' bodies to the demands of Roman culture.

The materialist historicism suggested by the deliberate disharmonies of its Titus, whose violence perhaps provoked all the more shock because he continued to invite amusement, continued in the production's treatment of the text's sense of gender difference. Warner's *Titus* emphasized, as the other RSC productions did not, that the patriarchal social order which transmitted Rome's rigid gender definitions was one of the material manifestations of Titus's absolute authority. This patriarchal authority of men over women was made powerfully visible in Titus's physical control over Tamora as he led her onstage. His assumption that he might rationally expect to rape her as the object of a coercive sexual exchange between him and her own people gained much of its theatrical point from the very lack of malice with which he alluded to it, half-submerging it within a larger speech on other imperial responsibilities.

The production also emphasized that Titus's patriarchal authority extended to his children, perceiving that the family depicted in Shakespeare's political plays is an institution designed to model most intimately the yielding to manifest authority. The shocking moment when Titus stabs his son Mutius for defying him in the matter of Lavinia's betrothal was made more legibly a part of the play's enshrinement of difference by its previous suggestion of the existence of a near-tribal solidarity between Titus's sons. It gesturally represented this group solidarity as Romans and as men of their family by having the actors stamp in booming ritual unison on the wooden stage at moments when the text most strongly evokes cultural distinction: as they enter with their father and his captives, as they proposed to accompany the emperor on a hunt, as they return from sacrificing Tamora's son. Given the care it took to establish the bonds of familial enterprise between Titus's sons, the production was able to make sense of one of the play's most difficult moments, that of Martius and Quintus's discovery of Bassianus's body in the pit in 2.3. The text describes Martius falling into the pit accidentally, telling his brother above what he discovers there, and Quintus then falling in after him. In Warner's production, Aaron told his story about the chance to trap a sleeping panther in the pit as he taunts the brothers; Martius fell into the pit as they chased him. Quintus was unable to pull his brother out of the pit because both of them were simply incapacitated with horror by their recognition of Bassianus' body; overcome himself, he falls in. In Warner's *Titus,* the scene became an affirmation of the brothers' shared sensibility and their empathy with each other as men of the same tribe. Its motivation was laid by the specific physicality Warner and her actors created to communicate the group identity of Titus's sons.

If common purpose between its men thus becomes one pillar of patriarchal society, Shakespeare's *Titus Andronicus* identifies the strict control of women's bodies, utterances, and social experiences as another. As the only daughter of her authoritarian family, chaste and obedient Lavinia's role is as fixed as her brothers': to be given by her father in marriage and thereby to reproduce the familial order of Roman politics. In the first act, after respectfully greeting her father on his return to Rome, she maintains her silence as he impulsively decides to give her to Saturninus despite a preexisting contract with Bassianus, and is absent from the stage during Titus's equally impulsive murder of her brother Mutius. More than a replication of social restrictions on female autonomy, Lavinia's silence and absence is itself the product of the "range of difference"[42] between men and women within patriarchal dramatic narrative: her social presence derives from her status as her father's dependent daughter. The later rape and mutilation of a daughter named for the legendary mother of the Roman people images the destruction of a familially ordered civilization.

Under Warner's careful establishment of the cultural contexts which manifested Rome's authority, Lavinia's fate became the production's most powerful evocation of the effects of that authority as it was exercised by men against women within Roman culture. Again, the production's use of movement and gesture, its design of physical action to embody abstract ideas, clarified the bond between power and its abuse. After being forced to observe the Roman men's participation in group rituals of solidarity in the first act, Tamora and her sons spontaneously improvised a parodic ritual of their own as she described to them Lavinia and Bassianus's supposed plot against her sanity in 2.3. Richard McCabe and Piers Ibbotson as Chiron and Demetrius mimed the "hissing snakes" and "swelling toads" which Estelle Kohler as Tamora insisted lay in wait to menace her in the forest. The virtuosity of this communal improvisation, Kohler's fevered narration apparently eliciting McCabe and Ibbotson's gestures, created the audience's amused recognition of just how deliberately "staged" and artificial it was. But when Chiron and Demetrius suddenly stabbed Bassianus at the end of their mother's speech, the laughter was stifled; the murder was made to seem as logical a result of the Goths' bastardized ritual as their humiliation and Mutius's death were of the Romans' assertion of cultural unity.

The Goths' ritual desecration continued into the production's treatment of Lavinia's rape and mutilation. The contrast between the appearance of Sonia Ritter as Lavinia as she appeared in the first act and as she entered after the crime was cruelly obvious. Beginning the play as a radiant young girl in a plain sand-colored gown, she was transformed into a crippled, helpless picture of torment, her gown smeared with greenish-gray mud. Rigid with pain and shock, her hands wrapped in rags, she lay on the floor as Chiron and Demetrius exultantly mocked her, writhing across the stage to imitate her prostrate posture. After spitting on her, they congratulated each other on the thoroughness of their triumph over her and left the stage.

From Ravenscroft into the twentieth century, theatrical excuses for not playing Lavinia's entrance in a "realistic" manner have turned on the scene's disturbing extremity, it being regarded as either too violent or too absurd to be performed as written. Warner's presentation, preceded by careful explication of the blind force of Rome's assertion of control over its citizens and enemies alike, insisting on presenting the rapists' desire to degrade their victim and Lavinia's unbearable pain and shock, proved generations of such genteel exception wrong. The audience's stunned silence was broken only by murmurs of disturbed distress. The Swan's small size forced the audience to contemplate the spectacle of Lavinia's victimization as her uncle spoke all forty-seven lines of his Ovidian lament, trying to understand and accurately name what has happened to her. Donald Sumpter's measured and sorrowful meditation juxtaposed against the sight of Ritter's powerfully-mimed agony and shame spoke both to the irreducibly material presence of the crime in the text, and to the inability of Warner's male Romans to empathize with Lavinia's predicament.

Brook and Nunn both shaped 3.1, in which Titus cuts off his hand in a fruitless attempt to save two of his surviving sons, on Titus himself, treating it as an opportunity to dramatize the effects of his family's mounting suffering on the development of his own tragic knowledge. In Warner, the scene instead enacted the gap of feeling between father and daughter, concentrating on what happens to Titus' sense of patriarchal entitlement after the integrity of his family, which was its social manifestation, is shattered. Here, the interplay between Lavinia's pain and enforced silence and Titus' mounting baffled rage revealed Rome's chilling indifference to the human costs of obedience to its will. Her father and her uncle conducted their confused speculation on how she met her fate between themselves, as she tried to stand before them unaided. Unable to communicate verbally with her father, Lavinia remained a feeling, thinking being who visibly shook when Titus cut off his hand, who wept in her helpless shame and grief for her father as he dilated upon his disillusion, who sought through kissing him to receive a comfort that his growing conviction of Rome's betrayal prevents him from granting her or even realizing that she desperately needs. As even the reasonable Marcus urged Titus to look on his family as a spur to revenge, Lavinia finally collapsed beside him as if under the weight of her father's emotional distance from her suffering, a suffering rooted in her own sorrow, her grief for her husband and brothers, and her dispossession from the sources of her value in Roman culture—very nearly from human expressiveness itself. The family banquet in 3.2 became the occasion for a more contained exposition of this kind of patriarchal deafness to a daughter's devastation: as Ritter mimed thirst, the others at the table struggled unsuccessfully to read her signs.

Warner's production shared with Nunn's an interest in exploring the cultural and political status of Shakespeare's Rome. In sharp distinction from Nunn's, however, Warner's *Titus* recognized the text's identification of patriarchal solidarity and military triumph over foreigners as its primary dominant expressions of the nature of Roman politics. Instead of the lavish attention paid in the Royal Shakespeare Theatre to the visual assertion that the growth of Roman social decadence somehow produced the play's violence, Warner concentrated on producing the social and political relationships in which the text grounds its savageries. Titus's domination of Rome's enemies and his assumption of the right to kill the child who defies him both speak to this Rome's construction of political absolutism as male. Indeed, the patriarchal quality of power in the play first becomes visible because of those against whom Titus wields it: a foreign woman, her children, and his own. Warner's Titus's dreamy suggestion of his entitlement to rape Tamora alludes to a sexual expression of the authority that his entrance on her sons' shoulders has already presented; her treatment of Chiron and Demetrius's rape of Lavinia and its effects on her family was a more explicit representation of this masculine power to define and control.

In following the text, Deborah Warner's *Titus Andronicus* discovered methods of articulating its grim vision of the exercise of power without accountability. It contextualized the play's marked interest in the relationship between parents and children, particularly Titus's bond with his only daughter, through its representation of imperial tragedy. In Warner's hands, Rome became a place where parents' exploitation and destruction of their own children was the brutally logical familial result of the empire's dedication to mastery. If Warner's production may accurately be said to have pursued historical relevance in presenting Shakespeare's first Roman tragedy, such relevance lay in its theatrical dilations of the play's concern with patriarchy as a model for authoritarian rule. The history of gender difference she found in *Titus Andronicus* became available primarily through her production's refashioning of its narrative, a refashioning she ironically accomplished not through large-scale directorial intervention like Brook's or Nunn's, but through the comparatively modest tactic of returning to a complete text, and her resourceful means of filling in the text's gaps through physical action. Her *Titus* began by implicitly repudiating the theatrical assumption that its horrors are gratuitous, inexplicable, and best left unexamined. The newness of Warner's *Titus* resided precisely in its insistent exposure of how gender operates as an instrument of cultural authority. In producing this version of Roman theatrical value through the Royal Shakespeare Company, her *Titus* also adumbrated a working methodology for decentralizing and reapportioning some of the authority which cultures exercise over how they will represent themselves to their citizens.

NOTES

1. See, for example, Juliet Dusinberre, *Shakespeare and the Nature of Women* (London: Macmillan, 1975), and Kathleen McLuskie, " 'The Emperor of Russia Was My Father': Gender and Theatrical Power," in *Images of Shakespeare: Proceedings of the Third Congress of the International Shakespeare Association,* ed. Werner Habicht, D. J. Palmer, and Roger Pringle (Newark: University of Delaware Press, 1988), 174–87.

2. Peter Brook's in 1955 and Trevor Nunn's in 1972 were the only full-length productions before Deborah Warner's in 1987. However, the company also produced John Barton's one-hour condensed version as part of a double bill with *The Two Gentlemen of Verona* in 1981.

3. Through at least the beginning of the 1980s the company's structure remained not only strongly hierarchical despite experiments in decentralizing authority, but according to Colin Chambers, *Other Spaces: New Theatre and the RSC* (London: Eyre Methuen, 1980), "a male-dominated hierarchy, with those who [were] definitely parents and those who [were] definitely children (and if they happen to be secretaries and women, which is most often the case, they will be servicing their wise, humanist 'fathers' with cups of tea or coffee)"(17). Chambers describes communist and feminist activist Buzz Goodbody's struggle to progress as a woman director at the RSC in the late 1960s and early 1970s (11–14, 26–33).

4. See Margaret Sheehy, "Why Aren't There More Women Directors?" *Drama* 151, no. 2 (1984): 12; Clare Venables, "The Woman Director in the Theatre," *Theatre Quarterly* 38 (1980): 3. Actress Harriet Walter, speaking in Carol Rutter's

fascinating *Clamorous Voices: Shakespeare's Women Today*, ed. Faith Evans (New York: Routledge, 1989), notes the contradictions arising from granting of directorial authority to individual female directors with male-dominated institutions: "It's easier to defy a male director. If [he] makes a mistake, there's only a slight possibility that his career will be damaged. It's a personal failure, but a limited failure. If a woman's production fails, though, in a sense she has failed for all women directors. It is still the case that every time we do something publicly we are under pressure to represent women, and all the choices we have to make have to be right because any flaws or failures in a production will be put down to our gender" (xxi). Walter's complaint speaks to my argument that gender bias is an institutional pressure that cannot be wholly addressed by the simple expedient of granting individual women authority over individual productions.

5. I cite J. C. Maxwell's Arden edition (London: Methuen, 1953; rev. ed. 1961), which was Warner's choice of text.

6. From Ravenscroft's address "To the Reader" in the 1687 edition. For fuller discussion, see G. Harold Metz, "The Stage History of *Titus Andronicus*," *Shakespeare Quarterly* 28 (1977): 154.

7. Feminist film and theater theorists have conducted much of the contemporary dialogue on relationships between gender and narrative structure. See, for example, Teresa de Lauretis, *Alice Doesn't: Feminism, Semiotics, Cinema* (Bloomington: Indiana University Press, 1984); Elin Diamond, "Refusing the Romanticism of Identity: Narrative Interventions in Churchill, Benmussa, Duras," *Theatre Journal* 37 (1985): 273–86; and Catherine Belsey, "Constructing the Subject: Deconstructing the Text," in *Feminist Criticism and Social Change: Sex, Class, and Race in Literature and Culture*, ed. Judith Newton and Deborah Rosenfelt (New York: Methuen, 1985), 45–64.

8. The text of *Titus* persistently presents the character of Aaron as a recognizably black, sub-Saharan African, referring to his "fleece of woolly hair" at 2.3.34, describing him as the empress's "raven-colored love" at 2.3.83, presenting his vow to persevere in his evil ways until "his soul" is "black like his face" at 3.1.205. Interestingly, Warner ignored these textual cues as her production gave the role to an actor of Greek ancestry; he was olive-skinned, but certainly not "raven-colored." This choice in a production otherwise committed to following the text opens interesting possibilities for discussion of how Warner's race as well as her sex may have worked to produce her vision of *Titus*. While Trevor Nunn's 1972 *Titus* remained oblivious to many of the text's treatments of gender, his Aaron was played by a black American actor, Calvin Lockhart.

9. Peter Brook, *The Shifting Point* (New York: Harper and Row, 1987), 5. Brook's reshaping of *Titus Andronicus* was an early expression of his interest in abstracting and distancing Shakespeare, an interest perhaps brought to its fullest flowering in his influential 1970 *Midsummer Night's Dream*, performed on trapezes against a draped white background. Warner saw the 1970 *Dream* as a thirteen-year-old schoolgirl and cited it as one of the experiences most strongly affecting her choice of a theatrical career. See Debbie Wolfe, "Alive and Kicking," *Drama* 158: no. 4 (1985): 12.

10. Peter Brook, *The Empty Space* (New York: Atheneum, 1968), 95.

11. Richard David, "Drams of Eale," *Shakespeare Survey* 10 (1957): 126. Kenneth Tynan's contemporary review, reprinted in *Curtains: Selections from the Drama Criticism and Related Writings* (London: Longman's Green and Co., 1961), remarked that Olivier's performance confirmed his presence as "pound for pound, the greatest actor alive" (105).

12. J. C. Trewin, *Peter Brook: A Biography* (London: Macdonald, 1971), 84.

13. Tynan, *Curtains,* 104 (italics mine).

14. See Margaret Tierney's interview of Nunn and Christopher Morley, the stage designer for the 1972 season, in *Plays and Players* 19, no. 12 (1972): 23–27.

15. Trevor Nunn and David Jones, letter to *The Times,* 5 Dec. 1972: 17. Nunn and Jones made this statement in defense of the company's role in the controversy surrounding its production of *The Island of the Mighty,* a play on Irish history by John Arden and Margaretta D'Arcy. Arden and D'Arcy charged that the RSC was diluting what they had conceived as the anti-imperialistic core of the play and that Jones, the director, had denied them contractually guaranteed rights to meet with the cast and crew. To protest what they regarded as an abrogation of their rights as workers in the theatrical process, they eventually picketed the opening and Arden accepted Nunn and Jones's invitation to address the audience after the opening. Nunn and Jones found Arden and D'Arcy's accusation that they fomented through the RSC "an imperialistic atmosphere" particularly unfair, asserting that they represented "a basically left-wing organization which has staged the work of . . . politically committed authors." Occurring as it did at the end of a season dedicated to the presentation of Nunn's perception of the Roman plays' political views, the dispute over *The Island of the Mighty* speaks suggestively to his resistance to particular kinds of political content in his Shakespeares. The quarrel, Nunn and Jones wrote, manifested "a tension, possibly within the Ardens themselves, between political and social convictions on the one hand and the demands of a complex work of the imagination on the other," delicately implying that the producers had in fact acted to rescue the play for art from the authors' failure to separate the claims of art from those of politics. That their politics and the artistic forms they chose to dramatize them were inseparable was precisely the point that Arden and D'Arcy argued; their later comments, particularly D'Arcy's, that their works on socialist and Irish subjects encountered a kind of effective censorship in the British theater support my observations here on the difficulties inherent in unfixing the deproblematized blandness of expressions of dominant culture. For a discussion of the political issues Arden and D'Arcy perceived at work in the mainstream theater's treatment of their works, see Catherine Itzin, *Stages in the Revolution: Political Theatre in Britain Since 1968* (London: Eyre Methuen, 1980), 24–38.

16. Itzin, *Stages in the Revolution* is the most comprehensive history of the British alternative theater movement. Also see Chambers, *Other Spaces,* for an account of the influence of political theater in the RSC. Perhaps one measure of RSC actors' continuing interest in securing a greater voice in the administration of the company and in the various kinds of financial, political, and critical controver-

sies in which it finds itself embroiled was the establishment of the Company Committee after the 1986 season. Brian Cox, who played Warner's Titus, discusses his tenure as a member of the committee in *Drama* 165 (1987): 15–16. Noting the company's decision to dedicate an evening performance of *The Merchant of Venice* attended by a minister of the South African government to "the disenfranchised black majority of South Africa, thereby nullifying the gentleman's presence and securing his tacit participation in an expression of anti-apartheid sentiments," instead of refusing to play if he remained, Cox observes that the company felt its political gesture to be wholly consistent with its artistic mission: "what are Shakespeare's works if not a debate of life and living, and to make these plays work you have to have a sense of life and living and the responsibility that goes with it. We cannot be expected to be separated from what we do; as what we do is what we are" (16).

17. Interview with Peter Ansorge, *Plays and Players* 17, no. 12 (1970): 16.

18. Nunn and Morley describe the changes in Tierney, *Plays and Players*, 26–27. See also Terry Coleman's interview of Nunn, *The Guardian*, 5 Aug. 1972: 8.

19. Graham Holderness, "The Albatross and the Swan: Two Productions at Stratford," *New Theatre Quarterly* 4 (1988): 152–158, suggests the bonds between ideology—in his case, ideologies of sexual difference—and performance space. See also Kathleen McLuskie, *Renaissance Dramatists* (Atlantic Highlands, N. J.: Humanities Press, 1989), 10–16.

20. Buzz Goodbody was responsible for this and other crowd scenes in "The Romans." See Peter Thomson, " 'What Has He Done to Rome That's Worthy Death?': A Review of the Roman Plays at Stratford in 1972, With a Note on Decision-Making," *Literary Half-Yearly* 14, no. 1 (1972): 26–37.

21. Reviews were decidedly mixed, dominated by discussion of the production's opening tableau of a Roman orgy (Nunn had his cast go see Fellini's *Satyricon* at the beginning of rehearsals), and by comment on John Wood's extravagant performance as Saturninus. Wood's work neatly visualized Nunn's conviction of the social decadence of *Titus*'s Rome, embodying a range of "deadly vigilance, petty rancour, and buffoonery" (Irving Wardle, *The Times*, 13 Oct. 1972: 15) that seems to have left many viewers slightly stunned, if appreciative. The showy relish of the court scenes in fact achieved such prominence that it threatened to eclipse, rather than merely balance, Colin Blakely's "rock-like performance" (Michael Billington, *The Guardian*, 13 Oct. 1972: 19) in the title role.

22. Germaine Greer, *Plays and Players* 20, no. 3 (1972): 39.

23. On *Titus*'s status as a Roman play, see Robert Miola, *Shakespeare's Rome* (Cambridge: Cambridge University Press, 1983), 1–17, 42–75.

24. Vera Gottleib, "Thatcher's Theatre: Or, After *Equus*," *New Theatre Quarterly* 4 (1988): 100. Gottleib was an organizer of a roundtable discussion and subsequent public symposium on the role of theater in a conservative political and economic climate held in London in 1988. The preliminary discussion is reported in *New Theatre Quarterly* 5 (1989): 113–22.

25. "Shakespeare Company Governor Resigns," *The Times*, 6 Dec. 1972: 3.

A Conservative Member of Parliament for the Stratford district resigned his largely ceremonial post as a member of the RSC's board of governors in angry reaction to Trevor Nunn's and David Jones's description of the company as "a basically left-wing organization" in their defense against John Arden and Margaretta D'Arcy's criticism in the quarrel over *The Island of the Mighty.* The financial crunch and the ideological pressures it may have exacerbated continued throughout the 1980s, and indeed may more accurately be described as the normal state of affairs. See, for example, Christopher Warman, "RSC Seeks Aid to Ease Cash Crisis," *The Times,* 16 Oct. 1982: 2g; and Michael Billington, "A Deficit is Haunting the RSC," *New York Times,* 16 June 1987: 24.

26. Besides Holderness ("The Albatross and the Swan"), other reviews which noted the concern of Warner's production with culture, gender, and politics include John Peter, "How the Link Was Missed," *Sunday Times,* 17 May 1987: G54; and Robert Hewison, "In a Tear-Wrenching Encounter with Terror," *Sunday Times,* 10 July 1988: C8. H. R. Woudhuysen's review, "Savage Laughter," *Times Literary Supplement,* 22 May 1987: 551, presents itself as an explicitly historicist discussion, prefacing its evaluation of Warner's production with remarks on the connections between Elizabethan public violence and Elizabethan political authority. See also C. L. Barber, "*Titus Andronicus:* Abortive Domestic Tragedy," in *The Whole Journey: Shakespeare's Power of Development,* ed. Richard P. Wheeler (Berkeley: University of California Press, 1986), 125–57.

27. Christopher J. McCullough discusses possible implications of the homogeneity of the educational and social backgrounds of RSC directors and administrators in his essay "The Cambridge Connection," in *The Shakespeare Myth,* ed. Graham Holderness (Manchester: Manchester University Press, 1988), 112–21.

28. Besides Wolfe ("Alive and Kicking"), interviews discussing Warner's career before her work with the Royal Shakespeare Company include Sheridan Morley, "Leading Lady Moves Centre-Stage," *Sunday Times,* 5 Jan. 1989: 8; and Robert Gore Langton, "Kick for *Coriolanus,*" *Plays and Players,* Sept. 1986: 18–19.

29. Langton, "Kick for *Coriolanus,*" 19.

30. Wolfe, "Alive and Kicking," 12.

31. Ibid., 13.

32. Langton, "Kick for *Coriolanus,*" 19.

33. Morley, "Leading Lady," 8. See James R. Hamilton, " 'Illusion' and the Distrust of Theatre," *Journal of Aesthetics and Art Criticism* 41 (1982): 39.

34. See the remarks of Christopher Morley and Trevor Nunn in Tierney, *Plays and Players,* 26–27.

35. Actress Paola Dionisotti in Rutter, *Clamorous Voices,* xxii.

36. In Rutter's *Clamorous Voices,* actress Juliet Stevenson notes that the company's workshops "are so overloaded that the set designs have to be submitted something like three months in advance. That means that the director has had to finish making all the visual design choices before beginning to explore the play with actors" (xxi–xxii). Ronald Hayman, "Subsidy: Its Effects on Policy and People at the National Theatre and RSC," *Theatre Quarterly* 2, no. 6 (1972): 63–71, notes that Christopher Morley's decision to costume a well-received

production of *The Revenger's Tragedy* entirely in black taffeta and his arrival at a single "white box" setting for the 1970 season were at least partially determined by material considerations: black taffeta was the cheapest fabric available in quantity, and the white room set was easy to work with on the frequent days when a matinee performance ended only an hour before the evening's show was scheduled to begin.

37. Descriptions of the new theater include Laurie E. Maguire, "The New Swan's First Season," *Theatre Notebook* 41 (1987): 101–107; and Peter Holland, "Style at the Swan," *Essays in Criticism* 36 (1986): 193–209.

38. Evaluations of the first year's productions at the Swan suggest that the company did not immediately learn to trust the new playing space or the deliberately unfamiliar texts reserved for playing there. See Holland, "Style at the Swan," 198–202, for a discussion of Barry Kyle's *The Two Noble Kinsmen,* and McLuskie, *Renaissance Dramatists,* 10–11, on Trevor Nunn's *Fair Maid of the West.*

39. Alan Dessen's valuable volume on *Titus Andronicus* in the *Shakespeare in Performance* Series (Manchester: Manchester University Press, 1989), notes this, 57. His discussion of Warner's production, 57–69, and in *Shakespeare Quarterly* 39 (1988): 222–25, are rather differently focused from my own.

40. When I saw Warner's *Titus* near the end of its run at the Swan, the wooden stage bore a faded bloodstain which I thought was part of the original design. Estelle Kohler, who played Tamora, told me in a brief conversation that the stain had actually accumulated over many performances and, to Bywater's annoyance, resisted determined efforts to scrub it away.

41. Warner's first production with Kick was Brecht's *The Good Woman of Setzuan.* For discussion of how employment of Brechtian technique might affect performances of gender, see Jill Dolan, *The Feminist Spectator as Critic* (Ann Arbor: UMI Research Press, 1988), 110–13; and Elin Diamond, "Brechtian Theory/Feminist Theory: Toward a Gestic Feminist Criticism," *Drama Review* 32 (1988): 82–94.

42. Lorraine Helms, "Playing the Woman's Part: Feminist Criticism and Shakespearean Performance," *Theatre Journal* 41 (1989): 192. Also see Douglas E. Green, "Interpreting her martyr'd signs': Gender and Tragedy in *Titus Andronicus,*" *Shakespeare Quarterly* 40 (1989): 317.

LIZBETH GOODMAN

Women's Alternative Shakespeares and Women's Alternatives to Shakespeare in Contemporary British Theater

This is an essay about some of the women who play, or choose not to play, Shakespeare's women in contemporary British theater. In looking at a variety of different kinds of feminist reinterpretations of Shakespeare, not only in theory but also in practice, it becomes clear that such factors as the performer's relationship to Shakespeare's women and issues such as social and economic support for new work by women must inform discussion of women's roles in (and in creating alternatives to) the Shakespearean canon.

Feminist critics from varying cultures, critical schools, and perspectives have begun re-viewing and partially dismantling the Shakespearean canon, in particular, deconstructing canonical images and structures. In this essay, only the most immediate element of deconstructing the canon is of concern: the practical effects of the construction of alternative Shakespeares and of women's alternatives to alternative Shakespeares.

British theater has left a legacy of practical obstacles for the female performer today: employment opportunities are obviously limited by perpetuation of a canon built around Shakespeare, whose parts for women are comparatively few and composed largely of supporting rather than leading roles. The tendency to re-produce the Shakespearean canon at the expense of new writing has obvious negative effects, such as relatively low levels of funding for young writers and new plays, and limited availability of space for these plays in the seasonal programs of the major subsidized national companies: the National Theatre and the Royal Shakespeare Company.

In regard to the limitations which perpetuation and re-production of the traditional canon has imposed upon women in the British theater, feminist playwright and performer Bryony Lavery has observed, "The theatre seems too much like a great museum run by male curators.

The glass exhibition cases are opened up and historic exhibitions taken out and shown to us all, if we can afford the entrance fee. . . . There are far too many good women actors for the amount of space in those glass cases. There is too much to say today to listen to the voices of the museum ghosts. . . . I am tired of my role as a cleaner in this museum. Most of the rubbish is dropped by men."[1] Lavery's observation can be applied to the canonization of Shakespeare. The question posed is not *how* to play Shakespeare but *whether* to play Shakespeare. The related and larger question is whether women writers may have something to say which is not contained in and cannot be extrapolated from a Shakespearean text: something which deserves funding, encouragement, performance, and review; whether strong female performers have the potential to create, in the act of performing, characters that move beyond the status quo and add up to more than the sum of their parts.

Nowhere is the gender-based hierarchy of theater studies brought out more strongly than in performance of Shakespeare. Most parts are played by men, except in the rare all-women's or mixed-cast experimental production, and most directors are men (with only a few notable exceptions such as Deborah Warner, Janet Suzman, and Phyllida Lloyd). Shakespeare can still be played—very successfully—by all-male casts, as in the 1991–92 international touring production of *As You Like It* directed by Declan Donnellan for Cheek by Jowl.[2] They also enrich the study of gender roles in the theater. All-female productions of Shakespeare might do the same but are not considered similarly "authentic" to Shakespeare. The mainstage rehearsal space for any Shakespeare performance is still likely to allow only a subordinate place for women and will in this sense be similar in many respects to a men's club or—in Lavery's terms—to a museum, in which most powerful roles (in performance and in terms of direction and production) are held by men. In fact, the upper echelons of direction, production, and administration of the national subsidized companies in Britain are, as they have always been, occupied almost exclusively by men.[3]

Sue Parrish and Sue Dunderdale found that out of the 620 plays produced in the major British repertoire companies and venues in 1982–83, only 42 (less than 6.8 percent) were written by women. Of these, 22 were written by Agatha Christie. Of the 42, 14 were produced in studios, none by Agatha Christie.[4] Therefore, only 6 plays (less than 1 percent of plays produced on main stages) were written by women other than Agatha Christie. A 1990 survey, conducted by researchers for a Channel Four television series on women as "Ordinary People" shows that, of 435 plays produced by the National Theatre, only 10 were written by women.[5] Thus, for all the talk about revolutions in the British theater, and for all the very real progress that has been made, it is evident that the area of Shakespearean performance remains one of the last bastions of patriarchal control over performance and over the perpetuation of the British acting tradition.

Since there is a limited and steadily decreasing amount of funding available to all British theater, the more that is spent on Shakespeare, the less that remains to be spent on the alternatives. But then, what exactly are the alternatives? In Britain, "alternative theater" (which can be compared to the American off-off-Broadway circuit) is often confused and conflated with terms such as "experimental theater" and "fringe theater." But the term "alternative theater" more accurately refers only to theaters (companies, productions, or venues) which fall outside the subsidized and commercial (West End) theater sectors.

It is not a haggling over terminology which is of interest here, but rather a more generalized understanding of what it means to be considered alternative to the British theater tradition. Such an understanding must be reached by consideration of women's perceived relationships to the concept of alternatives to Shakespeare, to the traditional canon, and to the term "alternative" itself. It is thus necessary to turn to a contemporary resource: the performers who create and recreate Shakespeare's women in British theater today. These performers inevitably hold widely differing views of their relationships to the Shakespearean canon, ranging from a sense of complicity with it to a need for distance, or even denial, of its legitimacy as an inheritance.

Inheriting False Fathers?
Performers' Approaches to the Shakespearean Patrimony

Deborah Levy, in her play *Pax,* creates the character of the "Hidden Daughter" who rejects her inheritance from "false fathers." In some sense, this notion of the false inheritance or inappropriate legacy of words and images from a patriarchal tradition is also relevant to a study of feminist performance of alternative Shakespeares, in that many of the varied approaches thereto include, or react against, just such an idea.

The perspectives of contemporary players of Shakespeare's women on the British stage are anything but uniform. It becomes clear in evaluating the views and statements of women in British theater—whether in personal conversation, public lectures, or any of the available published interviews and reviews—that despite differences in age, class, and political perspectives, many share a recognition of the alternative status of their own views vis-à-vis those of the so-called gatekeepers of the canon. The nature of this perception of difference, however, varies greatly from individual to individual.

The two performers chosen for this brief study are Fiona Shaw and Tilda Swinton: women who can be compared in some ways (for instance, both are known for important cross-dressing roles), and yet who must be contrasted in most respects. These women speak from very different perspectives, which is not surprising, given that they come from quite different backgrounds (Shaw is Irish and Swinton a descendant of the British upper middle class). Both have worked on the most "alternative" fringe stages as well as on the main stages of the RSC and the Royal National Theatre. Fiona Shaw is best known for her creative interpretations of women in the classics; Tilda Swinton for her alternative roles. Both are known for their film roles as well as theater work (Shaw was featured in *My Left Foot, Mountains of the Moon,* and *Three Men and a Little Lady;* Swinton in several of the films of Derek Jarman, including *Caravaggio, The Last of England,* the recent *Edward II,* Sally Potter's new film of Virginia Woolf's *Orlando,* and in the television work of John Byrne). While these tag descriptions of Shaw's and Swinton's work may facilitate discussion, what is most interesting about the comparison is the way in which the tags or labels will *not* fit.

Fiona Shaw purposefully sets out to confound simplistic descriptions and draws on her Irish heritage as an "alternative" to the British tradition. In her own words, "The history of the British theatre has little to do with me, because I am Irish."[6] The distinction between Irish and English tradition is generally recognized, but that between Irish and British tradition and history much less so. In this statement, Shaw reminds us that Ireland has its own rich history and tradition separate from those of England (as do Scotland and Wales). In locating herself outside the English or so-called British tradition, Shaw effectively marginalizes herself, and does so in a liberating way: her self-exclusion from that tradition thereby declares "outsider" status and provides the right to a "backdoor" entrance into the canon, or at least into performance thereof. In denying her part in the British Empire, she frees herself to experiment with its associated traditions.

Shaw also excludes herself from the expectations normally associated with modernity in performance, in one tongue-in-cheek observation: "The history of the eighteenth century is very familiar, as I effectively grew up with that in Ireland."[7] This sense of Shaw's distance from Englishness and modernity is employed to define her stance as a performer of Shakespeare today. Shaw's comments are an exercise in identity politics: they partially distance her "self" in performance from the Shakespearean canon and the British acting tradition. At the same time, however, Shaw is strongly in favor of contemporary reinterpretations of Shakespeare and argues that overemphasis on "women and Shakespeare," as on the theory of acting, may only distract the performer from the focus of her work—performing. Instead, she argues for emphasizing rhythm, presentation, power. The contradiction is apparent: in denying the importance of gender in performance, she opens the way to an active critique of gender stereotypes. Shaw's work continually shifts the boundaries of gender representation by showing that such boundaries are most pliable when they are not constantly reinforced by self-reflection.

A case in point was her 1989 interpretation of Shakespeare's Rosalind in Tim Albery's production of As You Like It. Shaw's Rosalind was among the strongest modern portrayals of a Shakespearean female character, despite her disclaimers about her relationship with Englishness, modernity, and the relationship of gender to performance. Rosalind is, of course, among the best-known and most frequently "reclaimed" of Shakespeare's cross-dressing women. In an earlier and much-discussed production, Shaw played Celia to Juliet Stevenson's Rosalind, a casting which allowed Shaw to develop (by contrast) her ideas of what Rosalind could be.[8] Shaw's Rosalind, in the Albery production, was self-possessed, strong but not "masculine" even when dressed in breeches: she was androgyny powerfully, and somehow erotically, personified.

The photograph from this production (fig. 2) illustrates Shaw's erotic androgyny more explicitly than words can: the photo shows Shaw seated, embraced by but not embracing Orlando (Adam Kotz). Both are on the ground, but neither is in a supplicant position. Nor do the two seem equal. Shaw is mud-splattered, Kotz is clean. Shaw is barefoot, Kotz wears shoes. Their hair is the same length and is combed back in similar styles. Shaw's features are more angular, her pose more possessed. Orlando's expression is more exaggerated, yet Rosalind's (Shaw's) is more engaging.

Body language in this isolated pose is indicative of the presentation of gender relationships in the play as a whole. This Orlando embraces Rosalind and (it seems) the idea of her, while she seems to embrace another idea. His eyes are rapturously closed, his smiling mouth wide open. Her eyes are open and directed into the distance, her mouth nearly closed in a grin. Orlando's body is directed at Rosalind's, and hers is angled slightly, with one foot pressed to the ground and the other loose but positioned for movement. In the tangle of arms, his are on top, touching hers, while her right hand touches her own grounded leg, and she curls the fingers of her left hand carelessly, as if unconscious of the overarching embrace.

In performance, perhaps more than in the photo, Shaw's presence is compelling. The gaze of the audience is literally redirected at her, whether

Fiona Shaw as Rosalind and Adam
Kotz as Orlando in *As You Like It,*
directed by Tim Albery. Photo by
Simon Annand.

she plays woman or man. She embodies a contradiction: a strong person
for whom a single gender cannot be read into either costume or gesture.
Similarly, as Shen Te in Deborah Warner's 1989 National Theatre production of Brecht's *The Good Person of Sichuan,* Shaw played both woman
and man, cross-dressing and thereby breaking down the borders between
genders, while somehow managing to avoid stereotypical presentation of
"feminine" and "masculine" characteristics. The character of Shen Te was
reshaped into something both more and less human, ending in a powerful
and believable presentation of a character in the context of a situation
which, so soon after the Tienanmen Square massacre, had very real
implications. The text was not altered, the action not curtailed. The play
was not anachronistically set. This was not an alternative Brecht, any
more than Albery's *As You Like It* was alternative Shakespeare. Yet Shaw's
roles in both productions *were* alternative: that is, they offered alternatives
to a dichotomy in the representation of gender, and instead presented an
intriguing ambiguity. In *As You Like It,* such a presence manipulates the
expectations of the audience: the transformation from "female" to "male"
which is key to Rosalind's role is deflated in its importance when both
sexes seem to be embodied in one performer.

The unique power of Shaw's presence stems from her performance of two genders and her ability to project an individual woman out of both. She appears not as a woman dressed as a man but as herself. It is not the costume which makes Shaw's Rosalind into a man; rather it is Shaw's personality which enlivens and supports both parts. It has been argued that women have long been cast as "other" in terms of representational conflation of the actress with her costume.[9] Shaw's characterization of Rosalind illustrates one way in which performers today may reclaim the power to wear the costume, rather than be subsumed into it. Her costume is not a sign representing her but rather a disguise she uses to subvert expectation. The process of creating alternatives as enacted by Shaw is built upon a recognition of a working dynamic between gender and power, which informs her characterizations of both female and male parts, and which is stressed in performance, where acting (in practice) takes priority over the (feminist) theory of performance. Shaw's presentation of androgyny contributes to a greater act of subversion that takes into account her personal context and ambivalence about elements of the British tradition, and thereby liberates her, as a performer, to create alternatives that are authentic both to the requirements of Shakespeare and to herself.

By contrast, Tilda Swinton takes a very different view of the dramatic possibilities of Shakespeare's female characters:

There are, as we know, very few deterministic women characters in the classics, in the sense of women who actually determine their own destinies. Some of the most interesting roles for women in Shakespeare, for instance, involve dressing up as boys. Rosalind, Viola, Portia. . . . but actually, I don't think that those roles should be played by women at all. I don't think those plays work today; the point is that the play was written for boys to play the women's parts. So in *As You Like It,* (as I see it) Rosalind can never be successfully played by a woman today: when Orlando falls in love with what we can patently see really is a boy (and it is a boy: albeit a boy playing a girl playing a boy) and Orlando thinks he's in love with this boy, then we have a real frisson. That's political. That's profound. To really stick a knife in modern Shakespeare, I think that *As You Like It* played with women reveals itself as rather a silly play: beautiful, nice poetry, lovely images, but it doesn't add up to much.

The battle when working with texts is the battle to get those texts to really work as plays. Plays really work as they were originally intended to work, and Shakespeare's plays were intended for men and boys. They weren't written for women. It would probably make life a great deal easier for actresses if Shakespeare were only played by men; then women would be free to play roles which mean something to them, which were written for them.[10]

Swinton is deliberately provocative in this statement, and in another interview, she admitted that she has always wanted to play Hamlet. Here, two points should be considered: there are powerful feminist interpretations of Shakespeare's women (Fiona Shaw's Rosalind included), and the implications of a statement such as "Shakespeare may be better played by men" are not necessarily negative and indeed potentially positive. Such a statement, taken out of context, might be read as support for any number of standard misogynist views of women's roles (on and off stage). But Swinton is adamant that her choice of so-called alternative roles is a choice *for* powerful roles in spite of the dominant press emphasis on what she chose *against:*

> In terms of the politics of choice: when you study my work—even when I study my work—on the face of it, it looks like a choice has been made. I suppose one has been made, in terms of relationship to career structure; you could say I actually chose against a certain course. . . . All this also applies to choosing roles, and in that sense there is a running commentary on my relationship to the established repertoire, but it's a negative commentary—not in terms of performance, but in terms of focus. . . . For example, when I did *Man to Man,* one of the basic lines of press inquiry was based on the titillation of the fact that I was 'the one who doesn't't', 'the one who left the R.S.C.'. That was the initial impact of all the hype. Only after that was there any interest in what I *did.*[11]

Furthermore, Swinton attributes some of that "press titillation" not only to her career decisions as such but also to her status as a young woman from the British upper middle class: "There was a shock that someone patently from the class into which I was born, with the credentials and the proportions, someone who could quite easily have been seen to be perfect fodder for R.S.C. life membership, chose against it, or at least questioned it. I suppose there is a personal-political element underlying the reaction: the sniff of sacrilege. That in itself was a press story."[12]

With Swinton's personal status vis-à-vis her "press identity" thus established as context, her earlier comments regarding the value of Shakespeare for the woman performer are recast in a more positive light. The idea is not that women cannot play Shakespeare well, but rather that they can do more, and might better move on to more challenging roles: perhaps those written for them by other women.

When women define themselves *as* the mainstream, the value system

which insists upon and defines a differentiation between the mainstream
and the alternative begins to fall apart. Such a disintegration or subversion
of values is illustrated by this extract on the topic of women vis-à-vis
mainstream and alternative theater, from another interview with Swinton:
"It all boils down to this: I've never been conscious of taking an alternative stance. My position is not alternative to me. . . . As far as I'm concerned,
there's nothing 'alternative' about my work at all. If I were to say that I'm
taking an alternative stance, that's saying that I consider myself less
powerful than someone else, less powerful than I could be. The work that
I'm doing is the work that I need to do in order to be at my most powerful
and most effective."[13]

Swinton is dissatisfied with the definitions assigned to her, imposed
upon her by producers, critics, audiences. She responds by offering her
alternative definitions. She considers herself neither more nor less than
"master" of her own theatrical possibilities, and is thus free to transfigure
herself (or her concept of self, and thereby her presentation of self in
performance), and to translate her own role from the object to the subject
position, at least within the playing space. When a woman, and especially
a performer, thus reacts to the limitations of an acting tradition, she
actively declares herself an agent of change, an actor.

If Swinton is not "alternative to self," it is because she defines herself as
the norm (at least for herself, when she herself is acting). She discards the
traditional measure of artistic value and creates her own. So did Shaw,
in her self-distancing from the British tradition. In declaring and affirming
her Irishness, Shaw defines a new norm, a unique starting place for the
development of identity and for the presentation of self in performance.
These two women have many more differences than similarities. It is,
however, their challenge to dominant value systems which allows for
comparison between them.

Organizing and Performing the Opposition:
Alternative Theater and Alternatives to Shakespeare

Thus far, individual writers and performers have been discussed vis-à-vis
their relationships with the Shakespearean canon, whether in terms of
complicity with the canon or denial of the value and relevance thereof.
There is another approach which is worth examining: the creation of
collective feminist alternatives to Shakespeare. Three notable but little-
documented projects can be seen as British feminist alternatives to
Shakespeare: they are Monstrous Regiment's productions of *Shakespeare's
Sister* (1980 and 1982), the Royal Shakespeare Company's Women's

Project (1984–87), culminating in the 1986 production of *Heresies,* and Women's Theatre Group's productions of *Lear's Daughters* (1987 and 1988).

Monstrous Regiment was formed as a feminist theater collective in 1975 by a small group of performers who were disillusioned with the limited opportunities available to women in both mainstream and fringe theater. In the company's words, they were "a group of professional actors who wanted to make exciting political theatre based on women's experience: tired of seeing that experience marginalised or trivialised, we wanted to take it out of the wings and place it at the centre of the stage."[14] One of the earliest British feminist theatre groups and one of the few original groups still operating in Britain, the Regiment was set up as a permanent collective committed to feminist and socialist ideals. Key founding members included Gillian Hanna, Mary McCusker, Chris Bowler, and Sue Beardon. Writers who worked with the Regiment early on included Bryony Lavery, Caryl Churchill, Sue Todd, and Michelene Wandor. Performers who have worked with the Regiment since 1976 are too numerous to list, but include women (and men) from the gamut of British theater: from Paola Dionisotti (known for her work with the RSC) to Sue Todd (known for directing the RSC Women's Project, as well as for work with the early women's Street Theatre Group, among others) to Ann Mitchell (known primarily for work in fringe, feminist theatre), to Caryl Churchill (whose early collaborative work with the Regiment, in both *Vinegar Tom* and the co-written cabaret *Floorshow,* was influential in her development as a playwright).[15] The link to the RSC is important: both Dionisotti and Todd were later involved in formation of the RSC Women's Project. Deborah Levy has worked with Women's Theatre Group in addition to the RSC and several other feminist companies. Similarly, Bryony Lavery has worked extensively with Monstrous Regiment and Women's Theatre Group.

Monstrous Regiment has been, in effect, a forum where many of the founders of the contemporary British "women in theater movement" met to share work and exchange ideas.

Initially, the Regiment had no permanent artistic director, and all policy decisions were made democratically. This structure has changed in recent years due to the financial necessity of decreasing numbers of full-time staff, but the working practices developed in the early years of the collective can still be seen to shape the Regiment's work. Monstrous Regiment has always taken account of contemporary political and social events in its work, has striven for a transcultural perspective, and has informed all its projects with an awareness of changes in feminist theory and practice. *Shakespeare's Sister* was one such project.[16]

The idea of "Shakespeare's Sister" is familiar from Virginia Woolf's *A Room of One's Own,* in which Woolf imagines that Shakespeare may have had a sister, who would have died unknown, not for lack of talent but rather because she was a woman. Shakespeare's Sister has since been a relatively popular figure in feminist writing which seeks to re-view the canon in search of a legacy of women writers, and the phrase has taken hold in more popular cultural forms, such as rock and punk music.

Monstrous Regiment described the play in this way in their press release: "Shakespeare's Sister is a tragic fantasy figure created by Virginia Woolf in 'A Room of One's Own.' She is a gifted woman, born in the wrong age and of the wrong sex and therefore never allowed the chance of self fulfillment. *Shakespeare's Sister* takes this image and explores it in relation to marriage today, measuring it against views of contemporary women. The play is a new departure for Monstrous Regiment in that it uses bizarre and surreal theatrical techniques. It is funny and disturbing, familiar and sad, showing us how little things have changed in the treatment of women and in their view of themselves."[17] This was not a play about Shakespeare, nor even an alternative Shakespeare, but rather a women's alternative to Shakespeare: a theatrical representation of women's lives. While the play was chosen by the Regiment partially because of its feminist political content, it is important to note that the play was not originally produced with a British audience in mind. Still, Monstrous Regiment saw the play's relevance to British, and particularly British feminist, audiences.

Shakespeare's Sister was developed from improvisations based on research, interviews, and newspaper articles about the status of women in Parisian society in the 1980s. The collaborative process of the play's development was similar, in some respects, to those of *Heresies* and *Lear's Daughters* (though both of those plays were scripted, the process of developing the script involved extensive input from performers in both cases). The act of choosing and producing the play was a radical transcultural act of reclamation: the fictional character created by an English woman (Woolf), claimed internationally by feminist critics and historians (primarily in America), recreated for the stage by a French theater company, and reclaimed by a British socialist-feminist company for production for a British audience. Similarly, the major impact of the RSC Women's Project was not generated by the play it eventually produced but rather by the project itself and by its development in relation to individual women engaged in re-viewing and playing Shakespeare. The RSC Women's Project, like Monstrous Regiment, chose to produce women's alternatives to Shakespeare rather than alternative Shakespeares.

The RSC Women's Project was formed in 1984–85 and disbanded in

1987. The Project was inspired primarily by three performers working for the Royal Shakespeare Company—Fiona Shaw, Juliet Stevenson, and Lindsey Duncan—with input from several other women who were performing for the RSC, and from directors, writers, and administrators from a range of other theater groups and associations, including Sue Todd and Angela Carter. The Project is most significant in that it represents the only avowedly feminist theater company to date which can be considered mainstream, in that it was generated from within the Royal Shakespeare Company and was thus subsidized as part of one of the established "Theatres National."

The history of the RSC Women's Project is little-documented and must be pieced together from statements made from memory by the individuals involved, and from reviews and collected press cuttings from the Project's only full production: Deborah Levy's *Heresies* in 1986. In fact, even the name of the group is debatable: it seems that the larger ideas and initiatives were known as the Women's Project (now commonly associated with the production of *Heresies*), and the women themselves were known as the RSC Women's Group.

The following information regarding the origins of the Project has been extracted from a long interview with Genista McIntosh, who was employed during the Project's gestation, first as an independent agent, and then as administrator for the RSC. McIntosh recalled,

> I think that what happened is that at a certain time in that company's life in Stratford, there was a company meeting at which some of those women challenged Terry Hands, Artistic Director, about there being so little work and provision for women in the company . . . in terms of insufficient positive discrimination for performers, directors, writers, designers, technicians, etc. They threw down a gauntlet to Terry, which he took up, primarily by saying that if that's how they felt, they should do something about it and he wouldn't stand in their way.
>
> They started to work. Initially, there were no limits imposed on their imaginative sweep. . . . Another round of discussions began about the *kind* of work that a Women's Group should do.[18]

It is precisely the issue of the kind of work which was done which is of interest to this discussion of women's alternatives to Shakespeare. *Heresies*, like *Shakespeare's Sister*, was not an all-women's production: it involved male performers as well. It was inspired by women and developed through a long workshop process run by women. It was written by a woman and directed by a woman. Also like *Shakespeare's Sister*, *Heresies* was not explicitly about Shakespeare and was certainly not derivative of any one play. That kind of direct approach to altering the Shakespearean canon came only later, for instance in the acclaimed 1987–88 productions by the Women's Theatre Group of *Lear's Daughters*.[19]

The earlier work of both Monstrous Regiment and the RSC Women's Project took a less direct approach to the Shakespearean canon, examining images and ideas which were less obviously associated with Shakespeare's plays, but more closely associated with the power of the Shakespearean image: that of the bard, the male genius, the patriarchal figure overshadowing the development of contemporary theater. Such work suggested that it was the Shakespearean image, rather than the plays, which had the most interesting impact on the lives and work of living women. The R.S.C. Women's Project recognized a significant gap in opportunities for women performers.

In McIntosh's words, "Within that group, there was a feeling about appropriation of Shakespeare having provided relatively few major opportunities for women. The very domination of the repertoire by Shakespeare inevitably limited the opportunities for women; and it was this which was originally meant to be challenged. . . . There was the natural emphasis on restructuring or deconstructing Shakespeare to provide more opportunities for the women in the company."[20] The Project experienced a setback in morale when two key members (Shaw and Stevenson) left the group to pursue other projects. Accounts of this event differ substantially, but all note that these professional career moves were questioned, not on professional grounds, but rather on personal/political grounds. This kind of conflict of interests and perspectives can be seen to be fairly characteristic of the British feminist theater movements of the seventies and eighties, and even of the early nineties. Personal career development was (and is) sometimes seen as disloyal to the collective project, a view which adds an element of tension to the act of choosing roles and thus helps to explain the divergence of views between women, like those discussed earlier, who come from different class backgrounds and different generations, and who therefore bear radically dissimilar relationships to British socialist-feminist ideals, and specifically to the notion of the collective and the definition of feminism.

This tension resulted in the remaining members of the Women's Project pulling closer together and beginning to focus their energies on bringing the project to fruition in a production: "At this point, Sue Todd reactivated her relationship with Deborah Levy: she and Deborah had worked together previously, I believe it was in the Monstrous Regiment. . . . At any rate, it turned out that Deborah had already been working on a play which fit the Project's ideals: a partially written piece which was highly experimental in form. That play was *Heresies,* which was the Project's only production."[21]

Briefly, *Heresies* was an ambitious project concerned with several overlapping themes, including the nurturing role often played by women, represented in terms of the notion of a "women's creativity." The central figure of the large cast was an architect, a figure which was developed in *Pax* and in some of Levy's earlier work, based on a polysemous image of a female builder.

Both *Pax* and *Heresies* are, at one level, plays about building images of women from pieces of narrative and bits of information, much like Virginia Woolf's construction of the character of Shakespeare's sister, and like Monstrous Regiment's re-creation of her in modern guise. Like Woolf and the Regiment's re-production of *Shakespeare's Sister, Heresies* emphasizes the value of many women working without recognition. Appropriately, *Heresies* was also a collaborative project to some extent. Though Levy wrote the script in full, she worked extensively with the performers before creating the characters who eventually shaped the play.

The play conveys the voices of individual women, all of whom try to create something: most importantly, a sense of self for public presentation. It is most interesting that the collective structure of the Women's Project which informed and influenced Levy's script for *Heresies* was seen by the critics as a weakness rather than a strength. Many mixed reviews of the play in performance reflect a certain cynicism about the feminist collective as an effective structure for the production of "good theater."[22] Overall, the most common criticism of the play suggested that it was "over-ambitious," due, perhaps, to an over-emphasis on collaboration. Yet this focus on project over play is appropriate to Levy's conception of the role of the play. She describes her style of writing, of piecing together her plays, as a process of "structuring the audience's attention" with regard to the actual theater space, and with awareness of the audience's active role in making the play, as similar to the playwright's "presence," and as opposed to the notable absence of the critic. In Levy's words, "the only thing the artist has going for her is that she is present and therefore potentially receptive, able to tap into what is around, and to make of it something new."[23]

Levy is critically aware of context. So was the RSC Women's Group as a whole. The Group was particularly determined that their production should be performed in a particular kind of space, with a particular place in the public realm of "structured attention": that is, on a main stage. Interestingly, though, *Heresies* was staged in the Pit, the RSC's London studio space for alternative work. Since *Heresies,* there have been no more all-women's productions at the RSC. More to the point, there has never been a woman director employed to work on the RSC main stage in

London (though Buzz Goodbody did a main stage production of *As You Like It* in 1973 in Stratford). There was not another main stage production directed by a woman until 1988, when Di Trevis also directed in Stratford, though Deborah Warner's acclaimed production of *Titus Andronicus* was staged at the Swan in Stratford-upon-Avon (a major venue, though not a "main stage") in 1987.

Such practical and material considerations are immediate to the task of placing a production like *Heresies* into its proper context. Just as the character of Shakespeare's Sister took on a new dimension when performed in English, and in England, by the socialist-feminist group Monstrous Regiment, so *Heresies* was perceived as actually heretical when produced by a group of women within the Royal Shakespeare Company. In this context, it is particularly interesting to consider *Lear's Daughters*, produced only a few years after *Heresies*, in smaller venues and with very limited resources.

Lear's Daughters was written by Elaine Feinstein and Women's Theatre Group and was specifically envisioned as a feminist rewriting of Shakespeare. As is the case with much group-devised work, it is difficult to say who actually "wrote" the working script for the play.[24] *Lear's Daughters* was commissioned in 1987 by Women's Theatre Group; Elaine Feinstein was offered the commission as writer, to work with members of the company, which at that time consisted of Gwenda Hughes, Janys Chambers, Hilary Ellis, Maureen Hibbert, and Hazel Maycock. All company members contributed to the workshops, and thus to the rewriting of the working script.

The play is a landmark in feminist "reinventing" of Shakespeare. It takes as its premise the notion that, to a female reader (and more specifically to a feminist reader), all of history as presented in standard texts may resemble a genealogy of "false fathers." When these false fathers are produced on stage, the fathers come to life, and the necessary feminist reaction is the creation of new mothers (just as, in theory, the "false universal" must be deconstructed and replaced within feminist criticism). *Lear's Daughters* questions the mainstream casting of Shakespeare as the "fit father" of the literary-dramatic canon. The focus is not on Lear but on his daughters, on the women who are affected by the events of the play: the Queen (who does not appear in the original), the three princesses, the Nanny (a new character: another mother figure), and the androgynous Fool (see Fig. 3).

The play is billed as "the story of women growing up in the kingdoms of their fathers." The gaze of the audience-spectator of the play is directed not only at the women in the story of Lear but at Lear's daughters as they might be seen today:

Fool (background) and Regan (foreground) in *Lear's Daughters*, 1987. Photo by Sheila Burnett.

> three daughters, locked in a room
> with
> two mothers, dead or gone missing
> and a
> Father, waiting outside
> three princesses, sitting in a tower
> with
> two servants, behind the door
> and a
> King holding the crown.

The daughter role and sister role are prioritized, and the mother role implied as part and parcel of both. The father in this stark picture figures as a threat, a shadow of vague and impersonal power, although (or perhaps because) he is neither seen nor heard; he is the embodiment of the "absent father" image of today's no-longer-nuclear families. The mother is also noticeable in her absence, but she is represented in the figure of another character, Nanny, and also in the grotesque image of the mother-figure—to whom the three princesses direct their speeches and actions in mimed sequences—represented by a tea towel hastily draped over a saucepan (metonymically representing the "other" missing crown). Nanny is both mother and servant, in the words of the play, "the mother who is paid." Fool is costumed and directed as a highly androgynous figure; s/he is the only character in the play who is even partially "male," and therefore, as if by rights, wears the managerial hat. Fool is both servant and stage manager.

The princesses are carefully balanced against each other in terms of character and color (multiracial casting is common to much of the Women's Theatre Group's work). In the first production, Cordelia was played by a blond, white woman, while Regan and Goneril were played by black women. This heightened the sense of petty favoritism which Lear expressed for Cordelia (a factor which is emphasized in the play in scenes which suggest that some sexual attraction may have motivated the favoritism and frightened young Cordelia into a permanently childlike and vocally reticent state). By contrast, Regan and Goneril seem (quite literally, given the racial counterplay) to be children of different fathers, or mothers. In the second production, however, all three sisters were played by black performers while both Nanny and Fool were played by white women. Fool was played in both productions by a white woman in whiteface wearing black and white: half of her suit of clothes designated as male and half as female. Lear himself is never seen. The implication was communicated in the second production, however, that he and (or) his dead wife or one of his mistresses—if indeed the daughters are of different mothers—must be (have been) black. The servants are white. These points are represented physically but not explored (this is not color-blind, but rather determinedly color-conscious casting).

The question of lineage informs the story of *Lear's Daughters* in sexual as well as racial terms. Little is known of the dead Queen, except that she suffered in childbirth. The promiscuity of Lear is common knowledge. His paternity, like his patriarchal right, is not questioned. The daughters' relationship with their father is one of fear and awed respect, notably tinged with embarrassment on the part of Cordelia, and with jealousy on the part of the other two. Theoretical questions of otherness, agency, and difference are thus enacted in this story of daughters, literally locked in the attic, growing together and apart in isolation from their mother and in a combination of fear and desire in relation to their father, and by extension—as he is the only man they have ever known—to men in general. Each sister symbolically insists upon her right to her own vision and version of the story. Each also seeks to wear the crown. In the final image of *Lear's*

Daughters, the crown is thrown into the air and caught by all three daughters at once. The shrinking spotlight highlights the black and white of hands on gold just before the final blackout.

Sweeping Up: On a Clear Stage

Feminist interpretation of Shakespeare creates a space for a critical deconstruction and reevaluation of mainstream values, as well as a physical space appropriate to the feminist project of reshaping and re-viewing gender roles. As Janelle Reinelt has observed, "Historicizing gender relations is a powerful way to change the field itself because it explicitly challenges the notion of transhistorical male and female modes of being and recovers a marginalized alternative narrative of women as active subjects determining the concrete course of human events."[25] The theater is the frame and impetus for active representation of ideas and language in three dimensions, in the public sphere. Crucial differences between women, and even between feminists, complicate any attempt to define "women's theater" or to locate its place in the history of representation. The critical perception of the female gaze, or the woman's view of self and self in performance, is still seen by many, and even by some women performers themselves, as alternative and therefore in danger of continual attack. This, in theatrical terms, sometimes renders it difficult to evaluate women's work (in the theater as in other sectors) in relation to standard (academic) measures. But Jill Dolan suggests that the theater is an appropriate site for the deconstruction of gendered forms of representation, not in spite of the difficulties here mentioned, but *because* of them. She writes, "The stage, then, is a proper place to explore gender ambiguity, not to cathartically expunge it from society, but to play with, confound and deconstruct gender categories. If we stop considering the stage as a mirror of reality we can use it as a laboratory in which to reconstruct new, non-genderized identities. And in the process, we can change the nature of theatre itself."[26]

Gender ambiguity is the essential point of interest in Shakespeare, at least in terms of the representation of women. The woman performer in Shakespeare is intrinsically, radically, perhaps definitionally alternative to the boy-man for whom the parts were written. She may choose to play those parts as a woman, or as a woman playing a man playing a woman, or not at all. She may choose to play them as if they were written for a woman, even specifically for her. She may choose to play them as if she is part of the circumstances of their production, or by reminding herself that she stands outside those circumstances, or by denying the relevance of any such considerations. She may see herself as a performer of alternative

Shakespeares or as an *actor* in the process of creating alternatives to Shakespeare.

All these perspectives incorporate one basic idea: that of including self in performance. All may be bases for radical reorganization of the operative set of values or structures by and through which women's work in the theater (and in other spheres) is evaluated. As the process develops and the boundaries shift, this radical inclusion of women may become part of the value system itself, and women's work may then be judged, not according to some predefined and imposed alternative scale of values, but rather according to criteria authentic to individual and collective perspectives, contexts, and ways of seeing. Then theory may have a firmer base in practice.

> Imagine a Theatre for Women somewhere in Warwickshire, by a river, well subsidized...
> Imagine a National Theatre somewhere in London, say by a river, well subsidized, putting on NEW plays... [27]

Or even better, imagine a theatrical climate in which this and other alternatives are all possible; a stage on which there is room for all.

NOTES

1. Bryony Lavery, "But Will Men Like It?" in *Women and Theatre: Calling the Shots,* ed. Susan Todd (London: Faber and Faber, 1984), 30–31.

2. The production, with an all-male multiracial cast, toured from July 1991 to March 1992. Another all-male British production of *As You Like It* was produced by the Royal National Theatre, directed by Clifford Williams, with Anthony Hopkins and Derek Jacobi, first performed at the Old Vic Theatre, 3 October 1967.

3. A study in 1986–87 showed that only 4.5 percent of artistic directors were women and 27.5 percent of senior administrators were women: "Updated Survey of Sex of Artistic Directors and Administrators Currently Working in Repertory Theatres in England and Wales," *Contacts,* no. 76, 1986/87. In 1983, the figures were even lower, particularly for the Theatres National (the RSC, the National Theatre, and the Royal Court Theatre): Sue Dunderdale and Sue Parrish, report for Conference of Women Theatre Directors and Administrators, 1982/83, published in *Drama,* no. 152, 1984.

4. Statistics compiled by Sue Dunderdale for the Conference of Women Theatre Directors and Administrators (C.W.T.D.A.), published in *Drama,* no. 152, 1984. Also see Sir Kenneth Cork, "Theatre Is for All: The Inquiry into Professional Theatre in England" [a.k.a. "The Cork Report"] (London: Arts Council of Great Britain, 1986), 44; and Caroline Gardiner, "What Share of the Cake: The Employment of Women in the English Theatre" (London: The Women's Playhouse Trust, 1987).

5. Findings from the survey were printed in the series booklet: *Ordinary People: Why Women Become Feminists,* ed. Derek Jones (London: Channel Four Television, 1990).

6. Fiona Shaw, a talk given at the DIVINA International Conference on "The Changing Representation of Women in the Theater," Turin, 4–5 June 1990; Shaw spoke as part of the British panel (also including Charlotte Keatley, Gabriella Giannachi and Lizbeth Goodman). The conference report appears in *New Theatre Quarterly* 7 (Feb. 1991): 97–99.

7. Ibid.

8. *As You Like It,* directed for the Royal Shakespeare Company by Adrian Noble in 1985. This production is discussed at length in Carol Rutter, *Clamorous Voices,* ed. Faith Evans (London: The Women's Press, 1988), 97–121.

9. Lesley Ferris, *Acting Women: Images of Women in the Theatre* (London: MacMillan, 1989).

10. Lizbeth Goodman, "Subverting Images of the Female: An Interview with Tilda Swinton," *New Theatre Quarterly* 6 (Aug. 1990): 222. This interview was compiled from a series of taped and untaped sessions, June–October 1989.

11. Ibid., 221. The reference is to Manfred Karge's *Man to Man,* performed by Swinton at the Royal Court Theatre, January 1988.

12. Ibid., 221.

13. Ibid., 222.

14. From the Monstrous Regiment company brochure, 1985. Also see the first Monstrous Regiment book: *Monstrous Regiment: A Collective Celebration,* ed. Gillian Hanna (London: Nick Hern Books, 1991), which includes four of the company's plays published for the first time. A long interview with Gillian Hanna appears in *New Theatre Quarterly* 6 (Feb. 1990): 43–56.

15. *Floorshow* was co-written by Caryl Churchill, Bryony Lavery, and Michelene Wandor in 1977–78. A complete list of contributors to and participants in Monstrous Regiment productions is included in the company brochure, 1985.

16. *Shakespeare's Sister,* based on an original production devised by Théâtre de l'Aquarium, Paris. Translated by Gillian Hanna for Monstrous Regiment. This version was first performed at the Institute of Contemporary Arts, London, for three weeks in December 1980: directed by Hilary Westlake, designed by Gemma Jackson, with a cast including Gillian Hanna and John Slade. Revived by the Regiment for a second (national touring) production in 1982: directed by Jan Sargent, designed by Gemma Jackson, with Patricia Donovan, Tony Guilfoyle, Gillian Hanna, Ann Haydn, Stephen Ley, and Mary McCusker.

17. Monstrous Regiment, Press Release for *Shakespeare's Sister,* 1980; unpublished, in the Monstrous Regiment company files. Reviews are also collected in the company archives.

18. From an unpublished interview with Genista McIntosh, who was Senior Administrator and artistic director–elect at the time of the interview, 2 May 1990. McIntosh has since been appointed Executive Director of the National Theatre.

19. *Lear's Daughters,* by Elaine Feinstein and Women's Theatre Group, in *Herstory, Vol. 1,* ed. Gabrielle Griffin and Elaine Aston (Sheffield: The Academic

Press, 1991). N.B.: In 1992, Women's Theatre Group changed its name to The Sphinx.

20. Unpublished interview with Genista McIntosh.

21. Ibid.

22. Reviews are collected in full in the Royal Shakespeare Company archives.

23. Deborah Levy, "Structuring the Audience's Attention," an unpublished seminar paper delivered to the Graduate Women and Literature Seminar, St. John's College, Cambridge, 7 Feb. 1990.

24. The authorship of the play is contentious, as the script which Feinstein contributed was significantly reworked in devising and rehearsal by the company. As a result, Feinstein's name appears on only some of the press releases and reviews for the show. The complicated question of 'copyright' for this and other British feminist plays is examined in detail in my book, *Contemporary Feminist Theatres* (London: Routledge, 1993).

25. Janelle Reinelt, "British Feminist Drama: Brecht and Caryl Churchill," unpublished conference paper, delivered at a conference on "Brecht: Thirty Years After," Toronto, Fall 1986.

26. Jill Dolan, "Gender Impersonation Onstage: Destroying or Maintaining the Mirror of Gender Roles?" in *Women and Performance* 2, no. 2 (1985): 10.

27. Lavery, "But Will Men Like It?" 31.

ANIA LOOMBA

Hamlet in Mizoram

GENTLEMAN: Her speech is nothing,
Yet the unshap'd use of it doth move
The hearers to collection; they yawn at it,
And botch the words up fit to their own thoughts,
Which as her winks and nods and gestures yield them,
Indeed would make one think there might be thought,
Though nothing sure, yet much unhappily.

HORATIO: 'Twere good she were spoken with, for she may strew
Dangerous conjectures in ill-breeding minds.

(*Hamlet* 4.5.7–15)[1]

This essay speculates upon the political unconscious of some recent performances of Shakespeare's *Hamlet* in India's northeastern border state of Mizoram that provide a remarkable instance of cross-cultural performance. The essay also reflects upon the methodological and theoretical difficulties that attend any critical unraveling of the purposes of playing. The almost obsessive Mizo playing of *Hamlet* has to do with the relationship between theater, power, and subversion; with the politics of subaltern appropriations of "master-texts"; and most importantly, with the intersection of gender relations with other social differentials. I will place the performances within their various contexts, which are provided by the current debates about subaltern resistance, by the history and contemporary ramifications of the Shakespeare myth in India, by Mizo cultural politics (especially gender politics), by the film that "captures" the enactment for British television, and finally, by my own academic discourse. The intersections and divergences between these suggest the ways in which *Hamlet* functions in Mizoram both as a display and a displacement of resistance.

Because of its obvious link with practices such as rituals, carnivals, and festivals, and because staging and display are central strategies of social negotiations, theater is a particularly rich site for exploring the relationship between power and its subversions. Traditional anthropology, even when sensitive to the turbulence within theatrical practices like ritual, had, on the whole, evaluated them as the means of preserving order. As many recent commentators have noted, it is not surprising that the shift towards focusing on their contestatory nature, towards seeing how meanings are challenged as well as enforced in their enactment, was in part effected by those (especially feminists) who were interested in marginalized groups, particularly women.[2] In the writing of social history, resistance has now begun to be located in ordinary life and everyday practices rather than solely within extraordinary moments such as riots and rebellion. While this shift too has been enabled by an investment in the study of "subaltern" peoples, it simultaneously criticizes some "subalternist" histories for continuing to neglect women, and in fact attributes this neglect to their concentration on violent confrontations, where women are often invisible.[3] Implicit in this critique is the belief, or at least a hope, that attention to the ordinary and the everyday will restore women to the arena of struggle. I will return to this later; here I only want to point out that although theater contributes to the language of the extraordinary (spectacular, dramatic), and provides metaphors for violent confrontation (the arena or theater of war), besides being the site for the reproduction of violence, as practice it belongs to everyday life rather than to what historians call extraordinary moments.

Both these shifts—towards examining the everyday manifestations of contestation and locating the confrontational aspects of ritual—are responsible for the increasing overlaps in anthropological, historical, and literary enquiries.[4] Both are also often attributed by historians to the influence of poststructuralist literary criticism, which emphasizes the instability and the precariousness of power.[5] This is somewhat paradoxical because precisely such an emphasis has been seen as contributing to a political quietism—especially within political criticism of the Renaissance, where the containment/subversion debates of poststructuralist theory have been most vigorously conducted. Oppositional impulses exist everywhere, and all of them are finally contained by the structures of authority. Within Renaissance studies, theater which showed every sign of "strewing dangerous conjectures" in its audience was, in the last analysis, seen as complicit with power structures.[6] Often positions in this debate are read as indices of the politics of the critics in question, so that those who emphasize containment are in some danger of being seen as complicit with authoritarian structures.[7]

The debates around this subject are by now sprawling and I will only recount them briefly (risking much reduction of complicated positions and arguments) in order to set one major context for evaluating cross-cultural performances. That opening up the sites and modes of resistance should be suspected of contributing to their containment is attributable to an apparent circularity in two shared perspectives: the first is what Lyotard calls an "incredulity towards metanarratives," and the second, a Foucauldian emphasis on the *interdependence* of power and resistance, which are theorized as entirely relational concepts. Both perspectives have enabled the insertion of oppositional histories and perspectives that metanarratives always historically excluded. If marginalized people are inserted into the very production of power, it can be seen as the precarious and thereby more contestable result of continuous negotiations. But power conceptualized as being diffuse and without an epicenter can be understood as either all-pervasive or somewhat benign. Moreover, human subjects, also conceived of as decentered, are potentially stripped of their agency.[8] If we position subordinate groups exclusively in relation to hegemonic structures and ideologies, we might seem to be implying that resistance is entirely an effect of power, which again seems to tilt the balance in favor of containment. The idea that subordinate groups are themselves active in the construction and reformulation of oppressive structures and ideologies can blunt the edge of exploitative realities, represent bitter confrontations almost as a sort of mutually agreed-upon game, and diffuse the hierarchy which attaches to "difference" into too comfortable a partnership, "or else, to alter Plato's parable / Into the yolk and white of the one shell."[9]

Cultural "re-visions" and appropriations—in fact all seizures of the book, all processes of "unlearning" and formulating alternative cultures— are especially vulnerable to such a circularity in conceptualizing resistance. Although in this essay I use "appropriation" in a narrow sense, it also encompasses the interaction of "Third World" societies with all Western thought—including Marxism, varieties of feminism, and modern science—or of feminism with poststructuralism. Appropriation is an integral part of all literary reception, and especially of theatrical practice. The heterogeneity of twentieth-century audiences and readers of Shakespeare, partly the result of colonial history, has especially spawned a variety of cross-cultural readings by conventionally marginalized readers. On the one hand they indicate cultural difference and the difference that makes to reading literature; on the other they are always in some danger (like anthropological analysis) of reading difference either to erase it or to resubscribe to Western cultural hegemony or to confirm the universality of dominant cultural phenomena and literary texts or human subjects. So obviously are cross-cultural enactments and readings dependent upon hegemonic culture that it is easy to write them off as "false consciousness." Caliban's curse is, of course, the well-worn symbol of this variant of the power/subversion dialectic: "You taught me language, and my profit on't / Is I know how to curse. The red plague rid you / For learning me your language."[10] Not only does Prospero's language make the curse possible, but in cursing, Caliban creatively uses ("the red plague" sounds like something he didn't learn from Prospero) and therefore perpetuates Prospero's language.

Precisely for this reason oppositional movements and theorists have continually debated the sources of revolutionary consciousness.[11] Surely Caliban's curse is made possible by more than Prospero's language. Is to probe this "more" necessarily to resurrect a romantic notion of oppositional culture? Foucault's analysis of power soberly reminds us that the marginalized are not, as Judith Walkowitz puts it, "left free to invent their texts."[12] Moreover, the idea of spaces *outside* structures of domination leading to the easy formation of oppositional communities disguises, as Rosalind O'Hanlon has argued, "the extent to which these 'communities' may themselves be fractured by relations of power."[13]

The categories O'Hanlon invokes—fragmentation, heterogeneity of social structures, and multiplicities of histories—are also central poststructuralist assumptions whose usefulness for marginalized groups and political struggle has been controversial. Do they induce intellectual angst and political paralysis and entrench existing exclusions, as some thinkers seem to believe? Nancy Hartsock, for example, contends that "those of us who are not part of the ruling race, class, or gender . . . need to know how it works" and that therefore "postmodernism represents a dangerous approach for any marginalised group to adopt."[14] On the other hand, as Jane Flax argues, perhaps "reality can have 'a' structure only from the falsely universalising perspective of the dominant group."[15] Similar differences exist among "Third World" critics as to the politics of relativism.

But a careful use of the idea of heterogeneity is conducive to a less pessimistic repositioning of the power/resistance dialectic. To say that power is not monolithic, but itself composed of various structures of domination, is not necessarily to deny their consolidation in effecting oppression, but to suggest, first, that none of them is autonomous. It has been pointed out often enough that the contradictions between them may catalyze the possibility of change. If there are various interlocking relations of power and resistance, no one of them is suffocatingly self-sufficient. Their coexistence makes it possible to acknowledge that resistance may draw on resources outside of a particular dialectic, even though these are themselves not free of relations of power. Prospero is not the whole of Caliban's history or identity—it is also Sycorax (among other factors), who, even though absent, shapes his curse. But no precolonial culture is merely precolonial; it is also permeated by its own hierarchies and oppressions, which surface and are renegotiated, rejuvenated, and challenged too in the new struggle against colonialism. Thus we are enabled to think of resistance as entirely bounded by specific cultural and historical parameters, and yet as being more than the effect of the power it contests. Stephen Greenblatt's oft-cited observation that "actions that should have the effect of radically undermining authority turn out to be the props of that authority" may (in some contexts) be usefully rewritten as "actions that radically undermine one sort of authority often turn out to be the props of another structure of authority."[16]

Finally, heterogeneity implies not just endless fragmentation, not just impossible relativism and what Mohanty calls "debilitatingly insular spaces" but also the possibility of new alliances, new comings together of ideas, cultures, peoples. From this point of view, appropriations are especially rich sites for those who want to also mark "the limits of otherness" and " 'a genuine dialogue' between anthropologist and native, the ex-coloniser and the ex-colonised."[17]

The Mizo *Hamlet* demonstrates some of this weaving, this divergence and coming together. It also indicates two other ways in which power is heterogeneously composed. The first has to do with the fact that although literary authority constitutes and is constituted by social or political authorities, all these are not identical, and challenges to them are often conflictual exercises. Secondly, the conflicts between gender and other forms of cultural difference become especially important in evaluating subversion. As mentioned earlier, a preoccupation with spectacular and extraordinary forms of confrontation, such as riots, rebellions, and organized political activity, often sidelines the gender politics of these moments and marginalizes women as social participants. Similar critiques have been made regarding the carnivalesque. Such disjunctures within "power" and "resistance," as these performances of *Hamlet* clearly reveal, disallow hasty conclusions about containment "in the final analysis."

Of the diverse and contradictory dimensions of the authority which the Mizo *Hamlet* could be subverting or resurrecting, the most obvious one is that of the Shakespeare myth, which has had a long and varied history in the Indian subcontinent. Elsewhere I have explored the ways in which the Indian dimension of the myth intersects with its Western counterpart.[18] This section will recount some of that history in order to suggest how the Mizo *Hamlet* marks a significant rupture within it.

As the privileged core of an English literary education which played a crucial role in the business of Empire, Shakespeare was, from the very first years of the setting up of British institutions, widely deployed in classrooms from Calcutta to Lahore.[19] Even in the mid-nineteenth century, this was a contested presence: on the one hand, Shakespeare (and English education in general) was seen as a vehicle for colonialism (Indians who "stand aloof" from their own people were described as "boxing themselves up with Shakespeare" instead of reading or writing in their own languages); on the other, Shakespeare and English education were "the blessings that Europe showers upon us," enabling those "who have drunk in that beauty" to "awake [sic] our poor countrymen."[20] Even before Shakespeare was included in the curriculum, his plays had begun to be staged in the theaters that the local Englishmen had set up. These theaters became models for the first public theaters in Calcutta. When in 1831 Prasanna Kumar Tagore founded his Hindu Theatre, the first performances consisted of selected scenes from *Julius Caesar.* In 1848, Calcutta saw a young Bengali called Baishnav Charan Auddy acting as Othello opposite an Englishwoman called Mrs. Anderson as Desdemona.[21] This may not seem remarkable until one recalls the vicious oppositions to a black Othello on the British stage,[22] or that at the same period social contact between Indian men and British women was minimal. The Parsi theaters of Bombay, too, were heavily influenced by Shakespearean performances, both in terms of story lines and the style of acting. They in turn shaped the popular Hindi cinema when it emerged at the turn of the century, so that the stamp of nineteenth- and early twentieth-century British Shakespearean performances are clearly visible in mainstream Bombay films right up to the present day. Indian cinema also offered more straightforward adaptations of the plays, including *Hamlet.*

I invoke these divergences to indicate that the Shakespearean legacy in post-independence India is not confined to academia, and to reiterate the surprisingly narrow confines within which Shakespeare is taught today. In the 1960s a well-known critic fervently prayed for the health of "the imperishable empire of Shakespeare"; in the late 1980s *The Tempest* continues to be read completely divorced from its colonial theme, and conferences are held proclaiming the universality of Shakespeare. The British Council's stock of BBC productions of the plays is in huge demand because, despite some changes in school syllabi, Shakespeare is still a solid part of Indian education at the higher level.[23] I am not in a position to offer any generalizations about the widespread adaptations and translations of Shakespeare's plays into Indian languages, of which no systematic study has been undertaken. These interacted far more vigorously with local politics and culture and are therefore less easy to categorize than the English-language performances of Shakespeare, which have largely existed within neocolonial parameters.[24] But English-language performances today cater to relatively truncated elite urban audiences, or are undertaken within university campuses. Despite this, they remind us that Shakespeare still implies, in upper-class circles, instant culture and value—in 1990, for example, a lavish Bombay production of *Othello* (to which I shall later return) not only played to packed halls in various Indian cities, with tickets at ten times the normal theater prices, but was patronized by audiences that often stay away from English-language plays. My point is that there is still a certain continuity of the Shakespeare myth from London to New Delhi, which certainly informs the understanding of the Delhi filmmaker as he captures the Mizo performances of *Hamlet*. These performances themselves, however, mark some of the points at which the myth is strained.

Let me quickly indicate the potential for these ruptures even within the colonial history of Shakespeare, which was not a simple matter of exporting an already-finished product. That the growth of literary studies in the metropolis was itself significantly molded by the colonial experience is evident from the way the universal Shakespeare of Western criticism took on a specific dimension, indeed was partly constructed, in colonial India. The Orientalist stereotype of a spiritual, emotional, transcendental India and the literary ideal of art as similarly "above" the mundane details of everyday existence were now brought together, in different ways, by British educationists and their Indian students, and even by those who were opposed to colonial education.[25] While English literature was often explicitly invoked to devalue Indian texts, at other times the two literatures (and specifically Shakespeare and the classical Sanskrit playwright Kalidasa) happily joined to celebrate this "world of the wonder and free power of life and not of its mere external realities."[26] Shakespeare as a poet who allowed his readers to "reach beyond eternity" could be co-opted as a special guru in a land of mysticism.

Such usages ironically undercut a Western copyright on either Shakespeare or Culture. Often, precisely because oppressive social practices are often shrouded in the rhetoric of universal humanism, women's movements, anti-racist struggles, and anti-colonial movements have strategically seized such rhetoric in spite of their divisions over whether to emphasize difference or sameness.[27] In any case, in nineteenth-century India, Shakespeare was a recurrent figure in these double-edged deployments of universalism, a means for pleading for the global *brotherhood*: Shakespeare says all men are equal, and Shakespeare is the most honorable man, so we are equal to you. The argument that Indians learned even their nationalism from English literature takes Indians' own statements to this effect at face value, rarely examining the rhetoric as possible strategy, conscious or otherwise. Moreover, the very other-worldliness of English literature was often followed by a demand for earthly equality—hence, wrote Isser Chander Dass of Hooghly College in 1851, "thoughts that reach beyond eternity [inspired by Milton, Shakespeare and Bacon in this case] . . . cannot but elevate the mind and awaken in it an aspiration after a purer state of being where all earthly distinctions should cease."[28] Subversive uses of the spiritual are of course widespread, and they inform Mizo performances of *Hamlet,* as I will later discuss.

A second rupture in the myth is potentially offered by the question of gender, which was intricately used in Orientalizing Shakespeare. Shakespeare's heroines were read as obedient, virtuous, passive daughters of nature. So were the heroines of Sanskrit drama. So, indeed, were the ideals of Indian womanhood selected from the vast repertoire of Indian myths and legends. Obviously there was no space for the *disobedience* of Shakespeare's women (or Middleton's or Webster's), much less for an examination of the historical context for such disturbances or of their effects on contemporary readers. Analogously, the disturbance offered by some heroines of Sanskrit theater was critically supressed, and similar erasure or marginalization or accomodative readings were the fate of the more contestatory female figures within Indian mythology.[29]

The coexistence of Shakuntala (the heroine of Kalidasa's play of the same name), Sita (the wife of Rama in the epic *Ramayana*) and Miranda (I have had students with all three names) as models for Indian women is remarkable for at least two reasons. First, it reiterates what other literary histories have already been mined to demonstrate: that canonical texts achieve that status partly by their fidelity (real or critically constructed) to patriarchal norms of femininity, which is a precondition for their marketability as universally valid models for human behavior. Second, it shows the ways in which both colonial and nationalist perspectives could be aligned on questions of femininity or the literary text, even though women and education/literature/culture were otherwise bitterly contested areas. The ideal of a passive Hindu wife served, for the British, both as a means of denigrating Indian culture and as a model for the construction of womanhood at home.[30] Conversely, at some moments of Indian nationalism, such an ideal became an emblem of Indian culture which could withstand the onslaughts of Westernization.[31] At other times, of course, both colonialist and native men became "liberators" of Indian women.[32] Such congruence of Western and indigenous patriarchal attitudes would position Indian women as best able to resist colonialism/nationalism as a binary opposition. In the nineteenth century there are some acute observations in their writings to this effect: "there is no hope for the women in India, whether they be under Hindu rule or British rule," or again, "we cannot blame the English government for not defending a helpless woman; it is only fulfilling its agreement made with the male population of India."[33] I was amused to find that, in an article written for a women's journal in 1918, Uma Nehru (who was married to Jawaharlal's cousin) indicted lascivious Indian men by comparing them to Hamlet: "Instead of pondering over 'To be or not to be' our Hamlet-like Indian youth is preoccupied with the weighty question: 'Should I lift the veil or not, and if I do, how much should I lift it?' "[34]

Although the preoccupations of Indian men are mocked by juxtaposing them with Hamlet's "deeper" questions, there is a shade of skepticism here about the endless pondering of men. Especially because at other times women explicitly ridiculed the pretensions of the Westernized Indian male, I wonder if *Hamlet* is unscathed by this somewhat confused analogy.[35]

Since patriarchalism was central to the process of universalizing the Western text whose colonial effects are evident, women are also potentially the most "resisting subjects" in the enterprise of rereading Shakespeare in contemporary India, as I have suggested elsewhere. Conversely, they are marginalized by other postcolonial appropriations.

These are some of the points at which recent Shakespearean criticism, with its interest in cultural difference, meets theories of colonial discourse, with their repeated debates over what constitutes subaltern agency. Such debates incorporate recent developments in ideas about language and ideology but also rehearse older controversies within nationalist movements concerning the relationship between native and foreign cultures, the value of Western education, and strategies of decolonization. As I mentioned earlier, these debates carry on today in postcolonial societies—over feminism, for example; or whether or not to use the English language; or, more to our purpose, whether or not to teach canonical English texts or use post-structuralist theory; whether teaching indigenous literatures can counter the burden of colonial education, and so on. The Mizo playing of *Hamlet* is necessarily embedded in both the Shakespeare myth and such postcolonial negotiations.

Pankaj Butalia's film *When Hamlet Came to Mizoram* (1989) documents one more attempt (shall we call it subaltern?), to deal with Shakespeare on the postcolonial stage.[36] I analyze the Mizo performances of *Hamlet* as reproduced and framed in the film, because the refraction of *Hamlet-drama,* as the Mizos call their version of the play, through the lens of this urban filmmaker, indicates at least part of the wide spectrum of postcoloniality and allows us to mark some of the other meanings of "authority" and "power" in that context. The filmmaker gazes at Mizoram through *Hamlet* rather than at Shakespeare in Mizoram. He is *not* interested in offering explanations about why the Mizos enact this play, but his implicit understanding of *Hamlet* and Shakespeare is located within the paradigms of conventional criticism. For him, as for some of the critics I outlined in the previous section, Shakespeare meets the Mizos in their common pursuit of the other world. His scopophilic gaze marginalizes women as he looks at the female body. Finally, he offers us only tantalizing glimpses of the performances. The divergence of his concerns from mine uncovers some of the problems of recording or representing subversion, in which questions of text, ethnography, and cinema are inevitably bound up with those of method.

When Hamlet Came to Mizoram suggests that contemporary Mizos—who are largely regarded by mainstream India as a strange mixture of the tribal and the Westernized—have lately become obsessed with Shakespeare's play. My talks with several groups of Mizo students confirmed the fact of this obsession; what is equally interesting is that for this filmmaker, it should have become the most powerful signifier of contemporary Mizo identity. First translated into the Mizo language about forty years ago, *Hamlet* is today performed in roadside theaters, in tiny town halls, and in the open air. Even more popular are tape recordings of the play, which blare out at little market kiosks and are duplicated in large numbers. In the film, the players wear T-shirts with "Hamlet" inscribed on them and claim that performing the play has profoundly affected their outlook on life. A man reads from a script to a crowd of children, asking them, "Will you avenge your father? The sword you choose should not be pointed but blunt. It should be dipped in poison. Do you understand? That's what a real king would say." Later, during their afternoon siesta, children murmur to each other:

> How now Ophelia?
> Your voice has changed and has become hoarse.
> Did you see it? Did you see my father?
> What's happening to you? I can't understand.
> When you died, on your grave
> Did I a ceremonial cloth place.
> My tears, mix'd with flowers
> Rain'd down on your grave.
> The season has come,
> Much to the joys of the young.
> The season is over,
> The young are still young,
> But the girls are fresh no more.
> I'm all right, my king,
> May God be with you.

These two sets of lines have not been penned by Shakespeare, nor do they correspond directly to a particular scene in *Hamlet:* yet they are central to *Hamlet-drama.* Both passages, like the audience of Ophelia's lunatic ramblings, freely "botch the words up to fit their thoughts." The first draws upon Claudius and Laertes's plan to kill Hamlet with a poisoned sword (act 4, scene 7), transforming Claudius's villainy into a sign of "real" kingship; the second recalls Ophelia's own song about the man who, on St. Valentine's day, "Let in the maid, that out a maid / Never departed more" (4.5.52–53).[37] Here the Mizo theater rewrites a scene which begins by talking about the dangers of such free botchings up which may, according to Horatio, "strew / Dangerous conjectures in ill-breeding minds" (4.5.14–15). What conjectures does *Hamlet* strew in its Mizo players, who appropriate a text which is itself obsessively concerned with the purposes of playing, with displayed and hidden enactment, and with the intersection of enacting and becoming?

"When Hamlet came to Mizoram," says the actor who plays the title role, "he became a Mizo." Not an Indian. A Mizo. *Hamlet-drama* is played out in India's own periphery, Mizoram, one of its many peripheries of which most "Indians" are only sporadically aware, and in ways that are well-recognized as central to colonial or patriarchal attitudes: tribals (especially northeastern ones) are a hazy confusion of the underdeveloped, childlike, inscrutable, wayward, uncontrollable, innocent, and above all strange. In the mainstream understanding, Mizoram must belong to India because it is good for Mizoram; "development" is measured by the degree to which peripheries melt into the center. The Mizos or their neighbors, the Nagas, are allowed representation mainly at India's Republic Day parades, or cultural festivals where they become living emblems of the "unity-in-diversity" theme so crucial to postcolonial Indian governance.[38] Their bright shawls and tribal dances may be foregrounded as evidence of India's infinite variety, but at the same time their cultural differences must not disturb the definition of what India is. One of Butalia's declared purposes in making the film was precisely to redress such biases.

That Mizoram is part of India today is itself the result of imperial governance, which shaped the present boundaries of a sprawling and previously loosely governed subcontinent. India's northeastern states are culturally closer to parts of Thailand, Burma, or Malaysia than to other parts of India. This cultural difference certainly includes, and more crucially, is perceived to include, a racial component. The Mizo leader Laldenga complained to pressmen in Delhi in November 1985 that his "flat nose" was an obstacle in his being recognized as an Indian. Mizos (who refer to themselves as a *Quom* or "nation") migrated, according to some sources, from Shanghai to Burma in the tenth century A.D. and from there to their present location about four hundred years later.

Economically, and in terms of postindependence "nation-building," Mizoram (like some other parts of the country) has been severely marginalized. Like other neighboring and predominantly tribal areas, it was the special target for large-scale missionary activity of all varieties. In the 1960s and early 1970s, some missionary groups, via the "international peace corps," became a route for international money, much of it funding guerilla activities. Missionary efforts in India were directed especially at those who were marginalized within Hinduism or who, like the tribals, existed outside its fold and that of other organized religions. Today, more than 90 percent of Mizos are Christians; the Welsh Mission Church is predominant, but there are over seventy others active in the region. The northeastern states have also received the persistent attention of Western "development" agencies, again often through missionaries. All this has resulted in a particular kind of Westernization in such peripheries—an infiltration of American fashion, music, and gadgets that reinforces the mainstream perception of Mizos as alien.

Gender is a crucial marker of differences between tribal and nontribal peoples, besides the fact that "tribal" occupies a position analogous to "woman" in their relationship to the mainstream. Such an analogy does not, however, blur the specificity of gender, because tribal society is itself not free of patriarchal oppression.[39] Although Mizo society was never matriarchal, it (like other tribal organizations) allows much more freedom and mobility to women than the more stratified "mainstream" does—both in sexual terms and in matters of property rights. In fact, this relative independence clearly feeds mainstream perception of tribals as animalistic and immoral. The recent shifts in Mizo gender relations (to which I will later return) have in part been the result of the following political developments.

Mizoram has long been the site of conflict between the Indian state, foreign missionaries, foreign funding agencies, local separatist movements, and their Mizo opponents. As in Nagaland, local separatist movements are both the target of the Indian military and the passage for foreign money and arms: both facts reinforce the dominant image of Mizos as a strange mix of uncivilized innocents and terrorists. Most of India's northeastern territories had long been the persistent site of violence—from and against the state. According to the report of a women's team investigating the area in 1982, an unaligned person is the potential target of both state and guerrilla violence. Most families have, at some point, lost someone in this warfare. Mizos themselves are suspicious about India. According to one report in a leading English newspaper, opposing political factions in the state all agree that Mizos must not take their differences to mainstream India: this battle is internal, and while Mizos may war with each other, none may betray their wrangles to "Indians." This seems to typify the Mizo response to India: Mizo students at my university informed me that there would be far more resistance to a Mizo's marrying an Indian than marrying a foreigner.

Indian nationalism, then, is not federal in nature. Its "secular" postures have always included an attempt to homogenize at the expense of cultural, linguistic, and ethnic variety. It has also included an openly communal element which, with increasing violence, mounts an offensive against religious minorities across the country. Both versions of nationalism are patriarchal, and both use the rhetoric of anticolonialism. What does this do to cultures like the Mizo, and how does it alter their relationship to colonialism and its texts?

Something is indeed rotten in the state of Mizoram. But what is the purpose of playing *Hamlet-drama* there? *When Hamlet Came to Mizoram* is not interested in such a question. It is, as the filmmaker reiterates, talking about, indeed rewriting, Mizoram.

After one screening of the film, there was a discussion between the director Butalia, students of my Renaissance drama class, and many Mizo students. It was unexpectedly polarized: my drama students (none of whom is a Mizo) accused Butalia of all the reductionism and ethnocentrism that is associated with traditional anthropology. The Mizo students said that they found it "incredibly moving and intelligent" and the only film by an Indian which understood "us as we are." When asked what accounted for this extraordinary fascination with *Hamlet* they said the reasons were "only emotional. We are a melancholy people, and that is why the play touches us, that is why it is more popular than other Western dramas such as *Romeo and Juliet* or *Salomé.*" But why is *Hamlet* played in Western costumes? "That's because we have no theatrical tradition of our own. In fact, we have no traditions at all, we aren't like the rest of India, you know. So we can make everything our own."

The Mizoram of the film is no doubt a far cry from the simple tribal territory of government-sponsored documentaries. But the choice of *Hamlet* performances as a signifier of contemporary culture shapes the film's Mizoram profoundly. The film has been financed by the British television company Channel Four. Its audiences are therefore predominantly either non-Indian, or urban Indians with a fair degree of contact with the West, like the filmmaker himself, or like me, who have grown up with Shakespeare at school, or university, or theater. That Shakespeare, which is both patriarchal and neocolonialist, directs the gaze of the filmmaker as it rests on Mizoram and "explains" it to his urban audiences.

The film constantly places the Mizo obsession with *Hamlet* within the context of the Christianization of Mizoram, juxtaposing scenes from the performances with the singing of hymns. The filmmaker contends, in discussions with his audiences, that the Mizos' relationship with Christianity and with *Hamlet* are analogous: Mizo culture has appropriated and

When Hamlet Came to Mizoram, 1989, directed by Pankaj Butalia. The shot of a crucifix on the Mizo landscape contributes to how the film places the Mizo obsession with *Hamlet* within the Mizos' relationship to Christianity.

transformed both and is not the passive recipient of either. But although the film shows how church practice is transformed by the enthusiasm, the rhythms, the exuberance, the physical movements of the singers into something very different from the solemn affair one witnesses in, say, the cathedral in New Delhi, this "distinctly Mizo" Christianity is not at all subversive because the film clearly implies that it directs Mizos into other-worldly interests.[40] Shakespeare was in fact the cause for some disagreement between missionary and secular British education in colonial India: despite the frequent assertions that he displayed "sound Protestant principles," he was initially not part of the missionaries' syllabus, which put their students at a disadvantage in public examinations, in which questions on Shakespeare were predominant.[41] But no such disjuncture between Christianity and *Hamlet* exists in the film, which ends, all too neatly, with Hamlet dying to the strains of "I Long for My Saviour's Face," so that *Hamlet* becomes a desire for escape, and its playing a transparent sign of the same. This reinscribes the Orientalist Shakespeare and, like that earlier deployment, deflects the tensions of contemporary social conditions.

"When Hamlet came to Mizoram, he became a Mizo." But then the actor playing Hamlet goes on to assert the very opposite—that playing makes a Mizo into a Hamlet: "It often happens that although I'm not Hamlet, I tend to think and act like him. . . . I often feel, I live in the play itself."

What kind of Mizo did Hamlet become when he came to Mizoram? Or what kind of Hamlet does the play make Mizos? The film suggests that it is a Hamlet truly weary of "all the uses of this world" (1.2.134). The interactions of Mizos with Christianity and with *Hamlet,* then, as articulated by the players, the film, and its Mizo audiences appear to rehearse many of the critical and cultural commonplaces of a universal Shakespeare, of cultureless tribals, of a Protestant *Hamlet.* The natives would appear to be ripe for Shakespearean lessons.

In the film, the actor playing Hamlet continues explaining his shaping by the performances. He says, "I've started distancing myself from people to ponder over things alone. . . . His mood takes over and makes me melancholy." He also states that *Hamlet* teaches him how to hide his real feelings, how to dissemble and not reveal himself easily. The Mizos I spoke to reacted to this by affirming that they were, in any case, "too complex for you to comprehend." I would, in other words, be unable to pluck out the heart of their mystery.[42]

Loss, separation, the importance of dissembling—these are the crux of the players' confessions. What kind of loss is this? A kind of universal loss, which is best articulated for the "melancholy people" by the crosscultural bard? A Protestant "loss," now available to Mizos via missionaries and again best expressed through *Hamlet?* Or is it a loss that both the Mizos and the film are remarkably silent about, a loss that must be related to the extraordinary contexts framing what is rotten in the state of Mizoram? Such a link can be established via the gender politics of both texts.

Dominant critical responses to *Hamlet* have fetishized its fetishization of inscrutability and mystery. At the heart of both fetishes, as Jacqueline Rose brilliantly demonstrates, lies unease about female sexuality.[43] But this anxiety is managed partly by superimposing the mystery of *men* (understood as *the* human predicament) upon the anxiety about women. *Hamlet* glamorizes male dissimulation chiefly by distinguishing it from its more transparent female variants such as verbosity (Hamlet will not "like a whore unpack my heart with words" [2.2.589]), deceit ("God hath given you one face and you make yourselves another" [3.1.146–47]), or simply madness without a method in it, like Ophelia's. In other words, the anxiety generated by female sexuality is deflected by being expressed as a philosophic doubt from which women are themselves excluded—they become the effaced catalysts of man's predicament.

When Hamlet Came to Mizoram, however, almost obsessively focuses on a wandering, lamenting Ophelia. I asked the filmmaker if this reflected the Mizos' preference for the scene. He said it was merely that he found "her movements most captivating." The film doesn't interrogate the relationship of women to this text. The actress playing Ophelia repeats twice that she "identifies" completely with the character because she herself would lament her father in the same way and be similarly affected by her brother's absence. Zos, a research student at Jawaharlal Nehru University, told me that "Mizo families are very close knit" and that for her this entirely explains both Ophelia and the actress playing her.[44]

Hamlet-drama, it seems to me, can be read by extending the vital connections between denial and obsession, fear and meaning that Jacqueline Rose makes in relation to *Hamlet* criticism, and by uncovering what the film and the players most vehemently suppress. The film's scopophilic gaze on Ophelia throws into sharp focus its coyness in looking at other aspects of Mizoram, notably its recent political history, which is also markedly missing in the responses of the players and of the Mizo audience of the film. Butalia himself acknowledges that he wanted to interrogate the actors' various statements about the reasons for playing. "I wanted to say you've changed because of all the other things that now make up your life, not just the play." But what are these things? Western notions of music and fashion? The influx of cars in the city of Aizawl? The recurrent crucifix on the landscape? At one screening, the filmmaker casually pointed out to me that one of the actors used to be part of the terrorist Mizoram National Front (MNF). This Front was originally formed in order to do relief work following a famine in the 1950s and finally spearheaded the separatist movement. Butalia explained away this marked exclusion of Mizo political life by saying that he "couldn't possibly follow up everything." The cameraman of the film, Ranjan Palit, was more vehement in his insistence that this could have no bearing on the performances: after all, Aizawl was now remarkably quiet, people were fed up with politics, and *Hamlet* wasn't a political play. The Mizo students agreed: "The separatist movements are more or less silent. Most Mizos are now interested in joining the government because there are hardly any other jobs available. Yes, we'll have to consider it too. Mizos aren't too interested in studies. What's the point of studying? There aren't any opportunities in Mizoram. Yes, we'll probably have to go away somewhere else."

It is this recent history of Mizoram that, *through the very silences, anxieties, and denials that surround it,* gives a specific meaning to loss, to terror, and to the importance of hiding what you are, to the inscrutability which Mizos seem to assert and value today. At one level *Hamlet-drama* is casually careless with the whodunit element in Hamlet's drama—it cuts out the play within the play, thus simplifying the idea of revenge and focusing more directly on the conflicts of identity. In other ways, though, the Mizo *Hamlet* extends the uses of mystery, of dissembling, suggested by the original play.

Tragedy, it has been suggested, masks defeat with glamor.[45] But *Hamlet-drama* is not simply a disguised fatalism. It is true that things are relatively quieter today on the northeastern front than before the government-MNF accord. But this quiet clearly hides deep resentment, which is of course adulterated by opportunism, exhaustion, and the desire to get on. Recent reports indicate the possibility that separatist sentiments, and guerrilla warfare, are hardly safely buried. If this is so, *Hamlet-drama* is enacted in a crucible of political unease. It therefore marks a time of waiting. I suggested earlier that theater itself is a sort of bridge between the everyday and the spectacular. The performances can be seen as negotiating between the failure of a more spectacular form of resistance and its possible resurgence. Such a negotiation requires that *Hamlet* be transformed into *Hamlet-drama*—tragedy (dismissed by Bakhtin as monologic) into a roadside carnival, its action slashed by everyday life.

Renaissance criticism has been for some time interested in emphasizing the proto-Brechtian episodic and folk elements of the drama of the period.[46] The Mizos punctuate and rewrite *Hamlet* for reasons far removed from Brecht. Their leading actor says that they have done the full play only rarely. The filmmaker told me that the selection of episodes depends on availability of actors: often Horatio is called away to his job as senior technician at Aizawl's only hospital, and Laertes doesn't turn up because of a fight with his girlfriend. The audiences seem unperturbed by such casual montage: in fact, *Hamlet-drama*'s popularity does not rest only on the performances. Its audio cassettes sell widely and are the noisy background to shopping and other daily business.

Such a popularity further removes *Hamlet-drama* from *Hamlet* in mainstream India. Even though English literature is consumed on a large scale (I once estimated that at least 20,000 students study it yearly in the University of Delhi alone) these numbers are still only a small and elite section of the general population. Although in absolute numbers the Mizo viewers may be smaller, certainly the film suggests that *Hamlet-drama* is consumed on a larger scale within that society at large. Moreover, the quality of the involvement is different. My students certainly do not lounge in bed reciting Shakespeare to each other, nor do they play it on their Walkmans. In Mizoram, *Hamlet-drama* approximates a cult film.

And yet it does not reproduce a colonialist Shakespeare. It does not confer "status" or "culture" upon the players or audience, who are only casually aware of the original or of Shakespeare's prestige. As Pankaj

Butalia informed me, Mizo academics who deal with Shakespeare in the school or university context probably disparage these performances and look down upon the translator of *Hamlet* into Mizo, Laldailova, sometimes called the Mizo Shakespeare. (Of course, Mizo academics themselves hardly exist for their counterparts in metropolitan centers like Delhi, who proudly publish a journal called *Hamlet Studies,* advertising it as the only journal in the world devoted to a single text!) *Hamlet-drama* breaks one continuity of the Shakespeare myth, where the burden is of the myth which must be upheld or subverted. Therefore, although (or perhaps because) there is no self-conscious attempt to "appropriate" in *Hamlet-drama,* no questioning of the imperial legacy of Shakespeare, and although translations and adaptations of Shakespeare on the formal stages of Delhi and Bombay often adapt the original for contemporary Indian audiences, the Delhi Shakespeare remains Western in a way that *Hamlet-drama* does not. It cannot therefore be analyzed within the framework I may use for looking at how *Hamlet* is taught at the University of Delhi, or at, say, a recent production of *Othello* on the Bombay stage.[47]

So Mizoram is further removed from Delhi than Delhi is from London. This distance, the differences between the players of *Hamlet-drama,* the filmmaker, the various audiences of the film, and me as a Shakespearean academic, makes it clear that "master-culture" (and therefore its subversion) is not a stable construct, especially as we move from colonialism to its aftermath. *Hamlet-drama* negotiates an authority whose legitimacy is derived from its stance of anticolonialism. But I do not want simply to suggest that nationalism replaces imperialism or neocolonialism as a concern in the "Third World."[48] Rather, the experience of nationalism in many postcolonial countries alters our understanding of colonialism itself.

And even this only partially explains the layering of the society in which the play is enacted. If *Hamlet-drama* is at all an oppositional phenomenon, it is only partially so, and reminds us also that everyday resistance as well as the carnivalesque often are new ways of marginalizing women. For the failure of Mizo insurrection was enacted on the traditional battlefield of arms and warrior men. But despite the traditional Mizo stories of male warriors, such a battlefield was partly created by the guerrilla-versus-state clashes, which, as the Mizo students I interviewed confirmed, edged Mizo women out to a fringe position, the watchers of dramas rather than actors. The Church also played a role in imposing patriarchal norms upon Mizo society: it battled (although somewhat ineffectually) to regulate sexual behavior to its own norms. It has been unable, however, to attach much guilt to premarital sex and to adultery. It is of course possible to see *Hamlet-drama* as communicating such sexual norms to its Mizo viewers. But its patriarchal effects are also more general and more subtle. *Hamlet* cloaks the failure of a certain sort of masculinity by offering—indeed glamorizing—another *equally masculine* alternative to the warrior-man. The playing of *Hamlet* is both the result and the means of shaping a more macho Mizo identity than before.

Hamlet also glamorizes individual, as opposed to collective, identity—the difference between and intersection of the two, suggests Anuradha Kapur, is also the traditional subject of tragedy: "at this intersection the sense of self is joined by narrativizing; it is also in that process dispersed in the structures of the world—religion, state, institutions, language."[49] *Hamlet-drama* betrays such a dispersal and betrays also the fact that its male, individual self is, after all, collectively produced in drama, and by the longing for a secure identity for the Mizo *Quom*. Finally, we must also ask, is *Hamlet-drama* Shakespeare at all? I think it also marks the point where negotiations, self-conscious or otherwise, transform the original to something else. This "new" product, I have shown, is not entirely free of the burden of its earlier connotations: its remarkable use of tragedy as a form of avoidance tactics severely rewrites colonial Shakespeare but also extends the power of the patriarchal bard. Its negotiations with the various authorities—of text, nation, and patriarchy—indicate the fluidity of the categories of "subversion" or "containment," indeed of subalternity itself, with which I began this essay. Although the exercise of reading it as such is inevitably vulnerable to some of the cultural reductionism that anthropologists or documentary filmmakers are routinely accused of, not to attempt it would be not only to succumb to poststructuralist angst but also to be intimidated by the "inscrutability" that *Hamlet* fetishizes.

NOTES

The generosity and patience of Pankaj Butalia made it possible for me to attempt this essay. I want to also thank Marianne Novy for making possible its presentation at various forums and for persistent queries about gender, Suvir Kaul for comments and encouragement, my students at Jawaharlal Nehru University for their responses, and, above all, Rajeswari Sunder Rajan for her considerable critical and editorial input.

1. *The Tragedy of Hamlet, Prince of Denmark,* ed. John Dover Wilson (Cambridge: Cambridge University Press, 1971). All quotations from the play are from this edition.

2. Nicholas B. Dirks, "Ritual and Resistance: Subversion as a Social Fact," in *Contesting Power, Resistance and Everyday Social Relations in South Asia,* ed. Douglas Haynes and Gyan Prakash (Delhi: Oxford University Press, 1991), 214; S. P. Mohanty, "Us and Them: On the Philosophic Basis of Political Criticism," *The Yale Journal of Criticism* 2, no. 2 (Spring 1989): 5. *The Reversible World,* ed.

Barbara Babcock (Ithaca: Cornell University Press, 1978), was a landmark with respect to a gender critique. See also Edward Said, "Representing the Colonized: Anthropology's Interlocutors," *Critical Inquiry* 15 (Winter 1989): 205–25; and James Clifford and George E. Marcus, *Writing Culture: The Poetics and Politics of Ethnography* (Delhi: Oxford University Press, 1990).

3. Rosalind O'Hanlon, "Recovering the Subject: *Subaltern Studies* and Histories of Resistance in Colonial South Asia," *Modern Asian Studies* 22, no. 1 (1988): 189–224; and "Issues of Widowhood: Gender and Resistance in Colonial Western India," in *Contesting Power,* ed. Haynes and Prakash, 62. "Subalternist" here refers in particular to the influential rewriting of South Asian history in the series *Subaltern Studies* edited by Ranajit Guha (Delhi: Oxford University Press, 1982–92).

4. See, for example, Louis A. Montrose, "The Purpose of Playing: Reflections on a Shakespearean Anthropology," *Helios* 7 (1980): 51–74.

5. See, for example, "Introduction: The Entanglement of Power and Resistance," in *Contesting Power,* ed. Haynes and Prakash, 1.

6. That Renaissance criticism has occupied a central position in debates about postmodernism is evident from Judith Newton, "*Family Fortunes:* 'New History' and 'New Historicism,'" *Radical History Review* 43 (1989): 5–22. See also Jonathan Dollimore, "Introduction: Shakespeare, Cultural Materialism and the New Historicism,'" in *Political Shakespeare: New Essays in Cultural Materialism,* ed. Jonathan Dollimore and Alan Sinfield (Manchester: Manchester University Press, 1985), and "Shakespeare, Cultural Materialism, Feminism and Marxist Humanism," *New Literary History* 21, no. 3 (Spring 1990): 471–93; Walter Cohen, "Political Criticism of the Renaissance," in *Shakespeare Reproduced: The Text in History and Ideology,* ed. Jean E. Howard and Marion O'Connor (New York: Methuen, 1987); Judith Newton, "History as Usual?: Feminism and the New Historicism," *Cultural Critique* 9 (Spring 1988): 87–121. Postmodernism is usefully summarized by Jane Flax, "Post Modernism and Gender Relations in Feminist Theory," in *Feminist Theory in Practice and Process,* ed. Micheline R. Makon et al. (Chicago: Chicago University Press, 1986).

7. Dollimore, "Shakespeare, Cultural Materialism, Feminism and Marxist Humanism," 476, resists this simple deduction of the critic's politics from the process she describes. He is referring in particular to the accusations of Carol Neely, "Constructing the Subject: Feminist Practice and the New Renaissance Discourses," *English Literary Renaissance* 18 (1988): 5–18. Neely's insistence on agency leads to a crude prioritization of gender over all other forms of social difference, as I argue in "The Colour of Patriarchy: Cultural Difference, Critical Difference and Renaissance Drama," in *Women, Race and Writing in Early Modern Europe,* ed. Patricia Parker and Margo Hendricks (Routledge, forthcoming).

8. See Mohanty, "Us and Them," 1–31. For feminist reservations about poststructuralism, see Judith Walkowitz, "Patrolling the Borders: Feminist Historiography and the New Historicism," *Radical History Review* 43 (1989): 23–43; and Nancy Hartsock, "Rethinking Modernism: Minority vs. Majority Theories," *Cultural Critique* 7 (Fall 1987): 187–206. For a "Third World" skepticism about

the same, see Kumkum Sangari, "The Politics of the Possible," *Cultural Critique* 7 (Fall 1987): 157–86.

9. W. B. Yeats, "Among Schoolchildren," in *The Selected Poems of W. B. Yeats,* ed. A. Norman Jeffares (London: Macmillan, 1962), 128. See Benita Parry, "Problems in Current Theories of Colonial Discourse," *Oxford Literary Review* 9 (1987): 27–58; Abdul R. JanMohamed, "The Economy of Manichean Allegory: The Function of Racial Difference in Colonialist Literature," *Critical Inquiry* 12 (1985): 59–87.

10. William Shakespeare, *The Tempest* 1.2.363–65, in *The Complete Works,* ed. Peter Alexander (London: Collins, 1951).

11. Lenin posed this problem in his *What Is To Be Done,* trans. S. V. and Patricia Utechin (London: Oxford University Press, 1963). Anticolonial movements have been for long preoccupied with the same issue.

12. Walkowitz, "Patrolling the Borders," 30.

13. O'Hanlon, "Issues of Widowhood," 62.

14. Hartsock, "Rethinking Modernism," 191.

15. Flax, "Postmodernism and Gender Relations," 63–64.

16. Stephen Greenblatt, *Shakespearean Negotiations* (Berkeley: University of California Press, 1988), 53.

17. Mohanty, "Us and Them," 15. For a sensitive attempt to recover a gendered subjectivity precisely *through* such decentering and fractures, see Zakia Pathak and Rajeswari Sunder Rajan, "'Shahbano,'" in *Feminist Theory,* ed. Malson, 249–73. Judith Newton and Deborah Rosenfelt argue that the provisionality of knowledge need not necessarily preclude political action, in *Feminist Criticism and Social Change: Sex, Class and Race in Literature and Culture* (New York: Methuen, 1985), xxiv.

18. Ania Loomba, *Gender, Race, Renaissance Drama* (Manchester: Manchester University Press, 1989).

19. For a discussion of English literary study and imperial rule see Gauri Viswanathan, *Masks of Power: Literary Study and British Rule in India* (London: Faber and Faber, 1989). See also *"The Lie of the Land": English Studies in India,* ed. Rajeswari Sunder Rajan (Delhi: Oxford University Press, 1991).

20. The celebratory lines were written by a student of Calcutta College, Nobin Chander Dass, in 1843 and are reproduced in *First Fruits of English Education, 1817–1857,* ed. Bhagaban Prasad Majumdar (Calcutta: Bookland Private Limited, 1973). The critique of alienated Indians is cited from an 1854 issue of the *Calcutta Review* by Viswanathan, *Masks of Power,* 160.

21. Sushil Kumar Mukherjee, *The Story of Calcutta Theatres, 1753–1980* (Calcutta: K. P. Bagchi and Company, 1982), 10.

22. See Ruth Cowhig, "Blacks in English Renaissance Drama and the Role of Shakespeare's *Othello,*" in *The Black Presence in English Literature,* ed. David Dabydeen (Manchester: Manchester University Press, 1985), 1–25.

23. *Shakespeare Came to India,* ed. C. D. Narasimhaiah (Bombay: Popular Prakashan, 1964), v. The Department of English, University of Delhi, hosted a conference with the theme "Shakespeare for All Time" in December 1988 where, with pitifully few exceptions, his universal relevance was reiterated.

24. The most well-known troupe was *Shakespeariana,* run during the first half of this century by the Englishman Sir Geoffrey Kendal, and the subject of Ivory-Merchant's 1965 film *Shakespearewallah.* Its performances were remarkable only for the range of audience they appealed to—Kendal was patronized by royalty and the intelligentsia as well as lower middle-class audiences which thronged to tiny theaters, often just tin shacks, all over the country to see the troupe perform. For an account of the company, see Geoffrey Kendal (with Clare Colvin), *The Shakespearewallah* (Middlesex: Penguin, 1986). Ivory-Merchant's film is discussed in John Pym, *The Wandering Company: 21 Years of Merchant-Ivory Films* (London: British Film Institute; New York: The Museum of Modern Art, 1983).

25. For Sister Nivedita, India was thus "a world in which men in loincloths, seated on door-sills in duty lanes, said things about Shakespeare and Shelley that some of us would go far to hear": *The Web of Indian Life* in *The Complete Works of Sister Nivedita,* 4 vols. (Calcutta: Ramakrishna Sharada Mission Sister Nivedita Girls School, 1967), 2:2.

26. Sri Aurobindo, "This Sheer Creative Ananda of the Life Spirit Which Is Shakespeare," in *Shakespeare Came to India,* ed. Narasimhaiah, 132. See also the essay by Isser Chander Dass of Hooghly College in *First Fruits,* ed. Majumdar.

27. See, for example, Michèle Barrett, "The Concept of 'Difference,' " *Feminist Review* 26 (Summer 1987): 29–91.

28. *First Fruits,* ed. Majumdar, 212.

29. See, for example, Sister Nivedita, "Of the Hindu Woman as Wife" and "Love as Strong as Death," in *The Web of Indian Life.* See also Uma Chakravarti, "Whatever Happened to the Vedic *Dasi?* Orientalism, Nationalism and a Script for the Past," in *Recasting Women: Essays in Colonial History,* ed. Kumkum Sangari and Sudesh Vaid (New Delhi: Kali for Women, 1989), 27–87.

30. Sister Nivedita's *Web of Indian Life* presents the passive Hindu wife as a model for all women; the *Church Times* reviewed it on 19 August 1904 with horror, reiterating the dominant colonial argument that the condition of Indian women made Western reform (especially through Christianity) a necessity.

31. Partha Chatterji, "The Nationalist Resolution of the Women's Question," in *Recasting Women,* ed. Sangari and Vaid, 233–53.

32. Gayatri Chakravorty Spivak, "Can the Subaltern Speak?" in *Marxism and the Interpretation of Culture,* ed. Cary Nelson and Lawrence Grossberg (Urbana: University of Illinois Press, 1988), 271–313. See also Lata Mani, "Contentious Traditions: The Debate on Sati in Colonial India," *Cultural Critique* 7 (1987): 119–56.

33. Qtd. in Chakravarti, "Whatever Happened," 74.

34. Vir Bharat Talwar, "Feminist Consciousness in Women's Journals in Hindi, 1910–20," in *Recasting Women,* ed. Sangari and Vaid, 227. I have retranslated this from the Hindi original cited by Talwar.

35. Mokshodayani Mukhopadhyay, for example, mocks the man who is

> transported with pride at the thought of his rank—
> But faced with a sahib [Englishman], he trembles in fear!
> Then he's obsequious, he mouths English phrases
> His own tongue disgusts him, he heaps it with curses.

"The Bengali Babu" (1882) reproduced in *Women Writing in India,* ed. Susie Tharu and K. Lalitha (New York: Feminist Press, 1990), 219.

36. The film's advertising copy reads as follows:

WHEN HAMLET CAME TO MIZORAM 1989/India/16mm/Col
Mizo (English subtitles) / 52 mins
Direction: Pankaj Butalia   Camera: Ranjan Palit
Sound: Suresh Rajamani, Pankaj Butalia   Editing Sameera Jain

In the North-East of India, near the Burma border, live the Mizo tribals. Ever since J. F. Laldailova, an interpreter in the British Army, translated some of Shakespeare plays into English, there has been a love-affair between the Bard and the Mizos. A few years ago a group of amateurs put up a performance of *Hamlet* which was a smash hit with the local population. A modified version of the play was then put on audio cassette which sold 3,000 copies in two weeks. The film documents this phenomenon as well as the environment within which it happens in the north-east of India where the Mizo tribals live.

37. I am grateful to Marianne Novy for drawing my attention to the parallels.

38. See my "Overworlding the 'Third World,'" *Oxford Literary Review* 13, nos. 1–2 (1991): 164–91.

39. See Manoshi Mitra, "Women in Santhal Society: Women as Property, Women and Property," in *Samya Shakti: A Journal of Women's Studies* 4–5 (1991): 213–27, for a cautious analysis of differences between tribal and mainstream Hindu social relations.

40. I am indebted to Marianne Novy for suggesting that that the Mizo relationship with Christianity as well as the nationalist usage of a transcendent literary text can be located alongside African-American use of spirituals, as described by Eugene Genovese in *Roll, Jordan, Roll* (New York: Random House, 1976). As I see it, the analogy is more appropriate to nationalist Shakespeare than to Mizo Christianity, at least as it is offered by the film.

41. Viswanathan, *Masks of Power,* 80; Majumdar, *First Fruits,* 138.

42. The Mizo students I interviewed at Jawaharlal Nehru University all emphasised this. Lal Biak Thanga's *The Mizos: A Study in Racial Personality* (Gauhati: United Publishers, 1978) cites the "strange behaviour" of various Mizo legendary and historical figures to conclude that "the root of the trouble in the Mizo country" may be connected to the fact that a "A Mizo is not easy to understand" (174–75).

43. Jacqueline Rose, "Sexuality in the Reading of Shakespeare: *Hamlet* and *Measure for Measure,*" in *Alternative Shakespeares,* ed. John Drakakis (London: Methuen, 1985), 95–118.

44. Interestingly, the legend of the death of Taitsana, "the idol of all Mizo youths," indicates that concern with female adultery has been central in Mizo culture. While this hero was still a small boy, his mother ran away with another man. When he was dying and in great agony, she came to be with him, but Taitsana said that his injury was nothing compared to the pain she had caused him by her sin (see Thanga, *The Mizos,* 107).

45. I thank Peter Erickson for suggesting to me "that the play functions as a refuge and escape and that the genre of tragedy helps to shape that escape in the mode of isolation, melancholy, even despair, thus lending dignity to a kind of fatalism or sense of inevitability" (personal communication).

46. See especially Jonathan Dollimore, *Radical Tragedy* (Brighton: Harvester, 1983); also Loomba, *Gender, Race, Renaissance Drama,* chapter 5.

47. Shakespeare's *Othello,* directed by Alyque Padamsee and featuring Kabir Bedi, was played at the Siri Fort Auditorium in New Delhi on 30 and 31 March 1991 to packed houses. There was no attempt to think about cultural differences within the play, or in the context of its staging, except at one point when Othello's doubts about Desdemona and resultant confusions are gathering momentum. Suddenly, he goes through the motions of reading *namaaz* (Muslim prayers), and cries of "Allah-ho-akbar" fill the stage. Stripped bare to the waist, Othello lashes his back with a whip, replicating the self-flagellation and grief of the faithful during the Muslim festival of Moharram, which marks the death of Prophet Mohammad. The whole point of the play is precisely that Othello thinks of himself as a Christian, as defender of the Venetian state, without which his schizophrenia has no meaning. In a production which otherwise paid no attention to Othello's racial difference, this sudden and token invocation of Islam served only as a grotesque and momentary parody of the differences which do pervade the play. Of course, there have been other, more serious attempts, to adapt Shakespeare, many of which have used non-linear, nonteleological aspects of Indian theatrical traditions which employ proto-Brechtian devices and ideas about communication, theatrical meaning, and so on.

48. Lata Mani, "Multiple Mediations: Feminist Scholarship in the Age of Multi-National Reception," *Feminist Review* 35 (Summer 1990): 22–41. Aijaz Ahmed, "Jameson's Rhetoric of Otherness and the 'National Allegory,' " *Social Text* 17 (1987): 3–25, takes Fredric Jameson to task for suggesting that nationalism is the burden of "third world" texts. Although my position is slightly different in that I do see nationalism as a major concern for postcolonial movements and intellectuals, and as a factor that in fact disturbs an understanding of postcoloniality as either homogeneous, or a simple hangover of colonialism, his point that it cannot be simply privileged is well taken.

49. See "Dialogue," *The Journal of Arts and Ideas,* Issues 20–21 (March 1991): 9.

PETER ERICKSON

Afterword: "Trying Not to Forget"

As the key phrase in its subtitle signals, *Cross-Cultural Performances: Differences in Women's Re-Visions of Shakespeare* is a sequel to *Women's Re-Visions of Shakespeare: On the Responses of Dickinson, Woolf, Rich, H.D., George Eliot, and Others.* Two major motifs in this second volume are those of theatrical production and race. In order to situate these two strands in a larger critical context, I shall construct a lineage for *Women's Re-Visions of Shakespeare* as a two-volume project, with particular reference to feminist, cultural materialist, and new historicist approaches and with special focus on their strategic deployment through the medium of essay collections.

The 1980s were an unusually productive and unusually turbulent period in Shakespeare studies: the decade's work constitutes a turning point in the history of Shakespeare criticism. This extraordinary ferment and upheaval are in large part a result of the emergence of feminist, cultural materialist, and new historicist modes as distinct critical constellations. Moreover, collections of essays, as a specific format, have played an important role in the development of these critical discourses. In the symbolic economy of literary criticism, collections have the potential to convey galvanizing, high-profile resonance because they concentrate intellectual energy and signal formations of institutional power. A collection makes particularly visible the process of networking by which scholarly positions are staked out. The collection as a critical mode thus has double impact as an intellectual and a professional force; it not only announces new intellectual directions but also expresses a collective action. This latter institutional dimension is magnified during an unsettled, exploratory phase such as characterizes the present situation in Shakespeare studies.

A monograph, of course, also participates in a group process and thereby displays an institutional aspect. The accumulation of footnotes, for example, implies a similar act of gathering and assembling, a local politics of citation that decides which names will be put into circulation. But this effect is far more dramatic in the case of a collection, where the process is not coordinated and mediated by one voice. The collocation of many voices in the same space creates a series of implied interactions that produce more vivid reverberations and crosscurrents. The acts of collection incorporated in collections of essays suggest small-scale, transient efforts to organize a canon of literary critics. Such momentary clusterings are subsumed by the larger ongoing process in which partially overlapping, partially competing networks constantly shift and reform. But in their moment the alliances crystallized by a particular collection constitute a critical movement.

In its defining moment, each of the three major lines of criticism established in the first half of the 1980s—feminist, cultural materialist, and new historicist—manifested itself in part through the vehicle of an identifiably movement-oriented collection. When situated in its context, the collective project signified by the two volumes of *Women's Re-Visions of Shakespeare* can be seen as a reconfiguration that cuts across and interweaves these three distinct lines. I now turn to specific instances of the present project's strongly marked relation to previous collections.

Feminist Shakespeare criticism was inaugurated by *The Woman's Part: Feminist Criticism of Shakespeare,* edited by Carolyn Ruth Swift Lenz, Gayle Greene, and Carol Thomas Neely (University of Illinois Press, 1980). This volume stands out as the most obvious antecedent of *Women's Re-Visions of Shakespeare.* Not only do the two projects have the same publisher, but the first volume of *Women's Re-Visions* contains essays by each of the three co-editors of *The Woman's Part,* as well as essays by two additional contributors, Marianne Novy and Madelon Sprengnether Gohlke. However, the significance of this undeniably strong connection should not be overemphasized to the exclusion of other important links, especially with regard to *Cross-Cultural Performances.* What is of particular interest here is how both volumes of *Women's Re-Visions* register changes that have occurred since the appearance of *The Woman's Part.*[1]

Cultural materialism in Shakespeare studies was established by the publication of *Political Shakespeare: New Essays in Cultural Materialism,* edited by Jonathan Dollimore and Alan Sinfield (University of Manchester Press, 1985) and reinforced by two related collections, *Alternative Shakespeares,* edited by John Drakakis (Methuen, 1985), and *The Shakespeare Myth,* edited by Graham Holderness (Manchester University Press, 1988).[2] As Carol Neely observes, feminist contributions by women in these three volumes are disproportionately small; hence the volumes' overall structures tend to marginalize women critics.[3] Ann Thompson, for example, is obliged to note the "tokenism" of her inclusion in *The Shakespeare Myth* (85).

Cross-Cultural Performances, however, holds out the prospect of a more productive affiliation with cultural materialism. First, this prospect is enacted by the presence here of Dympna Callaghan and Ania Loomba, whose books—*Women and Gender in Renaissance Tragedy* (Harvester Wheatsheaf, 1989) and *Gender, Race, Renaissance Drama* (Manchester University Press, 1989)—originated in work at Sussex University, the central location for cultural materialism in Renaissance studies.[4] Second, the powerful set of essays on British theater in the present volume follows from Alan Sinfield's pioneering analysis of the Royal Shakespeare Company in *Political Shakespeare* (158–81).[5] In sharp contrast with orthodox performance criticism, which too frequently becomes a reductive filtering device by which a play's complex textual and cultural significance is screened out and denied by deeming it unactable, Sinfield develops a materialist approach that focuses on the theater as a site where organizational power relations are played out and as a popular medium in which ideological meanings are purveyed or placed in conflict. This materialist perspective is strongly continued here in the essays by Juliet Hankey on Helen Faucit, Dympna Callaghan on Joan Littlewood, Joyce MacDonald on Deborah Warner, and Lizbeth Goodman on Fiona Shaw and Tilda Swinton.

In addition to the valuable bibliography on the theater they provide, what makes this subsection of essays illuminating is the detailed way they highlight issues of political control involving theatrical administrative hierarchies, the prevalence of male direction, and the unequal distribution by gender of acting roles, and the fine-pointed way they demonstrate the successful interventions, difficulties, and outright contradictions in women's attempts to speak within a tradition of Shakespearean performance. To move from the blatant repression of the "innocent ignorance" in Helen Faucit's nineteenth-century dramatization of female roles to the consciously oppositional strategies in the post–World War II period—from the founding of the Theatre Workshop in 1945 through the work of Monstrous Regiment, the Royal Shakespeare Company's Women's Project, and Women's Theatre Group in the 1980s—is invigorating.[6] But even more bracing is Lizbeth Goodman's articulation of a wider range of choices made possible by a positive rejection of the Shakespeare option—positive because it envisions an alternative to the limited spectrum offered by the various alternative Shakespeares: "The question posed is not *how* to play Shakespeare but *whether* to play Shakespeare. The related and larger question is whether women writers may have something to say which is not contained in and cannot be extrapolated from a Shakespearean text." In this regard, Goodman raises the issue of canonicity, to which I shall return.

The third critical mode, new historicism, was instituted by Stephen Greenblatt's *Renaissance Self-Fashioning* (University of Chicago Press, 1980). Its collective expression followed in *The Power of Forms in the*

English Renaissance, edited by Stephen Greenblatt (Pilgrim Books, 1982) and in the related founding of the journal *Representations,* whose first issue appeared in September 1983 and which led to a new collection, *Representing the English Renaissance,* also edited by Stephen Greenblatt (University of California Press, 1988). The link to the present volume is indirect since it requires the intervention of another prominent collection: *Rewriting the Renaissance: The Discourses of Sexual Difference in Early Modern Europe,* edited by Margaret W. Ferguson, Maureen Quilligan, and Nancy J. Vickers (University of Chicago Press, 1986). The mediating role of this collection is made possible by the inclusiveness of its critical perspectives.[7] The principal contribution of *Rewriting the Renaissance* was to insist on feminist historicism as an alternative to versions of new historicism that ignored or marginalized women. The spirit exemplified by the double emphasis on gender and history in the introduction by Margaret Ferguson is carried over into *Cross-Cultural Performances* by Ferguson's own lead essay, which sets the stage for much that follows.

Two points of contact between *Rewriting the Renaissance* and the two volumes of *Women's Re-Visions of Shakespeare* are especially pertinent. First, the titles themselves suggest the close proximity between the concepts of rewriting and re-visioning.[8] Second, the final turn from images of women in male-authored writing to actual women writers in the last two chapters of *Rewriting the Renaissance* prefigures the focus on women writers in *Women's Re-Visions.* As Margaret Drabble puts it, "the Shrew began to see how to rewrite the last act." The significance of this move for Shakespeare studies is that it broadens the social and historical scope of analyses of the "sex-gender system" (*Rewriting the Renaissance,* xxi). The system is no longer seen as expressed solely at the level of character in the patterns of power relations between male and female Shakespearean characters, but now extends to the institutions of authorship as differentially applied to men and women writers. The focus on women as authors makes clear that Shakespeare's authorship is gendered male.

One consequence of feminist Shakespeare criticism's encounter with new historicism has been increased emphasis on a new avenue of historical study—the study of representations of Shakespeare in the work of women writers from later historical periods. Such studies are historicist in that they strategically involve two different historical locations. But such studies also remain resolutely feminist not only because they concern a woman writer, but because they expand the possibilities for a critical perspective on Shakespeare. This expansion depends on an internal critique of feminism voiced here by Margaret Ferguson and Ania Loomba. What is needed is not only greater historical precision with respect to gender but also greater emphasis on multiple cultural variables. Exclusive focus on gender as the single key variable, constituted as a unified category, has been modified and complicated by increasing recognition that female gender is itself divided by structural patterns of race, class, national location, and sexual orientation,[9] and that idealized appeals to women's solidarity are liable to project white middle-class women's viewpoint as though it were universally shared.

The particular contribution that the present volume makes to the reconstitution of feminist criticism concerns the issue of race, which forms a main topic in the group of essays by Margaret Ferguson, Malin LaVon Walther, Valerie Traub, Diana Brydon, and Ania Loomba.[10] The vast historical reach of this collection is suggested by the leap from Aphra Behn's problematic image of the silenced black woman Imoinda in the late seventeenth century as addressed in Ferguson's opening essay to the contemporary examples of black women authors speaking for themselves in the essays by Walther and Traub on Toni Morrison and Gloria Naylor. The Shakespearean negotiations that Morrison and Naylor conduct in relation to *The Tempest* involve reimagining Miranda as black.[11]

Although Malin LaVon Walther does not discuss the commanding character of Thérèse as *Tar Baby*'s restoration of Sycorax, one implication of Walther's emphasis on Jadine as the key to Morrison's re-vision of *The Tempest* is that *Tar Baby* does not seek restitution simply by redoing the play's broken bond between Caliban and Sycorax through the sympathetic treatment of the collaboration between Son and Thérèse highlighted by the novel's ending. The novel's focal point is not Sycorax but Miranda. Walther's reading suggests to me that, rather than dismiss Jadine as Miranda, Morrison makes a substantial investment in her as a figure for Morrison as author; by means of the emotional locus provided by Jadine, Morrison is able to "bid a textual farewell to Eurocentric aesthetics" that frees her to write *Beloved*. In the case of Gloria Naylor, the figure of a black Miranda is vested in Mama Day. As Valerie Traub demonstrates, Naylor invokes the weight of Shakespearean tradition in order to evade it by giving Mama Day–Miranda a double name. By virtue of the more powerful name Mama Day, Miranda's generational position is transformed from that of innocent daughter to maternal authority.

In another revision that empowers a nonwhite woman to speak, the Indian Canadian lesbian feminist writer Suniti Namjoshi makes Caliban female in her poem "Snapshots of Caliban," as though imaginatively to recreate the space in which the difficult exchange between a white and a racially other woman foreclosed by Aphra Behn might take place.[12] In a different way, Martha Tuck Rozett's essay on Lillie Buffum Chace Wymanea also bears on Margaret Ferguson's account of Behn and of women's relations across racial differences. Wyman's revisionist view of Gertrude

becomes a means of recovering the absent mother that left her feeling, in
Rozett's words, a "motherless Ophelia"—of inventing a fantasy substitute
for "the idealized maternal presence" she never had. In light of the
information about Wyman's mother provided by the daughter's biography
of her, Wyman's revision of Shakespeare appears as an escape from her
mother's political activity, specifically as it involves the vexed interactions
of gender and race figured by the nineteenth-century abolitionist and
women's rights movements. If Wyman met Sojourner Truth and Frederick
Douglass through her mother's work, Wyman's own work on Shakespeare functions as a refuge that enables her to avoid the implications of
such meetings. In this sense, Wyman's Gertrude is an emblem of the
forgetting from which revisionist engagement with Shakespeare is not
automatically free. In our own contemporary terms, active remembering
of our political contexts, including race, requires a more substantial
breaching of the Shakespearean canon.

The most obvious example of the breaking down of the boundaries
that define the Shakespearean field occurs in Ania Loomba's account of
"*Hamlet* in Mizoram." To reach the geographically and culturally distant
point of Mizoram—"Mizoram is further removed from Delhi than Delhi is
from London"—Shakespearean influence is overextended, stretched beyond
recognition. Mizo rewriting "breaks one continuity of the Shakespeare
myth, where the burden is of the myth which must be upheld or subverted."
Shakespeare is not the issue: the Mizos are "only casually aware of the
original or of Shakespeare's prestige." Since *Hamlet-drama* inserts newly
improvised language that is not Shakespeare's and Mizo performances
take further liberties through an episodic format of "casual montage," the
Mizo version transforms *Hamlet* into "something else." This process of
dispersal is also evidenced in the fiction of Toni Morrison and Gloria
Naylor, where the vectors of appropriation reverse direction, Morrison
and Naylor freely recomposing, rather than being constrained by, the
Shakespearean traces on which they draw. In general, the overall effect of
the two volumes of *Women's Re-Visions of Shakespeare* is to foster
dispersal by repositioning Shakespeare through filling in blank spaces and
environing him with myriad contexts that were hitherto nonexistent.

As a two-volume project, *Women's Re-Visions of Shakespeare* tends to
challenge the Shakespearean circle by which everything is seen as originating with Shakespeare and therefore ultimately circles back and redounds
to his credit. The circumference can be indefinitely enlarged but the shape
and center will hold: the points on the expanding circumference continue
to be defined in relation to a Shakespearean center from which a controlling influence continues to radiate. But this circular image prevents us
from pursuing the full scope of the cultural politics involved in literary

re-vision. Because Shakespeare's position as the canon within the canon is so pivotal and because the net result of their re-visions is to decenter and reposition Shakespeare, the two volumes of *Women's Re-Visions of Shakespeare* participate in a much wider effort to question the structural implications of the established literary canon. It is extremely important to experience the emotional liberation that accompanies the realization that we are not condemned by the accreted historical weight of literary tradition to a fixed and inescapable canonical gaze, that we can instead rewrite our inheritance. At the same time, we must face with equal ardor questions about the limits and problems of this rewriting. In the space remaining, I want to address some of the difficulties that accompany canon revision, while leaving open the question of the extent to which these difficulties can be overcome.

One significant common element that the treatment of the two major topics of race and theater in this volume share is the concept of rewriting or re-vision. Yet there is no avoiding the pressures that counteract assertions of total freedom to rewrite. Even the Mizo culture described in Ania Loomba's essay cannot wholly escape the Shakespearean influence; for if the Mizos do not know Shakespeare's name, they nevertheless experience a powerful attraction to a traditional conception of his tragic mode. The genre, if not the author, is the message. The interview with the actor who plays Hamlet suggests that the appeal of tragedy lies in its capacity to provide both the vehicle and the cultural permission for the expression of solitude and melancholy. If Hamlet's melancholy allows the Mizos indirectly to voice a sense of loss connected specifically to their current political situation, this "political unease" is registered in the silences and denials that compose the drama's "political unconscious." Because *Hamlet-drama* enacts "both a display and a displacement of resistance," its effects work two ways: "If *Hamlet-drama* is at all an oppositional phenomenon, it is only partially so." The Mizos' use of *Hamlet* may then be as much a force of tradition as of liberation and thus calls into question the whole notion of rewriting.

The critique of rewriting, however, can be conducted on two quite distinct levels: the first is primarily philosophical, the second primarily social. This difference in approach leads to a crucial difference in emphasis: whereas the former portrays rewriting as a logical impossibility, the latter acknowledges the cultural and political obstacles that make rewriting extremely difficult—but not impossible. The philosophical approach is exemplified by Howard Felperin's contention that opponents of the canon are unwittingly caught in a metaphysical bind because all efforts at "decanonizing" are necessarily subject to a "boomerang effect" whereby "even the most negative critique works to reinforce its canonical object" so that "canonical text and anticanonical critique" are always "mutually reinforcing."[13] Failure to admit this paradox, Felperin warns, results in criticism that is not only self-deluded but literally self-destructive: "For any criticism bent on abolishing or dissolving the canon in the name of an 'egalitarian' politics or an 'interdisciplinary' theory is effectively committing suicide. . . . It will also discover, in the moment of recognition before death, that its attempt to dismantle the canon has only reinforced it" (xii). The problem is Felperin's use of this circular dilemma as a fixed formula that automatically applies in all cases. The exaggerated misrepresentation of canon revision as "abolishing or dissolving" suggests an attempt to circumvent or deny the substantial positive change that this revision has actually achieved. The threatening image of suicidal death, which is simply unconvincing when applied to the activity of canon revision, seems rather to express Felperin's own sense of anxiety about cultural change.[14] Against this anxiety, Felperin's assertion of a binding deconstructive law too neatly affords a protective distance.

Jonathan Crewe pursues the philosophical critique of rewriting in a completely different tone.[15] Where Felperin is hyperbolic, strident, and defensive, Crewe is restrained, circumspect, and serenely self-assured. For Crewe, the set of terms on which current criticism so frequently depends—rewriting, revision, representation, refiguring, reconstituting—carries an inherently problematic echo of the structure of the word Renaissance itself. These terms announce a break that is undercut by the inevitable indication built into the prefix "re-" of an insuperable connection with what came before. Thus Crewe's own use of the term "reconstruction" in his book's subtitle is counterbalanced by the explicit acknowledgment of "anterior forms" to which any reconstruction remains attached. Crewe's avowed commitment to "satiric criticism" (8–13) provides a valuable antidote to uncritically "romantic" versions of rewriting. Yet if this coolly satiric stance usefully avoids "*promising* too much" (12), it also includes its own form of complacency when "satire" and "romance" readily modulate into alignment with another pair of terms—"conservative" and "radical." The flat implication is that literary forms can be reworked but not fundamentally changed; the very word "rewriting" becomes a bell tolling us back to painful consciousness of the intellectual futility of all efforts at radically rewriting the Renaissance.[16] One can agree that there are intrinsic limits to our ability to reinterpret the materials of the Renaissance, but this agreement neither requires us to abandon all possibility of radical analysis nor predictably "preclude[s] any representation of the Renaissance as *radically* otherwise" (1). Crewe secures a "conservation of premises" (2) because in his mind there is only one Renaissance. Yet the term Renaissance is reopened when, in a larger view, it has multiple literary historical references, including the contemporary American Renaissance of minority literatures. The perspectival contrast and interplay between the Shakespearean Renaissance and this latest American Renaissance bring back the term "radical" from the intellectual banishment to which Crewe tries to consign it.

Despite their differences in style, Felperin and Crewe reach similar conclusions: both reject the claims of canon revision. Carla Frecerro, however, puts the critique of rewriting on a different basis:

> We are not simply rewriting history, "refiguring woman" in order to render her "visible." . . . Liberal humanist debates about whether or not women had roles to play in the economic and political life of the Renaissance, whether or not they were empowered within bourgeois society, beg the question of systematic class oppression and struggles for change. We know that some women were producers, and that some women have been economically and politically enfranchised. The uncovering of these facts by themselves has little effect on the notion of male superiority to the female, which includes the internalization of this ideology by women; such "discoveries" (like the white liberal "appreciation" of African-American culture) often serve class interests that resist the radical restructuring implicit in the designation of "women" as a category of struggle.[17]

Unlike Crewe, Frecerro gives credence to the potential for "radical restructuring" of the literary and the social order. Yet Frecerro's vision cannot be comfortably dismissed as naively utopian. As I understand it, no easy, absolute victory is anticipated; the struggle is ongoing, the results likely to be mixed. The chief distinction between Frecerro and Felperin or Crewe is that the difficulties Frecerro acknowledges are of a different order: though formidable, they do not invalidate the prospect of significant change.

In closing, I want briefly to note the difficulties that follow from using the term "multicultural" to characterize the conceptual and ideological framework within which current revisions of the literary canon are carried out.[18] Ania Loomba's essay here is insightful not only because of her cogent formulation of the oppressive political hierarchy that can hide behind the name of multiculturalism, but also because of her awareness of her own potential implication in this hierarchy through a "Calibanistic double bind." Loomba shows that the "nationalist appropriation of Shakespeare" in India absorbed the colonialist idea of universal Shakespeare, a cultural operation that helps to maintain postcolonial India as a society structured in dominance. Appeals to multiculturalism are used co-optively: "the Mizos are allowed representation mainly at India's Republic Day parades, or cultural festivals where they become living emblems of the 'unity-in-diversity' theme so crucial to postcolonial Indian governance. Their bright shawls or tribal dances may be foregrounded as evidence of India's infinite variety, but at the same time their cultural differences must not disturb the definition of what India is." A similar "politics of multi-culturalism" is repeated on an international scale when "minorities within the 'first world' begin to represent diverse 'Third World' contexts." The best multicultural intentions of revisionists within "the Anglo-American academy" can thus be inadvertently subjected and bent to the imposition of dominant global power structures.

With the intractableness of the problem of the political erasure of cultural difference in mind, I turn to two responses to this dilemma in the present volume. Two passages by Margaret Ferguson and Valerie Traub counterpoint each other as gestures of caution and of possibility. I evoke them not in opposition but in combination as the double parameter within which ongoing work may productively proceed. First, I want to repeat in my own voice, and from within a perspective positioned not only as white but also as male, heterosexual, and middle-class American, the sobering clause at the end of Margaret Ferguson's essay: "trying not to forget." I cite these terms of my identity in a contingently historical rather than an essentialist vein—not to proclaim a tragically inevitable helplessness but to say that even as I strive to redefine the meanings of my social locations, I do not want to refine them out of existence by means of a multicultural transcendence every bit as escapist as the standard traditionalist version of universalism. Second, I reiterate Valerie Traub's genre-based political distinction: "Such differences are not only oppressive, but fecund; not merely tragic in the effects of systematic inequalities in the distribu-tion of goods, jobs, services and opportunities, but comedic in the Shake-spearean sense of spawning imaginative visions of social reconstitution and regeneration." The hopeful appeal to comic inventiveness and fluidity as a political resource is important, but this promise will not be fulfilled unless equal attention is paid to the sharp reminders provided by Ferguson and Loomba.

NOTES

1. An overview of American feminist Shakespeare criticism through 1985 is provided by my entry in volume 2 of *Women's Studies Encyclopedia*, ed. Helen Tierney (New York: Greenwood Press, 1990), 314–18. More recent work includes Dympna Callaghan, Lorraine Helms, and Jyotsna Singh, *The Wayward Sisters: Shakespeare and Feminist Politics* (Cambridge, Mass.: Basil Blackwell,

1993); Margaret W. Ferguson, *Partial Access: Studies in Female Literacy in Early Modern France and England* (London: Routledge, forthcoming); Jean E. Howard, *Discourses of the Theater: The Stage and Social Struggle in Early Modern England* (London: Routledge, 1993); *The Matter of Difference: Materialist Feminist Criticism of Shakespeare,* ed. Valerie Wayne (Hemel Hempstead: Harvester Wheatsheaf, 1991); Valerie Traub, *Desire and Anxiety: Circulations of Sexuality in Shakespearean Drama* (London: Routledge, 1992); *Women in the Renaissance,* ed. Ann Rosalind Jones and Betty S. Travitsky, special issue of *Women's Studies* 19, no. 2 (1991). Forthcoming from Routledge are five volumes in the Feminist Readings of Shakespeare series, whose general editor is Ann Thompson.

2. For an account that shows *Political Shakespeare*'s roots in the revised Marxist approaches of Raymond Williams and Stuart Hall, see my review in *Shakespeare Quarterly* 37 (1986): 251–55.

3. Carol Thomas Neely, "Constructing the Subject: Feminist Practice and the New Renaissance Discourses," *English Literary Renaissance* 18 (1988): 9.

4. On Sussex University as an institutional context, see Jonathan Dollimore's evocation in his "Introduction to the Second Edition" of *Radical Tragedy: Religion, Ideology and Power in the Drama of Shakespeare and His Contemporaries* (London: Harvester Wheatsheaf, 1989), xi–xii.

5. Sinfield extends his analysis of British theater in "Making Space: Appropriation and Confrontation in Recent British Plays," in *The Shakespeare Myth,* ed. Holderness, 128–44; especially pertinent for the present collection is Sinfield's distinction between "re-reading" and "rewriting" (134). His work on the Royal Shakespeare Company is placed in a wider historical and social context in *Literature, Politics and Culture in Postwar Britain* (Berkeley: University of California Press, 1989), 249. Susan Carlson applies the concept of rewriting in her fine study, *Women and Comedy: Rewriting the British Theatrical Tradition* (Ann Arbor: University of Michigan Press, 1991), in which she distinguishes between "Women *in* Comedy," including Shakespeare's, and "Women *Writing* Comedy." Dympna Callaghan discusses "the problematic of feminist representation in Shakespearean theatre" in the specific instance of "Buzz Goodbody: Directing for Social Change," in *The Appropriation of Shakespeare: Post-Renaissance Reconstructions of the Works and the Myth,* ed. Jean I. Marsden (New York: St. Martin's Press, 1992), 163–81.

6. Although the work presented here focuses on British theater, a related American-based feminist theatrical reinterpretation is described in Sue-Ellen Case, *Feminism and Theatre* (New York: Methuen, 1988) and in *Performing Feminisms: Feminist Critical Theory and Theatre,* ed. Sue-Ellen Case (Baltimore: Johns Hopkins University Press, 1990). To cite a specific example: in the production of *Hamlet* directed by Normi Noel at Shakespeare & Company in Lenox, Massachusetts, in July 1991, Corinna May brilliantly played the roles of both Gertrude and Ophelia. The remarkable effect of this rewriting was to shift the emotional center of play. The female power normally dispersed by the separation of female roles was suddenly intensified by their unexpected concentration. May's performance in the part of Ophelia especially gained an electrifying critical edge.

7. The confluence of approaches in *Rewriting the Renaissance* is symbolically figured by the inclusion of feminists such as Coppélia Kahn, historicists such as Louis Montrose, and cultural materialists such as Peter Stallybrass, who taught at Sussex and who describes himself as "working within a British Marxist tradition" (*Cultural Studies,* ed. Lawrence Grossberg, Cary Nelson, and Paula A. Treichler [New York: Routledge, 1992], 610).

8. It is important to note that Ferguson modifies the scope of the term "rewriting" in her afterword to another collection, *Shakespeare Reproduced: The Text in History and Ideology,* ed. Jean E. Howard and Marion F. O'Connor (London: Methuen, 1987). Given the pressure of the shift in connotation from rewriting to reproducing, Ferguson qualifies the optimism of the former. Whereas in the introduction to *Rewriting the Renaissance* Ferguson endorses the activity of canon revision (xxi), in the afterword to *Shakespeare Reproduced* she questions its efficacy (276–79). The suggestion is less that the entire project of revision is invalid and must be abandoned, but that it needs to be made more attuned to structural obstacles. Ferguson's essay on Aphra Behn in the present volume can be read in part as a meditation on the tensions between rewriting and reproducing.

9. With regard to sexual orientation, Jonathan Dollimore remarks the relative neglect of sexualities, as distinct from heterosexual conceptions of gender, in American feminist Shakespeare criticism, in his "Shakespeare, Cultural Materialism, Feminism and Marxist Humanism," *New Literary History* 21 (1990): 471–93; and "Critical Developments: Cultural Materialism, Feminism and Gender Critique, and New Historicism," in *Shakespeare: A Bibliographic Guide,* ed. Stanley Wells (Oxford: Clarendon Press, 1990), 405–28. In an American context, this point has been developed by Bruce R. Smith, *Homosexual Desire in Shakespeare's England: A Cultural Poetics* (Chicago: University of Chicago Press, 1991) and by Valerie Traub, *Desire and Anxiety.* Also see Traub's review of W. Thomas MacCary's *Friends and Lovers* and Smith's review of Joseph Porter's *Shakespeare's Mercutio* in *Shakespeare Quarterly* 38 (1987): 520–22; and 42 (1991): 99–102.

10. Work that focuses on race and gender in the Renaissance includes Kim F. Hall, "Sexual Politics and Cultural Identity in *The Masque of Blackness,*" in *The Performance of Power: Theatrical Discourse and Politics,* ed. Sue-Ellen Case and Janelle Reinelt (Iowa City: University of Iowa Press, 1991), 3–18 (part of a manuscript in progress on race, gender, and power in early modern England); *Women, Race, Writing in the Early Modern Period,* ed. Patricia A. Parker and Margo Hendricks (London: Routledge, 1993). For a reading of the single occurrence of the word "race" in *The Tempest,* see Kwame Anthony Appiah's essay "Race," in *Critical Terms for Literary Study,* ed. Frank Lentricchia and Thomas McLaughlin (Chicago: University of Chicago Press, 1990), 278–79.

11. Elaine Showalter's *Sister's Choice: Tradition and Change in American Women's Writing* (Oxford: Clarendon Press, 1991) provides related commentary on Gloria Naylor (38–40) in the chapter tracing the afterlife of "Miranda's Story" in American literary history. Also important is the conclusion in the chapter's final paragraph: "Perhaps it is time to say that Shakespeare's American sister is *not* going to come" (41).

Michelle Cliff's "Caliban's Daughter: The Tempest and the Teapot," *Frontiers: A Journal of Women Studies* 12, no. 2 (1991): 36–51, focuses not on Miranda but on Ariel, whom Cliff associates with her own graduate work in the Italian Renaissance at the Warburg Institute (38–39). The result, in Cliff's graphic account, is that she gained a language but lost her voice. Recovery from the speechlessness in which Renaissance studies have left her is achieved by the imaginative recreation of "the Jamaican Sycorax" (47).

12. In the commentary preceding each section in *Because of India: Selected Poems and Fables* (London: Onlywomen Press, 1989), Namjoshi describes her transition from India to Canada and England and her evolution as a "lesbian feminist" (83). Another writer of Indian origin, Bharati Mukherjee, puts Shakespeare to satiric use in her novel *Tiger's Daughter* (Boston: Houghton Mifflin, 1972), in which the businessman Pronob's quotation of Prospero's "We are such stuff as dreams are made on" (61) signifies blithe adherence to a conservative status quo in the face of demonstrating workers who later assault him (210).

13. Howard Felperin, *The Uses of the Canon: Elizabethan Literature and Contemporary Theory* (Oxford: Clarendon Press, 1990), 181.

14. Felperin's recourse to the image of death is a rhetorical staple in traditionalist alarms: see also Alvin Kernan's *The Death of Literature* (New Haven: Yale University Press, 1990) and Richard Levin, "The Poetics and Politics of Bardicide," *PMLA* 105 (1990): 491–504. For further discussion, see my reviews of Felperin's book in *Renaissance Quarterly* 44 (1991): 613–16, and of Kernan's in *Criticism* 23 (1991): 263–65.

15. Jonathan Crewe, *Trials of Authorship: Anterior Forms and Poetic Reconstruction from Wyatt to Shakespeare* (Berkeley: University of California Press, 1990).

16. Crewe specifically cites *Rewriting the Renaissance* (167*n*6). However, an alternative to "rewriting" and its variants is provided by Cornel West's "Decentering Europe: A Memorial Lecture for James Snead," *Critical Quarterly* 33, no. 1 (Spring 1991): 1–19. The term "decentering" more emphatically signals its direction and thereby perhaps avoids the equivocal circling back on itself that lingers in a word with the "re-" prefix.

17. Carla Freccero, "Economy, Woman, and Renaissance Discourse," in *Refiguring Woman: Perspectives on Gender and the Italian Renaissance,* ed. Marilyn Migiel and Juliana Schiesari (Ithaca: Cornell University Press, 1991), 192–208; quotation from p. 194. I want to make explicit my own investment in rewriting as restructuring in Freccero's sense. My distinction between additive and transformative models of canon revision in *Rewriting Shakespeare, Rewriting Ourselves* (Berkeley: University of California Press, 1991), 6, 105, corresponds to Freccero's contrast between "rendering [women] 'visible' " and "radical restructuring."

18. I discuss multiculturalism and canon revision in the following: "Rather than Reject a Common Culture, Multiculturalism Advocates a More Complicated Route by which to Achieve It," *The Chronicle of Higher Education,* 26 June 1991: B1–B3; "What Multiculturalism Means," *Transition* 55 (1992): 105–14; "The Two Renaissances and Shakespeare's Canonical Position," *The Kenyon Review,*

n.s., 14, no. 2 (Spring 1992): 56–70; "The Question of the Canon: The Examples of Searle, Kimball, and Kernan," *Textual Practice* 6, no. 3 (Winter 1992): 439–515; "Multiculturalism and the Problem of Liberalism," *Reconstruction* 2, no. 1 (Fall 1992): 97–101.

Contributors

DIANA BRYDON teaches in the English Department at the University of Guelph. She is the author of *Christina Stead* (1987), the co-author, with Helen Tiffin, of *Decolonising Fictions* (1993), and the editor of the journal *World Literature Written in English,* and served as President of the Canadian Association for Commonwealth Literature and Language Studies from 1989 to 1992. She is the editor of the Canadian section of the forthcoming *Encyclopedia of Post-Colonial Literature in English.*

DYMPNA CALLAGHAN is an assistant professor in the Department of English and Textual Studies at Syracuse University, where she teaches feminist theory and Renaissance drama. She is the author of *Women and Gender in Renaissance Tragedy* (1989) and has completed a co-authored book, *The Weyward Sisters Go on Tour: Shakespeare and Feminist Politics* (1993), with Jyotsna Singh and Lorraine Helms.

MARGARET DRABBLE has written twelve novels, most recently *The Gates of Ivory* (1991). She also edited the *Oxford Companion to English Literature,* 5th edition (1985). She is currently working on a biography of the British novelist Angus Wilson.

PETER ERICKSON is the author of *Rewriting Shakespeare, Rewriting Ourselves* (1991) and *Patriarchal Structures in Shakespeare's Drama* (1985), and co-editor of *Shakespeare's "Rough Magic": Renaissance Essays in Honor of C. L. Barber* (1985).

MARGARET FERGUSON is a professor of English and Comparative Literature at the University of Colorado at Boulder, the author of *Trials of Desire: Renaissance Defenses of Poetry* (1983), and a co-editor of *Rewriting the Renaissance: Discourses of Sexual Desire in Early Modern Europe* (1986), and of *Re-Membering Milton: Essays on the Texts and the Tradition* (1987). She is currently completing a book called *Partial Access:*

Female Literacy and Literary Production in Early Modern France and England and editing Elizabeth Cary's *Mariam*.

LIZBETH GOODMAN is Lecturer in Literature (Theatre Specialist) at the Open University. She is the author of *Contemporary Feminist Theatres* (1993) and is a co-editor of *Imagining Women: Cultural Representations and Gender* (1992).

JULIE HANKEY is currently co-editing the theater-historical series "Plays in Performance," formerly published by Bristol Classical Press, but now being reissued and continued by Cambridge University Press. She has herself contributed the *Richard III* (1981) and *Othello* (1987) volumes to that series.

JUDITH LEE is an assistant professor in the Department of English at Rutgers University. She has published essays on the Renaissance epic, William Blake, Djuna Barnes, Virginia Woolf, Isak Dinesen, and the literary fantastic.

ANIA LOOMBA has published *Gender, Race, Renaissance Drama* (1989) and articles on Renaissance drama, current theories of colonial discourse, English literature in the Indian classroom, and the Indian women's movement. In 1992 she joined the English Department of the University of Tulsa.

JOYCE GREEN MACDONALD is an assistant professor at the University of Kentucky. She is working on a manuscript on the family-state analogy in early Shakespeare.

MARIANNE NOVY is a professor of English and Women's Studies at the University of Pittsburgh. She is the author of *Love's Argument: Gender Relations in Shakespeare* (1984) and the editor of *Women's Re-Visions of Shakespeare: On the Responses of Dickinson, Woolf, Rich, H.D., George Eliot, and Others* (1990). Her book about engagements with Shakespeare in George Eliot and other women novelists is forthcoming.

MARTHA TUCK ROZETT teaches at the State University of New York at Albany and is the author of *The Doctrine of Election and the Emergence of Elizabethan Tragedy* (1984) and a book on Shakespeare re-visions, *Talking Back to Shakespeare* (forthcoming).

VALERIE TRAUB is an assistant professor of Renaissance Drama and Gender Studies at Vanderbilt University. She has published *Desire and Anxiety: Circulations of Sexuality in Shakespearean Drama* (1992) and is at work on another project, *Staging Desire: Discourses of Female Erotic Pleasure in Early Modern England*.

MALIN LAVON WALTHER has published articles on Alice Walker and Toni Morrison and wrote her dissertation, "Embodying Beauty: Twentieth-Century American Women's Writers' Aesthetics," at the University of Wisconsin–Madison. She is an assistant professor at the University of North Carolina at Charlotte.

Index

Callaghan, Dympna, 7, 253
Cambridge University, 128–30
Canadian appropriations of Shakespeare,
   165–81
Carlisle, Carol, 50–51, 63
Carlson, Susan, 261n5
Carlyle, Thomas, 54, 56
Cartelli, Thomas, 103n21, 137
Case, Sue-Ellen, 10n7
Césaire, Aimé, 165, 166
Chace, Elizabeth Buffum, 73, 74, 79
Charles I, 26
Charles II, 18, 30
Cheney, Lynne, 6, 12n25
Christianity, 238–41, 244, 249n40, 250n47
Christie, Agatha, 207
Churchill, Caryl, 215
Cinderella, 93
Cixous, Hélène, 11n14
Clarke, Mary Cowden, 75, 76, 84n16
Class, 28, 111, 115, 121, 122,
   124–25n15, 170, 213, 232
Cleopatra, 4, 108, 159
Cleveland, John, 15, 19
Cliff, Michelle, 263n11
Cohn, Ruby, 104n24
Coleridge, Samuel Taylor, 54–55, 56, 57
Collaborative theater, 112–13, 118–20,
   122, 186, 192, 194, 215–20
Colonialism, colonial discourse, 25, 37,
   88–89, 137–40, 154, 165–81, 230–39,
   244–45
Constance (King John), 75
Cooper, Anna Julia, 4–5, 6, 12n16
Cox, Brian, 195, 203n16
Craik, Dinah Mulock, 51–52, 53, 60
Crewe, Jonathan, 258–59
Cromwell, Oliver, 24
Cross-dressing, 13n27, 92, 105n37, 209,
   210–13, 222
Cultural materialism, 251, 252–53
Cusack, Sinead, 7, 8
Cymbeline, 61, 130–36

Dabydeen, David, 180, 184n28
Dash, Irene, 8
Dass, Isser Chander, 233
Davenant, Charles, 22
Davis, David Brion, 43n13, 48n54
Davis, Henrietta Vinton, 5

Dekker, Thomas (Lusts Dominion), 29
Dench, Judi, 127
DeSalvo, Louise, 104n33
Desdemona, 19, 27, 31, 38, 39, 40, 44, 56,
   58, 111
Desmet, Christy, 75
Dinesen, Isak, Anecdotes of Destiny, 2,
   86–107
Dionisotti, Paola, 8, 215
Dolan, Jill, 223
Dollimore, Jonathan, 252, 261n4, 262n9
Donaldson, Laura, 167
Dowden, Edward, 103n13
Drabble, Margaret: 7, 8, 254; Garrick Year,
   136
Drakakis, John, 252
Dryden, John, 19–20, 31, 51, 66n5
Dunderdale, Sue, 207, 224nn3,4
Dusinberre, Juliet, 8

Edmund (Lear), in Naylor, 157–60
Eliot, George, 5, 12n19, 53, 65
Eliot, T. S., 131, 138–39
Erickson, Peter, 9, 10n5, 12n25, 13n27, 46,
   250n45
Eurocentrism, 137–49
Everyman, 131

Faucit, Helen, 7, 51–69, 253
Feinstein, Elaine, 220
Felperin, Howard, 257–58, 259
Ferguson, Margaret, 254, 255, 260, 262n8
Fiedler, Leslie, 139–40
Findlay, Timothy, 172–73
Flax, Jane, 230
Fletcher, George, 57–58, 63
Fletcher, John, 51, 66n5, 135
Foucault, Michel, 229, 230
Freccero, Carla, 259
Froula, Christine, 12n25
Fry, Christopher, 131

Gallagher, Catherine, 19–21, 31, 42n10,
   44n25
Garber, Marjorie, 13n27, 151
Gardiner, Judith Kegan, 44n24
Gates, Henry Louis, Jr., 151
Gautier, Théophile, 65
Gertrude (Hamlet): rewritten by Atwood,
   10–11n9; rewritten by Hurston, 2, 150,

31 5